COOKING WITH
CHOCOLATE

Essential Recipes and Techniques

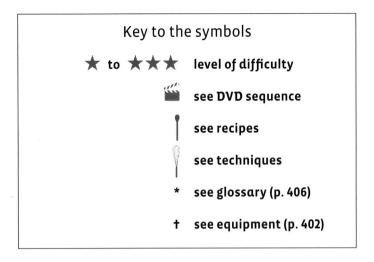

Key to the symbols

★ to ★★★   **level of difficulty**

      see DVD sequence

      see recipes

      see techniques

*   **see glossary (p. 406)**

†   **see equipment (p. 402)**

Frédéric Bau, Vincent Bourdin, Thierry Bridron, David Capy, Fabrice David, Philippe Givre, Julie Haubourdinn, Jérémie Runel, and Eve-Marie Zizza-Lalu all participated in the writing of this book.

Translated from the French by Carmella Abramowitz-Moreau
Graphics and Design: Alice Leroy and Audrey Sednaoui
Creation and technical follow-up of recipes: Julie Haubourdin
Copyediting: Penelope Isaac
Typesetting: Gravemaker+Scott
Proofreading: Helen Woodhall
Indexing: Carmella Abramowitz-Moreau
Color Separation: IGS-CP
Printed in China by Toppan

Originally published in French as *Encyclopédie du Chocolat*
© Flammarion, S.A., Paris, 2010

English-language edition
© Flammarion, S.A., Paris, 2011

87, quai Panhard et Levassor
75647 Paris Cedex 13

editions.flammarion.com

11 12 13 3 2 1

ISBN: 978-2-08-020081-5

Dépôt légal: 09/2011

Edited by Frédéric Bau,
Director of the École du Grand Chocolat Valrhona
Photographs by Clay McLachlan

COOKING WITH
CHOCOLATE
Essential Recipes and Techniques

Flammarion

How to use this book

Techniques (pp. 12–135)

All the basic techniques for working with chocolate, with specialist step-by-step explanations.

Level of difficulty

Video pictogram for the DVD sequences

Easily visible page numbering

Step-by-step photographs referring to the text

Cross-references to the equipment list

Cross-references to the glossary

Advice from the pastry chefs of the École du Grand Chocolat

References to recipes that use this technique

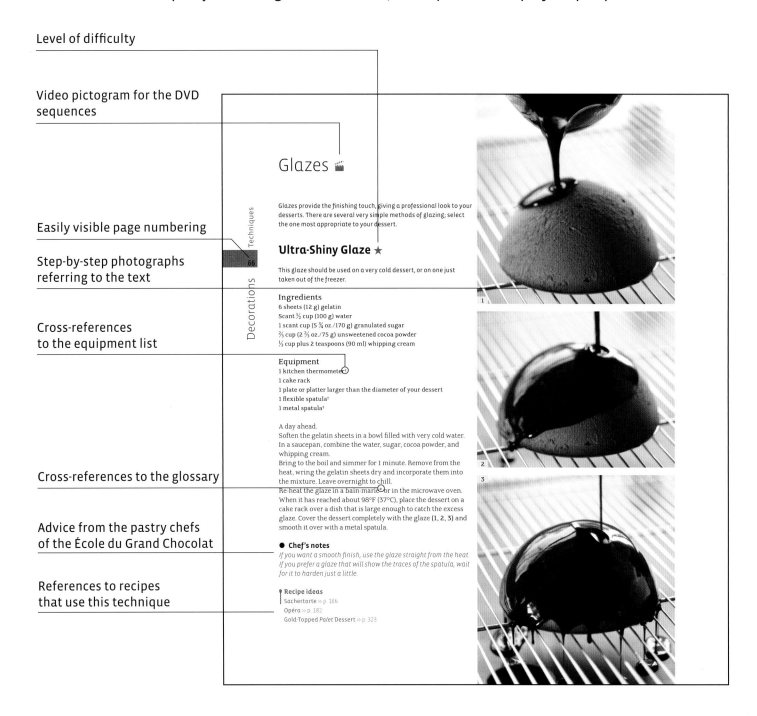

Techniques

Decorations

66

Glazes 🎬

Glazes provide the finishing touch, giving a professional look to your desserts. There are several very simple methods of glazing; select the one most appropriate to your dessert.

Ultra-Shiny Glaze ★

This glaze should be used on a very cold dessert, or on one just taken out of the freezer.

Ingredients
6 sheets (12 g) gelatin
Scant ½ cup (100 g) water
1 scant cup (5 ¾ oz./170 g) granulated sugar
⅔ cup (2 ⅔ oz./75 g) unsweetened cocoa powder
⅓ cup plus 2 teaspoons (90 ml) whipping cream

Equipment
1 kitchen thermometer
1 cake rack
1 plate or platter larger than the diameter of your dessert
1 flexible spatula†
1 metal spatula†

A day ahead.
Soften the gelatin sheets in a bowl filled with very cold water.
In a saucepan, combine the water, sugar, cocoa powder, and whipping cream.
Bring to the boil and simmer for 1 minute. Remove from the heat, wring the gelatin sheets dry and incorporate them into the mixture. Leave overnight to chill.
Re-heat the glaze in a bain-marie or in the microwave oven. When it has reached about 98°F (37°C), place the dessert on a cake rack over a dish that is large enough to catch the excess glaze. Cover the dessert completely with the glaze (1, 2, 3) and smooth it over with a metal spatula.

● **Chef's notes**
If you want a smooth finish, use the glaze straight from the heat. If you prefer a glaze that will show the traces of the spatula, wait for it to harden just a little.

❦ **Recipe ideas**
Sachertorte ›› p. 166
Opéra ›› p. 182
Gold-Topped *Palet* Dessert ›› p. 323

Recipes (pp. 156–399)

Over one hundred recipes created and tested by pastry chefs.

Easily visible page numbering

Level of difficulty

Ingredients

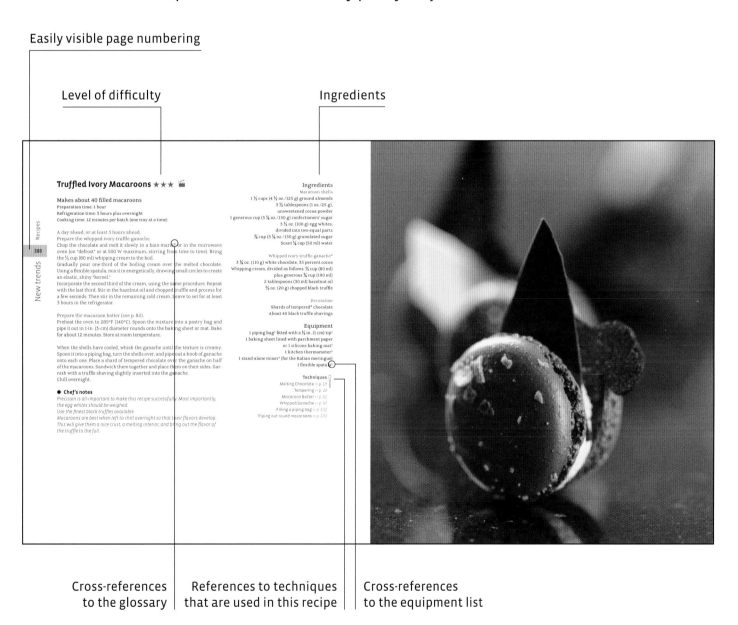

Truffled Ivory Macaroons ★ ★ ★

Makes about 40 filled macaroons
Preparation time: 1 hour
Refrigeration time: 3 hours plus overnight
Cooking time: 12 minutes per batch (one tray at a time)

A day ahead, or at least 3 hours ahead.
Prepare the whipped ivory-truffle ganache.
Chop the chocolate and melt it slowly in a bain-marie or in the microwave oven (on "defrost" or at 500 W maximum, stirring from time to time). Bring the ⅓ cup (80 ml) whipping cream to the boil.
Gradually pour one-third of the boiling cream over the melted chocolate. Using a flexible spatula, mix it in energetically, drawing small circles to create an elastic, shiny "kernel."
Incorporate the second third of the cream, using the same procedure. Repeat with the last third. Stir in the hazelnut oil and chopped truffle and process for a few seconds. Then stir in the remaining cold cream. Leave to set for at least 3 hours in the refrigerator.

Prepare the macaroon batter (see p. 82).
Preheat the oven to 285°F (140°C). Spoon the mixture into a pastry bag and pipe it out in 1-in. (3-cm) diameter rounds onto the baking sheet or mat. Bake for about 12 minutes. Store at room temperature.

When the shells have cooled, whisk the ganache until the texture is creamy. Spoon it into a piping bag, turn the shells over, and pipe out a knob of ganache onto each one. Place a shard of tempered chocolate over the ganache on half of the macaroons. Sandwich them together and place them on their sides. Garnish with a truffle shaving slightly inserted into the ganache.
Chill overnight.

● **Chef's notes**
Precision is all-important to make this recipe successfully. Most importantly, the egg whites should be weighed.
Use the finest black truffles available.
Macaroons are best when left to chill overnight so that their flavors develop. This will give them a nice crust, a melting interior, and bring out the flavor of the truffle to the full.

Ingredients
Macaroon shells
1 ½ cups (4 ½ oz./125 g) ground almonds
3 ½ tablespoons (1 oz./25 g),
unsweetened cocoa powder
1 generous cup (5 ¼ oz./150 g) confectioners' sugar
3 ½ oz. (100 g) egg whites,
divided into two equal parts
¾ cup (5 ¼ oz./150 g) granulated sugar
Scant ¼ cup (50 ml) water

Whipped ivory-truffle ganache*
3 ¾ oz. (110 g) white chocolate, 35 percent cocoa
Whipping cream, divided as follows: ⅓ cup (80 ml)
plus generous ¾ cup (190 ml)
2 tablespoons (30 ml) hazelnut oil
⅔ oz. (20 g) chopped black truffle

Decoration
Shards of tempered* chocolate
About 40 black truffle shavings

Equipment
1 piping bag† fitted with a ⅜ in. (1 cm) tip†
1 baking sheet lined with parchment paper
or 1 silicone baking mat†
1 kitchen thermometer†
1 stand-alone mixer† (for the Italian meringue)
1 flexible spatula†

Techniques
Melting Chocolate ⇒ p. 19
Tempering ⇒ p. 20
Macaroon Batter ⇒ p. 82
Whipped Ganache ⇒ p. 97
Filling a piping bag ⇒ p. 132
Piping out round macaroons ⇒ p. 132

Cross-references
to the glossary

References to techniques
that are used in this recipe

Cross-references
to the equipment list

Contents

Theory

Recipes

Appendixes

Foreword

Frédéric Bau

Executive Chef, Creative Director at the École du Grand Chocolat Valrhona

Dear Chocolate Lovers,

Before you dip into *Cooking with Chocolate*, I would like to share some thoughts with you.

When I founded the École du Grand Chocolat over twenty years ago, my intention was that it should set a benchmark for food artisans the world over, a place where they could come for training and to extend their knowledge.

Since then, the school has also become a place where we share our values and our expertise. It is open to self-taught chocolate connoisseurs and to amateurs who can enroll in our "Gourmet" training courses.

We were honored when Flammarion entrusted this book to us. We hope it will become a key reference work and that we have lived up to the challenge—after all, there are already many books that do justice to *Theobroma cacao*, the "food of the gods," as Linneaus dubbed the plant. However, this book is fundamentally different from other books already published on the subject.

First of all, it is a concentration of knowledge built up from the professional training we provide at the École du Grand Chocolat. We reveal the techniques for working chocolate in language that is easily comprehensible to nonprofessionals. These basic techniques comprise the first part of the book, and it is essential to master them to make the great classical recipes that incorporate confections, icings, ganaches*, and sponges. This book will also provide you with a symphony of pleasure for your palate, orchestrated by the chefs at our school and by some of the greatest names in the world of pastry, all centering on one magical ingredient: chocolate.

In the second section, we share over one hundred recipes, from the simplest and most basic to the most creative.

This book could not have been completed without the enthusiastic participation of my colleagues at the École du Grand Chocolat Valrhona.

Julie Haubourdin, my colleague in charge of the gourmet training courses, agreed to be the linchpin of the project. She used her considerable talent to "translate" our professional jargon into clear, precise language that everyone can understand. I hope that, as you turn the pages, enjoying Clay McLachlan's unique photos and Ève-Marie Zizza-Lalu's explicit instructions, you will be able to sense the associations of tastes and textures of each of our recipes, and our desire to share with you the culture of excellence that inspires us all.

On behalf of each and every member of the team, I wish you a tasty escapade into a world in which the inseparable duo of flavor and technique creates shared pleasures.

A passion to share

Pierre Hermé

Pastry Chef, Paris

From Antonin Carême to Gaston Lenôtre, and including Lucien Peltier, Gabriel Paillasson, Pascal Niau, and Yves Thuriès, great French pastry chefs have, one after another, left their indelible mark on the history of the craft.

For many long years, pastry making was a demonstrative art, with a decided tendency toward ornamentation. This approach is still alive, but now constitutes a separate area of our discipline, only one aspect of our profession, because the truth of the matter is that we do not construct elaborate *pièces montées* every day, but we make cakes, we make things to eat!

Today's pastry chefs focus on taste, flavors, textures, and temperatures. Gaston Lenôtre was the first to provide the impetus towards this focus on taste by emphasizing the ingredients—the quality of the basic components. The influence of Lucien Peltier and Pascal Niau were also decisive in orienting our profession towards a modern, highly demanding, and creative vision of the pastry that is sold in bakeries.

Pastry chefs must go through three stages: learning, mastering, and transmission. The phase during which all the techniques are acquired is indispensable for the chefs to shake themselves free of the basic reference system. Ultimately, we must use all we have learned in order not to reproduce what we have learned.

Of all the pastry chefs who have worked at my side, Frédéric Bau is without doubt the most talented and creative. Indefatigably inventive, unclassifiable, he combines his inspiration with virtuoso mastery, overturning traditions and exploring new horizons. His intimate knowledge of techniques and the canons of the profession constantly drive him to transform them to make them his own. When he makes his pastries, Frédéric Bau goes right to the heart of the matter: their taste. No artifices of decoration for him; his streamlined working methods preclude the excessive or uncalled-for decorations that so often clutter up pastries.

Chocolate is, of course, his favorite ingredient (and what else would one expect after twenty-two years with Valrhona?), but he is just as much at ease with sweet dishes as with savory, with fruits, spices, herbs, and all the other ingredients he comes across during his travels around the world, and particularly in Japan. Frédéric has an astounding way of taming an ingredient, understanding it, and then not only dreaming up a pastry but also a world to go with it.

By writing this book, which contains both techniques and delicious recipes and which will soon be a must-have volume for all chocolate lovers, Frédéric Bau, with his colleagues at the École du Grand Chocolat, will allow you to begin making desserts, from the simplest to the most sophisticated, that are normally the reserve of professionals. He shares his passion with you through original recipes, as well as those of his friends, some of today's finest pastry chefs and chocolatiers.

Techniques

Keep in mind

On the pages that follow, you'll find all the techniques you require to work with chocolate—tempering*, coating, decoration, and more—as well as a quick refresher course on pastry basics.

Check the percentage of cocoa in your chocolate

The quantities of chocolate you need will differ according to the cocoa percentage of the chocolate you use. This is because cocoa butter* (whose quantity will differ according to the cocoa percentage) acts to harden the preparation. A chocolate with 50 percent cocoa content and a chocolate with 70 percent cocoa content will give different results, particularly in terms of texture. In all the techniques we give here, we use Valrhona chocolate: Guanaja with 70 percent or 61 percent cocoa, Jivara, and Ivoire. Whenever possible, we include substitutes with different cocoa percentages.

For example:

Weigh the chocolate according to its cocoa content:
11 ¾ oz. (335 g) bittersweet chocolate, 70 percent cocoa
Or 13 oz. (370 g) bittersweet chocolate, 60 percent cocoa
Or 1 lb. 2 oz. (500 g) milk chocolate, 40 percent cocoa
Or 1 lb. 7 oz. (650 g) milk chocolate, 35 percent cocoa

Whipping cream

All whipping cream should have a minimum of 30-35 percent fat content, unless otherwise specified.

Refer to the glossary

All terms marked with an asterisk are explained in the glossary on p. 406-407.

Be precise and accurate

It is often said that a pastry chef never goes anywhere without his or her scales and thermometer. Pastry making and guesswork just do not go together, so follow the indications for weights and temperatures as given in the recipes. Measure all your ingredients carefully, and weigh them all, even liquids. When making the recipes in this book, use either imperial or metric measurements (rather than a combination of the two) for best results.

Make sure you have the right equipment

A kitchen thermometer† (or even better, an instant-read thermometer), an immersion blender†, a flexible rubber or silicone spatula†, a baking sheet, a piping or pastry bag† with tips†, and a rolling pin† are all essential utensils. You will even use your freezer in unexpected ways to facilitate assembling and unmolding.

Terms marked with a † are explained in the equipment list on p. 402-405.

Chocolate

Melting chocolate ★

There are certain fundamental principles when melting chocolate, and if you follow them, your liquid chocolate will be ready to use as a base in all sorts of recipes. There are also two absolute no-no's. Firstly, don't put a spoonful of water in the pot; contrary to popular belief, it will not aid the process. Secondly, never cook chocolate on direct heat.

In a bain-marie*

Using a serrated knife, chop the chocolate on a chopping board. You may also use couverture chocolate* in other forms, such as fèves, buttons, or pistoles. Place the chopped chocolate in a glass or metal heatproof bowl.
If you have a double boiler, half fill the bottom part with hot water. Otherwise, half fill a pot or saucepan with hot water. Place the bowl in this, ensuring that it does not touch the bottom of the saucepan. Place the saucepan (or double-boiler) over low heat and check that the water does not boil. As soon as the chocolate begins to melt, stir it continuously using a flexible rubber or silicone spatula† so that it melts evenly.

In a microwave oven

Place the chocolate pieces in a bowl designed for microwave use. Heat at 500 W maximum for one minute, remove from the oven, stir with a flexible spatula, and return to the heat for 30 seconds.
Mix again and repeat the procedure as many times as necessary, until the chocolate has melted completely.

● Chef's note
Melt bittersweet chocolate to a temperature of 131°F–136°F (55°C–58°C), and milk, white, and colored chocolate to a temperature of 113°F–122°F (45°C–50°C).

Tempering ★★★ 🎬

Tempering* chocolate involves putting it through a cycle of temperatures (heat/cooling/heat) that professionals call the "tempering curve." This cycle varies slightly depending on whether the chocolate is bittersweet, milk, white, or colored. Novices tend to believe that tempering is a complex process, but actually it is a relatively simple technique, and one that you will need for coating bonbons, making molded chocolate, and chocolate bars. The key is just to take your time and be precise. Chocolate artisans use the second phalanx of the index finger, or the upper lip, both of which act as natural thermometers. We advise buying a kitchen thermometer†, preferably an instant-read thermometer, which will enable you to follow the tempering curve precisely. This will guarantee a brilliant, melting, and breakable chocolate.

Why temper chocolate?

Tempering is the key to making small chocolates, bars, molded chocolate, and decorations. Merely melting a bar of chocolate is not enough for it to retain its qualities when used in another form, such as orangettes and mendiants. Only if the tempering is properly carried out will chocolate snap briskly, melt in the mouth pleasantly, and retain its gloss.

The reason for this is the large amount of cocoa butter* present in chocolate.

This fatty matter is complex and capricious. Insofar as a human attribute can be given to it, it can be described as "lazy!" Once it has melted, it cannot regain its stable crystalline form. This means that its component crystals are scattered. One result of this phenomenon is the "bloom"–the whiteish streaks–you sometimes see on slabs of chocolate.

This is not only rather unattractive (where has that lovely sheen gone?) but, more importantly, you won't hear that distinctive snap when you break off a square of a good bar of chocolate, and it will be a big disappointment when you taste it. The chocolate will not melt gently, it may be grainy, and its aromas will not develop nearly as well. To avoid these mishaps, all you need to do is to help the cocoa butter regain the stable crystalline form that helps it keep well, and which will make it snap, melt, and shine.

In a nutshell, tempering is not merely a question of good looks, but, more importantly, of good taste.

❘ Recipe ideas

Chocolate-Flavored Caramel Bonbons ›› p. 337
Mendiants ›› p. 341
Orangettes ›› p. 342
Fresh Fruit Chocolate Bars ›› p. 346
Coconut Bars ›› p. 349

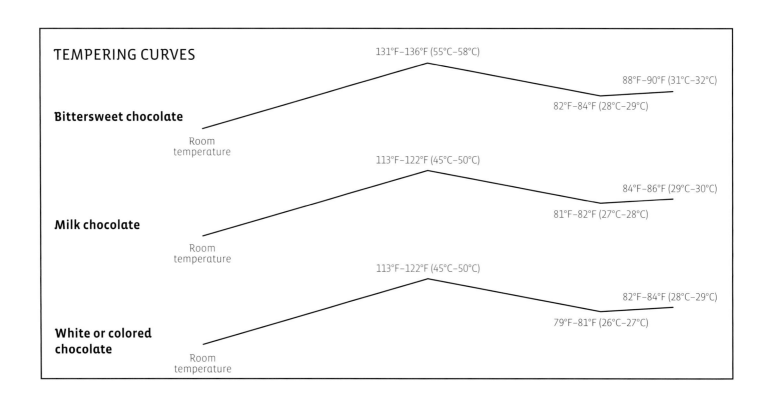

TEMPERING CURVES

Bittersweet chocolate
- Room temperature
- 131°F–136°F (55°C–58°C)
- 88°F–90°F (31°C–32°C)
- 82°F–84°F (28°C–29°C)

Milk chocolate
- Room temperature
- 113°F–122°F (45°C–50°C)
- 84°F–86°F (29°C–30°C)
- 81°F–82°F (27°C–28°C)

White or colored chocolate
- Room temperature
- 113°F–122°F (45°C–50°C)
- 82°F–84°F (28°C–29°C)
- 79°F–81°F (26°C–27°C)

Tempering by seeding ★ ★ ★

This tempering* method uses the addition of finely chopped pieces, disks, or pistoles of chocolate into already-melted chocolate. Adding stable, crystallized* chocolate lowers the temperature naturally, enabling regular crystallization of the chocolate mass. The method is a replacement for using a marble working surface or a cold-water bath.

Ingredient

14 oz. (400 g) chocolate

Equipment

1 serrated knife
1 kitchen thermometer†
1 flexible spatula†
1 food processor fitted with a blade attachment

Chop three quarters of the chocolate (10 ½ oz./300 g) on a chopping board, using a serrated knife. Even better, use couverture chocolate* in the form of fèves, buttons, or pistoles. Finely chop the remaining quarter (3 ½ oz./100 g) or process it with the blade knife attachment of a food processor. Place the roughly chopped chocolate in a bowl. Half fill a saucepan with hot water, and put the bowl over it, making sure that the bowl does not touch the bottom of the saucepan. Slowly heat the water, ensuring it does not boil.
Alternatively, use a microwave oven if you wish, but in "defrost" position or at 500 W maximum.
Stir regularly using a flexible spatula so that the chocolate melts smoothly. Check the temperature with a thermometer. When it reaches 131°F-136°F (55°C-58°C) for bittersweet, or 113°F-122°F (45°C- 50°C) for milk or white, remove the chocolate from the bain-marie*. Set aside one-third of the melted chocolate in a bowl, in a warm place. Add the remaining finely chopped quarter (4 oz./100 g) of the chocolate into the remaining two-thirds of the melted chocolate, stirring constantly.
Bittersweet chocolate should reach a temperature of 82°F-84°F (28°C-29°C); milk chocolate should reach 81°F-82°F (27°C-28°C); and white or colored chocolate should reach 79°F-81°F (26°C-27°C).
Then add the melted chocolate that you have set aside to increase the temperature. Bittersweet chocolate should reach 88°F-90°F (31°C-32°C); milk chocolate should reach 84°F-86°F (29°C-30°C); and white or colored chocolate should reach 82°F-84°F (28°C-29°C). Stir until the right temperature is reached.

● **Chef's note**

If the chocolate has attained the right temperature and there are still pieces of unmelted chocolate, remove them before increasing the temperature. If you leave them, the chocolate will thicken very quickly and become sticky because of over-crystallization.

Tempering in a bain-marie ★★★

This is as precise a method as tempering* by seeding*, but is a little more cumbersome because it requires two water baths, one hot water and one cold.

Ingredient
14 oz. (400 g) chocolate

Equipment
1 kitchen thermometer†

Chop the chocolate and melt it slowly over a bain-marie* (see p. 19).
Prepare the cold-water bath, adding a few ice cubes.
When the temperature reaches 131°F-136°F (55°C-58°C) if you are using bittersweet, or 113°F-122°F (45°C- 50°C) for milk or white chocolate, remove the bowl from the hot-water bath and place it over the cold-water bath.
Stir constantly so that the chocolate does not crystallize* too fast on the edges: this would "over-crystallize" the cocoa butter*. Check the temperature constantly. When it reaches approximately 95°F (35°C), remove the bowl from the cold-water bath.
Continue to stir. Bittersweet chocolate should reach 82°F-84°F (28°C-29°C); milk chocolate should reach 81°F-82°F (27°C-28°C); and white or colored, 79°F-81°F (26°C-27°C).
Return the bowl to the hot-water bath very briefly to increase the temperature. Bittersweet chocolate should reach 88°F-90°F (31°C-32°C); milk chocolate should reach 84°F-86°F (29°C-30°C); and white or colored chocolate should reach 82°F-84°F (28°C-29°C).
Remove from the hot-water bath, stirring as long as necessary to attain the right temperature, and then use immediately.

● **Chef's note**
Don't forget the phenomenon of "thermal inertia," which means that the ingredient will continue cooking after removal from a source of heat, or cooling after removal from a source of cold. Remove your bowl from the hot or cold-water baths before the desired temperatures are reached and keep stirring so that the chocolate is not too hot or too cold.*

1

2

3

4

Tempering using
a tempering stone ★★★

This is the kind of tempering* that has chocolate lovers drooling, as they watch TV programs where artisan chocolate makers spread and mix pounds of chocolate on a marble surface. You can use this method at home if you have a marble working surface and don't mind transforming your kitchen into a chocolate workshop for a few hours.

Ingredient

14 oz. (400 g) chocolate

Equipment

1 kitchen thermometer†
1 flexible spatula†
1 metal spatula†

Chop the chocolate and melt it slowly over a bain-marie* (see p. 19).
When the temperature of the chocolate reaches 131°F-136°F (55°C-58°C) if you are using bittersweet, or 113°F-122°F (45°C-50°C) for milk and white chocolate, pour two-thirds of it onto a marble slab (1, 2).
Keep the remaining third warm, either over the bain-marie, or in a warm place, but not over direct heat.
Using a flexible spatula and a metal spatula, keep spreading and turning the chocolate until the desired temperatures are reached (3, 4). Bittersweet chocolate must reach 82°F-84°F (28°C-29°C); milk chocolate must reach 81°F-82°F (27°C-28°C); and white or colored chocolate must reach 79°F-81°F (26°C-27°C).
Return the melted, stirred chocolate to a mixing bowl and gradually pour in the warm chocolate that was set aside until it reaches a temperature of 88°F-90°F (31°C-32°C) for bittersweet, 84°F-86°F (29°C-30°C) for milk chocolate, and 82°F-84°F (28°C-29°C) for white or colored chocolate.

● **Did you know?**

Most artisan chocolate makers have a tempering machine that puts their chocolate through the cycle of ideal temperatures. This makes it easier for them to coat confections.

Undercoating

Undercoating facilitates the handling of praline*, ganache*, *pâtes de fruits* (fruit jellies), and other fillings when you cut and coat them. It provides a protective layer, preventing fragile fillings from melting when they come into contact with the heat.

Before cutting ★★★

Ingredients
Tempered* chocolate (see p. 20)
Fillings for chocolate bonbons, uncut, such as ganache, praline, etc.

Equipment
1 spatula†

Spread a little tempered chocolate over the surface of your uncut ganache, praline filling, caramel*, or whatever you are coating. With a spatula, quickly spread the melted chocolate out into a very fine layer. This will make up the base of the bonbon you are coating (1).
Immediately cut it out to the desired shape. The fillings are now ready to be coated.

After cutting ★★★

Ingredients
Tempered* chocolate–more than you will use! (see p. 20)
Fillings for chocolate bonbons, cut out or molded

Equipment
1 pastry brush†

Using a pastry brush, spread out the tempered chocolate over the cut-out fillings (2, 3).
The fillings are now ready to be coated.

● **Chef's note**
Use the remaining tempered chocolate to make decorations (see p. 47)

❚ **Recipe ideas**
Sesame-Topped Choco-Cinnamon Ganaches ≫ p. 354

1

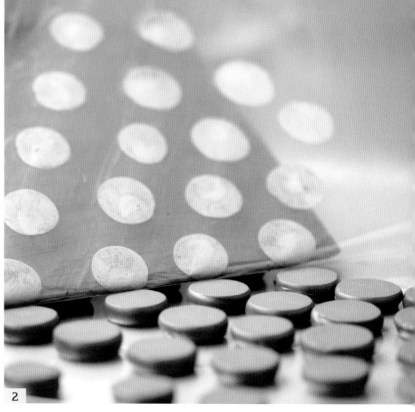

2

3

Coating ★★★ 🎬

Dipping a chocolate bonbon involves enclosing a filling such as ganache*, caramel*, *pâte de fruit* (fruit jelly), and so on in a fine layer of tempered* chocolate. This technique helps preserve the filling, adds a cracking texture, and enhances chocolate taste.

Ingredients
Tempered chocolate (see p. 20)
Fillings for chocolate bonbons, undercoated

Equipment
1 baking sheet lined with a plastic sheet or parchment paper
1 dipping fork[†]
1 chopstick (optional)

Place the undercoated side of the bonbon on the tines of a dipping fork and dip it in the tempered chocolate. Lower the tines into the chocolate to immerse it completely. Use the fork to retrieve the bonbon, and dip it in three or four times to create the suction that will prevent an overly thick layer of chocolate from forming.
Scrape the dipping fork against the edge of the mixing bowl so that the layer of chocolate on the base is not too thick.
Carefully place the bonbon on the prepared baking tray. If necessary, use a chopstick to slide it off the fork.

● **Chef's note**
Clean the dipping fork and chopstick regularly. If they accumulate too much chocolate, the bonbons will stick, and it will be hard to slide them off.

🍴 **Recipe ideas**
Crisp, Melting Bonbons ›› p. 334
Sesame-Topped Choco-Cinnamon Ganaches ›› p. 354
Chocolate-Coated Cherries and Pineapple Cubes ›› p. 360

Molding 🎬

Classic Molds ★ ★ ★

It's great fun to create molds the way great pastry chefs do. Begin by practicing with small molds to get the technique right. When you get the hang of it, try larger pieces.

Ingredient
Tempered* chocolate (see p. 20)

Equipment
Molds†
2 confectionery rulers† or similar device to hold the mold upside down
1 baking sheet lined with parchment paper
1 ladle

Clean the molds using cotton wool and 90° alcohol. It's essential to remove all traces of grease from the molds so that the chocolate is unblemished when turned out of the mold.
Place the rulers on a baking sheet lined with parchment paper. Pour the tempered chocolate into a large mixing bowl. Dip a ladle into the tempered chocolate and completely fill the mold so that the entire surface is covered (1).
Turn it upside down over the mixing bowl to remove the excess chocolate (2). Drain it off by shaking the mold gently and then place it upside down over the two rulers.
When the chocolate begins to set, turn the mold over again and remove the excess chocolate by leveling it with a kitchen knife so that the edges are neat and trim (3).
If you are making larger pieces, you can thicken the chocolate by filling the molds a second time once you have leveled off the excess chocolate.
Trimming is important because it allows the chocolate to retract to the size of the mold and also facilitates your task when you turn your pieces out of their molds.
Chill for 30 minutes. When you remove the molds from the refrigerator, wait a few minutes before turning them out.
If you wish to mold your pieces together, slightly warm a baking tray or the bottom of a saucepan. Lightly melt the edges of your chocolate pieces against the warmed metal (if you are using a saucepan, turn it upside down) so that you can use the melted chocolate like glue (4).

Recipe ideas

Mister Clown ›› p. 327
Betty the Baby Bear ›› p. 362
Sam the Snowman ›› p. 364
Daisy Easter Egg ›› p. 366

1

2

3

4

Making a gelatin mold ★ ★ ★

Choose whatever object you like to create a mold in the shape of your choice.

Ingredients
1 cup plus 1 scant ¼ cup (3 ½ oz./300 g) water
1 ½ cups (10 ½ oz./300 g) granulated sugar
Scant ½ cup (3 ½ oz./100 g) powdered gelatin
Tempered* chocolate (see p. 20)

Equipment
1 whisk†
1 bowl large enough to contain the piece you will be molding
1 kitchen thermometer†
Elastic bands

Pour all the water into a saucepan and heat over low heat. Combine the sugar and powdered gelatin and pour the mixture into the water, mixing with a whisk. Allow impurities (foam) to rise to the surface and remove them with a skimmer. Do not allow it to come to the boil, otherwise the gelatin will burn. When the liquid is perfectly clear, remove it from the heat.

Pour some of the gelatin mixture into a bowl and leave it to harden. Dip the base of the model you will be using for the mold (for example, a cocoa pod) into the liquid gelatin remaining in the saucepan and place it to set in the middle of the bowl. Leave to harden in the freezer.
While it is hardening, check that the remaining gelatin is at a temperature of about 113°F (45°C). It should be perfectly liquid, so either keep it warm or reheat it if necessary. Remove the bowl from the freezer and pour the liquid gelatin over the model. It should be about ½ in. (more than 1 cm) higher than the top of the model.
Leave to harden in the refrigerator for several hours.
When the gelatin mass has hardened well, cut the mold into two using a cutter. Carefully remove the model, ensuring you do not tear the mold.
To mold your chocolate, fasten the gelatin with elastic bands and make a hole through which to fill the gelatin shell with chocolate. Chill the mold well before each use, to between 37.5°F-43°F (3°C-6°C) so that the gelatin does not partially melt, which would leave deposits on the chocolate. Fill the cold mold with tempered chocolate. Then tap the mold a few times to ensure it is evenly distributed.
Remove any chocolate that has run out. Do not use any utensils that might damage the mold. Return it to the refrigerator for 3 to 5 minutes and release the chocolate from the mold. Note that this molded chocolate will not be shiny.

Bonbon fillings

Ganaches

A ganache* is made of chocolate and a liquid. Generally, the liquid is cream, but you will also find fruit pulp, soy milk, and so on. The ganache is an emulsion, which is a blend of fatty matter and water. The chocolate provides the fatty matter, and the cream, milk, or even fruit pulp provides the water. A ganache must be stable, elastic, and shiny.

Ingredients
Chocolate in quantities that depend on the cocoa percentage (see p. 15)
Full-fat whipping cream or milk or fruit juice
Butter, diced (optional)

Equipment
1 flexible spatula[†]
1 kitchen thermometer[†]
1 immersion blender[†]

Chop the chocolate and melt it in a heatproof bowl over a bain-marie or in the microwave oven (on "defrost" or at 500 W, stirring from time to time).
In a saucepan, bring the full-fat whipping cream, milk, or fruit juice to the boil.
Gradually pour one-third of the boiling liquid over the melted chocolate (1). Using a flexible spatula, mix it in energetically, drawing small circles to create an elastic, shiny "kernel."
Incorporate the second third of the liquid, using the same procedure. Repeat with the last third.
As soon as the ganache reaches a temperature of 95°F-104°F (35°C-40°C), add the diced butter, if using (2).
Blend using an immersion blender so that the mixture is smooth and perfectly emulsified* (3).

● Chef's notes
As soon as the liquid is added, the mass of chocolate thickens rapidly. In most cases, this is followed by a separation of the two, which gives rise to a grainy texture.
This is a perfectly normal occurrence and is due to the mass being saturated in fatty matter. Simply whisk vigorously.*
When the elastic, shiny "kernel" appears, this is the sign that the emulsion is beginning to form. This is the appearance that must be retained as you gradually incorporate the boiling liquid in three stages.
You may want to flavor your ganaches by infusing spices, zests, herbs, vanilla, or tea leaves in the cream. Ensure that you always have the required quantity of liquid for the recipe. Another option is essential oils.

● Did you know?
The texture of the ganache will vary with the recipe.
• For cut-out chocolate bonbons, use a ganache with a firm texture but one that melts easily.
• Molded chocolate bonbons or hollow molds should be filled with a ganache with a very soft, or even a liquid texture.
• Macaroons, desserts, and tarts require soft, creamy textures.*

Ganache for Hand-Dipped Centers ★★

Ganache* for hand-dipped bonbons, usually made in a confectionery frame (available at specialty stores and online), is the base for all sorts of coated chocolates: *palets d'or*, ganache fillings, *rochers** ("rock" cookies), and lollipops are some examples. Its consistency is firmer than that of ganache for molded bonbons and it is easy to fashion, roll, and manipulate into various shapes.

Ingredients

Weigh the chocolate according to its cocoa content:
11 ¾ oz. (350 g) bittersweet chocolate, 70 percent cocoa
Or 13 oz. (370 g) bittersweet chocolate, 60 percent cocoa
Or 1 lb. 2 oz. (500 g) milk chocolate, 40 percent cocoa
Or 1 lb. 7 oz. (650 g) white chocolate, 35 percent cocoa
1 cup (250 g) whipping cream
2 tablespoons (40 g) honey
5 tablespoons (2 ½ oz./70 g) butter, diced

Equipment

1 flexible spatula†
1 immersion blender†
1 confectionery frame† or brownie pan (see above)
1 baking sheet
1 kitchen thermometer†
1 sheet food-safe acetate†

Line a baking sheet with a piece of food-safe acetate and place the confectionery frame over it.
Chop the chocolate and melt it slowly in a bain-marie* or in the microwave oven (on "defrost" or at 500 W maximum, stirring from time to time).
Bring the whipping cream and honey to the boil in a saucepan. Slowly pour in one-third of the boiling mixture over the melted chocolate. Using a flexible spatula, briskly mix it in with a small circular movement to create an elastic, shiny "kernel." Then incorporate another third of the chocolate, using the same circular movement, and finally, the last third of the melted chocolate, still mixing with a circular movement.
As soon as the ganache reaches a temperature of 95°F-104°F (35°C-40°C), add the diced butter. Process with an immersion blender to ensure that the mixture is smooth and forms a perfect emulsion.
Immediately pour it into the frame. This type of ganache should ideally be stored at between 61°F-64°F (16°C-18°C) while it sets. Leave to set for 12 hours, then turn it out onto a sheet of parchment paper. Remove the frame and the acetate sheet.
It is now ready for undercoating (see p. 24) and coating (see p. 25).

● **Chef's note**
If you don't have a confectionery frame, use a brownie pan or dish just deep enough to pour your ganache to a thickness of under ½ in. (1 cm). Oil it and line with smoothed out plastic wrap.

❙ **Recipe ideas**
Chocolate-Pecan Ladyfingers ›› p. 246
Rose and Raspberry Lollipops ›› p. 344
Truffle Hearts ›› p. 350
Jasmine Truffle Logs ›› p. 353
Sesame-Topped Choco-Cinnamon Ganaches ›› p. 354

Raspberry Pulp Ganache
for Hand-Dipped Centers ★★

Adding fruit pulp to a ganache* subtly enhances the chocolate aromas. It is a technique that works well for all sorts of fruit pulps, such as raspberry, pear, peach, pineapple, and more.

Ingredients
Weigh the chocolate according to its cocoa content:
11 ¾ oz. (350 g) bittersweet chocolate, 70 percent cocoa
Or 13 oz. (370 g) bittersweet chocolate, 60 percent cocoa
Or 1 lb. 2 oz. (500 g) milk chocolate, 40 percent cocoa
Or 1 ½ lb. (700 g) white chocolate, 35 percent cocoa
9 oz. (250 g) raspberry pulp with 10 percent sugar
2 tablespoons (40 g) honey
5 tablespoons (2 ½ oz./70 g) butter, diced

Equipment
1 flexible spatula†
1 immersion blender†
1 confectionery frame† or brownie pan
1 baking sheet
1 kitchen thermometer†
1 sheet food-safe acetate†

Line a baking sheet with a sheet of acetate and place the confectionery frame or brownie pan on it.
Chop the chocolate and melt it slowly in a bain-marie* or in the microwave oven (on "defrost" or at 500 W maximum, stirring from time to time).
Heat the raspberry pulp with the honey in a saucepan. Be careful not to bring it to the boil, because the more it is heated, the less flavor it exudes. Slowly pour one-third of the hot mixture over the melted chocolate (1). Using a flexible spatula, briskly mix it in with a small circular movement to create an elastic, shiny "kernel." Then incorporate another third of the raspberry pulp, using the same circular movement, and finally, the last third, still mixing with a circular movement.
As soon as the ganache reaches a temperature of 95°F-104°F (35°C-40°C), add the diced butter. Process with an immersion blender to ensure that the mixture is smooth and forms a perfect emulsion.
Immediately pour it into the frame or pan (2). This type of ganache should ideally be stored at between 61°F and 64°F (16°C and 18°C) during its crystallization* phase.
Leave to set for 12 hours, then turn it out onto a sheet of parchment paper. Remove the frame and the food-safe acetate sheets and coat with a fine layer of chocolate to make an undercoat (see p. 24), then cut it out into the desired shapes.
Leave the cut-out ganache to crystallize for a further 24 hours.
Coat with tempered* chocolate (see p. 25).

● Chef's note
You will see that the ganache has a slightly grainy texture; this is due to the use of the raspberry pulp.

Classic Namachoco Ganache ★★

This recipe makes what is known as a "fresh" ganache*, one which must be eaten very quickly as it keeps no longer than twenty-four hours after it has crystallized*.

Ingredients
Weigh the chocolate according to its cocoa content:
6 oz. (175 g) bittersweet chocolate, 70 percent cocoa
Or 7 oz. (200 g) bittersweet chocolate, 60 percent cocoa
¾ cup (200 ml) whipping cream
4 tablespoons (60 g) butter
Granulated or caster sugar, confectioners' sugar, or unsweetened cocoa powder as needed

Equipment
1 flexible spatula†
1 immersion blender†
Plastic wrap
1 square dish, 8 in. (20 cm)
Or 1 confectionery frame† and 1 baking sheet

Line the square dish with plastic wrap, smoothing out all air bubbles and wrinkles.
Chop the chocolate and melt it slowly in a bain-marie*, or in the microwave oven (on "defrost" or at 500 W maximum, stirring from time to time).
Bring the cream to the boil in a saucepan. Slowly pour one-third of the boiling cream over the melted chocolate. Using a flexible spatula, briskly mix it in with a small circular movement to create an elastic, shiny "kernel." Then incorporate the next third, using the same circular movement, and finally the last third, still mixing with a circular movement.
As soon as the ganache cools to a temperature of 95°F-104°F (35°C-40°C), add the diced butter. Process with an immersion blender to ensure that the mixture is smooth and forms a perfect emulsion. However, be careful not to incorporate any air bubbles.
Immediately pour it into the frame or pan. Leave to set for 12 hours in the refrigerator.
Sprinkle with granulated or caster sugar, confectioners' sugar, or unsweetened cocoa powder, and cut out into the desired shapes.

● **Did you know?**
Namachoco ganache is widely used in Japan.

Ganache for Molded Bonbons ★★

This very creamy ganache* is particularly suitable for filling shells, molds, and tarts. Once it has crystallized*, it remains soft and retains its melt-in-the-mouth quality.

Ingredients
Weigh the chocolate according to its cocoa content:
6 oz. (175 g) bittersweet chocolate, 70 percent cocoa
Or 7 oz. (200 g) bittersweet chocolate, 60 percent cocoa
Or 8 oz. (230 g) milk chocolate, 40 percent cocoa
Or 12 oz. (340 g) white chocolate, 35 percent cocoa
⅔ cup (160 ml) whipping cream (35 percent fat content)
1 tablespoon plus 1 ¼ teaspoons (1 oz./30 g) honey
2 tablespoons (1 oz./30 g) butter, diced

Equipment
1 flexible spatula†
1 kitchen thermometer†
1 immersion blender†
1 piping bag†

Prepare your molds. Line them with chocolate (see Molds p. 26) (**1, 2**). Chop the chocolate for the filling and melt it slowly in a bain-marie* or in the microwave oven (on "defrost" or at 500 W maximum, stirring from time to time).
Bring the cream to the boil in a saucepan with the honey. Slowly pour one-third of the boiling cream and honey over the melted chocolate. Using a flexible spatula, briskly mix it in with a small circular movement to create an elastic, shiny "kernel." Then incorporate the next third, using the same circular movement, and finally, the last third, still mixing with a circular movement.
As soon as the ganache reaches a temperature of 95°F-104°F (35°C-40°C), add the diced butter. Process with an immersion blender to ensure that the mixture is smooth and forms a perfect emulsion.
Allow the temperature to cool to 81°F-82°F (27°C-28°C), then spoon it into the piping bag and pipe out into your chocolate-lined molds.
This ganache should ideally be stored at between 61°F-64°F (16°C-18°C) during its crystallization phase.
Leave to set for 12 hours, and then, if necessary, close the mold with tempered* chocolate. Allow the crystallization to continue for a further 24 hours.

● Chef's note
To flavor your ganache with a liqueur, add it when all the mixing is done. Dosage: 8–10 percent of the total mass of the ganache.

Various centers

Homemade Praline ★★

Praline* is a paste of nuts with a minimum of 50 percent almonds or hazelnuts, or a mixture of both, to which sugar is added. The nuts and sugar are cooked to enhance their flavor.
The cooked mixture is then cooled, ground, and worked further to make it as smooth as possible.

Ingredients
3 ½ oz. (100 g) hazelnuts
3 ½ oz. (100 g) blanched* almonds
¾ cup (5 ¼ oz./150 g) granulated sugar

Equipment
1 baking sheet or silicone baking mat†
1 rolling pin†
1 food processor fitted with a blade attachment

Preheat the oven to 300°F (150°C). Prepare a silicone baking mat or oil a baking pan. Roast the nuts for about 10 minutes, or until they are a nice amber color. Leave them to cool for a few minutes and peel* the hazelnuts. Keep in a warm place.
To prepare a caramel* using the dry method, preheat a large saucepan and pour in one-third of the sugar (¼ cup/50 g). Stir constantly until it reaches a uniform caramel color. Add the next third of the sugar, stirring constantly. Then pour in the remaining third, still stirring constantly, until the sugar caramelizes completely (1). Incorporate the warm roasted nuts (2), stirring quickly until thoroughly combined, and immediately smooth out over the oiled baking tray or silicone sheet (3). Leave to cool at room temperature.
Using a rolling pin, break up the praline into coarse chunks. Place the chunks into the bowl of a food processor and process until you have a smooth paste. If the motor of the food processor begins to heat, stop running it until it cools. This paste can be made in two or more stages.

● **Chef's note**
Use hazelnuts only to make a hazelnut praline.

❢ **Recipe ideas**
Hazelnut Praline Christmas Log ›› p. 306
Orange Blossom Ivory Mousse with a Praline Heart ›› p. 318
Rochers ("rock" cookies) ›› p. 368

Praline Filling
for Hand-Dipped Bonbons ★★

This is a confectionery classic. The method we give you here will enable you to prepare a homemade praline* base for bonbons to be coated in chocolate. Alternatively, you could use ready-made praline, which can be found in specialist stores.

Ingredients
3 ½ oz. (100 g) milk chocolate, 40 percent cocoa
7 oz. (200 g) homemade praline (see facing page)

Equipment
1 kitchen thermometer†
1 cold-water bath
1 confectionery frame† or lined brownie pan
1 baking sheet
1 sheet food-safe acetate† or parchment paper

Line a baking sheet with a sheet of food-safe acetate. Place the confectionery frame on it. Prepare a cold-water bath.
Chop the chocolate and melt it slowly in a bain-marie*, or in the microwave oven (on "defrost" or at 500 W maximum, stirring from time to time).
Incorporate the praline paste into the melted chocolate, making sure it is thoroughly blended. Cool the mixture down to 75°F (24°C): place the bowl of paste over a cold-water bath, stirring constantly. Then pour it into the prepared confectionery frame and leave it, ideally at a temperature range of 61°F–64°F (16°C–18°C), for 24 hours. Turn it out of the frame and remove the plastic or paper that covers it.
Give it an undercoat using tempered* chocolate (see p. 24). Cut out to the desired shapes and coat (see p. 25).

● **Chef's note**
If you use milk chocolate, there is less risk of fat bloom (see p. 147).

Praline Filling
for Molded Bonbons ★★

This praline* is designed to be poured into molds lined with hardened chocolate or inserted into chocolate or prebaked pastry shells.

Ingredients
1 ¾ oz. (50 g) milk chocolate, 40 percent cocoa
7 oz. (200 g) homemade praline (see opposite)

Equipment
1 kitchen thermometer†
1 piping bag†
1 cold-water bath

Have your molds lined with chocolate (see p. 26), or prebaked pastry shells, ready. Chop the chocolate and melt it slowly in a bain-marie* or in the microwave oven (on "defrost" or at 500 W maximum, stirring from time to time).
Incorporate the praline paste into the melted chocolate, mixing it thoroughly. Cool the mixture down to 81°F–82°F (27°C–28°C) by placing the bowl over the cold-water bath, stirring constantly.
With a piping bag, pipe out the praline filling into the chocolate-lined molds. Leave, ideally at a temperature range of 61°F–64°F (16°C–18°C), for 24 hours. Close the molded bonbons with tempered* chocolate (see p. 20).

● **Chef's note**
You will find ready-to-use praline at specialist stores.

Gianduja ★★

Gianduja is a paste comprising mainly roasted hazelnuts, chocolate, and sugar, to which a little milk may be added. It could be described as a chocolate in which some of the cocoa beans have been replaced by roasted hazelnuts.

Ingredients
9 oz. (250 g) whole hazelnuts
3 ½ oz. (100 g) milk chocolate, 40 percent cocoa
1 oz. (30 g) cocoa butter* (available at certain pastry shops, specialty stores, or online)
1 cup plus 1 scant cup (9 oz./250 g) confectioners' sugar

Equipment
1 food processor fitted with a blade attachment
1 kitchen thermometer[†]
1 cold-water bath

Preheat the oven to 300°F (150°C). Roast the nuts for about 10 minutes, until a nice amber color (see p. 134). Allow to cool for a few minutes, then peel* the hazelnuts.

Chop the chocolate and melt it slowly with the cocoa butter in a bain-marie* or in the microwave oven (on "defrost" or at 500 W maximum, stirring from time to time).

Place the roasted, peeled hazelnuts (1) in the bowl of a food processor with the confectioners' sugar and process until the mixture reaches the consistency of a paste. Add the melted milk chocolate and cocoa butter. Combine and transfer to a mixing bowl.

Cool the mixture down to 77°F-79°F (25°C-26°C) by placing the bowl over a cold-water bath, stirring constantly (2). Use the gianduja immediately, either pouring it into a confectionery frame or piping it out into chocolate-lined molds, or store it in an airtight plastic container, where you may keep it at room temperature for two weeks.

● **Did you know?**
The term gianduja comes from the Piedmont in Italy. It is believed to have originated from the name of a famous person of the region, Giandujotto.

Recipe idea
Gianduja-Topped Madeleines >> p. 284

1

2

Almond Paste ★★

Nothing can better homemade almond paste, but you will need a very sturdy food processor to make it—perfectly feasible at home for a small batch. Store it in the refrigerator and use it to make chocolate bonbons with an incomparably refined taste.

Ingredients
2 tablespoons (40 g) honey
⅔ oz. (20 g) glucose syrup
6 tablespoons (⅓ cup/90 ml) water
1 scant cup (6 ⅓ oz./180 g) sugar
13 oz. (375 g) whole blanched* almonds

Equipment
1 kitchen thermometer†
1 sheet food-safe acetate† or parchment paper
1 food processor fitted with a blade attachment
1 spatula†

In a saucepan, bring the honey, glucose syrup (1), water, and sugar to the boil.
Process the almonds in the bowl of your food processor (2) and add the boiling syrup. Process until the mixture reaches the consistency of a paste. The temperature should be 175°F (80°C). Place it on a sheet of food-safe acetate or parchment paper and continue mixing for a few minutes using a spoon or spatula, until the mixture is completely smooth (3). Store the paste in an airtight container at 39.2°F (4°C) (refrigerator temperature).

● Chef's note
This almond paste can be kept in an airtight container for about two months in the refrigerator.

❙ Recipe ideas
Almond Mousse, Milk Chocolate Heart,
and Honey-Softened Pears ›› p. 226
Mini Apple Chocolate Genoa Cakes ›› p. 255
Almond-Flavored Hot Chocolate ›› p. 266

3

Pistachio/Hazelnut Paste ★

All you need is an oven, a food processor, and a little grape-seed oil to make a uniquely flavorful, unctuous pistachio paste. And once you've tried it, you won't be able to use anything else!

Ingredients
7 oz. (200 g) green pistachios or peeled* hazelnuts
2 tablespoons (30 ml) grape-seed oil

Equipment
1 food processor fitted with a blade attachment

Preheat the oven to 300°F–325°F (150°C–160°C). Roast the nuts for about 10 minutes (see p. 134). Remove from the oven and allow to cool.
Pour the cooled nuts (1) into the bowl of your food processor with the grape-seed oil (2). Process until the paste reaches a smooth consistency (3). Store in an airtight container in the refrigerator for up to three weeks, or freeze in small quantities.

● **Chef's note**
Try dried plum (prune) kernel oil instead of grape-seed oil for an even tastier paste.

❘ **Recipe ideas**
Chocolate-Pistachio Loaf with Almond and Anise Streusel ›› p. 249
Hazelnut-Flavored Hot Chocolate ›› p. 267

2

1

3

Caramel Filling
for Hand-Dipped Centers ★ ★

This filling is made in the same way as ganache* for hand-dipping.
Caramel* paired with melted milk chocolate makes an ideal
combination.

Ingredients
3 ½ oz. (100 g) milk chocolate, 40 percent cocoa
Scant ¼ cup (50 g) water
2 ⅔ oz. (75 g) glucose syrup
Granulated sugar, divided as follows: 1 ¼ cup (240 g) and one scant
½ cup (80 g)
Generous ⅔ cup (5 ¾ oz./170 g) whipping cream
1 pinch salt
2 tablespoons (30 g) butter, cubed

Equipment
1 pastry brush†
1 kitchen thermometer†
1 confectionery frame† and 1 baking sheet lined with food-safe
acetate† or silicone baking mat†
Or 1 lined brownie pan

Place the frame on the lined baking sheet or the silicone
baking mat, or prepare the brownie pan.
Chop the chocolate.
In a saucepan, heat the water and glucose, and stir in the
1 ¼ cups (240 g) sugar.
Dip a pastry brush in water and brush the sugar crystals away
from the sides to dissolve all the sugar. Bring the mixture to a
temperature of 350°F (180°C) (1).
While it is heating, combine the cream, salt, and scant ½ cup
(80 g) sugar in another saucepan and bring to the boil. When
the water, glucose, and sugar mixture reaches the desired
temperature of 350°F (180°C), carefully add the cubed butter
(2). Stir briefly and then add the hot cream mixture (3) and the
chopped chocolate.
Stir continuously until the mixture reaches 250°F (120°C).
Pour the caramel into the confectionery frame (4) or brownie
pan. Leave to cool at room temperature for about 4 hours. Cut
into the desired shapes (5).

● Chef's note
*If you intend to coat your caramels, don't forget to give them an
undercoat of tempered* chocolate (see p. 24).*

❦ Recipe idea
Milk Chocolate *Palets* with Caramel ›› p. 274

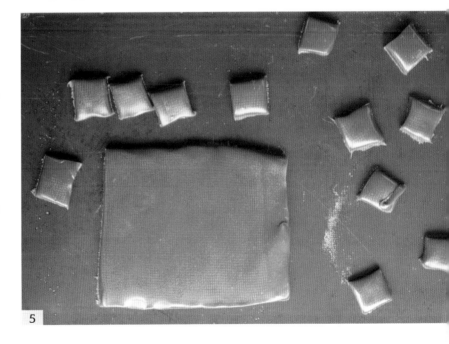

Chocolate Marshmallow ★★

There are several ways of making marshmallow. This is a simple, original recipe that uses gelatin, sugar, and honey as basic ingredients. You may flavor it with chocolate or all sorts of fruit coulis.

Ingredients

8 ½ sheets (17 g) gelatin
1 cup plus 3 tablespoons (8 oz./225 g) granulated sugar
½ cup (5 ¾ oz./170 g) honey, divided into 3 tablespoons plus 1 scant teaspoon (2 ½ oz./70 g) for the syrup, plus ⅓ cup (3 ½ oz./100 g)
⅓ cup (75 ml) water
3 ½ oz. (100 g) bittersweet chocolate, 70 percent cocoa

Equipment

1 kitchen thermometer[†]
1 baking sheet
1 confectionery frame[†] or baking pan, 8 × 8 in. (20 × 20 cm) square
1 flexible spatula[†]
Parchment paper

Line the baking pan with parchment paper and oil it lightly. Prepare another sheet of parchment paper to cover the pan and oil that too.

Soften the sheets of gelatin in a bowl filled with very cold water. In a saucepan, prepare a syrup. Cook the sugar, the 3 tablespoons plus 1 scant teaspoon (2 ½ oz./70 g) honey, and the water to a temperature of 230°F (110°C) **(1, 2)**.

Pour the scant ⅓ cup (3 ½ oz./100 g) honey into a bowl and pour the syrup over it. Wring the gelatin to remove the water and carefully dissolve it, without adding any water, in the microwave oven at 500 W, for about 10 seconds. Then pour it into the honey-syrup mixture and whisk* until the texture is foamy **(3)**.

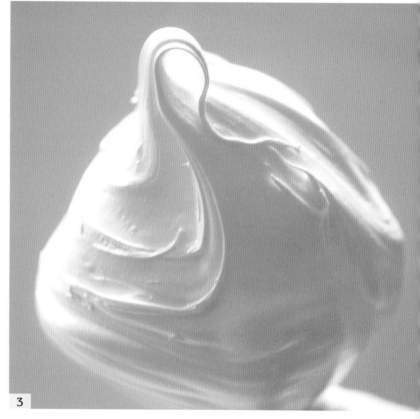

Chop the chocolate and melt it slowly in a bain-marie* or in the microwave oven (on "defrost" or at 500 W maximum, stirring from time to time).

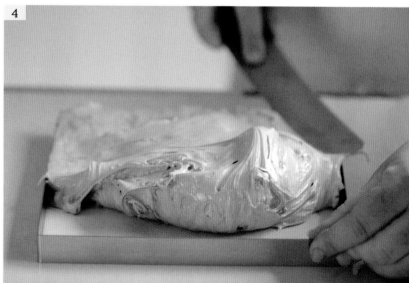

When the marshmallow paste is lukewarm (below 104°F or 40°C), incorporate the melted chocolate with a flexible spatula. Pour it immediately into the lined pan **(4)** and cover with the lightly oiled sheet of parchment paper, oiled side down.

Leave to crystallize* overnight. The next day, cut out strips using an oiled knife. Store in an airtight container for up to 4 to 5 days.

Recipe idea
Chocolate-Honey Marshmallow >> p. 338

Pâte de Fruits (jelled fruit) ★★

Fruit and chocolate go together wonderfully well, whether you use berries, deciduous, exotic fruits, or summer or fall fruit. *Pâte de fruits* can be used to fill chocolate bonbons and garnish many chocolate desserts.

Ingredients
Granulated sugar, divided as follows: 3 ½ tablespoons (1 ½ oz./40 g) to combine with the pectin plus 1 cup plus 2 tablespoons (7 ¾ oz./220 g)
1 ½ teaspoons (4 g) apple pectin (online or at specialty stores)
7 oz. (200 g) fruit pulp
⅔ oz. (20 g) glucose syrup (online or at specialty stores)
Juice of ½ lemon

Equipment
1 kitchen thermometer†
1 confectionery frame† or brownie pan
1 baking sheet or silicone baking mat†
1 sheet food-safe acetate†

If you are using pineapple, kiwi, or papaya, boil the fruit pulp before using. They contain a substance called a proteolytic enzyme that prevents jelling and is destroyed by heat. If it is still present, your fruit will not jel. So, if you opt for any of these fruits, bring to the boil and cool to 104°F (40°C) before proceeding with the recipe.
Line a baking sheet with a sheet of food-safe acetate and place the frame on the tray, or prepare your brownie pan.
Combine 3 ½ tablespoons (3 ½ oz./40 g) sugar with the pectin until thoroughly mixed.
In a saucepan, heat the fruit pulp to 104°F (40°C). Stir in the sugar-pectin mixture and continue to stir until the pulp begins to boil. Add the remaining 1 cup plus 2 tablespoons (7 ¾ oz./220 g) granulated sugar, still stirring constantly, and bring to the boil again. Add the glucose syrup, continuing to stir, and cook until the mixture reaches 221°F (105°C). Remove the saucepan from the heat straight away and stir in the lemon juice. Then pour it immediately into the frame or the brownie pan.
Leave to dry at room temperature for 24 hours, before coating. This confection keeps for 2 weeks.

● Chef's note
Flavor your fruit jellies by adding finely chopped herbs, grated citrus zest, or spice.*

❙ Recipe ideas
Chocolate, Coconut, and Passion Fruit Cakes ≫ p. 252
Bittersweet Chocolate Fondue ≫ p. 314

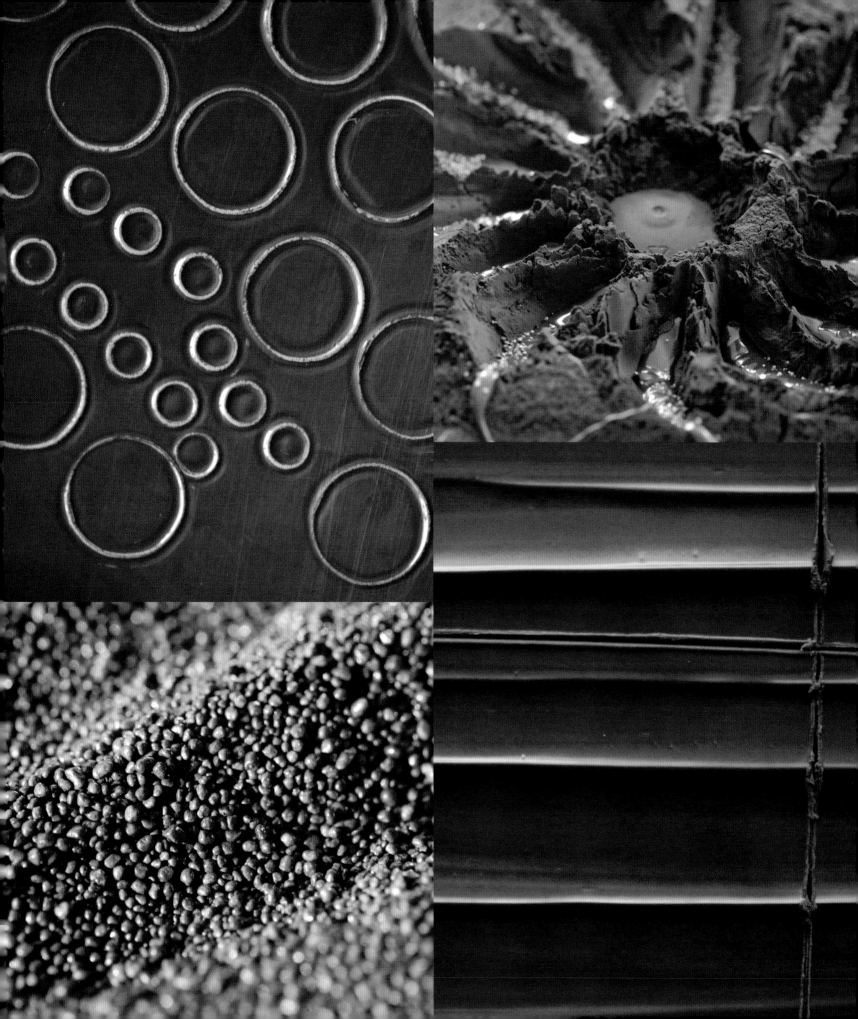

Decorations

Chocolate Decorations

Disks ★★★

Use this basic technique to make delicate chocolate disks of different sizes, as well as other decorations using differently shaped cookie cutters.

Ingredient
10 ½ oz. (300 g) chocolate

Equipment
1 baking sheet
2 sheets food-safe acetate†
1 cookie cutter†
1 metal spatula†
1 kitchen thermometer†
1 rolling pin†

Oil a plain flat baking sheet using a sheet of paper towel. Lay an acetate sheet over it and remove any air bubbles, so that the acetate is "stuck" to the baking sheet.
Temper* the chocolate (see p. 20).
Pour one-third of the tempered chocolate over the prepared tray. Cover it with the other sheet of plastic and roll it out to a thickness of ½ in. (1 mm) **(1)**.
When the chocolate just begins to harden, use the cutter to make disks of your chosen size. Press hard enough to make a good imprint of the circle **(2)**. Repeat the procedure with the rest of the chocolate. Place in a cool room at 63°F-64°F (17°C-18°C) for about 30 minutes to harden.
Carefully remove the top sheet of plastic and remove the chocolate disks, using the spatula if necessary.
Store in a cool, dry place in an airtight container.

● Chef's notes
To speed up the hardening of the chocolate, place it in the refrigerator for ten minutes, but don't forget that chocolate does not like humidity!
Chocolate may be stored for a considerable length of time (up to one year) so long as it is kept in a cool, dry place.

❦ Recipe idea
Jelled Milk Chocolate, Chestnuts, and Soy Foam ›› p. 382

1

2

Tuiles (Molded disks) ★ ★ ★ 🎬

Before chocolate hardens (crystallizes*), it will take on whatever shape you give it. If you curve it by placing it in a tuile mold or draping it over a rolling pin, you will have tuiles that will snap perfectly when you break them.

Ingredient

10 ½ oz. (300 g) tempered* chocolate (see p. 20)

Equipment

1 piping bag†
2 sheets food-safe acetate†, in strips
1 rolling pin†
1 tuile mold† (optional)

Fill a piping bag with tempered chocolate and pipe out small quantities onto a strip of acetate (1, 2).
Cover with a second strip of plastic and press down lightly with a rolling pin to make oval disks. Do not roll them out too thinly. Immediately separate the two strips (3) and drape them over the rolling pin or lay them in a tuile mold (4) to curve them. Leave to set.
Prepare several strips with tuiles of different diameters. Leave to harden for 5-10 minutes and then carefully detach the disks from the acetate strips (5).

🍴 **Recipe idea**
Black Forest ≫ p. 165

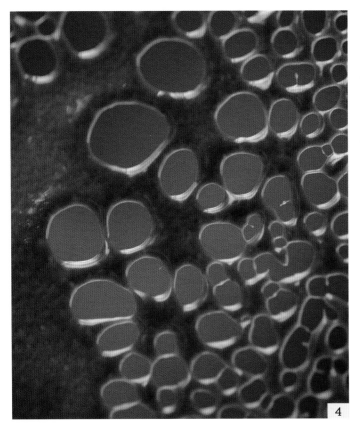

Opalines ★★★

These are often used to garnish individually served desserts.

Ingredients
½ lb. (225 g) pouring fondant* (online or at specialty stores)
5 ¼ oz. (150 g) glucose syrup (online or at specialty stores)
⅔ oz. (20 g) bittersweet chocolate, 70 percent cocoa, chopped

Equipment
1 flexible spatula†
1 silicone baking mat† or baking sheet lined with parchment paper
1 kitchen thermometer†
1 food processor fitted with a blade attachment
1 fine-meshed sieve† or sifter

In a saucepan, heat the pouring fondant and glucose syrup to 311°F-325°F (155°C-160°C). Incorporate the chopped chocolate using a flexible spatula. Pour the mixture over a silicone mat (1) or baking sheet lined with parchment paper. Leave to cool. Remove the paste when it has set and break it into pieces (2). Grind into a fine powder, seen here in extreme close-up (3). Preheat the oven to 285°F-300°F (140°C-150°C).
Sift the powder through a sieve onto the silicone baking mat. Do not make the layer too thin, otherwise your opalines will not hold. Bake until the powder melts and forms holes. Remove from the oven, leave to cool, and gently take off the baking mat (4). If you wish to make shapes, do so before baking. Use a toothpick to brush away the powder from around the shapes you are making, such as triangles, squares, and rectangles. Opalines must be stored in an airtight container, and even then will keep barely 24 hours.

Recipe idea
White Chocolate-Coffee Dessert with a Whiff of Dark Chocolate >> p. 229

Chocolate Plastic ★ ★

Chocolate plastic is a very malleable paste that should be used in a fairly thick layer. It can be used instead of almond paste for decorations.

Ingredients
9 oz. (250 g) bittersweet chocolate, 60 percent cocoa
Or 11 ½ oz. (325 g) white chocolate, 35 percent cocoa
Food coloring (optional)
7 oz. (200 g) glucose syrup

Equipment
1 baking sheet
1 kitchen thermometer†

Prepare one day ahead.
Chop the chocolate and melt it, with the food coloring (if using), in a bowl over a bain-marie* or in the microwave oven (on "defrost" or at 500 W, stirring from time to time).
In a saucepan, warm the glucose syrup to about 104°F (40°C). Carefully combine it with the (colored) chocolate (1). As soon as it is mixed through, remove from the heat and set aside at room temperature until the following day.

Knead* the mixture to soften it until you have perfectly smooth chocolate plastic (2).
Spread it out over a baking sheet (3) and cut it out into the shapes of your choice.

● **Chef's notes**
Because of the presence of cocoa butter in the chocolate, it's best to use food colorings that dissolve in fatty matter.
Chocolate plastic keeps for two months if wrapped tightly so it does not dry out.*

❚ **Recipe idea**
Lollipops >> p. 359

Teardrops ★ ★ ★ 🎬

Teardrops, commas, fans, or chocolate petals—choose your tools according to the shapes you want. This is definitely the type of decoration where practice makes perfect, so you will need to repeat the exercise until you get it just right. Whatever shape you decide on, it will be lovely!

Ingredient
10 ½ oz. (300 g) tempered* chocolate (see p. 20)

Equipment
Strips of parchment paper or food-safe acetate†
Kitchen knife, spatula†, triangular scraper†, etc.
1 tuile mold†
1 rolling pin†

Dip the corner of the blade of a kitchen knife or spatula (1) into the tempered chocolate. Place the flat of the blade firmly on the strip of parchment paper or acetate (2) and remove it quickly, drawing it away slightly. Repeat the procedure until you have filled the strip.
Leave to set at room temperature for 30 minutes (3), before removing carefully from the paper and using (4).

● Chef's notes
For curved teardrops, leave them to set on the strip of paper in a tuile mold or draped over a rolling pin.
To make rounded teardrops, use a thin spatula instead of a kitchen knife.
To create a wavy effect, dip one tip of a triangular scraper into the tempered chocolate and place it firmly on a strip of parchment paper or plastic. Slide it sharply to the right.

Palets ★★★

These small, flat *palets* that brighten up Christmas tables are prepared like chocolate disks. Embellish them with gold or silver leaf for a little glamour.

Ingredients
10 ½ oz. (300 g) tempered* chocolate (see p. 20)
Sheets of edible gold or silver leaf

Equipment
Strips of parchment paper or food-safe acetate[†]
1 piping bag[†]
1 confectionary ruler[†]

Spoon the tempered chocolate into the piping bag and pipe out small quantities onto the paper or plastic. Decorate with a small piece of gold or silver leaf and cover with a second strip of parchment paper or plastic. Flatten slightly with a ruler. Leave to set at room temperature for about 1 hour before using.

● **Chef's note**
You can also decorate the palets with crystallized flowers, chocolate granules, colored sugar, ground coffee, and so on.

Paper Decorating Cones ★★★ 🎬

The hidden artist in you gets a chance to draw with chocolate using a paper decorating cone.
Once you have mastered how to hold the cone and make the strokes, you can give free rein to your imagination!

Ingredient
10 ½ oz. (300 g) tempered* chocolate (see p. 20)

Equipment
Parchment paper for a paper decorating cone[†] and 1 piping bag[†] (optional for wider strokes)
Strips of parchment paper or food-safe acetate[†]
Tuile mold[†] or rolling pin[†] if making curved decorations

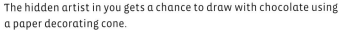

Prepare a parchment paper decorating cone (see Equipment, p. 402). Ensure the tip is properly closed and half fill it with tempered chocolate.
Cut off a small tip and press down on the chocolate to draw small circles or squares on the strips of parchment paper or plastic, crisscrossing the shapes with lines of chocolate. If you wish, sprinkle them with chocolate granules, colored sugar, and so on.
Leave to set for about 1 hour at room temperature before using. Carefully remove the decorations from the paper or acetate and place them on your cake.
For particularly thin, delicate decorations, draw them directly on the cake.

● **Chef's notes**
For curved decorations, use a tuile mold or a rolling pin.
You can use a piping bag for thicker decorations and a paper decorating cone for thinner ones.

1

2

Wavy Tiles ★ ★ ★

Chocolate is very flexible in its creative potential. When used as sculpting material, it fixes the light so you can play on contrasts between matte and shiny textures.

Ingredient
10 ½ oz. (300 g) tempered* chocolate (see p. 20)

Equipment
1 baking sheet
1 sheet food-safe acetate[†]
1 metal spatula[†]

Oil a perfectly flat baking sheet using a sheet of paper towel and stick a sheet of acetate to it, smoothing out all the air bubbles. Pour onto it a line of tempered chocolate (1) and spread it out with the spatula.
Before the chocolate hardens, make back-and-forth movements with the spatula to create a wavy effect. Then cut out rectangles or squares to the size you need (2). Allow to set for 30 minutes at room temperature before using.

● Chef's note
If you want to make smooth, shiny tile shapes, see the technique for disks (see p. 48).

3

Chocolate Cigarettes ★★★

This is an all-chocolate, refined version of the Russian cigarette. They are relatively simple to make as long as you choose the moment when they are sufficiently malleable.

Ingredient
Tempered* chocolate (see p. 20)

Equipment
1 metal spatula†
1 triangular metal pastry scraper†
Marble working surface, or other cool, smooth surface, such as tiling or a mirror.

Spread out the tempered chocolate on your cool working surface to a thickness of just under $\frac{1}{16}$ inch (2 mm). When it begins to set (the texture is just right when your finger can indent the chocolate easily), push it quickly away from you using the triangular scraper like a snow plough, pressing hard and keeping it firmly on the metal as you do so (1).
The chocolate will roll over itself and this will make your chocolate cigarette. Repeat the procedure as many times as necessary. If the chocolate hardens, you will not be able to continue. Instead scrape up the remaining chocolate and spread out some fresh tempered chocolate You may re-temper the chocolate if necessary.
Leave to harden for 30 minutes before using (2).

Powdered Decorations ★★★

Here is yet another way of exploiting the decorative potential of chocolate. Use powder or granules to create shapes as the inspiration takes you. Play with the textures of rough cocoa and shiny gold.

Ingredients
Unsweetened cocoa powder
Or granulated sugar
Or confectioners' sugar
Tempered* chocolate (see p. 20)

Equipment
1 ovenproof baking dish
Paper decorating cones† or 1 piping bag† (see Equipment, p. 402)
1 pastry brush†

Sift your chosen powder (cocoa, granulated sugar, or confectioners' sugar) into a baking dish. Fill the decorating cone with tempered chocolate and pipe out shapes in the powder. Leave to harden for 30 minutes before using. Remove the shapes from the dish and dust them off with the pastry brush.

● **Chef's note**
You can also make your shapes in the powder and then fill them with tempered chocolate.

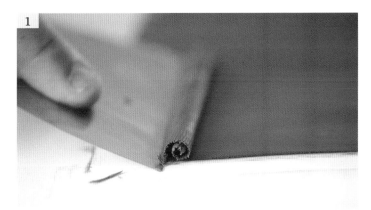

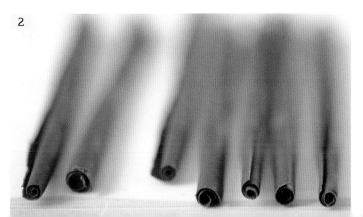

1

2

Ruffles ★ ★ ★

Ruffles are made in a similar fashion to chocolate cigarettes, but using a turning movement. You literally have to ruffle the chocolate, which then looks like drapery. Another case of practice makes perfect—even professionals sometimes have to make a special effort—so have confidence!

Ingredient
Tempered* chocolate (see p. 20)

Equipment
1 metal spatula[†]
1 triangular metal pastry scraper[†]
Marble working surface, or other cool, smooth surface, such as tiling or a mirror.

Spread the tempered chocolate out onto the cool surface to a thickness of just under $\frac{1}{16}$ in. (2 mm) (1). When it just begins to crystallize* (the texture is just right when your finger can indent the chocolate easily), place a finger firmly on a tip of the triangle and push the chocolate. It will ruffle naturally (2). Repeat the procedure as many times as you can. Should the chocolate harden, you will not be able to continue. Instead, scrape up the remaining chocolate and spread out some fresh tempered chocolate or re-temper what remains. Leave to set for 30 minutes before using (3).

3

Nougatine with Cocoa Nibs or Nuts ★★

This nougatine can be eaten on its own or used as a decoration. It brings together a blissful combination of a crisp, thin tuile, made mainly of sugar and butter, and the delicate crunch of cocoa nibs* (or nuts).

Ingredients
6 oz. (175 g) cocoa nibs or nuts of your choice
¾ cup (5 ¼ oz./150 g) sugar
¾ teaspoon (2 g) apple pectin
1 stick (125 g) butter
1 ¾ oz. (50 g) glucose syrup
2 teaspoons (10 ml) water

Equipment
1 food processor fitted with a blade attachment
1 silicone baking mat†
Rolling pin† (optional)

Preheat the oven to 375°F (190°C).
Chop the cocoa nibs or nuts roughly using the blade attachment of your food processor. In a saucepan, combine the sugar, pectin, butter, glucose, and water (1). Cook over low heat until the mixture is smooth. Add the cocoa nibs (2) or nuts to make the nougatine.
Drop small spoonfuls about 2 in. (5 cm) apart on the silicone baking mat (3) and bake for about 10 minutes (4).

● **Chef's note**
If you prefer curved shapes, like tuiles, drape the nougatines over a rolling pin as soon as you remove them from the oven. Use the same day.

❙ **Recipe idea**
❙ Crisp Shortbread and Nuts with Chocolate ›› p. 256
Chocolate, Coconut, and Passion Fruit Cakes ›› p. 252

Cocoa Cigarette Paste ★

These thin cigarette cookies are far easier to make than you might imagine. The chocolate recipe given here is a delicious variation on the classic cigarette cookie recipe.

Ingredients

7 tablespoons (3 ½ oz./100 g) butter
¾ cup (3 ½ oz./100 g) confectioners' sugar
3 tablespoons (⅔ oz./20 g) cocoa powder, unsweetened
Scant cup (2 ¾ oz./80 g) cake flour
3 egg whites

Equipment

1 pencil
Plastic wrap
1 whisk†
1 sieve†
1 piping bag†
1 silicone baking mat† or baking sheet

Cover the pencil in plastic wrap. Butter the baking sheet if using. Preheat the oven to 400°F (200°C). In a saucepan, melt the butter, whisking* it constantly, until it browns (*beurre noisette*).
Pour the melted butter into a mixing bowl. Lightly whisk the egg whites.
Sift the confectioners' sugar, cocoa powder, and flour together (1).
When the browned butter has cooled, add the sifted ingredients and half the egg whites, and combine.
Stir in the remaining egg whites, taking care not to overmix so that the mixture does not decrease in volume.
Using a spoon or piping bag, pipe out knobs of paste (2) onto the mat or baking sheet.
Use the back of a spoon to spread out the mixture to the desired shape (3).
Bake for 5-8 minutes.
To make the cigarette shapes, roll the cookies around the covered pencil as soon as you take them out of the oven (4). Should they begin to harden, return them briefly to the oven so they are soft enough to be rolled.

1

2

Other Decorations

Arlettes ★★

Arlettes are almost paper-thin disks of puff pastry.

Ingredients
7 oz. (200 g) puff pastry
½ cup (3 ½ oz./100 g) sugar
Confectioners' sugar for dusting

Equipment
1 rolling pin†
2 sheets of parchment paper

Cut the puff pastry into an 8 × 12 in. (20 × 30 cm) rectangle.
It should be about ⅕ in. (5-6 mm) thick.
Sprinkle it with the sugar. Using a rolling pin, roll it out again
to a thickness of ⅛ in. (3 mm). Roll the pastry up as you would
for a jelly (Swiss) roll (1) and place in the freezer for about 10
minutes to harden it slightly.
Preheat the oven to 350°F (180°C).
Cut it out into thin disks (2). Sprinkle them with confectioners'
sugar so that they do not stick when you flatten them (3). Place
them between 2 sheets of parchment paper. Use the rolling pin
to flatten them so that they are very thin. Bake for about 10
minutes, leaving them between the two sheets of parchment
paper, until they are a nice golden color.

❡ **Recipe idea**
Almond Mousse, Milk Chocolate Heart, and Honey-Softened Pears
» p. 226

3

Presentation Dishes

Chocolate Dish ★ ★ ★

Chocolate here is both container and content, so the whole plate can be eaten! The technique for making this requires some practice but the result is well worth the effort.

Ingredients
Water
A large quantity of ice cubes
Melted chocolate

Equipment
1 piping bag†

Half fill a large mixing bowl with water and ice cubes. When the melted chocolate has cooled and begins to thicken, pipe out thick squiggles into the well-chilled water **(1)** and immediately flatten the chocolate with your hand against the sides and bottom of the bowl to shape it into the form of a plate. Wait a few minutes and then remove it from the water **(2)**. Place it on some sheets of paper towel and dry well.

● **Chef's note**
You can decorate your plate with a colored chocolate velvet spray (available from specialty stores or online).

Compression ★ ★ 🎬

This technique is a variation on the theme of sculpted chocolate: think chocolate meets contemporary art.

Ingredients
A large quantity of ice cubes
Water
Melted chocolate
Edible gold luster dust

Equipment
1 cube-shaped mold† or square plastic box
1 piping bag†
1 pastry brush†
1 (full) bottle of water
Large, flat-bottomed mixing bowl

Fill a large, flat-bottomed mixing bowl with water and ice cubes so that you have really icy water to set your chocolate.
Place the cube mold or square box at the bottom of the mixing bowl. When the melted chocolate begins to cool and thicken, pipe it into the cube in fairly thick squiggles and immediately place the full water bottle into the center of the shape, so that the chocolate rises up round it to form the sides of your edible container.
Wait a few minutes before removing the cube from the water (1). Turn the chocolate out of the mold and place it on sheets of paper towel. Dry well.
Brush it with edible gold luster dust so that it looks realistically shiny (2).

Chocolate Thread Dish ★★★ 🎬

To produce this contemporary serving dish, you will need to wield the piping bag with assurance, making wide, continuous back-and-forth movements. Work quickly, and have confidence in your skills!

Ingredient
Tempered* chocolate (see p. 20)

Equipment
1 piping bag†
1 stainless steel round-bottomed bowl
1 sheet parchment paper

Place the bowl in the freezer. Fill the piping bag with tempered chocolate. To make the base of the bowl: pipe out disks of chocolate onto a sheet of parchment paper. Leave to crystallize* or set.

Remove the bowl from the freezer and turn it upside down on your work surface. Pipe out threads from one side to the other using a quick back-and-forth movement (1), to form a thick band of threads. When both base and dish are set, pipe a small amount of melted chocolate onto the bottom of your dish and place a disk on top to form the base. Leave to set (2).

Allow the chocolate dish to stay hardening on the bowl for about 1 hour (3).

Remove the set chocolate dish from the bowl and stand it upright. Fill it with your most delectable creations (4).

1

2

3

4

Molded Cup ★★★

Just like the sand used to mold bronze, cocoa powder can be used to make all sorts of shapes. Use cocoa as a cast and pour the tempered chocolate into the prepared molds.

Ingredients
Tempered* chocolate (see p. 20)
Unsweetened cocoa powder

Equipment
1 high-sided baking dish
1 small mixing bowl
1 ramekin
1 piping bag†

Sift the cocoa powder into the baking dish until it is about
2 in. (5 cm) deep. To create the base of the chocolate dish, place
the base of a small mixing dish firmly in the cocoa, and then
remove. Dip the rim of the ramekin into the cocoa powder and
then remove carefully to make a series of arcs radiating from
the base. Repeat to make 6-8 imprints.
Pipe tempered chocolate into the cast (1)–the arcs and
the central circle–and leave to set for about 1 hour before
assembling. Carefully remove the shapes and dust the cocoa
powder off. Glue the side shapes onto the base using tempered
chocolate (2).

Glazes 🎬

Glazes provide the finishing touch, giving a professional look to your desserts. There are several very simple methods of glazing; select the one most appropriate to your dessert.

Ultra-Shiny Glaze ★

This glaze should be used on a very cold dessert, or on one just taken out of the freezer.

Ingredients
6 sheets (12 g) gelatin
Scant ½ cup (100 g) water
1 scant cup (5 ¾ oz./170 g) granulated sugar
⅔ cup (2 ⅔ oz./75 g) unsweetened cocoa powder
⅓ cup plus 2 teaspoons (90 ml) whipping cream

Equipment
1 kitchen thermometer†
1 cake rack
1 plate or platter larger than the diameter of your dessert
1 flexible spatula†
1 metal spatula†

A day ahead.
Soften the gelatin sheets in a bowl filled with very cold water.
In a saucepan, combine the water, sugar, cocoa powder, and whipping cream.
Bring to the boil and simmer for 1 minute. Remove from the heat, wring the gelatin sheets dry and incorporate them into the mixture. Leave overnight to chill.
Re-heat the glaze in a bain-marie* or in the microwave oven. When it has reached about 98°F (37°C), place the dessert on a cake rack over a dish that is large enough to catch the excess glaze. Cover the dessert completely with the glaze (1, 2, 3) and smooth it over with a metal spatula.

🍴 **Recipe ideas**
Sachertorte ›› p. 166
Opéra ›› p. 182
Gold-Topped *Palet* Dessert ›› p. 323

Soft Bittersweet Glaze ★

This is a glaze that is aesthetically pleasing and will enhance any chocolate dessert. Use it on dishes that are either cold or at room temperature.

Ingredients
5 ½ oz. (150 g) bittersweet chocolate, 60 percent cocoa
Or 4 ⅔ oz. (130 g) bittersweet chocolate, 70 percent cocoa
1 cup (250 g) whipping cream
Scant 3 tablespoons (2 ¼ oz./60 g) honey
4 tablespoons (2 ¼ oz./60 g) butter, diced

Equipment
1 kitchen thermometer†
1 immersion blender†
1 cake rack
1 flexible spatula†
1 plate or platter larger than the diameter of your dessert
1 metal spatula†

Chop the chocolate and melt it slowly in a bain-marie* or in the microwave oven (on "defrost" or at 500 W maximum, stirring from time to time).
In a saucepan, bring the whipping cream and honey to the boil. Gradually pour one-third of the boiling liquid over the melted chocolate. Using a flexible spatula, mix in energetically, drawing small circles to create an elastic, shiny "kernel." Incorporate the second third of the liquid, using the same procedure. Repeat with the last third.
As soon as the ganache* reaches a temperature of 95°F-104°F (35°C-40°C), add the diced butter.
Blend for a few seconds using an immersion blender so that the mixture is smooth and perfectly emulsified*.
Place the dessert on a cake rack positioned above a dish large enough to catch the excess glaze.
Cover your dessert completely with the glaze (1) and smooth it over with a metal spatula (2).

● Chef's notes
If you want a smooth finish, use the glaze straight from the heat. If you prefer a glaze that will show the traces of the spatula, wait for it to harden just a little.

❢ Recipe idea
Chocolate Éclairs ›› p. 181

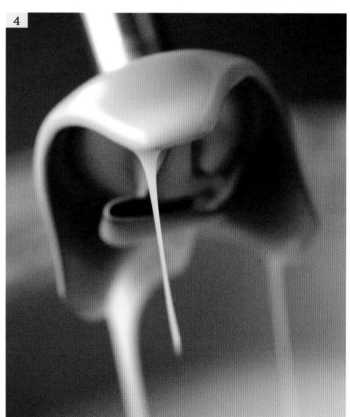

White Chocolate or Colored Glaze ★

This is an ivory variation of the ultra-shiny glaze that allows you to use interesting colors. It should be used over a very cold dessert, or one that has just been taken out of the freezer.

Ingredients
9 ⅓ oz. (265 g) white chocolate, 35 percent cocoa
2 sheets (4 g) gelatin
⅔ cup (175 ml) whipping cream
3 tablespoons (40 ml) water
1 ½ tablespoons (1 oz./30 g) glucose syrup
1 tablespoon plus 2 teaspoons (25 g) grape-seed oil
Food coloring of your choice, liposoluble

Equipment
1 kitchen thermometer†
1 cake rack
1 plate or platter larger than the diameter of your dessert
1 flexible spatula†
1 immersion blender†
1 metal spatula†

Chop the chocolate and melt it slowly in a bain-marie* or in the microwave oven (on "defrost" or at 500 W maximum, stirring from time to time).
Soften the gelatin in a bowl of very cold water. In a saucepan, bring the cream, water, and glucose syrup to the boil (1). Gradually pour one-third of the boiling liquid over the melted chocolate. (2). Using a flexible spatula, mix it in energetically, drawing small circles to create an elastic, shiny "kernel."
Incorporate the second third of the liquid, using the same procedure. Repeat with the last third (3). Wring the water out of the gelatin sheets and incorporate them, then add the grape-seed oil. If you are using food coloring, now is the time to incorporate it. Blend with an immersion blender until it is smooth and perfectly emulsified* (4), ensuring you do not incorporate any air bubbles. It can be kept in the refrigerator if you are not going to be using it very soon. If you chill it, re-heat the glaze over a bain-marie or in the microwave oven. When it reaches a temperature of about 98°F (37°C), the temperature at which it has to be spread, place the dessert on a cake rack positioned over a dish that is large enough to catch any excess glaze. Cover your dessert completely and smooth it over with a metal spatula.

● **Chef's note**
Use liposoluble colorings (ones that will dissolve in fat) because of the presence of cocoa butter in the chocolate.*

🍴 **Recipe idea**
Flore ›› p. 324

Chocolate Hazelnut Glaze ★

This beautiful, delicious glaze is a reminder that above all, a glaze should taste—and look—fabulous.

Ingredients
2 ¾ oz. (80 g) bittersweet chocolate, 70 percent cocoa
6 ⅓ oz. (180 g) hazelnut gianduja, homemade (see p. 40) or store bought
Generous ⅔ cup (175 g) whipping cream
3 tablespoons (40 g) water
1 ½ tablespoons (1 oz./30 g) glucose syrup
1 tablespoon plus 2 teaspoons (25 g) grape-seed oil

Equipment
1 kitchen thermometer†
1 cake rack
1 plate or platter larger than the diameter of your dessert
1 flexible spatula†
1 immersion blender†
1 metal spatula†

Chop the chocolate and gianduja and melt them slowly in a bain-marie* or in the microwave oven (on "defrost" or at 500 W maximum, stirring from time to time).
In a saucepan, bring the whipping cream, water, and glucose syrup to the boil.
Gradually pour one-third of the boiling liquid over the melted chocolate. Using a flexible spatula, mix it in energetically, drawing small circles to create an elastic, shiny "kernel." Incorporate the second third of the liquid, using the same procedure. Repeat with the last third. Add the grape-seed oil. Blend with an immersion blender until it is smooth and perfectly emulsified*, ensuring you do not incorporate any air bubbles.
You can keep this in the refrigerator if you are not going to be using it immediately. If you chill it, re-heat the glaze over a bain-marie or in the microwave oven. When it reaches a temperature of about 98°F (37°C), the temperature at which it has to be spread, place the dessert on a cake rack positioned over a dish that is large enough to catch any excess glaze. Cover your dessert completely and smooth it over with a metal spatula.

● **Chef's note**
Add chopped roasted hazelnuts or almonds for an even more intense taste experience.

Pastry doughs and sponges

Almond Shortcrust Pastry ★

This is a classic pastry that makes a perfect base for most chocolate-filled tarts. Its crumbly texture offsets the smoothness of chocolate to perfection. It never hurts to make extra, as it can be kept in the freezer for other occasions.
Makes one 9 in. (23 cm) tart shell, for 6–8 people.

Ingredients

1 stick (4 oz./120 g) butter, room temperature
Scant ½ teaspoon (2 g) salt
⅔ cup (3 ¼ oz./90 g) confectioners' sugar
3 tablespoons (½ oz./15 g) ground blanched* almonds
1 egg
Cake flour, divided as follows: ⅔ cup (60 g) plus 2 cups (180 g)

Equipment

2 sheets of food-safe acetate†

In a mixing bowl, soften the butter and mix with the salt, confectioners' sugar, ground almonds, egg, and ⅔ cup (60 g) cake flour.
As soon as the ingredients are mixed through, add the remaining flour and mix until just combined (1, 2). Roll the dough out to a thickness of ⅛ in. (3 mm) between two sheets of acetate (3) and place it in the freezer for 1 hour, ensuring that it is flat.

When the dough has completely hardened, peel off the sheets of acetate. Cut the dough out to the desired shape (4). Line the tart molds or leave flat if your recipe calls for this.
Chill for 30 minutes. Preheat the oven to 300°F–325°F (150°C–160°C). Bake the pastry for about 15 minutes, until golden.

Recipe ideas

Extraordinarily Chocolate Tart ›› p. 175
Golden Rules ›› p. 192
Walnut, Caramel, and Coffee-Chocolate Tart ›› p. 195
Sunny Pear and Chocolate Tart ›› p. 196
A Take on Tartlets ›› p. 198
Chocolate, Clementine, and Orange Blossom Water Tartlets ›› p. 201
Hazelnut Waves ›› p. 205
Warm Chocolate Tart ›› p. 210
Mont Blanc, Revisited ›› p. 305
Pear and Milk Chocolate Petits Fours ›› p. 321
Bittersweet Chocolate Bars, Salted Butter Caramel, and Crystallized Almonds ›› p. 332

Piped Shortbread Pastry ★

This shortbread dough is soft enough to be piped out into the shapes of your choice. It's a variation on the Spritz cookies of the Alsace region.
Makes about forty-five ½-oz. (15-g) cookies.

Ingredients
1 ⅓ stick (5 ¼ oz./150 g) unsalted butter, room temperature
¾ cup (3 ½ oz./100 g) confectioners' sugar
1 egg
1 tablespoon (15 g) whipping cream
2 ¼ cups (7 oz./200 g) cake flour
2 tablespoons (⅔ oz./20 g) cornstarch
1 pinch salt
1 pinch vanilla seeds or ground vanilla

Equipment
1 baking sheet
Parchment paper or molds† if using
1 piping bag† fitted with a plain or star-shaped tip†

Preheat the oven to 300°F-325°F (150°C-160°C). Line a baking sheet with parchment paper or prepare your molds. Sift the confectioners' sugar. Cream the softened butter with the confectioners' sugar and then incorporate the egg and cream. Add the flour, cornstarch, salt, and vanilla and mix until just combined. Do not overmix.
Spoon the dough into a piping bag and pipe out onto the lined baking sheet or into your molds.
Bake until the dough is a light golden color, about 15 minutes, depending on your oven.

❦ **Recipe idea**
Crisp Shortbread and Nuts with Chocolate >> p. 256

Breton Shortbread
with Chocolate Chips ★

Breton shortbread always has a generous proportion of butter, giving it a texture that is crisp, melting, and crumbly all at once. It is perfectly satisfying on its own, but balances extremely well with melting chocolate or fruit coulis.

Ingredients
2 egg yolks
Scant ½ cup (2 ¾ oz./80 g) sugar
5 ½ tablespoons (2 ¾ oz./80 g) butter, softened
1 cup plus 1 scant ¼ cup (4 ¼ oz./120 g) all-purpose flour
1 teaspoon (4 g) baking powder
¼ teaspoon (1 g) salt
Scant ½ cup (2 ⅔ oz./75 g) Valrhona chocolate pearls (roughly chopped chocolate or chocolate chips can be substituted if necessary)

Equipment
1 silicone mat† or 1 baking sheet lined with parchment paper
2 sheets food-safe acetate† (optional)

Preheat the oven to 350°F (170°C). Sift the flour with the baking powder and the salt.
Beat the egg yolks with the sugar (1, 2, 3) until the mixture is thick and pale. Soften the butter and incorporate it, then the sifted dry ingredients. Stir in the chocolate pearls or chips (4) until just combined.
Roll out the dough to a thickness of ¼ in. (5 mm). Rolling it between 2 sheets of acetate means you avoid sprinkling your pastry board and dough with too much flour. This will ensure that the cookies retain their crunch. Cut out to the desired shapes (5) and place them on the silicone mat or lined baking tray. Chill for 30 minutes. Bake for about 15 minutes, until golden.

● **Chef's note**
If you want to reproduce the authentic Breton palets, *bake them in small, ungreased pastry circles. The original cookies are of uniform thickness from the center to their straight edges.*

❘ **Recipe idea**
Coffee, Chocolate, and Vanilla Creams with Breton Shortbread ≫ p. 217

Spiced Dough ★

This cookie dough is flavored with cinnamon, making it an excellent pairing for the spicy notes of certain types of chocolate.

Ingredients
2 sticks (8 oz./250 g) butter
1 ¼ cups (8 oz./250 g) light brown sugar
⅓ cup (2 ½ oz./75 g) granulated sugar
1 egg
5 cups (1 lb./450 g) cake flour
1 tablespoon plus 1 scant tablespoon (½ oz./14 g) ground cinnamon
1 tablespoon plus 1 teaspoon (20 ml) whole milk

Equipment
Baking sheets
2 sheets food-safe acetate† (optional)
1 flexible spatula†
1 whisk†

Take the butter out of the refrigerator several hours before you begin baking and place it in a mixing bowl. When it has reached room temperature, use a flexible spatula to soften it (*pommade**). If you need to soften the butter more quickly, pop it into the microwave briefly or over a bain-marie*. Finish softening it with a spatula or a whisk.
Preheat the oven to 350°F (170°C). Sift the flour with the cinnamon and set aside.
Add the brown sugar and white granulated sugar to the butter and mix in well. Incorporate the egg and sifted flour and cinnamon (1, 2) Lastly, stir in the milk and mix until the dough is smooth (3, 4).
A trick is to roll the dough out, preferably between 2 sheets of acetate, to a thickness of just under ⅟₁₆ in. (2 mm), or thicker if you are making individual cookies, before chilling it for about an hour. Otherwise you can cover the dough in plastic wrap, chill for an hour, and roll it out after that. Cut it out to the desired shapes.
Bake for about 15 minutes.

❗ Recipe idea
Mandarin Marvels ›› p. 206

Choux Pastry ★★

Choux pastry is used to make the cream puffs of *religieuses* and for éclairs. It requires a certain skill to dry it out to just the right degree over the stove. The trick lies in knowing exactly when to take it off the heat.

Makes about 10 average-sized éclairs.

Ingredients
Scant ⅓ cup (75 ml) water
Scant ⅓ cup (75 ml) whole milk
Heaped ½ teaspoon (3 g) salt
¾ teaspoon (3 g) granulated sugar
4 tablespoons (60 g) butter
1 cup (3 ¼ oz./90 g) cake flour
3 eggs
1 beaten egg yolk, for the egg wash (optional)

Equipment
1 piping bag†
1 baking sheet lined with parchment paper
1 pastry brush†

Preheat the oven to 480°F (250°C).
In a saucepan, bring the water, milk, salt, sugar, and butter to the boil. Sift the flour into the liquid. The important step now is to dry it out: stir energetically until the moisture has evaporated. Remove from the heat and mix in the eggs, one by one (1). Stir thoroughly each time. When the batter is ready it should have a satin finish (2), like paint. If it is matte it is already too hard; if it is shiny it is too wet.
Spoon the batter into a piping bag and pipe out shapes (rounds for profiteroles, for example, and long shapes for éclairs) on a lined baking sheet (3). For a nice, finished result, brush the top of the dough with a beaten egg yolk, pressing down lightly with a fork.
Place the baking sheet in the oven and immediately switch off the heat.
As soon as the choux pastry begins to puff up and color, turn the heat back on to 350°F (180°C) and leave the pastries to dry out slowly for about 10 minutes.

Recipe ideas
Chocolate Profiteroles ›› p. 172
Chocolate Éclairs ›› p. 181

Pastry doughs and sponges

Brioche Dough ★ ★

Homemade brioche requires technique and time, but the smell as it wafts through your house will be reward enough—not to mention the compliments you'll get when it's eaten.
This recipe makes 1 large brioche or about 8 small ones.

Ingredients

1 tablespoon plus 2 teaspoons (25 ml) whole milk
⅕ oz. (6 g) fresh (compressed) yeast
2 ½ cups (9 oz./250 g) all-purpose flour
2 tablespoons (¾ oz./25 g) granulated sugar
1 teaspoon (5 g) salt
3 eggs plus 1 egg for the egg wash
1 ⅓ stick (5 ½ oz./150 g) unsalted butter, cubed

Equipment

1 stand-alone mixer† fitted with a dough hook
1 pastry brush†
1 kitchen thermometer†
1 chinois†

Slightly warm the milk in a small saucepan and dilute the yeast in it.
Pour the flour, sugar, salt, milk and yeast mixture, and the 3 eggs into the bowl of the mixer fitted with the dough hook (1). Knead* for about 15 minutes at low speed so as not to heat the mixture, until the dough pulls away from the sides of the bowl. Gradually add the cubed butter (2), and knead until the dough is smooth (3).
Cover it with a clean damp cloth and leave it to double in volume (4).
Punch the dough down until it returns to its original volume (this is to remove the air) and chill for 1 hour.
Shape the brioche into the desired shape or shapes. Place on a baking tray. Again, cover with a clean damp cloth until it doubles in volume.
Preheat the oven to 350°F (180°C).
To prepare the egg wash, beat 1 egg and strain it through a chinois.
Using a soft brush, glaze* the brioche dough twice with the egg.
Bake for about 15 minutes. Test for doneness with an instant-read thermometer: the core temperature should be 200°F (93°C).

❢ Recipe idea
Tropézienne Redux with White Chocolate ›› p. 202

Croissant Dough ★ ★ ★

Makes 8–10 croissants.

Begin your preparation a day ahead, early in the afternoon.
Prepare what is called the *détrempe** (the flour-and-water paste
needed before the addition of water):
Dissolve the yeast in ⅔ cup (150 ml) very cold water. Sift
the flour into a mixing bowl and incorporate the salt, sugar,
and dissolved yeast. Mix in the bowl of the mixer fitted with
a dough hook until you have a smooth dough. If it appears
somewhat hard, add a little water.
Leave to rise* at room temperature for 1 hour–1 hour 30
minutes, until it is approximately twice the volume.
Then deflate the dough by punching it with your fist. Leave to
rest in the refrigerator for 1 hour.
Soften the butter and shape it by placing it between 2 sheets
of parchment paper and applying pressure with a rolling
pin. It should measure about 4 × 7 in. (10 × 18 cm). Roll out
the *détrempe* into a 6 × 12 in. (15 × 30 cm) rectangle. Place the
flattened butter at the base of the dough **(1)**, at a distance of
about ½ in. (1 cm) from the bottom.
Fold the top of the dough over the butter and then fold the
dough supporting the remaining exposed butter back to
enclose it completely (the two ends of dough will meet). Roll out
the dough to a 6 × 12 in. (15 × 30 cm) rectangle, cover in plastic
wrap, and chill for at least 1 hour.
Remove from the refrigerator and place it so that the visible
fold is on your right. Roll it out again to the same size, a
6 × 12 in. (15 × 30 cm) rectangle. Fold it again (the third at the
top downwards, and then the lower third over that).
Cover in plastic wrap, and chill for at least 1 hour.
Repeat the procedure 3 times allowing the dough to chill, well
wrapped, for at least 1 hour between each procedure. Make
sure that you place the visible fold on your right each time you
begin rolling out–the fold should be rolled out lengthways.
When you have finished, leave it to rest for 1 further hour at
room temperature. Then roll it out to a width of 8 in. (20 cm)
and a thickness of ⅛ in. (3 mm).
Cut it out into 8 to 10 triangles, each with a base of about 4 ½ in.
(12 cm). Starting from the base of the triangle, roll each one up
to the tip **(3)**. Cover them with a cloth to prevent a crust from
forming. Leave to rise overnight until they have doubled in
volume. The next morning preheat the oven to 350°F (180°C).
Then carefully brush the tops with the egg and bake for about
20 minutes.

Ingredients
6 cups (1 lb. 5 oz./600 g) all-purpose flour
2 teaspoons (⅓ oz./10 g) salt
⅓ cup (2 ½ oz./70 g) granulated sugar
⅖ oz. (12 g) fresh (compressed) yeast
⅔ cup–¾ cup (150-200 ml) very cold water
2 ⅘ sticks (11 ¼ oz./320 g) butter
1 beaten egg yolk, for basting

Equipment
1 stand-alone mixer† fitted with a dough hook
1 pastry brush†
1 rolling pin†

● **Recipe idea**
Chocolate-Filled Croissant Cubes >> p. 280

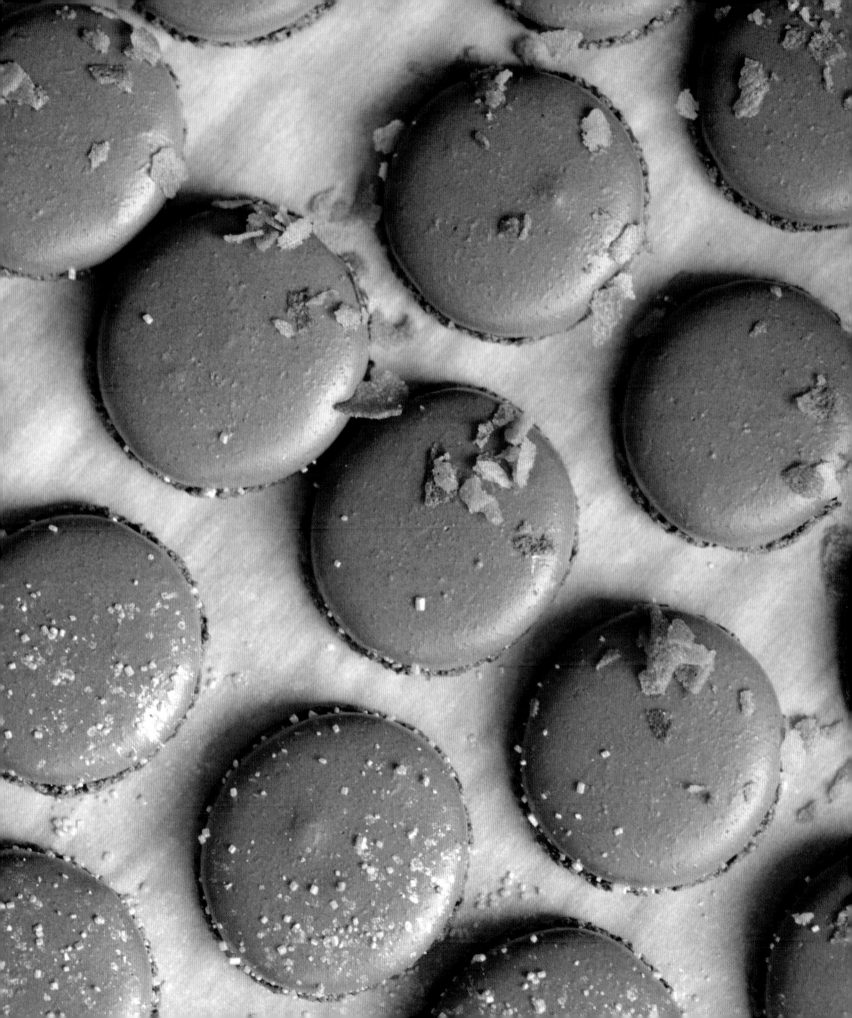

Macaroon Batter ★★

These delicate little cookies have been titillating the imagination of pastry chefs for many years now, and can be found in all manner of flavors. The macaroon* batter itself is simply colored to harmonize with the filling.
Makes about 40 individual macaroons

Ingredients
1 ¾ cups (5 ½ oz./150 g) blanched* ground almonds
1 generous cup (5 ½ oz./150 g) confectioners' sugar
¾ cup (5 ½ oz./150 g) granulated sugar
Scant ¼ cup (50 ml) water
3 ½ oz. (100 g) egg whites, weighed out into two equal parts
Powdered food coloring (optional)

Equipment
1 kitchen thermometer†
1 piping bag†
1 baking sheet lined with parchment paper or silicone mat†
1 stand-alone mixer† (for the Italian meringue)
1 flexible spatula†

Preheat the oven to 300°F (140°C). If your oven has smaller Fahrenheit increments, heat it to 285°F (preferable). Combine the ground almonds with the confectioners' sugar, but mix only briefly so that the almonds do not exude their oil.
To prepare an Italian meringue, cook the granulated sugar with the water to 230°F (110°C). While the mixture is heating, start whisking* half the egg whites to soft peaks (see p. 108). When the syrup has reached the right temperature, pour it gradually over the whisked egg whites, whisking as you do so. Continue beating until the mixture cools to 113°F (45°C). Then pour in the other half of the egg whites (1 ¾ oz./50 g), add the coloring if using, and the ground almonds combined with the confectioners' sugar. Stir in energetically with a flexible spatula until the batter is liquid and forms a ribbon.
Spoon the mixture into a piping bag and pipe it out onto the baking sheet or mat. Bake for about 12 minutes, depending on the size of your macaroons. Leave to cool at room temperature. Fill them when they have cooled and store in the refrigerator. Macaroons are best eaten the day after baking. That's when they will have a crisp shell, a soft center, and the strongest flavor.

❗ Recipe idea
Assorted Macaroons ›› p. 283

Cocoa Macaroon Batter ★★

Chocolate macaroons* include a small amount of cocoa powder. But whatever recipe you use, don't attempt to change the proportions and always weigh the eggs carefully.
Makes about 40 individual macaroons.

Ingredients
1½ cups (4 ½ oz./125 g) blanched* ground almonds
1 generous cup (5 ½ oz./150 g) confectioners' sugar
3 ½ tablespoons (¾ oz./25 g), cocoa powder, unsweetened
¾ cup (5 ½ oz./150 g) granulated sugar
Scant ¼ cup (50 ml) water
3 ½ oz. (100 g) egg whites, weighed out into two equal parts

Equipment
1 kitchen thermometer†
1 piping bag†
1 baking sheet lined with parchment paper or silicone mat†
1 stand-alone mixer† (for the Italian meringue)
1 flexible spatula†

Preheat the oven to 300°F (140°C). If your oven has smaller Fahrenheit increments, heat it to 285°F (preferable). Combine the ground almonds with the confectioners' sugar and cocoa powder, but mix only briefly so that the oil in the almonds does not come out.
To prepare an Italian meringue, cook the granulated sugar with the water to 230°F (110°C). While the mixture is heating, start whisking* half the egg whites to soft peaks (see p. 108). When the syrup has reached the right temperature, pour it gradually over the whisked egg whites, whisking as you do so. Continue beating as the mixture cools, until it reaches 113°F (45°C). Then pour in the other half (1 ¾ oz./50 g) of the egg whites, and the ground almonds with the confectioners' sugar and cocoa powder. Stir in energetically with a flexible spatula until the batter is liquid and forms a ribbon.
Spoon the mixture into a piping bag and pipe it out onto the baking sheet or mat. Bake for about 12 minutes, depending on the size of your macaroons. Keep at room temperature until cooled, then sandwich them together with the filling and store in the refrigerator. They are best eaten the day after baking.

❗ Recipe ideas
Assorted Macaroons ›› p. 283
Truffled Ivory Macaroons
›› p. 388

Chocolate *Financier* Batter ★

This batter includes not whole eggs, but the whites only. It is this, together with the ground almonds, which gives this preparation its characteristic light, soft texture.
Makes about 18 average-sized *financiers**, each 1 ½ oz. (40 g).

Ingredients
2 ¼ cups (6 ¾ oz./190 g) blanched* ground almonds
1 generous cup (5 ½ oz./150 g) confectioners' sugar
1 tablespoon (⅓ oz./10 g) cornstarch
1 ½ tablespoons (⅓ oz./10 g) cocoa powder, unsweetened
9 egg whites
⅓ cup (75 ml) whipping cream
1 ¾ oz. (50 g) bittersweet chocolate, 60 percent cocoa

Equipment
Baking sheets with *financier* molds
1 whisk†

Butter the molds, unless you are using silicone.
Combine the ground almonds, confectioners' sugar, cornstarch, and cocoa powder in a mixing bowl (**1, 2**). Lightly beat the egg whites with a fork to liquefy them. Combine the egg whites and whipping cream with the dry ingredients until just mixed. Set aside the batter.
Chop the chocolate and melt it slowly in a bain-marie* or in the microwave oven (on "defrost" or at 500 W maximum, stirring from time to time).
Pour a little of the batter over the melted chocolate, stirring energetically to combine. Then pour this mixture back into the remaining batter and fold in* carefully. Chill for at least 3 hours. This is an important stage in the recipe, as it will allow the *financiers* to rise well when baked.
Preheat the oven to 350°F (175°C). Pour the chocolate batter into the molds and bake for 15 to 20 minutes.
Leave to cool a little before turning the *financiers* out of their molds.

❙ Recipe idea
❙ Chocolate *Financiers*, Citrus Streusel, and Candied Orange Peel
>> p. 258

Basic Cake Batter ★

This is a classic recipe for a loaf cake that gives a nice, airy result and can be flavored as you wish. Just how moist or crisp is it depends on how you store it. Wrapped in plastic film, it will be moist; unwrapped, it will have a slight crunch when you bite into the crust.

Ingredients
5 tablespoons (2 ½ oz./70 g) butter
2 ¼ cups (7 oz./200 g) cake flour
1 teaspoon (4 g) baking powder
1 ¼ cups (9 oz./250 g) sugar
4 eggs
¼ teaspoon (1 g) salt
½ cup minus 1 tablespoon (110 ml) whipping cream
To flavor: your choice of vanilla, citrus zest*, etc.

Equipment
1 loaf pan, 10 in. (25 cm)
Parchment paper
1 whisk†

Preheat the oven to 300°F (150°C). Line the loaf pan with parchment paper.
Melt the butter and set it aside. Sift the flour with the baking powder. Whisk* the sugar, eggs, salt, and cream together in a mixing bowl (1, 2). Stir in the sifted flour and baking powder until the mixture is thoroughly combined. Stir in the melted butter. Add the flavor of your choice, if using.
Pour the batter into the lined pan and bake for about 45 minutes. Check for doneness with a cake tester or the tip of a knife, which should come out dry.

❗ **Recipe idea**
Cupcakes ›› p. 262

Chocolate Cake Batter ★

Use the best cocoa powder you can find: it will improve the flavor of your cake considerably.

Ingredients

2 ½ oz. (70 g) bittersweet chocolate, 70 percent cocoa
1 stick (4 ¼ oz./120 g) butter
1 ¾ cups (5 ½ oz./160 g) cake flour
2 ½ teaspoons (10 g) baking powder
¼ cup (1 oz./30 g) unsweetened cocoa powder
6 eggs
Scant ⅓ cup (3 ½ oz./100 g) acacia honey
1 scant cup (5 ¾ oz./170 g) granulated sugar
1 cup plus 3 tablespoons (3 ½ oz./100 g) ground almonds
⅔ cup (160 ml) whipping cream
Scant ⅓ cup (70 ml) rum

Equipment

1 loaf pan, 10 in. (25 cm)
Parchment paper
1 whisk†

Preheat the oven to 300°F (150°C). Line the loaf pan with parchment paper. Chop the chocolate and dice the butter **(1)**. Melt the chocolate and butter slowly in a bain-marie* or in the microwave oven (on "defrost" or at 500 W maximum, stirring from time to time).

Sift the flour with the baking powder and cocoa powder. Whisk* the eggs, honey, and sugar together in a mixing bowl. Stir in the ground almonds and the sifted dry ingredients and add the cream. Incorporate the melted chocolate and butter, and then the rum until just mixed through.

Pour the batter into the prepared pan **(2)**. Bake for about 40 minutes, or until a cake tester or knife tip comes out clean.

● Chef's note

You can also bake this batter on a jelly roll (Swiss roll) pan, in which case you should bake it at 350°F (180°C) for about 10 minutes. Use this method to cut out bases and layers for desserts.

❗ Recipe ideas

White Chocolate-Coffee Dessert with a Whiff of Dark Chocolate
>> p. 229
Cupcakes >> p. 262
Gold-Topped *Palet* Dessert >> p. 323
Flore >> p. 324
Mister Clown >> p. 327

Cocoa Ladyfingers ★

This light, airy long cookie with a crisp crust makes a wonderful accompaniment to soft chocolate textures and sorbets. Makes about one dozen 4 in. (10 cm) ladyfingers.

Ingredients

3 eggs, separated
⅓ cup (2 ⅔ oz./75 g) granulated sugar
Generous ¼ cup (1 oz./25 g) cake flour
3 tablespoons (⅔ oz./20 g) unsweetened cocoa powder
4 tablespoons plus 2 teaspoons (1 ⅔ oz./45 g) cornstarch
Confectioners' sugar for dusting

Equipment

1 piping bag†
1 flexible spatula†
1 whisk†

Preheat the oven to 400°F (200°C).
Whisk* the egg whites to soft peaks (see p.108), gradually adding the sugar as you whisk. Carefully fold in* the egg yolks with a flexible spatula. Then sift in the flour, cocoa powder **(1)**, and cornstarch, and combine **(2)**.
Spoon the batter into the piping bag and pipe out "fingers" about 4 in. (10 cm) long, leaving about ¾ in. (1.5 cm) between each one. Dust them with confectioners' sugar and wait a few minutes. Dust them a second time for an attractive "pearl" effect.
Bake for a few minutes only, until they are a nice golden color. These ladyfingers are best eaten fresh.

Almond or Hazelnut *Dacquoise* ★

This *dacquoise** sponge makes a base* for many types of chocolate dessert. It is light, crisp, and tasty.

Ingredients

⅓ cup (1 oz./30 g) cake flour
1 cup (3 oz./85 g) blanched* ground almonds or hazelnuts
¾ cup (3 ½ oz./100 g) confectioners' sugar
3 egg whites
¼ cup (1 ¾ oz./50 g) granulated sugar

Equipment

1 piping bag †
1 pastry cicle† or baking sheet
1 flexible spatula†
1 whisk†

Preheat the oven to 350°F-375°F (180°C-190°C).
Sift the flour with the ground almonds or hazelnuts and the confectioners' sugar into a mixing bowl.
Pour all the granulated sugar into the egg whites and immediately begin whisking* until the mixture forms soft peaks (see p. 108). Carefully fold in* the sifted dry ingredients with a flexible spatula. Spoon the batter into a piping bag and spread it out into a pastry circle or over a baking sheet, depending on what your recipe calls for.
Bake for about 10 minutes, until a nice golden color. Use very quickly or freeze.

❙ **Recipe ideas**
Royal ›› p. 170
Glasgow Cakes ›› p. 313
Almond *Dacquoise* with Semi-Confit Mandarins and Bittersweet Chocolate *Suprême* ›› p. 384

Cocoa Joconde Sponge ★★

A delicate, soft almond and cocoa sponge, this is used as the base*
for the popular multi-layered Opéra cake.

Ingredients
2 eggs plus 3 egg whites
¾ cup (2 ⅓ oz./65 g) ground almonds
½ cup (2 ⅓ oz./65 g) confectioners' sugar
2 tablespoons (1 oz./25 g) granulated sugar
1 tablespoon plus 2 teaspoons (25 g) butter
Generous ¼ cup (1 oz./25 g) cake flour
3 tablespoons (⅔ oz./20 g) unsweetened cocoa powder

Equipment
1 baking sheet, 12 × 10 in. (30 × 25 cm) lined with parchment paper
1 offset spatula†
1 flexible spatula†
1 hand-held electric beater†

Preheat the oven to 425°F (220°C). Beat together the 2 whole
eggs, ground almonds, and confectioners' sugar with an
electric beater until the mixture is pale and thick. In another
mixing bowl, whisk* the egg whites, adding the granulated
sugar gradually, until they form soft peaks (see p. 108).
Melt the butter and set aside. Sift the flour and cocoa powder
together. Fold in* one-quarter of the beaten egg whites into the
egg and almond mixture using a flexible spatula. Then incorporate
the sifted dry ingredients and the remaining egg whites. Continue
mixing and then incorporate the melted butter (1).
Using an offset spatula, spread the batter over the baking sheet
(2, 3) and bake for 6-8 minutes. Use quickly or freeze.

❙ Recipe idea
Opéra >> p. 182

Chocolate-Almond Streusel ★

This crumb recipe adds texture to many desserts, and is often an interesting component in *verrines*, layered desserts in shot glasses.

Ingredients
Generous ⅓ cup (2 ⅔ oz./75 g) light brown sugar
1 cup less 1 tablespoon (2 ⅔ oz./75 g) ground blanched* almonds
1 ½ tablespoons (10 g) unsweetened cocoa powder
Scant cup (3 oz./85 g) cake flour
1 good pinch (3 g) fleur de sel
5 tablespoons plus 1 teaspoon (2 ⅔ oz./75 g) butter, chilled

Equipment
1 baking sheet

Combine the brown sugar, ground almonds, cocoa powder, flour, and fleur de sel in a mixing bowl. Cut the butter into small dice and mix it into the preparation using your hands until it forms a crumbly texture (1).
Chill for at least 30 minutes.
Preheat the oven to 300°F-325°F (150°C-160°C). Spread the crumbs out onto the baking sheet and bake for about 10 minutes, until nicely browned.

● Chef's notes
If you prefer more regularly shaped streusel crumbs, form the mixture into a ball before chilling, and then push it through a frying basket (2).
Streusel crumbs may be frozen raw or baked. If baked, heat them in the oven to restore their original crunch.

Recipe ideas
Cilantro-Scented Pineapple-Mango Tart ≫ p. 209
Mini Molten Chocolate Cakes with *Verrines* of Softened Bananas and Chocolate Granita ≫ p. 224
Chocolate-Pistachio Loaf with Almond and Anise Streusel ≫ p. 249
Chocolate *Financiers*, Citrus Streusel, and Candied Orange Peel ≫ p. 258
Jelled Milk Chocolate, Chestnuts, and Soy Foam ≫ p. 382
Almond *Dacquoise* with Semi-Confit Mandarins and Bittersweet Chocolate *Suprême* ≫ p. 384

Chocolate Genoa Loaf ★★

This type of "beaten" batter rises when baked. Genoa loaf flavored with chocolate makes an excellent base for desserts, as well as being a special treat when eaten on its own with tea or coffee.

Ingredients

2 ⅔ oz. (75 g) milk chocolate, 40 percent cocoa
3 tablespoons plus 1 teaspoon (50 g) butter
⅓ cup (1 oz./30 g) cake flour
½ teaspoon (2 g) baking powder
5 ⅔ oz. (160 g) almond paste (see p. 41)
3 eggs
2 teaspoons (10 ml) anise-flavored liqueur
2 ½ oz. (70 g) pearl sugar (coarse sugar grains)

Equipment

A stand-alone mixer† fitted with a paddle attachment
1 kitchen thermometer†
1 piping bag† (optional)
1 whisk†
1 loaf pan or baking sheet with rectangular cake molds†

Preheat the oven to 325°F-350°F (160°C-170°C).
Melt the butter. Chop the chocolate and melt it in a bowl over a bain-marie* or in the microwave oven (on "defrost" or at 500 W, stirring from time to time). Stir in the hot melted butter.
Sift the flour and baking powder together and set aside.
Slightly warm the almond paste in the microwave oven, then place it in the bowl of your mixer. Whisk* the eggs in a bowl placed over a bain-marie. When the temperature reaches 122°F (50°C), pour the eggs gradually over the almond paste, beating constantly (1). As soon as the mixture is smooth, carefully fold in* the sifted flour and baking powder, then the liqueur, and finally, the melted chocolate and butter mixture. To maintain the volume of the batter, it's best to pour a little of it into the melted chocolate and butter mixture to ensure that the two textures are similar before combining the two mixtures.
Fill the cake molds (2) or mold.
Sprinkle with the pearl sugar and bake for about 14 minutes if making small cakes, a few minutes longer for one large cake (about 1 in./2 cm high), which you may bake in a brownie pan.

Recipe idea
Mini Apple Chocolate Genoa Cakes >> p. 255

Soft Almond or Coconut Sponge ★

This sponge is softer than the *dacquoise** (see p. 86) and makes an interesting base* for chocolate and fruit desserts.

Ingredients
6 egg whites, divided (2 plus 4)
⅔ cup (2 oz./55 g) ground blanched* almonds or finely ground coconut
Generous ¼ cup (1 oz./25 g) cake flour
Scant ½ cup (2 oz./55 g) confectioners' sugar
1 tablespoon (15 ml) whipping cream
⅓ cup (2 ½ oz./70 g) granulated sugar

Equipment
1 jelly roll (Swiss roll) pan
1 silicone baking mat† or baking sheet lined with parchment paper

Preheat the oven to 350°F (180°C). Lightly beat the 2 egg whites. Combine the ground almonds or coconut, flour, and confectioners' sugar with 2 egg whites and the whipping cream.
Whip* the 4 remaining egg whites to soft peaks, gradually pouring in the sugar as you whip. Carefully fold* the beaten egg whites into the first mixture.
Spread out the batter on a lined baking sheet or silicone baking mat and bake for about 10 minutes, until golden.

● Chef's note
This sponge may be frozen.

❦ Recipe idea
Klemanga ≫ p. 308

Plain Jelly Roll (Swiss Roll) ★

This sponge barely colors when baked. Do watch out that it does not overbake and harden: it must be soft so that you can roll it.

Ingredients
Generous ½ cup (1 ¾ oz./50 g) cake flour
4 eggs, 2 whole and 2 separated
Granulated sugar, divided as follows: scant ½ cup (2 ¾ oz./80 g) plus 2 ½ tablespoons (1 oz./30 g)

Equipment
1 jelly roll (Swiss roll) pan
1 whisk†

Preheat the oven to 350°F (170°C). Sift the flour and set aside. Whisk* the 2 whole eggs and 2 egg yolks with the scant ½ cup (2 ¾ oz./80 g) sugar until the mixture is pale and thick. Whisk the remaining egg whites and sugar to soft peaks (see p. 108). Carefully fold* this into the first mixture and pour in the sifted flour. Stir until just combined. Spread the batter out onto the pan and bake for about 5-7 minutes until springy to the touch.

❦ Recipe idea
Hazelnut Praline Christmas Log ≫ p. 306

Cocoa Jelly Roll (Swiss Roll) ★

Use the finest quality unsweetened cocoa powder you can find for an optimal result.

Ingredients

Scant ½ cup (1 ½ oz./40 g) cake flour
¼ cup (1 oz./30 g) unsweetened cocoa powder
6 eggs, 3 whole and 3 separated
½ cup plus 1 tablespoon (3 ¾ oz./110 g) granulated sugar
3 ½ tablespoons (1 ⅔ oz./45 g) brown sugar

Equipment

1 jelly roll (Swiss roll) pan
1 offset spatula†
1 whisk†

Preheat the oven to 425°F (210°C). Sift the flour and cocoa powder together and set aside. Beat together the 3 whole eggs and 3 egg yolks with the granulated sugar until the mixture is pale and thick. Whisk* the 3 egg whites together with the brown sugar until they form soft peaks (see p. 108).

Carefully fold* the beaten egg whites into the first egg mixture. Pour in the sifted flour and cocoa powder and mix through (1). Spread the batter out over the pan (2) and bake for about 15 minutes. The sponge is done when the tip of a knife comes out clean, but the surface should remain soft to the touch.

Flour-Free Chocolate Sponge ★

This sponge has a rich chocolate taste and an extraordinary texture. However, it's best used as a layer in a multi-textured dessert for added contrast. Make sure you spread it out very thinly to bake.

Ingredients

1 oz. (30 g) bittersweet chocolate, 60 percent cocoa
2 teaspoons (⅓ oz./10 g) butter
1 egg, separated
2 ½ teaspoons (10 g) sugar

Equipment

1 silicone baking mat† or baking sheet lined with parchment paper

Preheat the oven to 350°F (180°C).
Chop the chocolate and melt it slowly with the butter in a bain-marie* or in the microwave oven (on "defrost" or at 500 W maximum, stirring from time to time).
While it is melting, whisk* the egg white with the sugar until it forms soft peaks (see p. 108). Stir in the egg yolk, then carefully fold in* the melted chocolate and butter.
Pour the batter over the lined baking sheet or mat.
Bake for about 5 minutes. It will drop from a height of under ½ in. (1 cm) to about ⅛ in. (3 mm) when it cools.

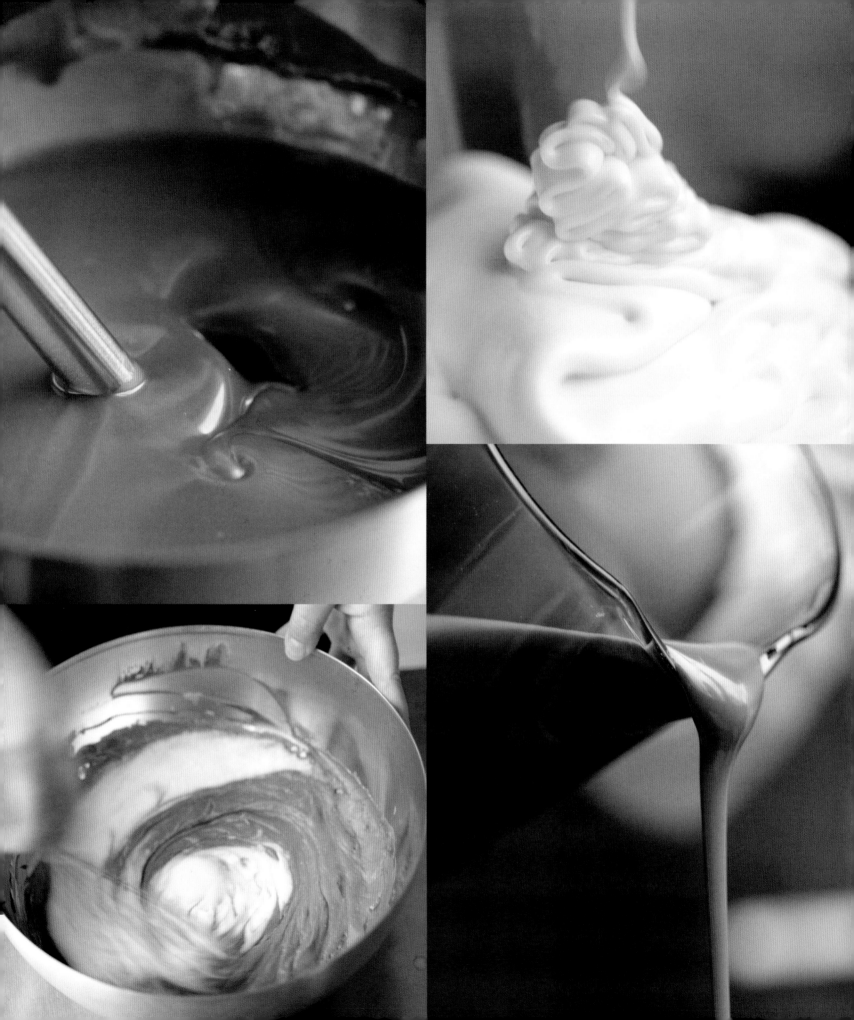

Creamy textures

WHAT IS AN EMULSION?

We make emulsions to reduce the sensation of fat on the palate, to achieve smooth, creamy textures, and for optimal preservation. When it comes to chocolate, emulsifying* the mixture will produce a chocolate mousse or ganache* that has a true taste of chocolate and a very creamy texture.

An emulsion is the mixture of two liquids that do not combine naturally, such as water and oil. To understand the principle of an emulsion, try a quick experiment: pour some oil into a glass of water and stir with a spoon. In just a few seconds, you will see that the oil is floating at the top of the water! When we emulsify two substances, we disperse one of them into the other in the form of minuscule droplets.

There are two types of emulsion. For the first type, we incorporate oil into water. When we make mayonnaise, the oil, in what is known as the "oily phase," is progressively incorporated into the mixture of egg yolk, vinegar, and mustard, known together as the "aqueous phase." For the second type, we incorporate water into oil. For a ganache, we incorporate the chocolate, the "oily phase," into liquid such as cream, milk, fruit juice, or coffee (the "aqueous phase").

When you make a mayonnaise, you gradually add the oil to the yolks and mustard until you have a shiny, elastic texture. If you continue to add oil (that last drop that is the one too many), the emulsion becomes saturated in fat and separates. The texture is no longer homogenous, far from it. At this point the mayonnaise looks ruined: professionals say that the mixture has separated or split. In fact, to remedy the situation, all you need to do is add a little liquid (water, lemon juice, or vinegar) and beat hard, and once more the homemade mayonnaise is restored to full glory.

This is quite unlike what happens with ganache. We start off with a saturated fat base, and then progressively pour the liquid–milk or whipping cream–into the chocolate. This is why, as soon as we pour a little liquid over the chocolate, the mass rapidly thickens. And this is why you should never put two tablespoons of water in with your chocolate to melt it. Adding water leads, usually, to separation.

In the initial phase of the emulsion, the ganache will not look very attractive, and that is quite normal. There is no reason to panic and add liquid faster. Instead, you should take your time to make the emulsion, ensuring you have the elastic "kernel" that means the emulsion is well on its way to forming, and stir energetically while you gradually add the liquid, just as you would gradually add oil to a mayonnaise.

Mixing energetically with small circular movements in the very center of the mixture ensures that the globules of fat and water droplets are organized regularly and homogenously. This homogeneity stabilizes the emulsion and reduces the impression of fat on the palate. It results in smooth, creamy, melting textures.

So, to make the perfect ganache, follow an infallible rule to incorporate the oily phase into the aqueous phase correctly: this is the "three thirds*" rule.

THE "THREE THIRDS" RULE

· Chop the chocolate and melt it slowly in a saucepan over a bain-marie* or in the microwave oven (on "defrost" or at 500 W maximum, stirring from time to time).
· Bring the liquid (cream or milk and honey, vanilla, or other ingredients) to the boil in a saucepan.
· Slowly, pour one-third of the boiling mixture over the melted chocolate.
· Using a flexible spatula[†], energetically mix the liquid into the chocolate, drawing small, quick circles in the center to create a shiny, elastic "kernel."
· Incorporate the second third of the liquid and mix in exactly the same way. Pour in the remaining third, using the same stirring technique.
· Check the temperature: it should be over 95°F (35°C).
· Use an immersion blender[†] to finish the emulsion process.

Ganache for Tarts and Desserts ★

This ganache* comprises only chocolate, whipping cream, and honey. Its relatively soft texture makes it a perfect filling for tarts and certain desserts. This recipe will fill a tart for 6–8 servings.

Ingredients
Weigh the chocolate according to its cocoa content:
7 oz. (200 g) bittersweet chocolate, 70 percent cocoa
Or 9 ½ oz. (270 g) bittersweet chocolate, 60 percent cocoa
Or 1 lb. (450 g) milk chocolate, 40 percent cocoa
Or 1 lb. 5 oz. (600 g) white chocolate, 35 percent cocoa
1 ¼ cups (300 ml) whipping cream
2 ½ tablespoons (1 ¾ oz./40 g) honey

Equipment
1 immersion blender†
1 flexible spatula†

Chop the chocolate and melt it slowly in a bain-marie* or in the microwave oven (on "defrost" or at 500 W maximum, stirring from time to time).
Bring the cream and honey to the boil in a saucepan.
Gradually pour one-third of the boiling mixture over the melted chocolate.
Using a flexible spatula, energetically mix the liquid into the chocolate, drawing small, quick circles in the center to create a shiny, elastic "kernel."
Incorporate the second third of the liquid and mix in exactly the same way. Pour in the remaining third, using the same stirring technique. Use an immersion blender to finish the emulsifying* process.

● Chef's notes
This ganache can be frozen; otherwise it should be incorporated immediately into a preparation: pour it into a baked tart shell or use it in a dessert such as the palet d'or *for a perfectly smooth finish. Leave to rest for about 3 hours before serving.*
If you intend to use it for a jelly roll (Swiss roll) or a Genoa sponge, leave it to set slightly at room temperature for 1–2 hours before spreading it out with a spatula.

Recipe ideas
Sachertorte ›› p. 166
Extraordinarily Chocolate Tart ›› p. 175
Golden Rules ›› p. 192
Walnut, Caramel, and Coffee-Chocolate Tart ›› p. 195
Mandarin Marvels ›› p. 206

Whipped Ganache ★★

Whipped ganache* is an innovation of the École du Grand Chocolat Valrhona. It is unctuous and an excellent substitute for traditional butter cream. It is widely used by pastry professionals today.

Ingredients
Weigh the chocolate according to its cocoa content:
3 ¼ oz. (90 g) bittersweet chocolate, 70 percent cocoa
plus 1 cup less 2 ½ tablespoons (7 oz./200 ml) whipping cream
Or 4 oz. (110 g) bittersweet chocolate, 60 percent cocoa
plus 1 cup less 1 tablespoon (7 ¾ oz./220 ml) whipping cream
Or 5 ⅓ oz. (150 g) milk chocolate, 40 percent cocoa plus 1 cup
plus 2 teaspoons (9 ¼ oz./260 ml) whipping cream
Or 5 ⅔ oz. (160 g) white chocolate, 35 percent plus 1 cup
plus 1 tablespoon (9 ½ oz./270 ml) whipping cream
½ cup less 1 tablespoon (110 ml) whipping cream

Equipment
1 immersion blender†, 1 flexible spatula†
1 whisk† or hand-held electric beater†

Chop the chocolate and melt it slowly in a bain-marie* or in the microwave oven (on "defrost" or at 500 W maximum, stirring from time to time). Bring the ½ cup minus 1 tablespoon (110 ml) whipping cream to the boil in a saucepan. Gradually pour one-third of the boiling cream over the melted chocolate. Using a flexible spatula, energetically mix the cream into the chocolate, drawing small, quick circles in the center to create a shiny, elastic "kernel." Incorporate the second third of the cream and mix in exactly the same way. Pour in the remaining third, using the same stirring technique. Use an immersion blender to finish the emulsifying* process. Pour in the quantity of cold cream indicated for the type of chocolate you are using. Stir in, cover with plastic wrap flush with the surface of the ganache, and chill for a minimum of 3 hours.
Whisk* the ganache at medium speed until it reaches the consistency of a thick cream (1, 2). If you whisk it at high speed, it will lose its light, creamy texture and become fatty.

● **Chef's note**
You can flavor the ganache by infusing tea leaves, vanilla, spices, or herbs in the scant ½ cup (110 ml) cream.

Recipe ideas
Opéra ›› p. 182
Tropézienne Redux with White Chocolate ›› p. 202
Cupcakes ›› p. 262
Assorted Macaroons ›› p. 283
Hazelnut Praline Christmas Log ›› p. 306
Manhattan Cappuccino ›› p. 317

Basic Custard (*crème anglaise*) ★★

This recipe is used as the base for the various *crémeux* and certain mousses.

Ingredients
3 egg yolks
¼ cup (1 ¾ oz./50 g) granulated sugar
1 cup (250 ml) whole milk
1 cup (250 ml) whipping cream

Equipment
1 kitchen thermometer†
1 immersion blender†

Whisk* the egg yolks (1) and sugar together until pale and thick.
Pour the mixture into a saucepan and add the milk and cream (2). Cook slowly over low heat, stirring constantly, until the mixture coats the back of a spoon and has thickened slightly. The temperature should be between 180°F-187°F (82°C-86°C) (3). It is best, however, to remove the saucepan from the heat as soon as the thermometer shows 180°F (82°C), because the temperature will continue to rise (the law of thermal inertia*; see p. 22). If you do not have a thermometer, a sure method of knowing when the custard is ready is to dip a wide spatula (or wooden spoon if using) into the custard and draw a horizontal line with your finger across the back. When the line stays visible, i.e. when the custard does not immediately drip down to cover it, your custard is done.
As soon as you have removed the custard from the heat, pour it into a deep bowl and process it briefly with an immersion blender for a smooth, creamy texture.

● Chef's notes
If the pouring custard has curdled, it has overcooked. Filter it through a sieve and then process it briefly with an immersion blender; this will remedy the problem, though the texture will not be quite as silky as a perfectly prepared custard.
Leftover custard may be frozen (immediately) but because the recipe contains egg yolks, it will only keep for 1 to 2 days in the refrigerator.

❙ Recipe ideas
Layered *Verrines* of Coffee, Chocolate, and Vanilla Creams with Breton Shortbread ›› p. 217
Crisp Triple Chocolate Cake ›› p. 310

Basic *Crémeux* ★★

This cream is extremely useful when putting desserts together, as you can flavor it as you wish. Makes about 2 cups (600 ml).

Ingredients
2 sheets (4 g) gelatin
6 egg yolks
½ cup (3 ½ oz./100 g) sugar
2 cups (500 ml) whipping cream

Equipment
1 kitchen thermometer†
1 immersion blender†

Soften the gelatin sheets in cold water. Whisk* the egg yolks with the sugar until thick and pale. Pour the mixture into a saucepan and stir in the cream. Cook over low heat, stirring constantly, until the mixture coats the back of a spoon. It should thicken slightly and the temperature should be between 180°F and 183°F (82°C-84°C). Remove the saucepan from the heat as soon as the thermometer shows 180°F (82°C), as the temperature will continue to rise (thermal inertia*, see p. 22). Wring out the water from the gelatin sheets and stir it in until completely dissolved. Immediately remove from the heat and pour into a deep mixing bowl. Process for a few seconds with an immersion blender for a smooth, creamy texture.

● Chef's notes
For a caramel flavor, use 2 additional tablespoons (1 oz./25 g) granulated sugar. Prepare a caramel* using the dry method over low heat. At the same time, start heating half the cream, without letting it boil. When the sugar has caramelized, pour half the heated cream over it, stirring as you do so. Continue to stir until the caramel has completely dissolved in the cream. Immediately remove from the heat and pour in the remaining cold cream mixed with the egg yolks and sugar. Proceed with the recipe.
For a honey flavor, use 2 ½–3 ½ tablespoons (50–75 g) honey instead of the ½ cup (100 g) sugar.
For a liqueur flavor, allow the mixture to cool before incorporating any liqueur so that the flavor does not evaporate with the heat.
For a herb or spice flavor, infuse the leaves or spice in the cold whipping cream for 24 hours before preparing the crémeux, or in the hot cream if you are making an infusion that requires heat. You may lose some of the cream when you make the infusion (through straining or evaporation); ensure that you add just the amount you need to have the quantity called for in the recipe. This cream keeps no longer than 2 days in the refrigerator.

❢ Recipe idea
Flore ›› p. 324

Chocolate *Crémeux* ★★

Adding chocolate to the basic *crémeux* recipe makes for a perfect base that will allow you to create delicious, multi-textured desserts.

Ingredients
Weigh the chocolate according to its cocoa content:
6 ¾ oz. (190 g) bittersweet chocolate, 70 percent cocoa
Or 7 ½ oz. (210 g) bittersweet chocolate, 60 percent cocoa
Or 9 oz. (250 g) milk chocolate, 40 percent cocoa
Or 8 oz. (225 g) white chocolate, 35 percent cocoa, plus 1 ½ sheets (3 g) gelatin
5 egg yolks
¼ cup (1 ¾ oz./50 g) granulated sugar
1 cup (250 ml) whole milk
1 cup (250 ml) whipping cream

Equipment
1 kitchen thermometer†
1 flexible spatula†
1 immersion blender†

A day ahead of using the *crémeux*, melt the chocolate slowly (1) in a bain-marie* or in the microwave oven (on "defrost" or at 500 W maximum, stirring from time to time).
Soften the gelatin in cold water if you are using white chocolate. Whip* the egg yolks and sugar together until thick and pale. Pour the mixture into a saucepan with the milk and cream (2) and cook over low heat until it coats the back of a spoon and is slightly thickened. The temperature should be between 82°F and 84°F (28°C–29°C).
Wring the water out of the gelatin sheets and incorporate it at this stage. Remove the saucepan from the heat and pour the custard into a deep bowl. Process for a few seconds with an immersion blender until the texture is smooth and creamy. Slowly pour one-third of the hot custard over the melted chocolate (3). Using a flexible spatula, energetically mix one-third of the cream into the chocolate, drawing small, quick circles in the center to create a shiny, elastic "kernel." Incorporate the second third and mix in the same way. Pour in the remaining third, again using the same stirring technique. Use an immersion blender to finish the emulsifying* process (4).
Pour it into a bowl and cover with plastic wrap flush with the surface (5) to prevent a skin from forming. Chill overnight and use within 1 to 2 days.

❙ Recipe ideas
Opéra ≫ p. 182
A Take on Tartlets ≫ p. 198
White Chocolate-Coffee Dessert with a Whiff of Dark Chocolate ≫ p. 229
Exotic Fruit with Lime-Scented White Chocolate ≫ p. 233

1

2

Vanilla Pastry Cream
(crème pâtissière) ★

This is one of the most frequently used creams in pastry making.
It's perfect as a bed in tarts in which fruits can nestle.

Ingredients
2 vanilla beans
1 ¾ cups (450 ml) whole milk
Scant ¼ cup (50 ml) whipping cream
3 egg yolks
2 ½ tablespoons (1 oz./25 g) cornstarch
2 tablespoons plus 2 teaspoons (15 g) cake flour
¾ cup (5 ¼ oz./150 g) granulated sugar

Equipment
1 immersion blender†
1 whisk†

Slit the vanilla beans lengthways and scrape out the seeds into
the milk and cream to be boiled. Whisk* together the egg yolks,
starch, flour, and sugar until pale and thick.
Bring the milk and cream to the boil in a saucepan. Mix in
a little of the hot liquid with the egg combined with the dry
ingredients. When it is thoroughly blended, pour it back into
the remaining hot milk and cream. Cook over low heat, stirring
constantly, until the mixture thickens (1).
Leave it to simmer briefly, still stirring constantly so that the
cream does not stick to the bottom of the saucepan. It should
become even creamier; most important, it should have a shine
(2).
Process briefly with an immersion blender so that the cream is
completely emulsified*.

● Chef's notes
*For a more pronounced vanilla flavor, leave the vanilla beans to
infuse in the cream a day ahead in the refrigerator.
Cornstarch reacts to heat: if the cream is not simmering properly,
it will not thicken.*

❗ Recipe idea
Hazelnut Waves >> p. 205

Chocolate Pastry Cream
(*crème pâtissière au chocolat*) ★

This is the star ingredient of chocolate éclairs.
This recipe makes enough to fill at least 10 éclairs
(1–1 ½ oz. or 30–40 g per éclair).

Ingredients
3 oz. (85 g) bittersweet chocolate, 70 percent cocoa
Or 3 ½ oz. (95 g) bittersweet chocolate, 60 percent cocoa
2 egg yolks
1 tablespoon (⅓ oz./10 g) cornstarch
2 ½ tablespoons (1 oz./30 g) granulated sugar
1 cup minus 2 tablespoons (220 ml) whole milk
Scant ¼ cup (50 ml) whipping cream

Equipment
1 immersion blender†
1 whisk†
1 flexible spatula† (optional)

Chop the chocolate and melt it slowly in a bain-marie* or in the microwave oven (on "defrost" or at 500 W maximum, stirring from time to time).
Whisk* the egg yolks with the cornstarch and sugar until thick and pale.
Bring the milk and cream to the boil. Pour a little into the egg yolks combined with the dry ingredients and mix thoroughly. Return the saucepan to the heat. Pour the diluted egg mixture into the saucepan and cook over low heat, stirring constantly with a whisk until it thickens. Continue cooking for a few more minutes, still stirring so that the cream does not stick to the bottom of the saucepan. It should become creamier; most importantly, it must be shiny.
Slowly pour one-third of the hot cream over the melted chocolate (1). Using a whisk or flexible spatula, mix in energetically (2), drawing small circles to create an elastic, shiny "kernel."
Incorporate the second third of the liquid, using the same procedure. Repeat with the last third.
Blend briefly using an immersion blender so that the mixture is smooth and perfectly emulsified*.

❚ **Recipe ideas**
Chocolate Éclairs ›› p. 181
Chocolate-Filled Croissant Cubes ›› p. 280

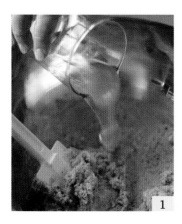

Vanilla-Scented Almond Cream ★

This is the recipe traditionally used in the *galette des rois*, the Kings' cake eaten for Twelfth Night, and the *pithiviers*.

Ingredients
5 oz. (150 g) almond paste (see p. 41)
2 eggs
1 vanilla bean
5 tablespoons plus 1 teaspoon (2 ⅔ oz./75 g) butter, softened
1 tablespoon (⅓ oz./10 g) cornstarch
¼ cup (⅔ oz./20 g) ground almonds
2 ⅔ oz. (75 g) vanilla pastry cream (see p. 102)

Equipment
1 whisk†

Soften the almond paste slightly in the oven or in the microwave (on "defrost" or at 500 W, stirring from time to time). Then incorporate the eggs into the almond paste one by one (1), mixing well each time.
Slit the vanilla bean lengthways and scrape out the seeds into the mixture. Add the softened butter (*beurre en pommade**). Lightly whisk* the mixture so that it does not separate and then sift in the cornstarch (2) and ground almonds (3).
Blend the cold pastry cream into the mixture. Use immediately, or chill until needed, no more than 1 to 2 days.

Chocolate Panna Cotta ★

Ingredients
2 sheets (4 g) gelatin
¾ cup (200 ml) whole milk
1 ¼ cups (300 ml) whipping cream
Weigh the chocolate according to its cocoa content:
4 oz. (110 g) bittersweet chocolate, 70 percent cocoa
Or 4 ½ oz. (130 g) bittersweet chocolate, 60 percent cocoa
Or 5 ½ oz. (160 g) milk chocolate, 40 percent cocoa
Or 6 ⅙ oz. (175 g) white chocolate, 35 percent cocoa

Equipment
1 immersion blender†
1 flexible spatula†

Soften the gelatin in a bowl of very cold water. Bring the milk
and cream to the boil. When the gelatin has softened, wring out
the water and dissolve it in the milk-cream mixture. Remove
from the heat as soon as it has dissolved. Chop the chocolate
and melt it slowly in a bain-marie* or in the microwave oven
(on "defrost" or at 500 W maximum, stirring from time to
time). Slowly pour one-third of the hot mixture over the melted
chocolate. Using a flexible spatula, briskly mix it in with a small
circular movement to create an elastic, shiny "kernel." Then
incorporate another third of the hot liquid, using the same
circular movement, and finally, the last third, still mixing with
a circular movement. Process with an immersion blender to
ensure that the mixture is smooth and perfectly emulsified*.

● Did you know?
As the name panna cottta *indicates, the traditional Italian
dessert is a cooked cream. In this recipe, the gelatin brings about
a similar result using a very simple method.*

❘ Recipe ideas
Tonka Bean-Scented Ivory Panna Cotta with Strawberry Coulis ›› p. 234
Bittersweet Chocolate Panna Cotta with Thai-style Lemongrass
Foam ›› p. 237

Namelaka ★

The Namelaka is a particularly unctuous cream that sets slowly. Use
it in *verrines* or add scoops of it to the top of desserts.

Ingredients
Weigh the chocolate according to its cocoa content:
9 oz. (250 g) bittersweet chocolate, 70 percent cocoa, plus 2 ½
sheets (5 g) gelatin
Or 12 ⅓ oz. (350 g) milk chocolate, 40 percent cocoa, plus 2 ½
sheets (5 g) gelatin
Or 12 oz. (340 g) white chocolate, 35 percent cocoa, plus 2 sheets
(4 g) gelatin (the sugar in white chocolate means less is needed)
¾ cup (200 ml) whole milk
1 ½ teaspoons (10 g) glucose syrup
1 ⅔ cups (400 ml) whipping cream

Equipment
1 immersion blender†
1 flexible spatula†

Chop the chocolate and melt it slowly in a bain-marie* or in the
microwave oven (on "defrost" or at 500 W maximum, stirring
occasionally). Soften the gelatin in a bowl of very cold water.
Bring the milk to the boil in a saucepan. Wring the water out
of the gelatin. Add the glucose syrup and gelatin to the boiling
milk and stir until just dissolved. Remove from the heat. Slowly
pour one-third of the hot mixture over the melted chocolate.
Using a flexible spatula, briskly mix it in with a small circular
movement to create an elastic, shiny "kernel." Then incorporate
another third, using the same circular movement, and finally
the last third, in the same way. Stir in the cold whipping
cream. Process with an immersion blender to ensure that the
mixture is smooth and perfectly emulsified*. Leave to set in the
refrigerator. Keep chilled and use within 1 to 2 days.

● Did you know?
Namelaka means "ultra-creamy" in Japanese.

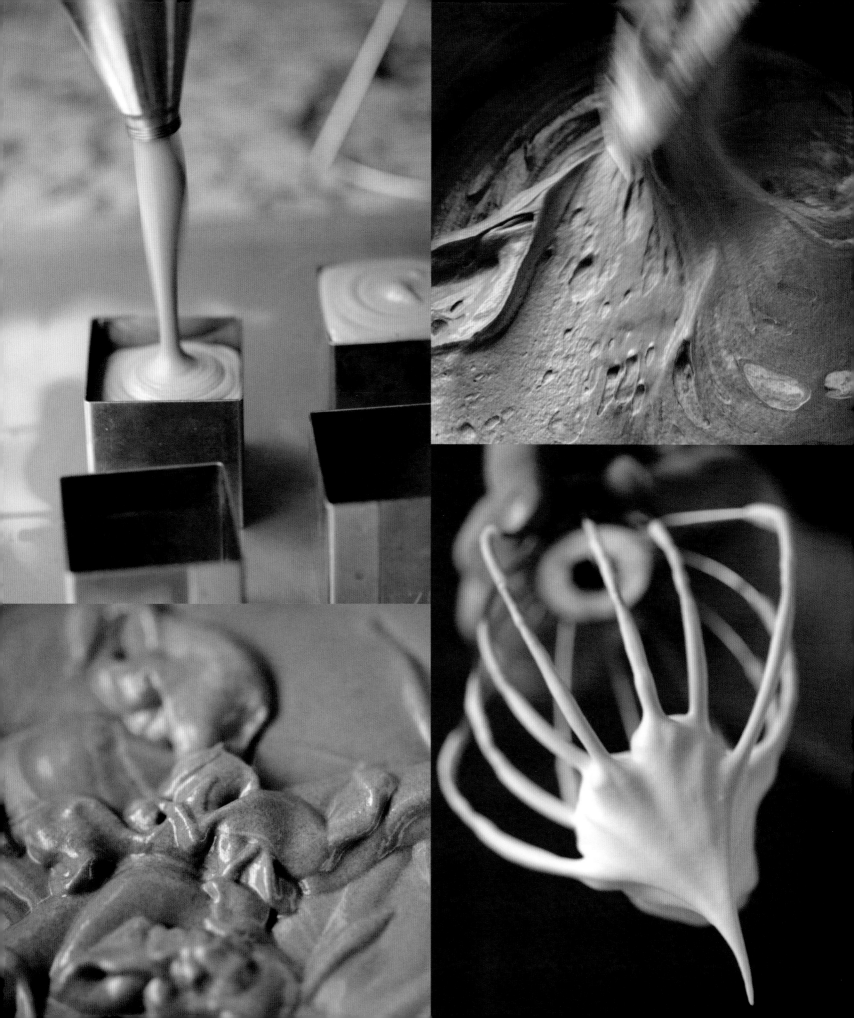

Mousses

THE WHIPPING PROCESS

Whipping or whisking* involves incorporating air into an ingredient that can contain it, such as egg white or full fat whipping cream. The purpose of whipping is to achieve light textures, with volume, that do not deflate–or, at least, not immediately. In other words, whipping is the art of getting whites to rise to form peaks and to create a foamy cream.

It is impossible to achieve good whipping results at high speeds. The stability of the whipped product is due to the architecture of the air bubbles inside the mixture. High speed causes large air bubbles to form in an anarchic form; they are therefore not durable and result in a fragile result. However, when medium speed is used, the air bubbles become smaller and smaller, thus offering greater resistance to any shock the mixture might be subjected to.

Any ingredient whisked at medium speed will thus have greater durability.

Whisking egg whites

First, make sure that the bowl is perfectly dry and free of grease. Whisk the egg whites with an electric beater† at medium speed. Stop beating when the egg whites reach the soft peak stage–they will form little waves, and bend slightly when you take the beater out of the bowl. The texture should be like shaving foam for men or styling mousse for women. Do not beat the egg whites into stiff peaks (when the egg whites remain upright when you lift the beater out of the bowl)–this is not necessary.

Egg whites whipped like this are lighter, more stable, and easier to combine with other ingredients. If we continue to whip, they will begin to collect on the whisk or beater and little grains will form–the whites go grainy.

Whisking whipping cream with a butterfat content of 30 to 35 percent

When whisking well-chilled whipping cream at medium speed, its volume increases. Lightly whipped, foamy whisked cream contains the most possible air, and this is the stage at which it is ideal to make a chocolate mousse, for example. The volume has increased by 220 percent. If we continue to whip, not only will we no longer imprison any air, but the volume will diminish. The cream is transformed into Chantilly cream, which is to say that its volume is now only 160 percent of the original. If we continue to whisk, it will change into butter!

● Chef's notes

The colder the cream is, the easier it is to whisk.
Don't attempt to whisk a low-fat liquid cream. This is an impossible task because it has insufficient butterfat content.
In milk and white chocolate recipes, gelatin is used to harden the mixture, compensating for the lack of cocoa butter.*

Chocolate Mousses

Each mousse here has a different intensity and should be tasted and used differently. Take into account variations in temperature, texture, "length" in the mouth, and so on.

These differences will enable you to customize your creations and allow you to balance textures and flavors.

A good chocolate mousse should be light, melting, and not fatty.

All chocolate mousses should set for at least 12 hours in the refrigerator. Most should be eaten at room temperature, so remember to take them out of the refrigerator 30 minutes before serving, except for the egg-free mousse and the soy chocolate mousse.

Egg White-Based Chocolate Mousse ★

This is the chocolate mousse our grandmothers used to regale us with. Airy and rich in chocolate, it gives a sensation of gentle melting.

Ingredients
Weigh the chocolate according to its cocoa content:
10 ½ oz. (300 g) bittersweet chocolate, 70 percent cocoa
Or 11 ⅔ oz. (330 g) bittersweet chocolate, 60 percent cocoa
Or 13 ¾ oz. (390 g) milk chocolate, 40 percent cocoa, plus 1 ½ sheets (3 g) gelatin
Or 13 ¾ oz. (390 g) white chocolate, 35 percent cocoa, plus 3 sheets (6 g) gelatin
Scant ⅔ cup (150 ml) whipping cream
3 egg yolks (2 ⅛ oz./60 g)
6-7 egg whites (7 oz./200 g)
¼ cup (1 ¾ oz./50 g) granulated sugar

Equipment
1 kitchen thermometer†
1 hand-held electric beater† or stand-alone mixer†
1 immersion blender†
1 whisk† or flexible spatula†

Chop the chocolate and melt it slowly in a bain-marie* or in the microwave oven (on "defrost" or at 500 W maximum, stirring from time to time). If you are using milk or white chocolate, soften the gelatin in very cold water. Bring the cream to the boil in a saucepan, then remove from the heat. Wring the water out of the gelatin, if using, and dissolve it into the cream. Slowly pour one-third of the hot cream over the melted chocolate (1). Using a whisk or flexible spatula, briskly mix it in with a small circular movement to create an elastic, shiny "kernel." Then incorporate another third, using the same movement, and finally, the last third, still mixing as before. Beat in the egg yolks (2). Process with an immersion blender to ensure that the mixture is smooth and perfectly emulsified*. In the meantime, start whisking* the egg whites with the sugar in the bowl of a stand-alone mixer until they form soft peaks. When the chocolate mixture cools to 95°F-113°F (35°C-45°C) for white or milk chocolate, or 113°F-122°F (45°C-50°C) for bittersweet chocolate mousse, fold in* a quarter of the whisked egg whites, then carefully fold in the rest (3).
Chill for 12 hours (4). The mousse will not keep longer than 24 hours because of the raw egg yolks.

❡ **Recipe ideas**
Bittersweet Chocolate Mousse ≫ p. 186
Chocolate Crown with Winter Fruit and Nuts ≫ p. 221

Egg-Free Chocolate Mousse ★

This is an extremely light mousse that uses milk and gelatin. It should be eaten straight from the refrigerator.
Prepare a day ahead, or at least 12 hours before needed.

Ingredients
Weigh the chocolate according to its cocoa content:
10 oz. (285 g) bittersweet chocolate, 70 percent cocoa, plus 1 ½ sheets (3 g) gelatin
Or 11 ⅔ oz. (330 g) bittersweet chocolate, 60 percent cocoa, plus 2 sheets (4 g) gelatin
Or 12 oz. (340 g) milk chocolate, 40 percent cocoa, plus 2 ½ sheets (5 g) gelatin
Or 1 lb. ½ oz. (470 g) white chocolate, 35 percent cocoa, plus 5 sheets (10 g) gelatin
1 cup (250 ml) whole milk
2 cups (500 ml) whipping cream, well chilled

Equipment
1 kitchen thermometer†
1 whisk† or hand-held electric beater†
1 flexible spatula†

Chop the chocolate and melt it slowly in a bain-marie* or in the microwave oven (on "defrost" or at 500 W maximum, stirring from time to time).
Soften the gelatin in a bowl of very cold water.
Bring the milk to the boil in a saucepan. Wring the water out of the gelatin and incorporate it into the hot milk. Immediately remove from the heat.
Slowly pour one-third of the hot mixture over the melted chocolate (1). Using a flexible spatula, briskly mix it in with a small circular movement to create an elastic, shiny "kernel" (2). Then incorporate another third of the hot liquid, using the same circular movement, and finally, the last third, still mixing with a circular movement.
Using either a whisk or an electric beater, whisk* the well-chilled cream until it is lightly whipped (for technique see p. 108) (3). When the chocolate mixture reaches 95°F-113°F (35°C-45°C) for white or milk chocolate, or 113°F-122°F (45°C-50°C) for bittersweet chocolate mousse, fold in* the lightly whipped cream carefully with a flexible spatula. Chill for at least 12 hours.

● Chef's notes
This mousse is ideal for people who are allergic to eggs.
It keeps for 1 to 2 days in the refrigerator and can be frozen.

⟊ Recipe ideas
Chocolate Mousse and Creamy Caramel in a Spoon ≫ p. 240
Flore ≫ p. 324

Chocolate Chantilly Mousse ★

Chocolate Chantilly makes a somewhat dense mousse, a little dry, with a very pronounced chocolate taste. It works well with a *crémeux* (see pp. 99 and 100).

Ingredients
Weigh the chocolate according to its cocoa content:
11 ¼ oz. (320 g) bittersweet chocolate, 70 percent cocoa
Or 12 ¾ oz. (360 g) bittersweet chocolate, 60 percent cocoa
Or 14 oz. (400 g) milk chocolate, 40 percent cocoa
Or 1 lb. (450 g) white chocolate, 35 percent cocoa, plus 3 sheets (6 g) gelatin
Well-chilled whipping cream, divided as follows: 1 ¾ cups (400 ml) plus ¾ cup (200 ml)

Equipment
1 kitchen thermometer†
1 whisk† or hand-held electric beater†
1 flexible spatula†

Prepare at least 13 hours ahead of time.
Chop the chocolate and melt it slowly in a bain-marie* or in the microwave oven (on "defrost" or at 500 W maximum, stirring from time to time).
For a white chocolate mousse, soften the gelatin in a bowl of very cold water.
Using a whisk or an electric hand beater, whip* the 1 ¾ cups (400 ml) chilled cream till it is lightly whipped (for technique see p. 108). Set aside in the refrigerator.
Heat the ¾ cup (200 ml) whipping cream in a saucepan to a simmer. Remove from the heat, squeeze the water from the gelatin sheets, and incorporate them, if using, until just dissolved. Slowly pour one-third of the hot mixture over the melted chocolate (1). Using a flexible spatula, briskly mix it in with a small circular movement to create an elastic, shiny "kernel" (2). Then incorporate another third of the hot liquid, using the same circular movement, and finally, the last third, still mixing with a circular movement. Check the temperature at this stage: it should be 113°F-122°F (45°C-50°C), whatever type of chocolate you use, so that the chocolate does not harden into little chips when you incorporate the cream.
Carefully fold in* the lightly whipped cream with a flexible spatula (3). Chill for about 12 hours. Remove from the refrigerator 1 hour before serving to bring it to room temperature.
This mousse keeps for 2 days in the refrigerator, and freezes well.

Recipe ideas
Klemanga >> p. 308
Pear and Milk Chocolate Petits Fours >> p. 321
Mister Clown >> p. 327

Custard-Based Chocolate Mousse ★★

This intensely chocolate mousse is very creamy and pairs wonderfully with various types of fruit.

Ingredients
Weigh the chocolate according to its cocoa content:
11 ½ oz. (325 g) bittersweet chocolate, 70 percent cocoa
Or 12 ¾ oz. (360 g) bittersweet chocolate, 60 percent cocoa
Or 1 lb. 3 ¾ oz. (560 g) milk chocolate, 40 percent cocoa
Or 1 lb. 2 oz. (500 g) milk chocolate, 35 percent cocoa plus 2 ½ sheets (5 g) gelatin
2 egg yolks
2 tablespoons (1 oz./25 g) granulated sugar
½ cup plus 1 teaspoon (130 ml) whole milk
Well-chilled whipping cream, divided as follows: ⅔ cup (150 ml) plus 1 ¾ cup (400 ml)

Equipment
1 kitchen thermometer†
1 immersion blender†
1 flexible spatula†
1 whisk† or hand-held electric beater†

Chop the chocolate and melt it slowly in a bain-marie* or in the microwave oven (on "defrost" or at 500 W maximum, stirring from time to time). If you are making a white chocolate mousse, soak the gelatin in a bowl of very cold water.
Prepare the pouring custard (*crème anglaise*).
In a mixing bowl, beat the egg yolks with the sugar until thick and pale. Pour this mixture into a saucepan, add the milk and ⅔ cup (150 ml) whipping cream, and simmer over low heat. The liquid should thicken slightly and coat the back of a spoon. The temperature should be between 180°F-183°F (82°C-84°C). Remove from the heat and pour the custard into a deep mixing bowl. Process for a few seconds with an immersion blender for a smooth, creamy texture. If using the gelatin, incorporate it at this stage. Gradually pour one-third of the hot custard over the melted chocolate. Using a flexible spatula, mix it in energetically, drawing small circles to create an elastic, shiny "kernel." Incorporate the second third of the custard, using the same procedure. Repeat with the last third. Process with an immersion blender for a smooth, creamy texture.
Using a whisk or an electric beater, whip* 1 ⅔ cup (400 ml), well-chilled cream until it is just lightly whipped (for technique see p. 108). When the chocolate-custard reaches a temperature of 113°F-122°F (45°C-50°C), fold in* one-third of the softly whipped cream. Carefully fold in the remaining cream with a flexible spatula. Chill for 12 hours.

● Chef's note
It is important to thin the chocolate-custard mixture with one-third of the softly whipped cream to bring it to a texture similar to that of the cream. This enables you to retain maximum volume when folding in the rest.

❘ Recipe ideas
Royal ›› p. 170
Iced Hazelnut-Chocolate Mousse and Lemon-Lime Cream ›› p. 295
Glasgow Cakes ›› p. 313

Pâte à Bombe Chocolate Mousse ★★★

An intense chocolate mousse with a sweet, creamy texture that can be served on its own.

Ingredients

¾ cup (200 ml) whipping cream, well chilled
Weigh the chocolate according to its cocoa content:
5 ⅓ oz. (150 g) bittersweet chocolate, 70 percent cocoa
Or 6 oz. (170 g) bittersweet chocolate, 60 percent cocoa
Or 8 oz. (230 g) milk chocolate, 40 percent cocoa, plus 1 ½ sheets (2.5 g) gelatin
Or 9 oz. (250 g) white chocolate, 35 percent cocoa, plus 2 sheets (4 g) gelatin

Pâte à bombe*
3 egg yolks
1 egg
Scant ¼ cup (1 ½ oz./45 g) sugar
2 tablespoons (30 ml) water

Equipment

1 kitchen thermometer†
1 whisk† or hand-held electric beater†
1 flexible spatula†

Using a whisk or an electric beater, whisk* the chilled cream until it is just lightly whipped (for technique see p. 108).
Chop the chocolate and melt it slowly in a bain-marie* or in the microwave oven (on "defrost" or at 500 W maximum, stirring from time to time).
If you are making a milk or white chocolate mousse, soften the gelatin in a bowl of very cold water.
Prepare the *pâte à bombe*. Whisk the egg yolks, egg, sugar, and water together in a mixing bowl until the sugar has just dissolved. Place the bowl over a bain-marie and stir constantly until the mixture reaches 180°F (82°C). Remove the bowl from the bain-marie. If you are using gelatin, wring out the water and incorporate it into the hot mixture. Whisk until it cools down to a warm temperature.
Now combine the ingredients. When the chocolate-cream mixture is at a temperature of about 113°F-122°F (45°C-50°C), whisk in a third of the lightly whipped cream until the texture is elastic and it is shiny. If the temperature is not right at this stage, the chocolate will form grains. Slightly reheat over the bain-marie or in the microwave oven. Then carefully fold in* the remaining cream using a flexible spatula, and then the warm *pâte à bombe*. Chill for about 12 hours. This mousse keeps 1-2 days in the refrigerator.

Chocolate Soy Mousse ★

This mousse has an extremely foamy texture and a very refreshing feeling in the mouth. An added advantage is the fact that it is free of animal fat.

Ingredients

5 ¼ oz. (150 g) bittersweet chocolate, 70 percent cocoa
3 egg whites
⅓ cup (2 ⅔ oz./75 g) granulated sugar, divided
1 ¼ cups (300 ml) liquid soy cream
Scant teaspoon (3 g) agar-agar
2 vanilla beans
Generous ⅔ cup (180 ml) soy milk

Equipment

1 whisk† or hand-held electric beater†
1 flexible spatula†

Chop the chocolate and melt it slowly in a bain-marie*or in the microwave oven (on "defrost" or at 500 W maximum, stirring from time to time).
Whisk* the egg whites with half the sugar until they form soft peaks. Using a whisk or an electric beater, whisk the soy cream until it becomes foamy, like lightly whipped cream. Combine it with the remaining half of the sugar and the agar-agar.
Slit the vanilla beans lengthways and scrape out the seeds. Leave them to infuse in the soy milk for a few minutes, then filter. Vanilla here balances the taste of soy, but you may use any flavor of your choice.
In a saucepan, bring the soy milk with the sugar and agar-agar to the boil. Gradually pour one-third of the boiling mixture over the melted chocolate.
Using a flexible spatula, mix in energetically, drawing small circles to create an elastic, shiny "kernel."
Incorporate the second third of the liquid, using the same procedure. Repeat with the remaining third. Fold in* one-third of the whisked egg whites to lighten the density of the chocolate-soy mixture, then carefully fold in the remaining egg whites. Chill for 12 hours.

● **Chef's note**
Agar-agar has to boil in order to jellify the mixture. However, it cannot be frozen: if you do freeze a mousse containing agar-agar, the mousse will not hold and will exude water as it defrosts.

Chocolate Bavarian Cream ★★

This is a melting type of mousse, and one of the least chocolatey. It is a practical mousse to use in desserts with several components and can be frozen.

Ingredients
Weigh the chocolate according to its cocoa content:
5 ¼ oz. (150 g) bittersweet chocolate, 70 percent cocoa
Or 5 ⅔ oz. (160 g) bittersweet chocolate, 60 percent cocoa
Or 6 ¾ oz. (190 g) milk chocolate, 40 percent cocoa
3 sheets (6 g) gelatin
1 cup plus one scant ½ cup (350 ml) basic custard (see p. 98)
1 ¾ cups (450 ml) whipping cream, well chilled

Equipment
1 kitchen thermometer†
1 flexible spatula†
1 whisk† or hand-held electric beater†

Chop the chocolate and melt it slowly in a bain-marie* or in the microwave oven (on "defrost" or at 500 W maximum, stirring from time to time) (1).
Soften the gelatin sheets in a bowl of cold water (2).
Prepare the pouring custard (*crème anglaise*).
Use a little of the hot custard to melt the gelatin. When the mixture is smooth, incorporate it into the remaining custard. Slowly pour one-third of this hot custard over the melted chocolate.
Using a flexible spatula, mix in energetically, drawing small circles to create an elastic, shiny "kernel."
Incorporate the second third of the liquid, using the same procedure. Repeat with the remaining third, still using the same procedure. Using a whisk or an electric beater, whisk* the chilled cream until it is lightly whipped (for technique see p. 108).
When the chocolate-custard mixture cools to 113°F-122°F (45°C-50°C), fold in* one-third of the lightly whisked cream. Then carefully fold in the remaining cream using a flexible spatula. Chill for 12 hours (3).

3

Ice creams, sorbets, and sauces

Chocolate Ice Cream ★ ★

This is a recipe for a deliciously creamy homemade ice cream that is particularly rich in chocolate.
Serves 8–10

Ingredients
6 ⅓ oz. (180 g) bittersweet chocolate, 70 percent cocoa
2 ¾ cups (660 ml) whole milk
1 tablespoon plus 1 teaspoon (20 ml) whipping cream
¼ cup (1 oz./30 g) powdered milk
⅓ cup (2 ½ oz./70 g) granulated sugar
3 tablespoons (2 ⅛ oz./60 g) honey

Equipment
1 immersion blender†
1 ice-cream maker†
1 kitchen thermometer†
1 cold-water bath
1 whisk† or flexible spatula†

Chop the chocolate, or use chocolate buttons, fèves, or pistoles (1) and melt it slowly in a bain-marie* or in the microwave oven (on "defrost" or at 500 W maximum, stirring from time to time). Heat the milk, cream, powdered milk, sugar, and honey in a saucepan (2) to boiling point, blending them with a whisk (3). Gradually pour one-third of the boiling liquid over the melted chocolate. Using a whisk or flexible spatula, mix in energetically, drawing small circles to create an elastic, shiny "kernel."
Incorporate the second third of the liquid, using the same procedure. Repeat with the last third.
Blend for a few seconds using an immersion blender so that the mixture is smooth and perfectly emulsified*.
Return the mixture to the saucepan and heat over medium heat, stirring constantly until it reaches 185°F (85°C).
Leave it for 2 minutes at this temperature, still stirring constantly, to pasteurize what will be your ice cream.
Cool rapidly by pouring it into a bowl placed over a larger bowl filled with ice cubes. Leave to rest overnight in the refrigerator so that the flavors develop (professionals call this "maturing"). Pour the mixture into the ice-cream maker, following the manufacturer's instructions for your machine, and store at 0°F (-18°C). This ice cream keeps for no longer than 2 weeks.

Recipe ideas
Chocolate Profiteroles ›› p. 172
Crisp Almond Cookies with Chocolate Ice Cream and Caramel and Passion Fruit Sauce ›› p. 299

Cocoa Nib Ice Cream ★ ★

The pronounced flavor of cocoa nib* ice cream is as surprising as the color is light!
Serves 12–15

Ingredients
5 ¼ oz. (150 g) cocoa nibs
3 cups (750 ml) whole milk
1 cup less 1 tablespoon (225 ml) whipping cream
Scant ½ cup (2 oz./55 g) powdered milk
Scant cup (6 oz./170 g) granulated sugar
2 egg yolks
2 teaspoons (15 g) honey

Equipment
1 ice-cream maker†
1 kitchen thermometer†
1 cold-water bath

Preheat the oven to 300°F (150°C). Heat the cocoa nibs for about 10 minutes.
Combine the milk, cream, powdered milk, sugar, egg yolks, and honey (1) in a saucepan. Heat, but do not boil because of the egg yolks, and add the cocoa nibs (2).
Stir constantly until the mixture reaches 185°F (85°C).
Cool rapidly by pouring it into a bowl placed over a larger bowl filled with ice cubes. Leave to rest overnight in the refrigerator so that the flavors develop (mature).
Filter the mixture, pour it into the ice-cream maker, following the directions, and store at 0°F (-18°C).

● Chef's note
Cocoa nibs are obtained from roasted, shelled cocoa beans. Roasting brings out their particularly pleasant, and even unexpected, notes. They are sold by certain artisan pastry makers, by Valrhona, as well as at professional pastry supply stores.

Recipe idea
Chocolate-Coated Cocoa Nib Eskimo Pie with Roasted Almonds and Peanuts ›› p. 290

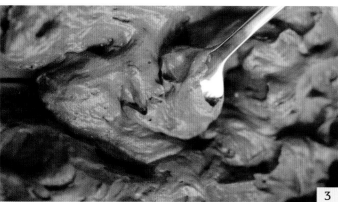

Chocolate Parfait ★★

This recipe illustrates an interesting technique for an iced dessert
that does not require an ice-cream maker.
Serves 6–8

Ingredients
3 egg whites
½ cup (3 ½ oz./100 g) sugar
5 ¼ oz. (150 g) bittersweet chocolate, 70 percent cocoa
Or 8 oz. (225 g) bittersweet chocolate, 60 percent cocoa
Or 7 oz. (200 g) milk chocolate, 40 percent cocoa
Or 8 oz. (225 g) white chocolate, 35 percent cocoa
¾ cup (200 ml) whipping cream

Equipment
1 kitchen thermometer†
1 whisk†
8 molds† or small glasses

Prepare a Swiss meringue. Whisk* the egg whites with
the sugar in a heatproof bowl over a bain-marie* until the
temperature reaches 131°F-140°F (55°C-60°C) (1). Then remove
from the heat and whisk until it reaches room temperature (2).
Meanwhile, chop the chocolate and melt it slowly in a bain-
marie or in the microwave oven (on "defrost" or at 500 W
maximum, stirring from time to time).
Lightly whisk the whipping cream (for technique see p. 108).
Take one-quarter of this cream and fold* it into the chocolate
until the texture is elastic and shiny.
Slightly reheat the mixture over the bain-marie or in the
microwave. The temperature should be 95°F-104°F (35°C-40°C).
Carefully fold in the Swiss meringue, and then fold in the
remaining lightly whipped cream (3).
Arrange the mixture in molds or small glasses (4) and freeze
for at least 3 hours. This parfait will keep for a maximum of
1 week in the freezer.

Recipe idea
Iced Chocolate Parfait and Cappuccino Sauce >> p. 292

Chocolate Granita ★

Granitas have an iced, crackly texture, and if you include this as one of the components of your desserts, you will be able to make interesting temperature and textural contrasts.

Ingredients

6 oz. (170 g) bittersweet chocolate, 70 percent cocoa
Or 6 ¾ oz. (190 g) bittersweet chocolate, 60 percent cocoa
2 ¾ cups (650 ml) water
1 ½ tablespoons (10 g) powdered milk
⅔ cup (4 ½ oz./125 g) granulated sugar
1 heaped tablespoon (1 oz./25 g) honey

Equipment

1 dish large enough to pour the mixture out to a depth of just over 1 in. (3 cm)
1 flexible spatula†
1 immersion blender†

Chop the chocolate and melt it slowly in a bain-marie* or in the microwave oven (on "defrost" or at 500 W maximum, stirring from time to time).
Heat the water, powdered milk, sugar, and honey in a saucepan and leave to simmer for 2 minutes.
Gradually pour one-third of the syrup over the melted chocolate. Using a flexible spatula, mix in energetically, drawing small circles to create an elastic, shiny "kernel." Incorporate the second third of the liquid, using the same procedure. Repeat with the last third.
Blend for a few seconds using an immersion blender so that the mixture is smooth and perfectly emulsified*.
Pour it into a dish to just over 1 in. (3 cm) thick (1). Place in the freezer for at least 3 hours, scratching regularly to form the crystals (2). If you don't scratch the granita regularly, it will just become a solid chunk of iced chocolate!

Recipe idea

Mini Molten Chocolate Cakes With *Verrines* of Softened Bananas and Chocolate Granita >> p. 224

Bittersweet Chocolate Sorbet ★ ★

Sorbet, unlike ice cream, comprises water and a little powdered milk, making for a light, fresh chocolate experience.
Serves 6

Ingredients
11 ½ oz. (325 g) bittersweet chocolate, 70 percent cocoa
4 cups (1 liter) water
2 tablespoons (20 g) powdered milk
1 ¼ cups (9 oz./250 g) sugar
2 ½ tablespoons (50 g) honey, preferably acacia or multifloral

Equipment
1 immersion blender†
1 ice-cream maker†
1 kitchen thermometer†
1 flexible spatula†

Chop the chocolate and melt it slowly in a bain-marie* or in the microwave oven (on "defrost" or at 500 W maximum, stirring from time to time).

Combine the water, powdered milk, sugar, and honey in a saucepan (1) and bring to the simmer. Leave to simmer for 2 minutes.

Gradually pour one-third of the syrup over the melted chocolate. Using a flexible spatula, mix it energetically, drawing small circles to create an elastic, shiny "kernel" (2). Incorporate the second third of the liquid, using the same procedure. Repeat with the last third.

Blend for a few seconds using an immersion blender so that the mixture is smooth and perfectly emulsified*.

Return the mixture to the saucepan and heat, stirring constantly, to 185°F (85°C).

Immediately pour it into a bowl over a larger bowl filled with ice cubes to cool it down.

Leave to rest (mature) overnight in the refrigerator to develop the flavors fully.

Place in an ice-cream maker, following the directions, and freeze at 0°F (-18°C).

● Chef's note
It's best to use a fairly neutral honey, such as acacia or multifloral, so as not to overpower the taste of the chocolate.

1

2

Milk Chocolate Sorbet ★★

Milk chocolate and a little powdered milk give a sweeter result, with notes of caramel and honey, like the treats we enjoyed as children.
Serves 12–15

Ingredients
13 ¾ oz. (390 g) milk chocolate, 40 percent cocoa
4 cups (1 liter) water
⅔ cup (2 ¾ oz./80 g) powdered milk
Scant ⅔ cup (120 g) sugar
3 tablespoons plus 1 scant teaspoon (2 ½ oz./70 g) honey

Equipment
1 immersion blender†
1 ice-cream maker†
1 kitchen thermometer†
1 flexible spatula†

Chop the chocolate and melt it slowly in a bain-marie* or in the microwave oven (on "defrost" or at 500 W maximum, stirring from time to time).
Bring the water, powdered milk, sugar, and honey to the simmer in a saucepan and simmer for 2 minutes.
Gradually pour one-third of the simmering liquid over the melted chocolate. Using a flexible spatula, mix in energetically, drawing small circles to create an elastic, shiny "kernel."
Incorporate the second third of the liquid, using the same procedure. Repeat with the last third.
Blend for a few seconds using an immersion blender so that the mixture is smooth and perfectly emulsified*.
Return the mixture to the saucepan and heat again, stirring constantly, until it reaches 185°F (85°C).
Cool rapidly by pouring it into a bowl over ice cubes. Leave to rest (mature) overnight to develop the flavors fully.
Place in an ice-cream maker, following the manufacturer's directions, and freeze at 0°F (-18°C).

Ivory Sorbet ★★

Last but not least in the series of chocolate sorbets—this is ivory colored and even milkier than the two previous sorbets.
Serves 12–15

Ingredients
1 lb. 3 ½ oz. (550 g) white chocolate, 35 percent cocoa
4 cups (1 liter) water
1 cup plus 3 ½ tablespoons (5 oz./140 g) powdered milk
3 ½ tablespoons (1 ½ oz./40 g) sugar
¼ cup (3 ¼ oz./90 g) honey

Equipment
1 immersion blender†
1 ice-cream maker†
1 kitchen thermometer†
1 flexible spatula†

Chop the chocolate and melt it slowly in a bain-marie* or in the microwave oven (on "defrost" or at 500 W maximum, stirring from time to time).
Heat the water, powdered milk, sugar, and honey and simmer for 2 minutes.
Gradually pour one-third of the simmering syrup over the melted chocolate. Using a flexible spatula, mix in energetically, drawing small circles to create an elastic, shiny "kernel."
Incorporate the second third of the liquid, using the same procedure. Repeat with the last third.
Blend for a few seconds using an immersion blender so that the mixture is smooth and perfectly emulsified*.
Return the mixture to the saucepan and reheat, stirring constantly, until it reaches 185°F (85°C).
Cool rapidly by pouring it into a bowl over ice cubes. Leave to rest (mature) overnight to develop the flavors fully. Process the mixture in ice-cream maker, following the manufacturer's instructions and then freeze at 0°F (-18°C).

Chocolate Sauce ★

Chocolate sauce makes everything better. It's the finishing touch for any number of iced desserts and is the indispensable ingredient in classic dishes, drizzled over Poire Belle Hélène, banana splits, and profiteroles. The quality of your chocolate makes all the difference, so use the best you can.

Ingredients
Weigh the chocolate according to its cocoa content:
3 oz. (85 g) bittersweet chocolate, 70 percent cocoa
Or 3 ¼ oz. (90 g) bittersweet chocolate, 60 percent cocoa
Or 4 ¾ oz. (130 g) milk chocolate, 40 percent cocoa
Or 5 oz. (140 g) white chocolate, 35 percent cocoa
½ cup minus 1 ½ tablespoons (100 ml) whole milk
A little sugar (optional)

Equipment
1 immersion blender†
1 kitchen thermometer†
1 flexible spatula†

Chop the chocolate and melt it slowly in a bain-marie* or in the microwave oven (on "defrost" or at 500 W maximum, stirring from time to time).

Bring the milk to the boil.
Gradually pour one-third of the boiling milk over the melted chocolate. Using a flexible spatula, mix in energetically, drawing small circles to create an elastic, shiny "kernel." Incorporate the second third of the milk, using the same procedure. Repeat with the last third.
Blend for a few seconds using an immersion blender. Serve hot, or reserve in the refrigerator.
Milk and white chocolate sauce should be served at 68°F-77°F (20°C-25°C); bittersweet chocolate should be served at 95°F-104°F (35°C-40°C).

● Chef's note
If you wish, you may sweeten bittersweet chocolate sauce by adding a little milk chocolate or sugar.

❦ Recipe ideas
Chocolate Profiteroles ›› p. 172
White Chocolate-Coffee Dessert with a Whiff of Dark Chocolate ›› p. 229

Ice creams, sorbets, and sauces

Chocolate-Caramel Sauce ★★

Chocolate and caramel are one of the most timeless and delicious pairings in the world of desserts.

Ingredients
7 ¾ oz. (220 g) milk chocolate, 40 percent cocoa
2 cups minus 2 tablespoons (470 ml) whipping cream
1 heaped tablespoon (1 oz./25 g) glucose syrup
1 ¼ cups (8 ½ oz./240 g) sugar
5 tablespoons plus 1 teaspoon (2 ⅔ oz./75 g) butter

Equipment
1 flexible spatula†
1 kitchen thermometer†
1 immersion blender†

Chop the chocolate and melt it slowly in a bain-marie* or in the microwave oven (on "defrost" or at 500 W maximum, stirring from time to time).
Bring the cream and glucose syrup to a simmer. While this mixture is heating, prepare a caramel* using the dry method, and bring the sugar to 356°F–365°F (180°C-185°C).
Carefully add the butter (don't burn yourself), and gradually pour the hot caramel over the cream and glucose syrup mixture. Bring this to the boil.
Gradually pour one-third of the boiling liquid over the melted chocolate. Using a flexible spatula, mix in energetically, drawing small circles to create an elastic, shiny "kernel."
Incorporate the second third of the liquid, using the same procedure. Repeat with the last third.
Process for a few seconds using an immersion blender.
Leave to crystallize* in the refrigerator for a few hours before using.

● **Chef's note**
Customize this sauce with spices, zest, juiced ginger or passion fruit, citrus juices, and more.*

● **Did you know?**
Glucose syrup prevents granulated sugar from forming crystals again in the caramel.

Recipe ideas
Cactus-Shaped Churros and Ginger-Scented Milk Chocolate Sauce
›› p. 219
Chocolate-Vanilla Marbled Waffles ›› p. 222
Crisp Almond Cookies with Chocolate Ice Cream and Caramel and
Passion Fruit Sauce ›› p. 299

Mastering further techniques

Marbling

For an attractive marbled cake, pour one-third of the vanilla batter into your loaf pan. Using a piping bag†, pipe half of the chocolate batter lengthways down the center. Cover this with one-third of the vanilla batter, and then pipe in the other half of the chocolate batter in another line down the center. Cover with the remaining vanilla batter.

Making the perfect loaf cake

For a loaf cake to rise to its optimum height, leave the batter overnight in the refrigerator just before baking. Then dip a triangular scraper† (or similar object) in a little melted butter and make an incision ½-¾ in. (1-2 cm) deep in a line down the center from one end to the other. This will result in a nicely risen cake with a good crust. When you remove it from the oven, leave it for a few minutes in the pan before you turn it out onto its side to cool. This will ensure that it remains straight, and it's a method that works whether your loaf pans have straight or inclined sides.

Filling a piping bag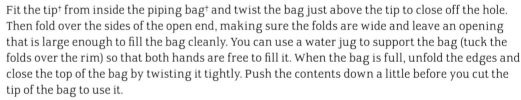

Fit the tip† from inside the piping bag† and twist the bag just above the tip to close off the hole. Then fold over the sides of the open end, making sure the folds are wide and leave an opening that is large enough to fill the bag cleanly. You can use a water jug to support the bag (tuck the folds over the rim) so that both hands are free to fill it. When the bag is full, unfold the edges and close the top of the bag by twisting it tightly. Push the contents down a little before you cut the tip of the bag to use it.

When you are not piping out the mixture, make sure you hold the bag with the tip upwards!

● **Chef's notes**
Hold your piping bag with the hand you use to write.
Do not overfill it, as that makes it harder to manipulate it.
You can also use a clothes peg to close it before filling and refilling.

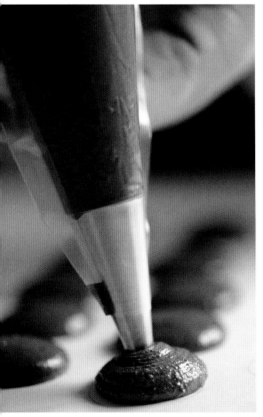

Piping out round macaroons

Hold the piping bag† perpendicular to the sheet of parchment paper. It should just about be in contact with the sheet. Press down without moving until you have the desired size of macaroon*. Stop the pressure and lift up the bag by flicking your wrist.

Lining a tart dish

Use buttered molds[†], either pastry circles[†] (without a base, used by professionals) or molds with bases. Metal molds give a crustier shell than porcelain or ceramic molds.

Classic method (1)
Roll out the dough to a size just slightly larger than that of your mold. Drape the dough over a rolling pin[†] to move it from the board to the mold; this will enable you to position it correctly. Now unroll the dough over the mold. Press down lightly with your thumbs so that the dough sticks to the sides. Trim the edges with a knife and chill according to the recipe instructions.

Lining base and sides separately (2)
Roll out the dough and cut out a disk using the pastry circle as a cutter. Gather the remaining dough into a ball, roll it out, and cut out strips to line the sides of the tart mold. Place the disk on the baking sheet and brush the sides of the pastry circle with water. Press the strips onto the side, pressing lightly with your thumbs. Trim the edges with a knife and chill according to the recipe instructions.

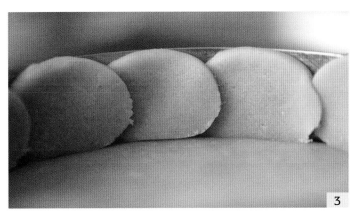

Lining with a scalloped pattern (3)
Roll out the dough and cut out a disk using the pastry circle as a cutter. Shape a log just over 1 in. (3 cm) in diameter and freeze for a few minutes to harden it slightly. This will enable you to cut out "slices" about $\frac{1}{16}$-$\frac{1}{8}$ in. (3-4 mm) thick. Overlap the slices like scales around the side of the circle. This will make an attractive scalloped border.

Without a mold
Cut out a disk, square, rectangle, or any other shape of your choice from the rolled-out dough. Place it on a baking sheet and pinch the edges between your thumb and index finger to create a rippled effect.

Whisking egg whites

Make sure that your bowl is perfectly clean, dry, and grease-free. It is always best to whisk* egg whites at medium speed to ensure that air is incorporated in fine bubbles, giving delicacy and stability to the structure.

If you whisk at high speed, the air is not incorporated in the same way, resulting in a more fragile, less stable mixture, usually with less volume. The eggs must be whisked until they form soft peaks, not stiff peaks, contrary to popular belief (and practice!).

The peaks they form will bend over slightly, instead of remaining pertly straight. The texture will be similar to that of shaving foam or styling mousse. When egg whites are whisked to this stage, it is relatively easy to incorporate them into other mixtures.

Softening butter

Wouldn't it be wonderful if butter were always soft enough to use immediately? But softened butter takes time and energy, so take it out from the refrigerator a few hours before you need it and place it, unwrapped, in a mixing bowl. Use a flexible spatula† to work it energetically.

If the butter remains hard, put it in the microwave oven for just a few seconds on low power, being careful not to melt it, or over a bain-marie*. Finish softening it with the spatula or a whisk†. In French, this is known as *beurre pommade**.

Roasting nuts

Roasting nuts is the best way of bringing out their flavors.
It is best to use low to medium heat (350°F or 150°C) so that the nuts are the same color both inside and out. This is the sign that they have been well roasted.

Place the nuts in an oven preheated to 350°F (150°C) for 10 to 15 minutes, until they turn a nice amber color.

Making the perfect chocolate mousse

Troubleshooting:
"My chocolate mousse is often grainy."
Be careful to reheat your chocolate mixture slightly before you incorporate the whisked egg whites or whipped cream. If the mixture has already cooled and you add a large quantity of egg whites or cold cream, the chocolate hardens and forms grains.

"There's liquid egg white at the bottom of my mixing bowl."
Make sure that you whisk your egg whites until they form soft peaks, when they should bend over slightly. If they are whisked to the firm peak stage, mixing them with the chocolate will deflate them, and deflated egg whites liquefy.

"My mousse is too firm or too liquid."
Have you used chocolate that has the cocoa content given in the recipe? If necessary, change the weight of the chocolate you are using according to its cocoa content (see The Cocoa Percentage p. 144).
The cocoa butter* contained in chocolate is what is known as a hardener. Depending on how much cocoa butter you include in your recipe, you may have too much or too little of the hardener, and hence a texture that is either too firm or too liquid.

"My mousse is dry and/or grainy."
Have you emulsified* the chocolate properly with the liquid, following the rule that specifies it should be incorporated by thirds* (see p. 95)?
Each time you prepare the emulsion, don't forget this rule: gradually pour one-third of the boiling liquid over the melted chocolate. Using a flexible spatula†, mix it in energetically, drawing small circles to create an elastic, shiny "kernel." Incorporate the second third of the liquid, using the same procedure. Repeat with the last third.

Mastering further techniques

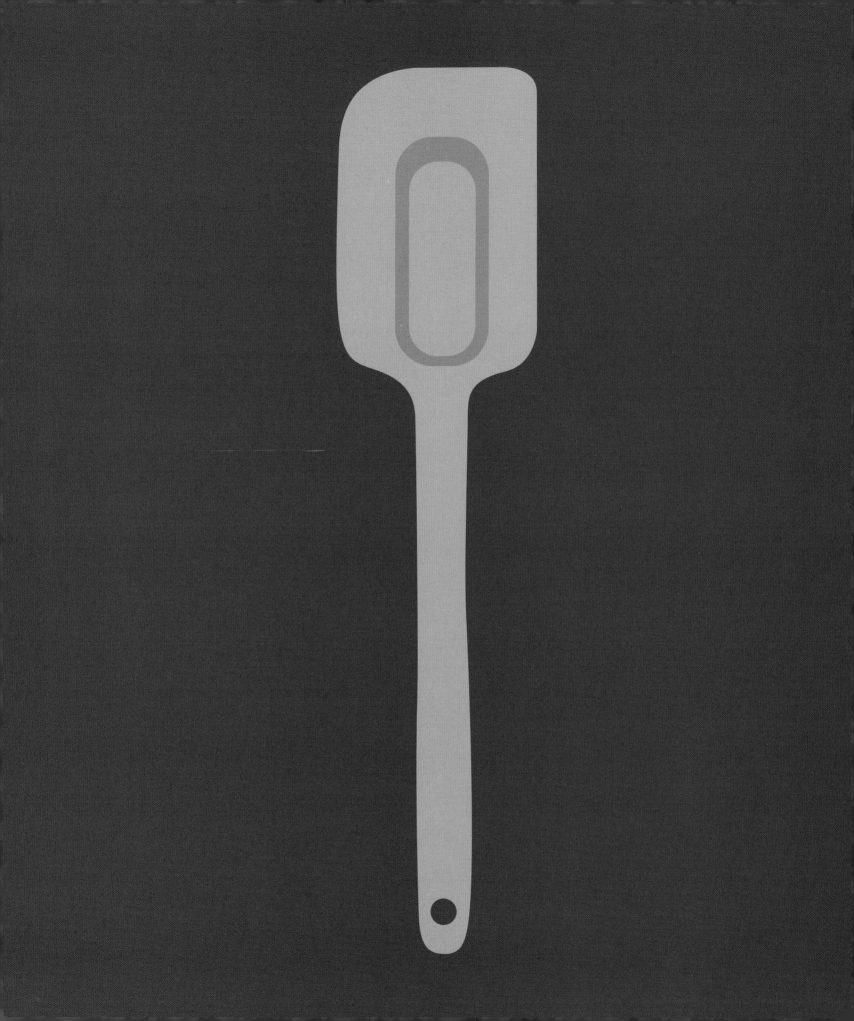

Theory

The secrets
of a quality chocolate

At first sight, there is no difference between one bittersweet chocolate with a cocoa content of 80 percent and another bittersweet chocolate with the same cocoa content. And yet, in some cases, there may be a world of difference. From one make to another, from one origin to another, from one manufacturing process to another, the aspect, the aromas, the texture, and the melting quality may vary radically. Where do these differences stem from? They are due to a number of parameters that are hard to imagine when you take that delicious bite into your favorite bar.

The terroir

The concept of terroir in chocolate-making was virtually unknown until the early 1990s. It is now taken as a given among connoisseurs. Chocolate comes from the cocoa pod, the fruit of the cocoa tree. The beans are, of course, agricultural crops, and like all agricultural crops they are influenced by the combination of factors that together make up what we call terroir: origin, choice of varieties, environment, and expertise. There are three main varieties of cocoa trees—Criollo, Forastero, and Trinitario—and each produces cocoa with different characteristics. Forastero, for example, is considered more bitter and astringent, while Criollo is regarded as mellower, with notes of berries, nuts, and honey. These subtle differences underpin the construction of the taste of chocolate. In addition to the variety of the tree, the environment is also an important factor. The amount of sunlight that reaches the trees influences the polyphenol content, and rain plays a role in fermentation. And, of course, the work of the farmers can radically modify the aromas of the product. When the pods are cleaved open, and during the processes of fermentation and drying, the slightest bit of inattention might well produce an unwanted aroma, such as a taste of mold or smoke, or excess acidity.

So all these factors, which vary from one plantation to another and from one year to another, have an influence on the final aroma. Yet they are not enough to guarantee the quality of a chocolate. Just like a wine producer who makes optimal use of his terroir to imprint his signature on his wine, a master chocolatier who knows how to get the most out of his plantations will leave his mark on a good chocolate.

Expertise

On cocoa plantations you will find an empirical know-how transmitted down through the generations. It is used for the harvesting techniques, the fermentation, and the drying. These age-old practices are still alive and well in the producing countries, and in no danger of disappearing, even if the scientific knowledge required to create the right conditions to grow the best possible produce also exists.

The transformation of bean to bar, on the other hand, follows a well-trodden, codified industrial process. The technological innovations developed by the major chocolate manufacturers over the nineteenth century gave chocolate the texture and aromas that we know today, light years away from the pre-Columbian chocolate made of grated cocoa, flavorings, and spices, and consumed as a drink. A quick overview of the significant names in the production of chocolate highlights François Louis Cailleur, the Swiss inventor of the chocolate bar in 1820; his compatriot, Philippe Suchard, who developed a *mélangeur* to combine sugar with cocoa; and then Charles-Amédée Kohler, yet another Swiss, who in 1831 put hazelnuts into the paste. Also around this time, Casparus Van Houten of the Netherlands extracted cocoa butter* from the rest of the mass, which he ground to powder. In 1849, Henri Nestlé, a German pharmacist living in Switzerland, invented powdered milk and at the same time launched chocolate milk. But it is Rodolph Lindt to whom we owe two major discoveries in 1879: the conching technique and the addition of cocoa butter, both of which have given chocolate its now characteristic silky texture.

The various stages of chocolate making have remained relatively unchanged, but the roasting and conching techniques depend on the knowledge and skills of master chocolate makers, and it is their familiarity with cocoa that allows them to understand the parameters that will result in the desired aroma and texture.

TERROIRS AND AROMAS Unlike wine, it is difficult to link a terroir to a chocolate taste, primarily because the varieties of cocoa are less distinct than those of vines.
In the plantations, farmers have cultivated their own mixtures, often by borrowing plants from a neighbor or grandfather. In addition, research on cocoa plants has concentrated on increasing yields and combating disease rather than on defining aromatic profiles. But chocolate artisans and groups of chocolate lovers have been increasingly emphasizing the links between terroir and taste. Perhaps this trend will develop to the point where appellations of origin will be established.

Creativity

Strange as it may seem, the creation of a chocolate involves working to a recipe. Labels on mass-produced bars sometimes give us the impression that it is all very simple: a minimum cocoa percentage, indicating the presence of cocoa paste and cocoa butter; sugar, a little soy lecithin, natural extract of vanilla—and nothing else. The adjectives used to describe chocolate—intense, elegant, sleek, subtle, sublime—rarely give any indications of the provenance and the quality of the cocoas used. And for good reason: all the

information is based on the percentages of cocoa and sugar. Variations of taste depend on the varieties of cocoa, the origins, and the way in which they are worked (see The Cocoa Percentage, p. 144).

Although they do not talk about it, industrial chocolate producers must ensure that the aromas of a 60, 70, or 80 percent cocoa chocolate are always uniform. To do so, they must determine a mixture of beans with identical or equivalent aromas.

Master chocolate makers behave like cellar masters who have to guarantee the stability of a blend, for example the assembly of a single malt and single grains that makes a whisky identical whenever it is produced over time. Certain artisan chocolatiers and even a few industrial producers, such as Valrhona and, more recently, Nespresso, go even further, showcasing the characteristics of each terroir by defining a veritable aromatic profile of the chocolate. They seek to establish a typical taste when they work on the composition.

In 1987, Valrhona was the first to launch a *grand cru* chocolate, created entirely from Caribbean Criollo cocoas. In 1998, Valrhona went even further when it developed the first single-origin domain chocolate: Gran Couva 60 percent from Trinidad. The entire range, divided into three large families, always emphasizes the importance of the provenance. Blended *grands crus* combine cocoas of various plantations in various producing countries, terroir *grands crus* comprise cocoas from a single producing country, and single-origin chocolate comes from a single plantation. The mouth-feel of a 70 percent Andoa bittersweet (a blend of *grands crus*) is completely different from that of a 68 percent Nyangbo (a single origin *grand cru*), not in terms of intensity, but in terms of aroma, texture, and "color." The first has a little bitterness, with notes of citrus fruits and roasted coffee, while the second is decidedly more "chocolatey," with notes of mild spices and roasted nuts.

The work of master chocolatiers involves finding exactly what proportion of chocolate and sugar, and which cocoa associated with another, will give the very best result. Today, there are clearly two major trends in the chocolate industry: those who favor a return-to-childhood chocolate, with a well-roundedness, sweetness, and accentuated vanilla notes; and those who seek out authenticity, the raw nature of the original cocoa, and who are happy to bring out the bitterness of the beans in the final product. Between these two extremes, an infinite number of combinations is possible. The chocolatier, like an organist pulling on the stops of the instrument, strives to modulate the aromas, working on the range from the most powerful to the freshest, the most bitter to the mildest, the most floral to the fruitiest.

Green beans

Roasted beans

Cocoa nibs*

Cocoa liqueur
(pure paste)

Cocoa mass
(pure paste plus sugar)

Refined, pulverized
cocoa mass

Chocolate

From bean to bar

To understand how a bar of chocolate gets to us from the cocoa tree, let's follow the progress of a handful of beans from a Venezuelan plantation to Valrhona's production facilities in Tain-l'Hermitage, in the Drôme region of France.

In the hot and humid climate of Venezuela, just as in the entire equatorial zone, cocoa trees flourish and their fruits ripen twice yearly, between November and January, and then again between May and July. The pod is a long fruit, about the size of a melon. Its thick shell protects the precious cocoa beans, which are contained in a gelatinous pulp. This white, sweet-sour pulp, which tastes something like a litchi or custard apple, is eaten raw by the locals. When the husk has been opened to extract the contents, the fresh beans (or seeds) are spread out in large bins or crates for the first stage of their transformation. This is the crucial fermentation phase, when the beans develop the underpinnings to what will be the chocolate aromas. Now a classic chain of chemical reactions ensues: yeast formation transforms the sugar into alcohol (anaerobic alcoholic fermentation); then the farmers rotate the beans for two to eight days, depending on the variety, to accelerate aeration, which helps the development of bacteria (acetic fermentation).

When the farmer considers that the fermentation is complete, he places the beans out on racks to dry in the sun. This is a critical time, for they must be prevented from rotting and turned over regularly, and covered if it rains. The moisture content drops from 80 percent to 5 percent.

Our seeds, now nestling in burlap bags, are transported to Europe, where they undergo a second transformation. At this stage, although it is hard to know what their taste is, their defects, such as bitterness, or a taste of mold or smoke, can be detected. An experienced nose can even make out aromas of fruit and flowers.

At the Tain-l'Hermitage chocolate factory, just as in all food-processing business, the arrival of the cocoa begins with a stringent quality control. We take samples of beans, we analyze them, we rid them of their bacteria, we cut, and we prepare an extract of the chocolate to establish the aromatic profile of the batch. And we compare it to the standard of products of the same provenance (Venezuela, Brazil, Ecuador, Côte d'Ivoire, and others).

The beans that are accepted then begin a rollercoaster ride within massive machines interconnected by tubes and conveyer belts that are constantly fed with a product that will eventually come out as a fat, smooth ribbon of chocolate ready to be molded.

Stage one: Roasting

This is very similar to the process still to be seen at some coffee sellers who use an old-fashioned roaster. The seeds are roasted at temperatures ranging from 250°F to 300° F (120°C–150°C) for a duration of 15 to 40 minutes—the chocolate maker will decide what is required to bring out the maximum aromas. Roasting is the final stage of transformation of cocoa, begun a few weeks earlier when the fermentation was carried out at the plantation. The sugars caramelize* and combine with the amino acids to produce the components of the chocolate aroma.

Stage two: Crushing

Under the weight of crushing hammers, the beans are freed of their shells and are reduced to minute particles of just a small fraction of an inch. The shells are evacuated using a system of sifting and ventilation. The small remaining shards are called cocoa nibs*: small, bitter, crunchy pieces that do not yet taste of chocolate. The nibs are bagged and sorted according to their origin while they await selection to be used as an ingredient in a specific type of chocolate that will be developed. For example, our Venezuelan beans for use in Araguani 72 percent, a terroir grand cru, will be incorporated in quantities that depend on the recipe developed by the master chocolate makers.

Stage three: Grinding

At this stage, nothing has been added to the nibs. They enter a mill to be finely pulverized. What comes out is a rough powder that melts in the mouth but that has the texture of a praline*. It is called cocoa paste, cocoa liqueur, or cocoa mass. But it still does not have the taste of chocolate; it is bitter, acidic, and a little grainy. Now is the time to add the necessary proportion of sugar, that indispensable complement to the cocoa percentage. It is also the moment when powdered milk is added to milk chocolate. This takes place in vast mixers where the sugar is incorporated into the paste. The mass that emerges is now chocolate paste, in the form of block. These sandy-textured blocks give us an initial idea of what the finished product will taste like.

Stage four: Refining

The raw chocolate paste is reduced to fine particles when ground by five to seven rollers spaced out at various intervals, and which work at various speeds. The size of the particles is reduced from 500 to 14 microns, resulting in a silky powder that just evaporates in the mouth. Chocolate as we know it is not far off.

Stage five: Conching

This procedure was invented by Rodolph Lindt in the late nineteenth century. Conching considerably improves the texture of chocolate, bringing out all its aromatic force. In a vat at a temperature of 176°F (80°C), the machine churns and agitates the chocolate paste continuously for one to three days. The heat and friction heat the fatty particles and liquefy the chocolate. During this process the cocoa butter* (see There's Cocoa Powder and Cocoa Powder, below) is added into the conch. This ingredient—chocolatiers will never divulge its proportions—binds the chocolate, increasing its unctuousness, something like an emulsion. Valrhona, like most other manufacturers, also adds soy lecithin, an emulsifier* that plays the same role as cocoa butter, as well as natural vanilla extract to finish the aromas.

Then comes the final stage: tempering*. Chocolate undergoes a temperature curve that takes it from 113°F (45°C) to 82.4°F (28°C) before being increased again to 90°F (32°C). This ideal curve, determined by the physics of the chocolate, gives it perfect stability. The fatty molecules are evenly distributed around the dry molecules, and the chocolate will now have the snap needed to cut it, the crunch between your teeth, and the uniform, smooth, melting texture that dissolves in the mouth. All that remains is to mold the black, ivory, or white jewel into any of a tremendously diverse range of forms: bars, buttons for professionals, tasting squares, Easter eggs, original molds, and many more.

THERE'S COCOA POWDER AND COCOA POWDER The powder ground from cocoa nibs is not the same as the powder that results from the separation of the dry matter and cocoa butter. The former results from the grinding of the whole bean; it is one of the stages of the production of chocolate and contains a mixture of cocoa and cocoa butter naturally present in the bean. The latter is made separately, often in a different factory, during a procedure that involves pressing the cocoa mass to separate the cocoa butter from the dry extract. The powder from this is used as the base for cocoa powder. Cocoa butter is used as an ingredient in chocolate factories and is also used to make some cosmetics.

Tasting: a revelation for the palate

Even consumers with an exceptional palate would be astonished to discover the range of nuances that describe the aromatic profile of a chocolate. Using chromatographic techniques, scientists have officially established over 400 aromatic notes in our black gourmet fruit. Chocolate experts, however, use only a limited number of characteristics—about fifty—to draw up the profile of a chocolate. Let us take a voyage into the heart of these aromas.

Major producers have developed customized tasting criteria, but all take the words of wine tasting as inspiration. And this is quite logical, for the yeasts and bacteria that play a role in the development of the aromas of chocolate and wine are identical.

Yet enologists readily acknowledge that it is far harder to taste a chocolate than it is a wine because of the presence of cocoa butter*, a factor that intrudes on one's perception.

If one is not to miss all the chocolate aromas contained in cocoa butter, one must melt the substance correctly when it is being tasted. If the tempering* has not been properly carried out, this can be complicated. If the fatty molecules are not correctly distributed around the dry molecules, melting does not take place as it should and the aromas are not completely liberated on the palate. Once again, we see how technique plays a role in the impact chocolate has on the senses.

At Valrhona, tasting sessions are of primordial importance. Some twenty people participate daily. The "cocoa-theque," created in the 1980s, is based on the work of an in-house jury comprising expert judges on a rotating basis and who undergo a yearlong training course. They first have to learn to identify and recognize simple aromatic molecules from the vials used by aroma specialists, containing aromas such as peach, red berries, licorice, and leather. Then they must transfer and apply this learning to the complex texture of chocolate. Lastly, they have to work on a shared scale of perceptions to enable them to profile a chocolate with as much objectivity as possible.

If you would like to try a tasting experience, wait until a considerable period after a meal has elapsed. Take a small piece of chocolate and observe its color and its snapping texture. It must be shiny, smooth, and break cleanly. Sniff it and begin by looking for its most obvious aromas. Then leave it to melt slowly in your mouth. Analyze your perceptions in terms of the main families of aromas: acidic, bitter, chocolate, fruity, sweet, caramel, spicy, etc. For each one, try to grade its intensity on a scale of one to eight.

You can take your tasting experience further by specifying the type of fruity aroma (fresh, dry, red, yellow) and look out for the sensations that follow directly from the texture: does its aftertaste linger long; is it fatty, dry, melting, astringent?

If you repeat the experiment with several chocolates of different brands with varying cocoa percentages, you will discover unexpected subtleties and become more demanding. And if this seems like a difficult exercise, rest assured that even experts admit that they lose their references very quickly—after just a few weeks without any activity—even if they have studied the art for an entire year.

The cocoa percentage

The more cocoa, the better the chocolate.... Any number of gourmets believes this; so do some professionals. Yet the cocoa percentage indicated on a bar of chocolate is no guarantee of quality. A chocolate is delicious, seductive, surprising because of the balance it offers between the proportion of the cocoa fruit and the sugar it contains—just as marmalade or strawberry preserves are good because of a harmonious balance between fruit and sugar.

Just as in a good wine or good olive oil, what is important—and in fact essential in chocolate—is the origin of the fruit, the cocoa bean. It is the terroir, the way in which it has been cultivated, fermented, dried, and then worked and transformed with the great care, sensitivity, and talent that people can provide. The Tanche olive tree, a variety planted and meticulously cultivated in Nyons, France, gives a particularly delicious olive oil, but the same olive tree planted in Greek orchards or harvested differently would produce an oil that is radically different in taste, color, and texture.

The same is true of cocoa. Venezuelan cocoa beans will not give the same chocolate as beans from Madagascar. So it makes no sense to select a chocolate based on its cocoa percentage; this would be just as ridiculous as choosing a wine for its color or its alcohol content.

Asking someone if he or she prefers a 60, 70, or 80 percent chocolate is the same as asking if they prefer a wine with 10 or 12 percent alcohol. It is far better to ask wine lovers about a Saint-Joseph or Hermitage red, or even better, suggest one or other producer.

The pastry chefs at Valrhona consider that chocolates with a cocoa content ranging from 60 to 75 percent, which means a maximum 40 percent to 25 percent sugar, are well balanced in terms of percentages and taste. A good milk chocolate can also be appreciated, even if it contains a higher sugar content, on condition that it is indeed composed of chocolate and milk, and not simply of sugar with a little cocoa and a little milk.

COEUR DE GUANAJA 80% VALRHONA Experts have created new chocolates that belie theory with extraordinary technical characteristics. This is the case with Coeur de Guanaja 80 percent, created by Valrhona.

Cocoa bean, paste, and butter

The percentage of cocoa given on a bar indicates a total percentage of cocoa, meaning the products of the cocoa tree. To continue our analogy with olive trees, just as olives can be transformed into tapenade paste, so cocoa beans can be transformed into cocoa paste. Olive trees produce olive oil, and cocoa trees produce fatty matter—cocoa butter*. They are equally noble products but their uses are very different. Logically, the richer a chocolate is in cocoa, the more cocoa butter it contains, because a cocoa bean holds 50 to 55 percent cocoa butter.

To produce what is called couverture chocolate*, used as a "cover" (to coat the fillings of chocolate bonbons), it is necessary to add a percentage of cocoa butter to the cocoa paste, and the quantity depends on the manufacturers. This cocoa butter, a noble fat, makes the chocolate more fluid and is a factor in providing the finished product with its snapping quality and appetizing satiny gloss. As long as it is added in reasonable quantities, it will boost the pleasure of the tasting experience.

The role of a hardener

Our ganaches*, mousses, and other treats all get their necessary "hardening" from cocoa butter. And that is why—whether one is a professional or an amateur—the cocoa percentage of the chocolate is relevant when making recipes; in fact, it is fundamental. The more cocoa a bar contains, the more cocoa butter it has, and therefore, the more the chocolate will have a hardening effect on the recipe. That is why 3 ½ oz (100 g) of chocolate will have a variable hardening effect depending on its cocoa percentage content.

If the cocoa percentage of a chocolate you want to use is nowhere near the one indicated on a recipe, the recipe may well be a flop. This book, particularly in the Techniques section, suggests variations that will enable you to use milk chocolate or white chocolate. Changing a chocolate will certainly change the texture and taste of a dessert, but use this freedom with care!

Bittersweet chocolate

When you see "70 percent cocoa" on a bittersweet Valrhona chocolate bar, do you know what comprises the remaining 30 percent? Less than 0.5 percent is natural vanilla and lecithin; the rest is, quite simply, sugar—about 30 percent. The 70 percent cocoa comprises about 80 to 90 percent cocoa paste (beans, therefore) and added cocoa butter.

Milk chocolate

Sugar plays a more significant role in milk chocolate, and the cocoa bean has a lesser role, making way for powdered milk. The percentage of cocoa nevertheless indicates the quantity of products that are grown on the cocoa tree.

White chocolate

White chocolate is actually ivory, the original color of cocoa butter. It contains no cocoa paste, so the cocoa butter flavors and colors the chocolate with its pigments and forceful tannins. In the case of white chocolate, the cocoa percentage is entirely cocoa butter! The remainder comprises sugar and powdered milk.

Storing chocolate

How should you store chocolate?
Never in the refrigerator! Moisture is one of chocolate's worst enemies, causing streaks of white (see How to avoid bloom, below). A well-wrapped chocolate in a dark, dry place will keep for a long time without losing any of its aromas.

Keep chocolate bonbons in a box, if possible. They should be kept in an airtight container or covered with plastic wrap. Since chocolate is a product that contains fat, it tends to entrap the odors that surround it (like onions) and loose its own, just as a badly stored spice will do.

Keep chocolate in a cool room, if you can. The ideal storage temperature ranges from 61°F to 64° F (16°C–18° C), but it will do very well between 72°F and 75° F (22°C–24°C).

How to avoid bloom
Temper* your chocolate correctly. Tempering (see the method on p. 20) ensures that the crystals of the cocoa butter* are stabilized and homogenized. It prevents these crystals from moving towards the edge of the chocolate—the cause of white streaks. So it is important to follow the temperature curves given to make a smooth, glossy, streak-free chocolate.

Store your chocolate in the right conditions. If the storage temperature fluctuates, or exceeds 75°F (24°C), fat bloom will appear. On the other hand, if the storage temperature descends below 59°F (15°C) or worse, if you leave it in the refrigerator, the condensation of the water will cause the sugar to recrystallize*, leading inevitably to sugar bloom. Here's how you can distinguish between fat bloom and sugar bloom: rub the surface of the chocolate lightly, and if the white streaks disappear, you will know that it is fat bloom.

What can you do to restore a chocolate that has bloom? Have you left a chocolate bar in the car one sunny summer afternoon? It's fine to eat it, preferably transforming it so that it regains some of its taste qualities. Once it has cooled down, use it to make a ganache* or a mousse, or temper it and remold it into a bar or chocolate bonbons, such as mendiants or orangettes.

Reading the fine print

Since the directives issued by the European Parliament in 1973, chocolate composition and labeling have been harmonized throughout the member countries. The various types of chocolate—including bittersweet, milk, white, and powder—are classified according to the presence of cocoa (cocoa butter and cocoa paste). The term "chocolate" implies a minimum of 35 percent of total dry cocoa solids (cocoa butter and dry non-fat cocoa solids). Milk chocolate contains a minimum of 25 percent of total dry cocoa solids.

Industrial manufacturers who do not produce their chocolate using beans but instead buy cocoa paste must mention it in the composition. Thus you will see "cocoa paste" instead of "cocoa beans" on such products.

Since August 1, 2003, a decree authorizes the use of vegetable fats other than cocoa butter, such as illipe, palm oil, and shea. The label must indicate the use of these additives, specifying that the chocolate contains vegetable fats in addition to cocoa butter. Chocolate made using traditional methods must be labeled as having "pure cocoa butter."

Chocolate myths: true or false?

The quality depends on the cocoa percentage

False >> The percentage indicates the proportion of cocoa (paste and butter) in the bar, but gives no indication of the country of origin, the quality of the cocoa, or the expertise of the master chocolate maker.

The higher the percentage of cocoa, the more bitter the chocolate

False >> When 70 percent cocoa is shown on the label of a bar, the remaining percentage indicates the sugar. One might think that the more cocoa there is, the less sugar. However, the cocoa itself varies greatly in taste. Some beans produce a mellower, sweeter chocolate than others. Consequently, there are some 80 percent cocoa chocolates that are quite inedible, and some 85 percent cocoa chocolates that are powerful and aromatic without being bitter.

Cocoa butter* is added to chocolate

True >> The cocoa butter added at the end of the manufacturing process forms a film of lipids that gives chocolate its unctuousness and facilitates the work of artisan chocolate makers. On average, about 10 percent cocoa butter is added to the chocolate paste, but the overall proportion of cocoa butter is considerably higher as it is already present in the chocolate paste.

White chocolate contains no chocolate paste

True >> To make white chocolate, only cocoa butter, sugar, and powdered milk are required. These components explain the absence of chocolate pigmentation and the sweetness of white chocolate, which contains only 20 to 30 percent cocoa butter in addition to 55 percent sugar.

Soy lecithin is a useless, low-grade additive

False >> It is an emulsifier* that binds the cocoa butter, the cocoa paste, and the sugar, just as egg yolk binds the ingredients in mayonnaise. There is very little lecithin in chocolate—less than 1 percent—and it is known to be a very healthy product.

Couverture chocolate* is good-quality chocolate

True and false! >> It is the basis for all the chocolates bought by professionals. It is called "couverture" (from the French verb *couvrir*, to cover) because it is used to coat chocolate bonbons and to make molds. There is only one difference, and that is in its presentation form: couverture chocolate may be sold in large chips or buttons, or in bars.

A chocolate that has whitened should be thrown out

False >> Whitening, or streaking, is a change in the appearance of the chocolate that has very little influence on the taste. It is a reaction due to inappropriate storage conditions or inadequate tempering*, but it is not toxic. Chocolate that has whitened is edible.

Chocolate can be tempered at home

True >> Equipped with a kitchen thermometer† and patience, you can of course temper chocolate in your own kitchen. This book is here to help you (see p. 20)!

Manual tempering with a tempering stone is a guarantee of good chocolate

False >> This tempering technique, which usually springs to mind when one thinks of the artisan chocolatier, is not necessarily a guarantee of quality. The temperature curve is respected just as well, if not better, in an electronic tempering machine. And, in fact, most of today's artisans use such a machine.

How to create a dessert

Creating a dessert involves using your heart, your imagination, and your senses. A successful dessert of your own creation might conjure up a childhood memory, evoke a flavor, emotion, aroma, color, or shape that is meaningful to you and that will convey something to others.

Your priority must be delicious food
Your creation should not elicit more questioning than pleasure. A dessert may be intriguing and awaken the desire to discern its various flavors, but this should never overpower the simple pleasure of tasting it.

Remember to stay simple
Remember the old adage of the importance of leaving well alone. Sometimes, one is tempted to accumulate the ingredients rather than work toward a harmonious, balanced creation. It's important not to confuse complexity with originality. Try to limit yourself to three different flavors—or five, at most—so that each one can be clearly identified.

Work on the architectural aspect
An architect would never construct a twenty-story building without a foundation. Bear this in mind when you construct your desserts. Logic dictates that you work from the most solid layer, at the base, to the lightest, at the top.

But why play by these "technical" rules?
Our love for certain ingredients might tempt us to dream up a nut nougatine atop a creamy, melting chocolate mousse. But stop! Take into account the mechanical reality. When you cut your dessert, you'll crush the mousse completely. It's quite simple: all you need to do is place the nougatine between the sponge base* and the mousse.

Try creating a surprise
Be audacious! Combine unusual and unexpected flavors. Create surprises with complementary textures and flavors—a hot soufflé with a cold sorbet, or a sour passion fruit jelly accompanied by a milk chocolate mousse for a note of sweetness.

If at first you don't succeed, try, try again
Another well-known adage, and true in the kitchen as well. If you don't get your dessert right the first time, it's not serious. Roll up your sleeves again, pick up your spatula† and whisk†, and try again, rectifying any errors you might have made. It's not often that a professional manages to get it right the first time either.

Combine technique and imagination
A successful dessert is the result of a fine balance between ideas and technique. When you have learned the basics, you can give free rein to your imagination. Technique is indispensable, but it provides only the foundation and the tools for your creativity.

Nuts

Walnuts from Grenoble

Brazil nuts

Sicilian pistachios

Piedmont hazelnuts

Cashew nuts

Pecan nuts

Provençal almonds

Macadamias

Pine nuts

Dried fruit

Dates

Apricots

Raisins

Dried plums (prunes)

Figs

Spices and flowers

Cinnamon

Star anise

Lavender

Piment
d'Espelette

Tonka bean

Szechuan pepper

Cardamom

Nutmeg

Tahiti vanilla bean

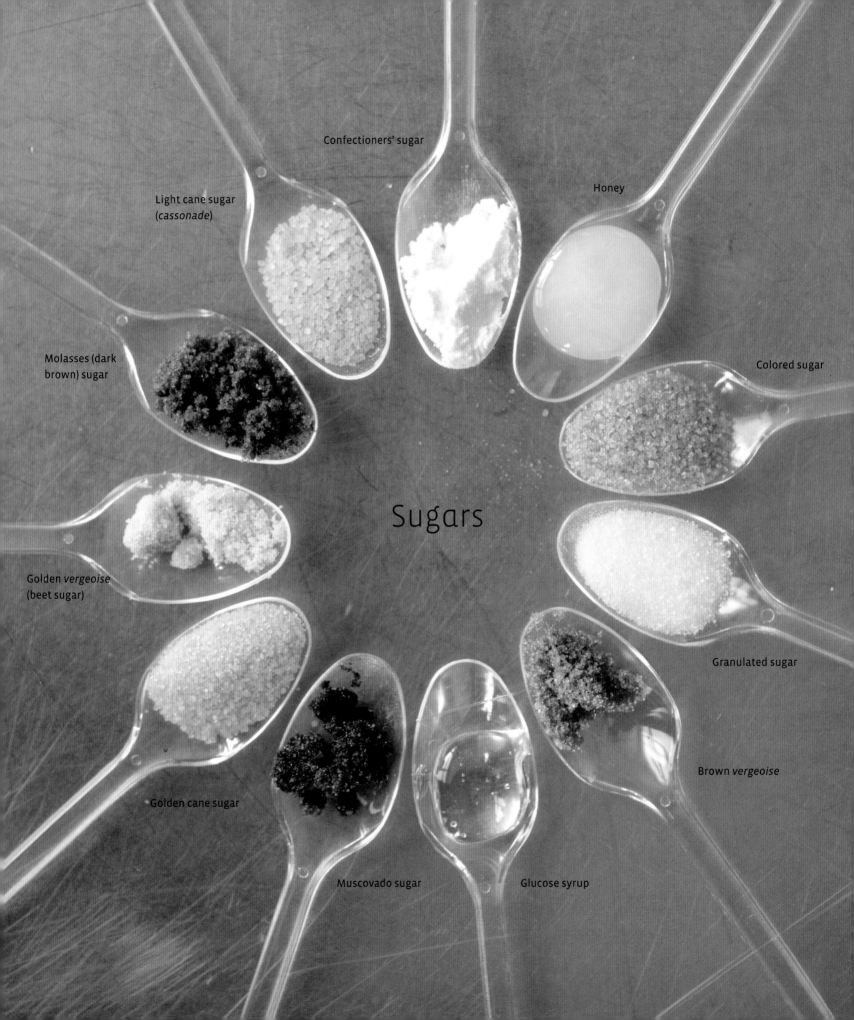

Light cane sugar (*cassonade*)

Confectioners' sugar

Honey

Molasses (dark brown) sugar

Colored sugar

Sugars

Golden *vergeoise* (beet sugar)

Granulated sugar

Golden cane sugar

Brown *vergeoise*

Muscovado sugar

Glucose syrup

Blue flower
Earl Grey

Rooibos tea

Jasmine tea

Tea
and
coffee

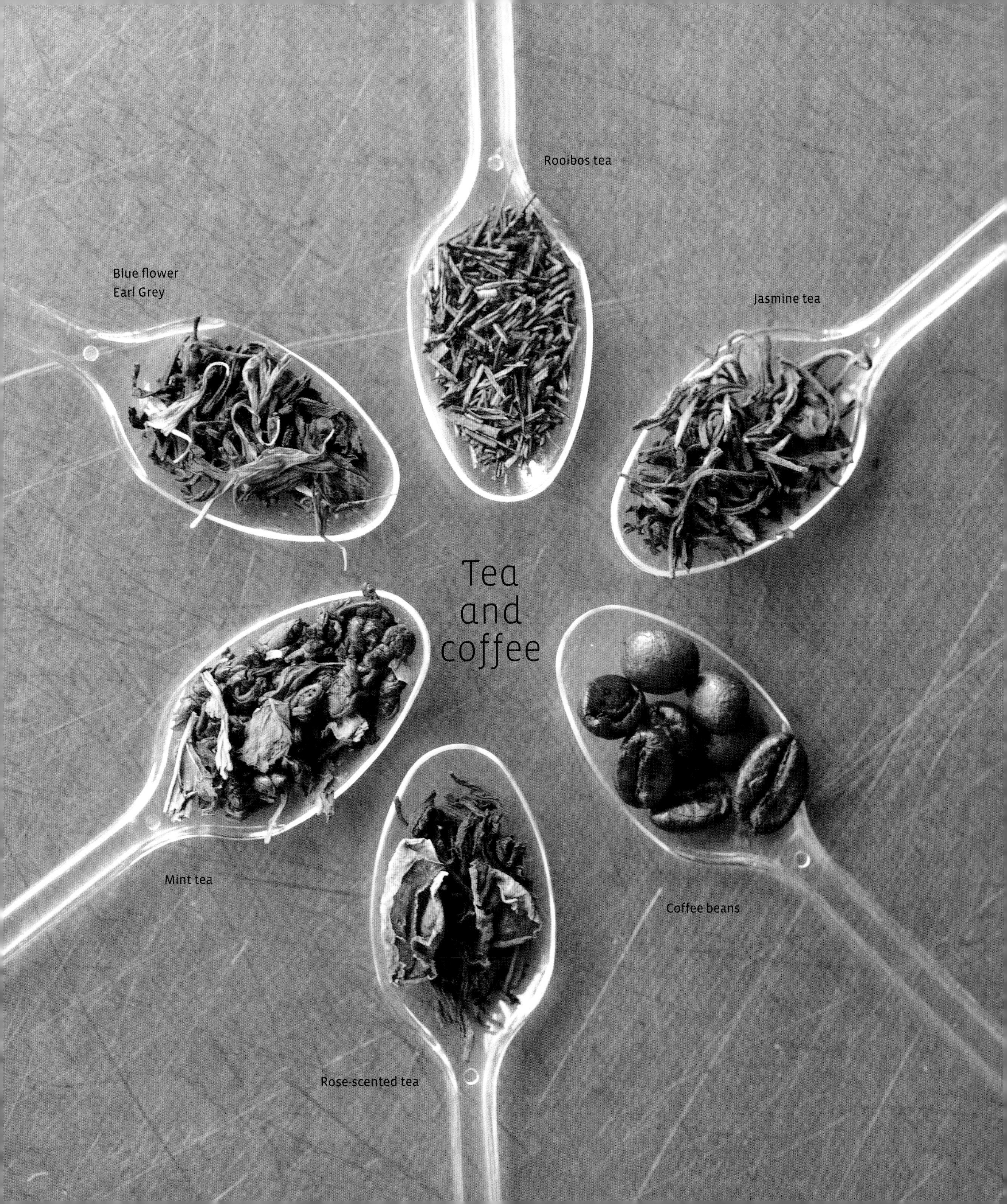

Mint tea

Coffee beans

Rose-scented tea

Recipes

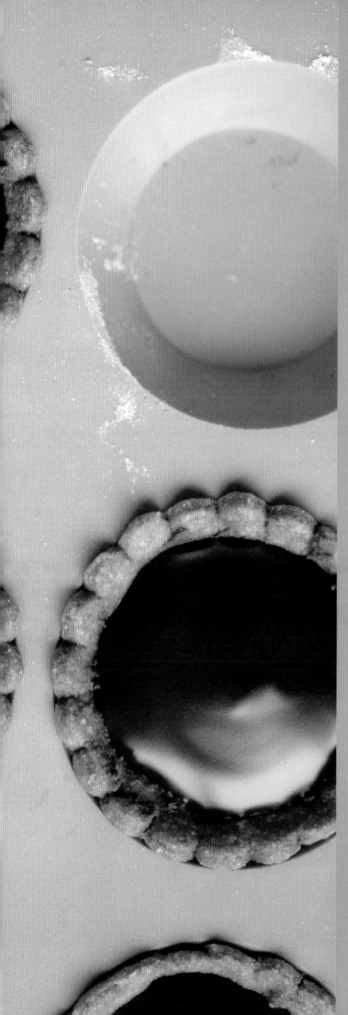

A few words of advice

Before you attempt any of the recipes in this section, take the time to read the advice we give here.

Read the recipe from beginning to end
Before you start making the recipe, read it through from beginning to end. Check that you have all the ingredients at hand as well as the necessary equipment. And ensure that you have enough time to make it. If you need to refer back to the Techniques section, remember to use the proportions given in the recipe you are making, as those in the first section are only given as guidelines.

Be precise
It is often said that pastry chefs go nowhere without their scales† and thermometer†. Pastry making and approximation do not make good bed-fellows! Make sure you follow the indications for weights, volumes, and temperatures.

Weigh all the ingredients
Be precise with liquids and eggs (1 yolk weighs about ¾ oz. or 20 g and 1 white weighs about 1 oz. or 30 g). This may seem a painstaking process at first, but just minor differences when you start may make quite a big difference to the end result. Unless otherwise specified, "eggs" refer to hens' eggs with an average weight of 2 oz. (55-57 g), "large" in the USA and Canada, "medium" in the UK.

Make sure you have the necessary equipment (see p. 402)
A kitchen thermometer, or probe, an immersion blender†, a flexible spatula†, a baking sheet, a piping bag†, and a rolling pin† are all indispensable. Your freezer will also be very useful in the preparation of some of the dishes, facilitating the assembly and unmolding of certain desserts.

Select your chocolate carefully
The quantities of chocolate you need will vary depending on their cocoa percentage (see p. 144). Cocoa butter* acts as a hardener, and a chocolate with a 50 percent cocoa content will not yield the same result as one with a 70 percent content, particularly in terms of texture. All the recipes on the pages that follow were created using Valrhona chocolate: Guanaja with 70 or 61 percent cocoa, Jivara, or Ivory. Whenever possible, we have given guidelines for variations using different chocolates.

Cooking/freezing times
Cooking, chilling, and freezing times vary with the material used. Always keep a careful eye on what you're preparing and follow the instructions.

Enjoy!
This book contains all the secrets and tips for successfully making the recipes. Be daring, have fun, and try out your own variations. The possibilities are endless (see p. 151).

The great classics

Frédéric Cassel

presents his recipe

My love for pastry was born quite fortuitously, in the neighborhood where I grew up. My parents had a delicatessen, and next door was a pastry shop. Their cakes were quite delicious, and their daughter was charming.

Very soon, I wanted to make pastry-making my profession.

I began working with sugar: large decorations, roses, cakes for weddings and other special occasions. The artistic dimension still remains important for me: I like to taste with my eyes before I eat. After seven years with Fauchon, in Paris, I set up shop in the town of Fontainebleau with my wife. I never make the same dessert twice, and try to awaken the curiosity of my clients, drawing them to ephemeral creations. Today, my team and I elaborate on seasonal themes. We create a new *macaron* (macaroon*) each month, and respect the seasonality of our ingredients. So there are no *fraisiers* (strawberry layer cake with mousseline cream) in winter, but we do have a lily of the valley *macaron* in spring, and a sacramental wine *macaron* for communions!

Coeur de Guanaja-Filled Religieuses

Choux pastry. Preheat the oven to 350°F (180°C). Sift the flour.
Combine the water, milk, sugar, salt, and butter in a saucepan and bring to the boil. Pour in the sifted flour and immediately begin mixing with a wooden spoon until the dough pulls away from the sides of the saucepan. This is how you dry the dough; removing excess moisture will allow it to rise well when baked. Remove from the pan when the dough is dried out, and incorporate the eggs one by one, stirring constantly. Spoon the dough into a piping bag. Line a baking sheet with a sheet of parchment paper and pipe out the shapes of your choice (balls for puff pastries and rectangles for éclairs). For optimal baking, make sure you leave enough space between them, at least 4 in. (10 cm). Bake for 30 to 40 minutes.

Coeur de Guanaja pastry cream. Chop the chocolate on a board. Bring the milk and cream to the boil. Whisk* the egg yolks, sugar, and cornstarch together until the mixture thickens and becomes pale. Then incorporate this mixture into the hot milk and cream and return to the heat. Bring to a simmer over medium heat, stirring continuously, and simmer for 1–2 minutes. Incorporate the chopped chocolate. Set aside in a bowl and cool in the refrigerator. Using a piping bag, fill the choux pastries with chocolate pastry cream.

● **Chef's note**
Top with good-quality pouring fondant.

Makes 6 *religieuses*

Ingredients
Choux pastry
1 cup (3 oz., 90 g) cake flour
⅓ cup (75 ml) water
⅓ cup (75 ml) whole milk
2 pinch granulated sugar
1 pinch salt
4 tablespoons (60 g) butter
3 eggs

Coeur de Guanaja Pastry Cream
3 oz. (84 g) bittersweet Coeur de Guanaja chocolate, 80 percent cocoa
¾ cup (200 ml) whole milk
3 tablespoons (40 ml) whipping cream, 35 percent fat content
1 ¼ oz. (36 g) egg yolks
2 ½ tablespoons (1 oz., 30 g) granulated sugar
1 level teaspoon plus 1 scant teaspoon (6 g) cornstarch

Decoration
Pouring fondant* (*fondant pâtissier*)

Equipment
1 piping bag†
1 baking sheet
1 whisk†

Ingredients

Chocolate sponge
Generous ¼ cup (1 oz./25 g) cake flour
3 tablespoons (⅔ oz./20 g) unsweetened cocoa powder
4 eggs: 2 whole, 2 separated
⅓ cup (2 ⅔ oz./75 g) granulated sugar
2 ½ tablespoons (1 oz./30 g) light brown sugar

Light kirsch-flavored cream
1 sheet (2 g) gelatin
1 vanilla bean
¾ cup (200 ml) full-fat whipping cream
1 heaped tablespoon (15 g) sugar
1 tablespoon plus 1 teaspoon (20 ml) kirsch
1 jar of griottes cherries, net weight 7 oz. (200 g)

Kirsch syrup
1 ¼ cups (300 g) syrup from the jar of cherries
2 tablespoons plus 2 teaspoons (40 ml) kirsch

Bittersweet chocolate ganache*
6 oz. (175 g) bittersweet chocolate, 60 percent cocoa
⅔ cup (150 ml) full-fat whipping cream

To decorate
Chocolate tuiles (see p. 49)
Confectioners' sugar

Equipment
1 large baking sheet
1 pastry circle†, 6 ½ in. (16 cm) diameter
1 pastry brush†
1 colander, 1 whisk†, 1 spatula†

Black Forest ★★ 🎬

Serves 6-8
Preparation time: 2 hours
Cooking time: 10 minutes
Refrigeration time: 1 hour

Prepare the kirsch syrup.
Thirty minutes before you need them, drain the cherries in a colander placed over a bowl. Add the kirsch to the syrup from the jar.

Prepare the chocolate sponge.
Preheat the oven to 350°F (180°C). Sift the flour and cocoa together and set aside. In a mixing bowl, whisk* the 2 egg yolks, 2 eggs, and sugar until pale and thick. Whisk the 2 egg whites with the light brown sugar. Gradually combine the two mixtures, first folding in* a little of the egg yolk mixture to the egg white mixture, and then carefully folding in the remaining egg whites.
Pour in the sifted dry ingredients and fold in until just combined.
Pour the batter onto the baking sheet and bake for 7 to 8 minutes. The texture should be spongy and the tip of a knife should come out dry. Leave to cool.

Prepare the light kirsch-flavored cream.
Soften the gelatin in a bowl of very cold water. Slit the vanilla bean lengthways and scrape out the seeds with the tip of a knife. Wring the water out of the gelatin sheets. Heat 3 tablespoons of whipping cream in a saucepan to dissolve the gelatin.
Whisk the rest of the whipping cream with the sugar and vanilla seeds. Just before the cream reaches a Chantilly texture, fold in the cream and gelatin mixture as well as the kirsch. Continue whisking until you have a light Chantilly cream texture.

Use the pastry circle to cut out 3 disks of chocolate sponge. Place the first disk on a cake rack and with a pastry brush moisten it with the kirsch syrup. Use a spatula to spread out half the kirsch-flavored cream and arrange half the cherries evenly on this layer. Place the second disk above this and repeat the procedure. Top with the third disk of chocolate sponge and chill.

Prepare the bittersweet chocolate ganache (see p. 96) using the proportions given here.
Pour the ganache over the cake so that it is completely glazed*. Chill for 1 hour. Arrange the chocolate tuiles on the ganache so that the cake is entirely covered. Dust lightly with confectioners' sugar.

● Chef's note
The Black Forest can be prepared ahead of time and frozen, but do not decorate it with the tuiles until it has defrosted.

🥄 **Techniques**
Tuiles ›› p. 49
Ganache for Tarts and Desserts ›› p. 96

Sachertorte ★★

Serves 6-8

Preparation time: 1 hour 10 minutes
Cooking time: about 10 minutes
Freezing time: 12 hours
Refrigeration time: 6 hours

A day ahead

Prepare the ultra-shiny glaze (see p. 66). Use the proportions given opposite. Leave overnight to chill.

Prepare the Sacher cocoa-chocolate sponge.

Soften the almond paste slightly in the microwave oven. Mix in the ⅓ cup (2 ½ oz./70 g) sugar. Then incorporate the egg yolks one by one, followed by the whole egg. Whisk* the egg whites, gradually incorporating the remaining sugar, until they form soft peaks. Preheat the oven to 350°F (180°C). Sift the flour and cocoa powder together and set aside. Chop the chocolate and melt it slowly in a bain-marie* or in the microwave oven (on "defrost" or at 500 W maximum, stirring from time to time). Incorporate the butter. Carefully fold in* a little of the whisked egg whites to lighten the chocolate mixture, then mix in the almond paste and egg mixture. Carefully stir in the sifted dry ingredients. Lastly, fold in the remaining whisked egg whites. Pour the batter out thinly over a lined baking sheet or silicone baking mat and bake for about 10 minutes. It should be spongy and the tip of a knife or cake tester must come out dry.

Prepare the dried apricot purée.

Simmer the dried apricots in a little water for 15 minutes and drain them. Add the apricot liqueur and blend until smooth.

Prepare the bittersweet chocolate ganache (see p. 96).

Add the cubed butter at the end, when the ganache has cooled to 95°F-104°F (35°C-40°C). Process with an immersion blender.

To assemble.

Cut the chocolate sponge into three even layers to fit into your cake ring. Line the baking sheet with parchment paper and position the cake ring on it. Place the first layer of sponge in the ring. Weigh out about one-third of the apricot purée (2 ½ oz./70 g) and brush the surface of the sponge with it. Then spread out a layer of ganache, about 3 ½ oz. (100 g), and place another layer of sponge above it. Brush the surface with another layer of apricot purée and spread out another 3 ½ oz. (100 g) of ganache. Finish with the third layer of sponge. Smooth out the remaining ganache over this with a spatula so that the surface is perfectly smooth. Place in the freezer for 12 hours.

The next day.

Remove the ring. Reheat the glaze in a bain-marie or in the microwave. When it has reached 98°F (37°C), place the still-frozen Sachertorte on a cake rack over a large dish. Cover it completely with the glaze and smooth it with a spatula. Decorate with edible gold leaf. Refrigerate for at least 6 hours, but make sure it has completely defrosted before serving.

Ingredients

Sacher cocoa-chocolate sponge
7 oz. (200 g) almond paste (see p. 41)
Granulated sugar, divided as follows: ⅓ cup (2 ½ oz./70 g) plus scant ⅓ cup (2 ¼ oz./65 g)
5 egg yolks
1 jumbo (USA) or extra-large (UK) egg, 2 ⅔ oz. (75 g)
2 egg whites (75 g)
Generous ½ cup (1 ¾ oz./50 g) cake flour
3 ½ tablespoons (1 oz./25 g) unsweetened cocoa powder
1 ¾ oz. (50 g) bittersweet chocolate, 70 percent cocoa
3 ½ tablespoons (1 ¾ oz./50 g) butter

Dried apricot purée
½ lb. (240 g) dried apricots
2 tablespoons plus 1 teaspoon (35 ml) apricot liqueur

Bittersweet chocolate ganache*
5 ½ oz. (150 g) bittersweet chocolate, 70 percent cocoa
1 cup minus 1 tablespoon (235 ml) whipping cream
1 heaped tablespoon (1 oz./25 g) honey
3 ½ tablespoons (1 ¾ oz./50 g) butter, cubed

Ultra-shiny glaze
6 sheets (12 g) leaf gelatin
Scant ½ cup (100 g) water
1 scant cup (6 oz./170 g) granulated sugar
⅔ cup (2 ⅔ oz./75 g) unsweetened cocoa powder
⅓ cup plus 1 tablespoon (3 oz./90 g) whipping cream

Decoration
A few flakes of edible gold leaf

Equipment
1 cake or mousse ring, 7 in. (16 cm) diameter
1 baking sheet lined with parchment paper or 1 silicone baking mat†
1 immersion blender†
1 kitchen thermometer†
1 pastry brush†
1 spatula†
1 cake rack

Techniques
Glazes ›› p. 66
Ganache for Tarts and Desserts ›› p. 96

Royal ★★

Serves 6-8

Preparation time: 2 hours
Cooking time: 10-12 minutes
Refrigeration time: 6 hours
Freezing time: 13 hours.

Prepare the almond *dacquoise*.
Preheat the oven to 350°F-375°F (180°C-190°C).
Sift the flour with the ground almonds and the confectioners' sugar into a mixing bowl.
Begin whisking* the egg whites with the granulated sugar, until soft peaks form (see p. 134). Carefully fold in* the sifted dry ingredients with a flexible spatula. Spread it out evenly over the lined jelly pan or silicone mat. Bake for about 10 minutes, until a nice golden color.

Prepare the crisp praline.
Chop the chocolate and melt it slowly in a bain-marie* or in the microwave oven (on "defrost" or at 500 W maximum, stirring from time to time). Crush the wafer biscuits (*crêpes dentelles*). Incorporate the praline into the melted chocolate, and then carefully stir in the crushed *crêpes dentelles*. Cut the *dacquoise* base* out into a circle just slightly smaller than the pastry circle and cover it with the crisp praline. Place in the refrigerator.

Prepare the custard-based chocolate mousse (see p. 114).
Use the proportions given opposite.

To assemble.
Position the *dacquoise* and crisp praline layer in the center of the circle. Pour in the chocolate mousse, ensuring that you reserve a little for the decoration. Place in the freezer immediately. As soon as the mousse begins to harden a little, prepare decorations for the top with the remaining mousse. Freeze for about 12 hours.
Remove the pastry circle and spray the dessert with the chocolate velvet spray. Place in the refrigerator for at least 6 hours. Serve it only when it is completely defrosted.

● Chef's note

When you prepare the chocolate mousse, check the temperature of the chocolate mixture before adding the lightly whipped cream. If it is too cold, the mousse will separate and form "nuggets" of chocolate. If it is too hot, the cream may well melt.

Techniques

Melting Chocolate >> p. 19
Almond *Dacquoise* >> p. 86
Custard-Based Chocolate Mousse >> p. 114

Ingredients

Almond *dacquoise**
Generous ⅓ cup (1 ¼ oz./35 g) cake flour
1 cup plus 3 tablespoons (3 ½ oz./100 g) ground almonds
Scant cup (4 ¼ oz./120 g) confectioners' sugar
6 egg whites (6 oz./170 g)
⅓ cup (2 oz./60 g) granulated sugar

Crisp praline*
⅔ oz. (20 g) milk chocolate, 40 percent cocoa
1 ½ oz. (40 g) crushed *crêpes dentelles*, an extremely friable, fine wafer-like biscuit, a Breton specialty
3 ½ oz. (100 g) homemade praline (see p. 38)

Custard-based bittersweet chocolate mousse
3 ¾ oz. (110 g) bittersweet chocolate, 70 percent cocoa
1 egg yolk
2 ½ teaspoons (⅓ oz./10 g) sugar
Scant ¼ cup (50 ml) whole milk
Whipping cream, divided as follows: ⅔ cup (150 ml) plus ¾ cup (200 ml)

Edible chocolate velvet spray

Equipment

1 stainless steel cake or pastry circle†,
6 ½ in. (16 cm) diameter
1 jelly (Swiss) roll baking pan lined with parchment paper or silicone baking mat†
1 kitchen thermometer†
1 whisk†
1 flexible spatula†

Chocolate Profiteroles ★★

Serves 6-8
Preparation time: 1 hour 20 minutes
Cooking time: 20 minutes
Refrigeration time: overnight
Freezing time: 30 minutes to 3 hours, depending on the ice-cream maker

A day ahead, make the chocolate ice cream (see p. 120).
Use the proportions given opposite.

The next day, prepare the choux pastry.
Preheat the oven to 480°F (250°C).
In a saucepan, bring the water, milk, salt, sugar, and butter to the boil. Sift the flour into the liquid. The important step is to dry it out: stir energetically until the moisture has evaporated. Remove from the heat and mix in the eggs, one by one. Stir thoroughly each time. When the consistency is right, it will have a satin sheen, like paint. Spoon the batter into a piping bag and pipe out little rounds, just over ⅓ oz. (12 g) or 1 in. (2.5 cm) in diameter per choux on a lined baking sheet. For a nice finished result, brush the top of the dough with a beaten egg yolk and press down lightly with a fork. Scatter over a few sliced almonds.
Place the baking sheet in the oven and immediately switch off the heat.
As soon as the choux pastry begins to swell and color, turn the heat back to 350°F (180°C) and leave the pastries to dry out slowly for about 10 minutes.

Prepare the chocolate sauce.
Chop the two sorts of chocolate and melt them slowly in a bain-marie* or in the microwave oven (on "defrost" or at 500 W maximum, stirring from time to time). Bring the milk and cream to the boil. Gradually pour a third of the boiling liquid over the melted chocolate. Using a flexible spatula, mix in energetically, drawing small circles to create an elastic, shiny "kernel." Incorporate the second third of the liquid, using the same procedure. Repeat with the last third. Process briefly using an immersion blender. Chill until serving.

Prepare the vanilla-scented Chantilly cream.
Slit the vanilla bean lengthways and scrape out the seeds into the well-chilled cream. Whip* the cream with the sugar and vanilla seeds until it reaches the consistency of a Chantilly cream.

To assemble.
Begin heating the chocolate sauce. Cut the tops off the choux pastries using a serrated knife. Place three pastries in each plate. Fill one with the vanilla Chantilly cream and the two others with the chocolate ice cream. Lightly sprinkle the tops with sugar and replace them over the fillings. Alternatively, cover with chocolate disks (see p. 48). Serve with hot chocolate sauce.

● **Chef's note**
You may also fill the choux pastries with ice cream ahead of time and freeze them. Just remember to take them out 5 minutes before serving.

Ingredients

Choux pastry
Scant ⅓ cup (75 ml) water
Scant ⅓ cup (75 ml) milk
Heaped ½ teaspoon (3 g) salt
¾ teaspoon (3 g) granulated sugar
4 tablespoons (60 g) butter
1 cup (3 oz./90 g) cake flour
3 eggs plus 1 egg yolk
A handful of sliced almonds for garnish

Chocolate sauce
1 ½ oz. (40 g) bittersweet chocolate, 60 percent cocoa
⅓ oz. (10 g) milk chocolate, 40 percent cocoa
⅓ cup (80 ml) whole milk
⅓ cup (80 ml) whipping cream

Bittersweet chocolate ice cream
3 ¼ oz. (90 g) bittersweet chocolate, 70 percent cocoa
1 ¼ cups (300 ml) whole milk
2 tablespoon plus 1 teaspoon (35 ml) whipping cream
2 tablespoons (½ oz./15 g) powdered milk
3 ½ tablespoons (1 ½ oz./40 g) sugar
1 ½ tablespoons (1 oz./30 g) honey

Vanilla-scented Chantilly cream
1 vanilla bean
⅔ cup (170 ml) whipping cream, well chilled
1 heaped tablespoon (15 g) sugar

Equipment
1 piping bag†
1 baking sheet lined with parchment paper
1 kitchen thermometer†
1 ice-cream maker†
1 cold-water bath
1 flexible spatula†
1 immersion blender†
1 serrated knife
1 pastry brush†

Techniques
Choux Pastry ›› p. 77
Chocolate Ice Cream ›› p. 120
Chocolate Sauce ›› p. 127

Ingredients

Almond shortcrust pastry
1 stick (4 oz./120 g) butter, room temperature
Scant ½ teaspoon (2 g) salt
⅔ cup (3 ¼ oz./90 g) confectioners' sugar
3 tablespoons (½ oz./15 g) ground
blanched* almonds
1 egg
Cake flour, divided as follows: ⅔ cup (2 oz./60 g)
plus 2 cups (6 oz./180 g)

Bittersweet chocolate ganache*
12 ⅓ oz. (350 g) bittersweet chocolate,
70 percent cocoa
1 cup (250 ml/250 g) whipping cream
1 tablespoon (15 ml) acacia honey
3 tablespoons plus 1 teaspoon (1 ¾ oz./50 g)
butter, diced

A little melted chocolate to brush the tart shell

Equipment

1 tart mold†
1 kitchen thermometer†
2 sheets food-safe acetate† or parchment paper
1 immersion blender†
1 pastry brush†
1 flexible spatula†

Extraordinarily Chocolate Tart ★

Serves 6–8
Preparation time: 1 hour
Cooking time: 20 minutes
Freezing time: 30 minutes
Refrigeration time: 2 hours 30 minutes

Prepare the almond shortcrust pastry.
Soften the butter (see p. 134), and combine it with the salt, confectioners' sugar, ground almonds, egg, and ⅔ cup (2 oz./60 g) cake flour. As soon as the ingredients are mixed through, add the remaining flour, and mix quickly, until just combined.
Roll out the dough to a thickness of ⅛ in. (3 mm) between 2 sheets of acetate or parchment paper. Place it, completely flat, in the freezer for 30 minutes.
When the dough has hardened, peel off the sheets and cut it out to the desired shape. Line your tart mold or pan with the dough and return it to the refrigerator for 30 minutes (so it retains it shape during baking), then preheat the oven to 300°F–325°F (150°C–160°C) and bake until it turns a nice golden color, about 15 minutes. Leave to cool for about 15 to 20 minutes.

Prepare the bittersweet chocolate ganache.
Chop the chocolate and melt it slowly in a bain-marie* or in the microwave oven (on "defrost" or at 500 W maximum, stirring from time to time).
Bring the cream to the boil with the honey.
Gradually pour one-third of the boiling cream over the melted chocolate. Using a flexible spatula, mix in energetically, drawing small circles to create an elastic, shiny "kernel."
Incorporate the second third of the cream-honey mixture, using the same procedure. Repeat with the last third.
When the temperature cools to 95°F–104°F (35°C–40°C), stir in the diced butter. Process for a few seconds using an immersion blender so that the mixture is smooth and perfectly emulsified*.

At this stage, brush a fine layer of melted chocolate over the cooled tart shell to seal it. As soon as it has hardened, pour the ganache into the shell and chill for about 2 hours. Serve it at room temperature.
Be sure to eat this tart the day you make it if you want to enjoy the crisp pastry and creamy ganache at their best.

Techniques
Almond Shortcrust Pastry ›› p. 72
Ganache for Tarts and Desserts ›› p. 96

Chocolate-Vanilla Marble Loaf ★

Serves 6-8
Preparation time: 20 minutes
Cooking time: 50 minutes to 1 hour

Prepare the vanilla batter.
In a mixing bowl, combine the egg yolks with the sugar. Add the cream. Slit the vanilla bean lengthways and scrape out the seeds into the mixture. Sift in the flour and baking powder and incorporate them into the batter, then stir in the melted butter. Set aside.

Prepare the chocolate batter.
Chop the chocolate and melt it slowly in a bain-marie* or in the microwave oven (on "defrost" or at 500 W maximum, stirring from time to time).
In a mixing bowl, combine the egg yolks with the sugar, then stir in the cream. Sift the flour, cocoa powder, and baking powder together into the mixture and stir in. Then stir in the melted chocolate and grape-seed oil until just blended.

Preheat the oven to 300°F (150°C). Line the loaf pan with parchment paper. For a really attractive marbled pattern (see p. 132), pipe out one-third of the vanilla batter over the bottom of the pan. Then pipe out half of the chocolate batter lengthways through the center.
Cover this with one-third of the vanilla batter and pipe out the remaining half of the chocolate batter lengthways through the center. Cover it with the remaining vanilla batter. Dip a spatula into a little melted butter and run it lengthways along the batter, making an incision about ½ in. (1-2 cm) deep so that the cake rises nicely.
Bake for 50 minutes to 1 hour, until the tip of a knife or cake tester comes out clean.
Turn the cake out onto a cake rack and leave it for about 10 minutes on its side so that it retains its shape.

Techniques
Melting Chocolate ›› p. 19
Marbling ›› p. 132

Ingredients
Vanilla batter
8 egg yolks
1 cup plus 2 tablespoons (7 ¾ oz./220 g) granulated sugar
½ cup (120 ml) whipping cream
1 vanilla bean
1 cup plus generous ¾ cup (5 ¾ oz./165 g) cake flour
¾ teaspoon (3 g) baking powder
4 ½ tablespoons (2 ⅓ oz./65 g) butter, melted and cooled

Chocolate batter
2 ½ oz. (70 g) bittersweet chocolate, 70 percent cocoa
4 egg yolks
Scant ⅔ cup (4 ¼ oz./120 g) sugar
Scant ⅓ cup (70 ml) whipping cream
Scant cup (2 ¾ oz./80 g) cake flour
2 teaspoons (5 g) unsweetened cocoa powder
½ teaspoon (2 g) baking powder
1 tablespoon plus 1 teaspoon (20 g) grape-seed oil

A little melted butter to dip the spatula (optional)

Equipment
1 cake pan, 10 in. × 5 in. × 3 in. (8 cm × 30 cm × 8 cm)
2 piping bags†
1 spatula†

Ingredients

4 ½ oz. (125 g) bittersweet chocolate,
70 percent cocoa
7 tablespoons (3 ½ oz./100 g) butter,
plus a little extra to grease the molds
4 eggs
¾ cup (5 ¼ oz./145 g) granulated sugar
Generous ½ cup (1 ¾ oz./50 g) cake flour

Equipment

8 molds†, 2 ½-3 in. (6-8 cm) diameter
1 whisk†
1 sieve†

Molten Chocolate Cakes ★

Serves 6-8

Preparation time: 20 minutes
Cooking time: 10-12 minutes

Butter the molds. Preheat the oven to 375°F (190°C).

Chop the chocolate and melt it slowly in a bain-marie* or in the microwave oven (on "defrost" or at 500 W maximum, stirring from time to time). Stir in the butter.

Whisk* the eggs with the sugar until pale and thick. Add the chocolate-butter mixture, then sift in the flour. Stir until just combined and pour into the molds. Bake for 10-12 minutes.

Turn them out into plates and serve immediately.

● Chef's notes

These little cakes can be prepared ahead of time and kept in the refrigerator until ready to be baked.
Accompany them with a fruit coulis, a pouring custard, or ice cream.

Technique
Melting Chocolate ›› p. 19

Homemade Chocolate Spread ★

Serves 6-8

Preparation time: 30 minutes
Cooking time: 10 minutes

Sterilize your jars before using them: leave them in a 200°F (90°-95°C) oven for 20 minutes.
Preheat the oven to 300°F (150°C). Place the almonds and hazelnuts in the oven and roast until they are a nice amber color right through. This should take about 10 minutes.
Leave them to cool and rub the hazelnuts between your hands to remove the skins.

Combine the milk, powdered milk, and honey in a saucepan and bring the mixture to the boil.

Grind the almonds and hazelnuts in the bowl of a food processor until they are reduced to a paste.
Chop the milk and bittersweet chocolates and melt both slowly in a bain-marie* or in the microwave oven (on "defrost" or at 500 W maximum, stirring from time to time).

Add the melted chocolate to the nut paste in the food processor and pour in the boiling milk-honey mixture. Process briefly. Strain the mixture through a chinois and pour it into jars.

● **Chef's note**

This homemade chocolate spread will keep no longer than a week in the refrigerator.

Techniques
Melting Chocolate >> p. 19
Roasting Nuts >> p. 134

Ingredients

1 ½ oz. (40 g) whole blanched* almonds
5 ⅔ oz. (160 g) whole hazelnuts
1 ¾ cups (400 ml) whole milk
½ cup (2 ¼ oz./60 g) powdered milk
2 tablespoons (40 g) honey
5 ½ oz. (150 g) milk chocolate, 40 percent cocoa
Either 5 ½ oz. (150 g) bittersweet chocolate, 60 percent cocoa
Or 5 oz. (140 g) bittersweet chocolate, 70 percent cocoa

Equipment

1 food processor fitted with a blade attachment
1 chinois†
Small jelly jars

Ingredients

Chocolate pastry cream

3 oz. (85 g) bittersweet chocolate,
70 percent cocoa
1 tablespoon (¼ oz./10 g) cornstarch
2 ½ tablespoons (1 oz./30 g) granulated sugar
2 egg yolks
1 cup minus 2 tablespoons (220 ml) whole milk
Scant ¼ cup (50 ml) whipping cream

Choux pastry

Scant ¼ cup (50 ml) water
Scant ¼ cup (60 ml) whole milk
1 pinch table salt
1 pinch sugar
2 tablespoons plus 2 teaspoons (40 g) butter
⅔ cup (2 oz./60 g) cake flour
2 eggs

Soft chocolate glaze

4 ½ oz. (130 g) bittersweet chocolate,
70 percent cocoa
½ cup minus 1 ½ tablespoons (100 ml)
whipping cream

Equipment

Baking sheets
Sheets of food-safe acetate† or parchment paper
1 kitchen thermometer†
1 piping bag† fitted with a small plain tip†
1 immersion blender†

Chocolate Éclairs ★★

Serves 6-8

Preparation time: 1 hour
Cooking time: 20 minutes
Refrigeration time: 1 hour

Prepare the chocolate pastry cream (see p. 103).
Set aside in the refrigerator.

Prepare the choux pastry.
Preheat the oven to 480°F (250°C).
Use the ingredients given opposite to prepare the choux pastry batter (see p. 77).
Spoon the batter into a piping bag and pipe out the pastry in éclair shapes, or pipe out three small puff pastries side by side to form a line as long as a traditional éclair. Place in the oven and switch off the thermostat immediately. As soon as the dough begins to puff up and color, turn the heat back on to 350°F (180°C) and leave the pastries to dry out slowly for about 10 minutes.

Prepare the soft chocolate glaze.
Chop the chocolate and melt it slowly in a bain-marie* or in the microwave oven (on "defrost" or at 500 W maximum, stirring from time to time). In a saucepan, bring the whipping cream to the boil. Combine the cream with the melted chocolate using the "three-thirds"* procedure (see p. 95). Blend for a few seconds using an immersion blender, making sure you do not incorporate any air bubbles. Set aside in the refrigerator.

To assemble.
Spoon the pastry cream into a piping bag fitted with a small plain tip and pipe it into the éclairs. Heat the glaze just slightly–it should be at a temperature of 82°F-86°F (28°C-30°C)–and glaze* the rounded tops of the éclairs. Refrigerate until you serve them.

● **Chef's note**
If you wish, you may freeze your choux pastry either raw or baked. If the éclairs are already baked, defrost them in the oven at 375°F–400°F (190°C–200°C) to restore their crispness.

Techniques
Soft Bittersweet Glaze ≫ p. 67
Choux Pastry ≫ p. 77
Chocolate Pastry Cream ≫ p. 103

The great classics

Opéra ★★

Serves 8
Preparation time: 2 hours
Cooking time: 8 minutes
Refrigeration time: 3 hours 30 minutes
Freezing time: overnight

A day ahead.
Prepare the ultra-shiny glaze (see p. 66) and chill overnight.

Prepare the whipped white chocolate-coffee ganache.
Make the espresso coffee. Chop the chocolate and melt it slowly in a bain-marie* or in the microwave oven (on "defrost" or at 500 W maximum, stirring from time to time). Gradually pour one-third of the hot coffee over the melted chocolate. Using a flexible spatula, mix it in energetically, drawing small circles to create an elastic, shiny "kernel." Incorporate the second third of the coffee, using the same procedure. Repeat with the last third. Incorporate the cold whipping cream and leave to set for at least 3 hours in the refrigerator.

Prepare the cocoa Joconde sponge (see p. 87).
Spread out the batter over the lined baking sheet and bake for 8 minutes, until springy to the touch. Cut out into three rectangles to fit into your cake mold.

Prepare the bittersweet chocolate *crémeux* (see p. 100).
Use the ingredients listed opposite.
Leave to set for at least 3 hours in the refrigerator.

Prepare the coffee syrup.
Make the espresso and mix in the sugar.

To assemble.
Line a baking sheet with parchment paper and position the cake ring on it. Place a layer of sponge in the mold and moisten it with coffee syrup using a pastry brush. Whip* the ganache until it is a light Chantilly texture. Spread out half over the first layer of sponge. Place another layer of sponge over the ganache and moisten it with coffee syrup. Spread out the other half of the chocolate-coffee ganache. Place the third layer of sponge over this and moisten it with coffee syrup. Cover the dessert with bittersweet chocolate *crémeux*, making sure the top is smooth, and leave in the freezer overnight. When the Opéra is frozen, remove the cake ring. Place it on a cake rack over a dish that is large enough to catch the excess glaze and cover it with ultra-shiny glaze (see p. 66). Leave it to defrost in the refrigerator.

● **Chef's notes**

Trim the edges of the Opéra with a sharp knife when it is still slightly frozen for a professional finish.
When you make a whipped chocolate-coffee ganache, you are using the same technique as is used for the whipped ganache; the coffee replaces the cream that allows the emulsion* to take place.

Ingredients

Cocoa Joconde sponge
2 eggs
3 egg whites
¾ cup (2 ⅓ oz./65 g) ground almonds
½ cup (2 ⅓ oz./65 g) confectioners' sugar
2 tablespoons (1 oz./25 g) granulated sugar
Generous ¼ cup (1 oz./25 g) cake flour
3 tablespoons (⅔ oz./20 g)
unsweetened cocoa powder
1 tablespoon plus 2 teaspoons (25 g) butter

Whipped white chocolate-coffee ganache*
½ cup minus 2 tablespoons (100 ml) espresso coffee
5 oz. (140 g) white chocolate, 35 percent cocoa
1 cup minus 2 tablespoons (220 ml)
whipping cream, chilled

Bittersweet chocolate *crémeux*
3 ¾ oz. (110 g) bittersweet chocolate, 70 percent cocoa
2 egg yolks (1 ⅔ oz./45 g)
1 ½ tablespoons (⅔ oz./20 g) granulated sugar
½ cup minus 1 tablespoon (110 ml) whole milk
½ cup minus 1 tablespoon (110 ml) whipping cream

Coffee syrup
1 cup plus 1 tablespoon (265 ml) espresso coffee
3 tablespoons (35 g) granulated sugar

Ultra-shiny glaze
6 sheets (12 g) leaf gelatin
Scant ½ cup (100 g) water
1 scant cup (6 oz./170 g) granulated sugar
⅔ cup (2 ⅔ oz./75 g) unsweetened cocoa powder
⅓ cup plus 1 tablespoon (3 oz., 90 g)
whipping cream

Equipment

1 square cake ring, 9 ½ in. × 13 ½ in. (24 × 34 cm)
(adjustable rings available online)
1 flexible spatula†
1 baking sheet, 13 in. × 28 in. (34 cm × 72 cm)
lined with parchment paper
1 pastry brush†, 1 kitchen thermometer†
1 cake rack, 1 metal spatula†

Techniques
Ultra-Shiny Glaze ›› p. 66
Cocoa Joconde Sponge ›› p. 87
Whipped Ganache ›› p. 97
Chocolate *Crémeux* ›› p. 100

Ingredients

A little butter, melted, to grease the soufflé molds
A little sugar to sprinkle the greased molds
5 ½ oz. (150 g) bittersweet chocolate,
70 percent cocoa
4 eggs, separated
½ cup (3 ½ oz./100 g) sugar
1 heaped teaspoon unsweetened cocoa powder
1 heaped teaspoon cornstarch
1 cup minus 3 tablespoons (200 ml)
whipping cream

Equipment

1 pastry brush[†]
6 individual soufflé molds[†] or ramekins
1 whisk[†]
1 flexible spatula[†]

Chocolate Soufflé ★★

Serves 6

Preparation time: 20 minutes
Cooking time: 10-12 minutes
Refrigeration time: 30 minutes

Using a pastry brush, carefully butter the molds with butter. Then sprinkle them all over with sugar, turning them upside down to remove the excess. Set aside in the refrigerator.

Chop the chocolate and melt it slowly in a bain-marie* or in the microwave oven (on "defrost" or at 500 W maximum, stirring from time to time).

Slowly start whisking* the egg whites, gradually adding the sugar. Continue until they form soft peaks.

Sift the cocoa powder and cornstarch together. Pour the cold cream into a saucepan and add the sifted ingredients. Bring to the boil, stirring constantly so that the liquid does not stick. When it simmers and starts to thicken, remove from the heat and slowly pour one-third over the melted chocolate. Using a flexible spatula, mix it in energetically, drawing small circles to create an elastic, shiny "kernel." Incorporate the second third of the liquid, using the same procedure. Repeat with the last third.

Add the egg yolks, whisking energetically until the texture is smooth and shiny. Carefully fold in* one-third of the whisked egg whites with a spatula. When the consistency has been lightened, so to speak, carefully fold in* the remaining egg whites.

Fill the molds up to the top, cleaning the rim so that the batter does not stick to it and so that the soufflés can rise straight up. Chill until they are to be baked.

About 30 minutes before serving the dessert, preheat the oven to 425°F (210°C-220°C).

Remove the soufflés from the refrigerator and bake for about 10 to 12 minutes, until well risen with a nicely done crust. Serve immediately.

Technique
Melting Chocolate >> p. 19

Bittersweet Chocolate Mousse ★

Ingredients
Chocolate mousse
10 ½ oz. (300 g) bittersweet chocolate,
70 percent cocoa
Scant ⅔ cup (150 ml) whipping cream
3 egg yolks (2¼ oz., 60 g)
6–7 egg whites (7 oz./200 g)
¼ cup (1 ¾ oz./50 g) granulated sugar

Chocolate sauce
3 oz. (85 g) bittersweet chocolate, 70 percent cocoa
½ cup minus 2 tablespoons (100 ml) whole milk

Equipment
1 kitchen thermometer[†]
1 whisk[†] or hand-held electric beater[†]
and, if possible, 1 stand-alone mixer[†]
1 immersion blender[†]
1 flexible spatula[†]

Serves 6–8
Preparation time: 15 minutes
Refrigeration time: 12 hours

Prepare the chocolate mousse.
Chop the chocolate and melt it slowly in a bain-marie* or in the microwave oven (on "defrost" or at 500 W maximum, stirring from time to time).
Bring the cream to the boil in a saucepan. As soon as it reaches the boil, remove from the heat. Slowly pour one-third of the hot cream over the melted choco-late. Using a flexible spatula, briskly mix it in with a small circular movement to create an elastic, shiny "kernel." Then incorporate another third of the hot cream, using the same circular movement, and finally, the last third, still mixing with a circular movement.
Stir in the egg yolks until the mixture is perfectly smooth.
Whisk* the egg whites, together with a little of the sugar, to soft peaks. When they reach this stage, mix in the remaining sugar and whisk until they are shiny. When the chocolate mixture has cooled down to 113°F-122°F (45°C-50°C), fold in* one-quarter of the whisked egg whites to lighten the mixture, then carefully incorporate the remaining egg whites. Chill for 12 hours.

Prepare the chocolate sauce.
Chop the chocolate and melt it slowly in a bain-marie or in the microwave oven (on "defrost" or at 500 W maximum, stirring from time to time). Bring the milk to the boil.
Gradually pour a third of the boiling milk over the melted chocolate. Using a flexible spatula, mix in energetically, drawing small circles to create an elas-tic, shiny "kernel."
Incorporate the second third of the milk, using the same procedure. Repeat with the last third.
Blend for a few seconds using an immersion blender.
Thirty minutes before serving, remove the mousse from the refrigerator to bring it to room temperature. Serve with warm or chilled sauce.

● **Chef's note**
Because this mousse contains raw egg yolks, it keeps no longer than 24 hours.

Techniques
Melting Chocolate ›› p. 19
Egg White-Based Chocolate Mousse ›› p. 110
Chocolate Sauce ›› p. 127

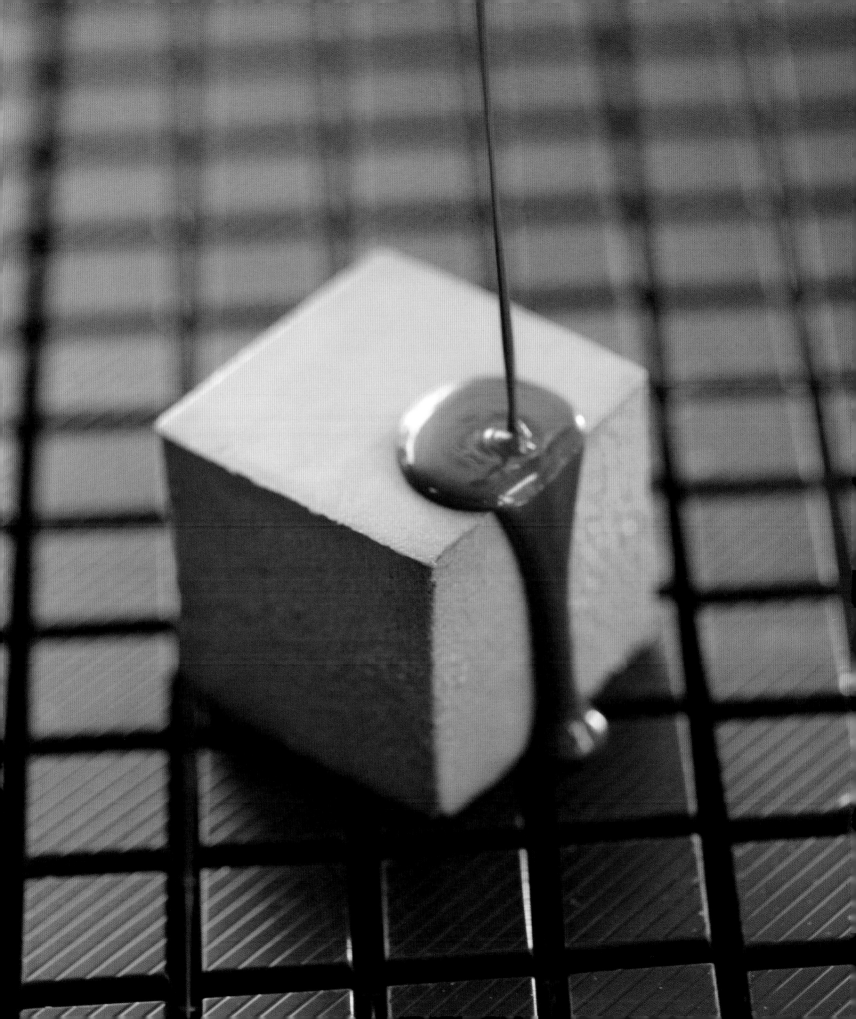

Tarts and tartlets

Éric Léautey
presents his recipe

I love chocolate. There are many reasons for this, the main one being its healing properties: it chases away the blues, gives us a lift, boosts our morale, and is the most innocuous of addictions, allowing us to tread the path between vice and great pleasure.

I also love chocolate because it reminds me of my afternoon snacks, when I would bite into a slice of bread with a good square of chocolate, and sniff the delicious aroma wafting out of the hot drink that I would find on my return from school. These emotions have stayed in my olfactory memory, and encourage me to include them in some of my recipes, such as this chocolate tart, eaten warm.

And it is a multifaceted food whose palette of flavors and colors inspires me to widen my horizons, combining bitter, spicy, and fruity tastes, bittersweet chocolate, white, and milk chocolate.

Creamy Caramel Chocolate Tart

Pastry shell. Combine the flour, confectioners' sugar, vanilla seeds, and salt. Add the chilled diced butter. Rub the butter into the other ingredients until you have fine crumbs. When the butter is completely incorporated, stir in the 1 oz. (30 g) egg. Form the dough into a ball, being careful not to overwork it. Flatten it slightly with a rolling pin. Cover it in plastic wrap and chill for 30 minutes.

Creamy caramel filling. Heat the confectioners' sugar in a nonstick frying pan over low heat until it forms a very light caramel. Deglaze it with the whipping cream, bring to the boil, and remove from the heat. Whisk* in the diced butter and leave to cool a little. In a mixing bowl, whisk the ½ oz. (15 g) egg yolk with 1 generous tablespoon (15 g) sugar until pale and thick. Pour the warm caramel over this mixture. In another mixing bowl, whisk the egg white until it forms soft peaks and then whisk in the remaining sugar until the peaks are firmer. Carefully fold* the egg white into the caramel mixture with a flexible spatula.

Chocolate ganache. Chop the chocolate into small pieces. Bring the cream to the boil and pour it over the chopped chocolate. Combine with a flexible spatula, add the cold milk to lower the temperature, and incorporate the beaten egg.

Assembling. Preheat the oven to 350°F (180°C). Place the pastry circle on the silicone baking mat or on a lined baking sheet. Line the circle with the pastry dough. Prick it with a fork and bake for 15 minutes. Trim the edges before filling the shell. Pour the creamy caramel into the tart shell and bake for a further 10 minutes. Switch off the oven.
Then pour the ganache over the caramel, making sure it flows over the back of a spoon so that the two mixtures do not combine. Return the tart to the cooled oven for 15 minutes. Remove the tart and leave it at room temperature for 30 minutes.

Decoration. Prepare a caramel with the confectioners' sugar in a frying pan. Leave it to rest before dipping the almonds into it, lifting them up to form caramel threads. Leave them to cool on a sheet of parchment paper and then decorate the tart with them.

● **Chef's note**
Use a heated knife to cut this tart.

Equipment
1 rolling pin†
1 whisk†
1 flexible spatula†
1 pastry circle†, 7 in. (18 cm) diameter
1 silicone baking mat† or baking sheet lined with parchment paper

Serves 6

Ingredients
Shortcrust pastry
1 ⅓ cups (4 ½ oz./125 g) cake flour
Scant ½ cup (2 ¼ oz./60 g) confectioners' sugar
1 Tahiti vanilla bean, slit, seeds scraped
A pinch of fleur de sel
4 tablespoons (60 g) butter, well chilled and diced
1 oz. (30 g) beaten egg, preferably organic

Creamy caramel* filling
Generous ½ cup (2 ¾ oz./75 g) confectioners' sugar
3 tablespoons (40 ml) heavy whipping cream,
40 percent fat content
3 ½ tablespoons (1 ¾ oz./50 g) salted butter
1 egg, separated
2 heaped tablespoons (30 g) granulated sugar, divided

Chocolate ganache*
1 ¾ oz. (50 g) bittersweet chocolate, 70 percent cocoa
3 tablespoons (40 ml) whipping cream, 40 percent fat
content
¼ cup (60 ml) whole milk
½ oz. (15 g) beaten egg, preferably organic

Decoration
¾ cup (1 ¾ oz./50 g) confectioners' sugar
10 unblanched* almonds

Golden Rules ★★

Serves 6-8
Preparation time: 1 hour
Cooking time: 20 minutes
Refrigeration time: 3 hours 30 minutes
Freezing time: 1 hour

Prepare the almond shortcrust pastry.
In a mixing bowl, soften the butter and mix with the salt, confectioners' sugar, ground almonds, egg, and 1 cup (3 ¼ oz./90 g) cake flour.
As soon as the ingredients are mixed through, add the remaining flour and mix until just combined. Roll the dough out to a thickness of ⅛ in. (3 mm) between two sheets of acetate and place it in the freezer for 1 hour, ensuring that it is flat. When the dough has completely hardened, remove the sheets of acetate. Cut out a long rectangle of dough and place it between 2 buttered stainless steel square rulers on a lined baking sheet. Press the sides against the rulers to form a hollow running down the center.
Chill for 30 minutes.
Preheat the oven to 300°F-325°F (150°C-160°C) and bake until the pastry is a nice golden color. When it has cooled, drizzle a stripe of orange or grapefruit preserves down the center.
Close each end of the hollow with plastic wrap or aluminum foil.

Prepare the bittersweet chocolate ganache.
Chop the chocolate and melt it slowly in a bain-marie* or in the microwave oven (on "defrost" or at 500 W maximum, stirring from time to time).
Bring the cream to the boil in a saucepan.
Gradually pour one-third of the boiling cream over the melted chocolate. Using a flexible spatula, energetically mix the cream into the chocolate, drawing small, quick circles in the center to create a shiny, elastic "kernel."
Incorporate the second third of the cream and mix in exactly the same way. Pour in the remaining third, using the same stirring technique. As soon as the ganache cools to a temperature of 95°F-104°F (35°C-40°C), add the diced butter. Process with an immersion blender so that the mixture is smooth and perfectly emulsified*.
Spoon or pipe out the ganache into the hollow. Rap the baking sheet lightly to ensure that the ganache is level and leave in the refrigerator to set for 3 hours. When the ganache has hardened, remove the aluminum foil or plastic wrap on either end and cut the "rules" to the desired size. Decorate with edible gold leaf.

● **Chef's notes**
If you wish, try other types of preserves and change the sizes of the molds. Use the freezer to harden the dough and facilitate cutting out.
This tart is best eaten at room temperature.

Techniques
Melting Chocolate ›› p. 19
Almond Shortcrust Pastry ›› p. 72
Ganache for Tarts and Desserts ›› p. 96

Ingredients
Almond shortcrust pastry
1 ½ sticks (6 ⅓ oz./180 g) unsalted butter, plus a little extra for the rulers (or molds)
1 pinch table salt
1 cup (5 oz./140 g) confectioners' sugar
Generous ½ cup, (1 ¾ oz./50 g) ground blanched* almonds
1 egg
Cake flour, divided as follows: 1 cup (3 ¼ oz./90 g) plus 3 cups (9 ½ oz./270 g)

3 tablespoons orange or grapefruit preserves

Bittersweet chocolate ganache*
Either 5 ½ oz. (150 g) bittersweet chocolate, 70 percent cocoa
Or 5 ⅔ oz. (160 g) bittersweet chocolate, 60 percent cocoa
Generous ½ cup (150 ml) whipping cream
3 tablespoons plus 1 teaspoon (50 g) salted butter, diced

Decoration
Edible gold leaf

Equipment
2 confectionery or four-sided rulers†, ½ in. (1 cm) high
1 baking sheet, 1 piping bag†
2 sheets of food-safe acetate† or parchment paper
1 kitchen thermometer†
1 immersion blender†, 1 flexible spatula†

Ingredients

Almond shortcrust pastry

1 ½ sticks (6 ⅓ oz./180 g) unsalted butter,
plus a little extra for the mold
1 pinch table salt
1 cup (5 oz./140 g) confectioners' sugar
Generous ½ cup, (1 ¾ oz./50 g) ground
blanched* almonds
1 egg
Cake flour, divided as follows: 1 cup (3 ¼ oz./90 g)
plus 3 cups (9 ½ oz./270 g)

Walnut and caramel* layer

2 ¼ oz. (60 g) milk chocolate, 40 percent cocoa
1 ¾ oz. (50 g) walnuts
½ cup minus 1 tablespoon (110 ml) whipping cream
⅓ cup (2 ½ oz./70 g) granulated sugar
2 tablespoons (30 g) butter

Coffee ganache*

2 ¾ oz. (80 g) bittersweet chocolate,
60 percent cocoa
Scant ⅓ cup (70 ml) whipping cream
1 ½ teaspoons (10 g) acacia honey
1 tablespoon (15 g) instant coffee granules
1 tablespoon (15 g) butter

Equipment

1 tart mold†, 8 in. (20 cm) diameter
1 kitchen thermometer†
2 sheets of food-safe acetate† or parchment paper
1 flexible spatula†

Walnut, Caramel, and Coffee-Chocolate Tart ★★

Serves 8

Preparation time: 45 minutes
Cooking time: 20 minutes
Refrigeration time: 2 hours 30 minutes
Freezing time: 1 hour

Prepare the almond shortcrust pastry.

In a mixing bowl, soften the butter and mix with the salt, confectioners' sugar, ground almonds, egg, and 1 cup (3 ¼ oz./90 g) cake flour. As soon as the ingredients are mixed through, add the remaining flour and mix until just combined. Roll the dough out to a thickness of ⅛ in. (3 mm) between two sheets of acetate and place it in the freezer for 1 hour, ensuring that it is flat.
Butter the tart mold. When the dough has completely hardened, remove the sheets of acetate. Cut out the dough to the shape of the tart mold and position it carefully. Place the lined tart mold in the refrigerator for the dough to rest for 30 minutes.
Preheat the oven to 300°F-325°F (150°C-160°C) and bake until the pastry is a nice golden color, about 20 minutes. Leave to cool.

Prepare the caramelized walnuts.

Chop the milk chocolate and roughly chop the nuts. Bring the cream to the boil. Place one-third of the sugar in a heavy-bottomed saucepan. Cook until it forms a light caramel. Add the next third of the sugar and stir. When this quantity has reached the same color–a light caramel–add the last third of the sugar.
When the caramel is ready, carefully add the butter and hot cream, taking care not to splash yourself as the caramel is very hot. The cream is heated before adding so the caramel doesn't harden. Leave to boil briefly.
Incorporate the chopped chocolate and then stir in the chopped nuts. Pour the mixture into the cooled tart shell and set aside. It will harden very quickly.

Prepare the coffee ganache.

Chop the chocolate and melt it slowly in a bain-marie* or in the microwave oven (on "defrost" or at 500 W maximum, stirring from time to time).
Bring the cream, honey, and instant coffee to the boil. Gradually pour one-third of the boiling mixture over the melted chocolate. Using a flexible spatula, mix it in energetically, drawing small circles to create an elastic, shiny "kernel." Incorporate the second third of the liquid, using the same procedure. Repeat with the last third.
Keep an eye on the temperature. As soon as the ganache cools to 95°F-104°F (35°C-40°C), add the butter, mixing in thoroughly. Process briefly.
Pour it directly over the walnut-caramel layer and leave to set for about 2 hours in the refrigerator.

Techniques

Melting Chocolate >> p. 19
Almond Shortcrust Pastry >> p. 72
Ganache for Tarts and Desserts >> p. 96

Sunny Pear and Chocolate Tart ★★

Serves 8

Preparation time: 45 minutes
Cooking time: 30 minutes
Refrigeration time: 1 hour 30 minutes

Prepare the almond shortcrust pastry.
In a mixing bowl, soften the butter (see p. 134) and mix with the salt, confectioners' sugar, ground almonds, egg, and 1 cup (3 ¼ oz./90 g) cake flour. As soon as the ingredients are mixed through, add the remaining flour and mix briefly, until just combined. Cover in plastic wrap and chill for about 1 hour. Butter the tart mold. Roll the dough out to a thickness of ⅛ in. (3 mm) and line the tart pan. Roll out the remaining pieces of dough to just under 1/16 in. (2 mm) and using differently sized cookie cutters, cut out small disks to use for decoration. Chill all the dough for 30 minutes; this will prevent it from shrinking during baking.
Preheat the oven to 300°F-325°F (150°C-160°C) and bake until the pastry is a nice golden color, about 15 to 20 minutes. The disks will bake quickly—keep an eye on them so you can remove when they are the right color and leave them to cool.

Prepare the honey-softened pears.
Peel the pears, cut them in halves, and then cut them into 4 or 5 pieces, depending on their size. Using a kitchen knife, remove the core and seeds, making sure the cut pieces are all the same size. Heat the honey slightly in a saucepan until it just begins to caramelize*.
Add the pear pieces and turn them over in the honey to coat them. Leave to cook gently for 2 to 3 minutes and set aside, drained.

Prepare the chocolate flan.
Chop the chocolate. Pour the milk and cream into a saucepan. Slit the half vanilla bean and scrape the seeds out into the liquid. Bring the mixture to the boil, remove from the heat, and allow to cool down until it is just warm. Whisk* in the egg, then the sugar and chopped chocolate. Process until thoroughly combined and set aside.
When the tart shell is the right color, ensure that the oven temperature is lowered to 300° (150°) if you have used the higher temperature. Arrange the pear slices attractively around the shell. Pour the chocolate flan in, pouring into the center, and continue baking for 10 to 12 minutes.
As soon as the flan has set, remove the tart from the oven and leave to cool at room temperature. Then place it in the refrigerator for at least 1 hour. Bring to room temperature before serving.

Technique
Almond Shortcrust Pastry ≫ p. 72

Ingredients

Almond shortcrust pastry
1 ½ sticks (6 ⅓ oz./180 g) unsalted butter, plus a little extra for the mold
1 pinch table salt
1 cup (5 oz./140 g) confectioners' sugar
Generous ½ cup, (1 ¾ oz./50 g) ground blanched* almonds
1 egg
Cake flour, divided as follows: 1 cup (3 ¼ oz./90 g) plus 3 cups (9 ½ oz./270 g)

Honey-softened pears
4 finely flavored pears, such as Bartlett (Williams' Bon Chrétien) or Doyenné du Comice
Scant ⅓ cup (3 ½ oz./100 g) honey

Chocolate flan
¼ cup plus 1 teaspoon (65 ml) whole milk
½ cup (125 g) whipping cream
½ vanilla bean
1 egg
2 tablespoons (1 oz./25 g) granulated sugar
1 ½ oz. (40 g) bittersweet chocolate, 70 percent cocoa

Equipment
1 tart mold† or pan, 8 in. (20 cm) diameter
Cookie cutters† or small glasses, various sizes
Plastic wrap, 1 rolling pin†, 1 whisk†

A Take on Tartlets ★ ★

Serves 8

Preparation time: 45 minutes
Cooking time: 20 minutes
Refrigeration time: overnight
Freezing time: 30 minutes

A day ahead, prepare the bittersweet chocolate *crémeux*.
Chop the chocolate and melt it slowly in a bain-marie* or in the microwave oven (on "defrost" or at 500 W maximum, stirring from time to time).
While it is melting, prepare the custard (*crème anglaise*).
Whisk* the egg yolks and sugar together. Pour this mixture into a saucepan with the milk and cream and cook over low heat until it coats the back of a spoon and is slightly thickened. The temperature should be 180°F-183°F (82°C-84°C). Remove the saucepan from the heat and pour the custard into a deep bowl. Process for a few seconds with an immersion blender until the texture is smooth and creamy. Slowly pour one-third of the hot custard over the melted chocolate.
Using a flexible spatula, energetically mix the cream into the chocolate, drawing small, quick circles in the center to create a shiny, elastic "kernel."
Incorporate the second third of the custard and mix in exactly the same way. Pour in the remaining third, using the same stirring technique. Use an immersion blender to finish the emulsifying* process.
Pour it into a bowl and cover with plastic wrap flush with the surface to prevent a skin from forming. Chill overnight.

The next day, prepare the almond shortcrust pastry.
In a mixing bowl, soften the butter (see p. 134) and mix with the salt, confectioners' sugar, ground almonds, egg, and 1 cup (3 ¼ oz./90 g) cake flour.
As soon as the ingredients are mixed through, add the remaining flour and mix until just combined.
Roll the dough out to a thickness of ⅛ in. (3 mm) between two sheets of acetate. Cut out 16 disks with the cookie cutter or glass and place them in the freezer for 1 hour, ensuring that they are flat. When the dough has completely hardened, remove the sheets of acetate and place the disks on a baking sheet. Return to the refrigerator to chill for 30 minutes. Preheat the oven to 300°F-325°F (150°C-160°C) and bake until the pastry is a nice golden color, about 15 minutes.
Place on a cooling rack and when they have cooled, spoon the chocolate *crémeux* into a piping bag fitted with a large plain tip. Pipe out a nicely rounded scoop onto the shortcrust pastry. Place another disk of pastry above it and press down lightly until the *crémeux* is evenly distributed, right to the edge of the pastry. Repeat the procedure with the remaining disks of pastry.

● Chef's note

The crémeux *needs to be well set for you to make evenly shaped scoops.*

Techniques

Melting Chocolate ≫ p.19
Almond Shortcrust Pastry ≫ p.72
Chocolate *Crémeux* ≫ p.100

Ingredients

Bittersweet chocolate *crémeux*
4 ¼ oz. (120 g) bittersweet chocolate,
70 percent cocoa
3 egg yolks
2 tablespoons (1 oz./25 g) granulated sugar
½ cup plus 1 teaspoon (130 ml) whole milk
½ cup plus 1 teaspoon (130 ml) whipping cream

Almond shortcrust pastry
1 ½ sticks (6 ⅓ oz./180 g) unsalted butter
1 pinch table salt
1 cup (5 oz./140 g) confectioners' sugar
Generous ½ cup, (1 ¾ oz./50 g) ground
blanched* almonds
1 egg
Cake flour, divided as follows: 1 cup (3 ¼ oz./90 g)
plus 3 cups (9 ½ oz./270 g)

Equipment

1 kitchen thermometer†
1 flexible spatula†
1 whisk†
1 immersion blender†
2 sheets of food-safe acetate† or parchment paper
1 baking sheet
1 round cookie cutter† or 1 glass,
2-2 ½ in. (5-6 cm) diameter
1 piping bag† fitted with a large
plain ½ in. (14-16 mm) tip†

Ingredients

Dried clementines

Scant ½ cup (100 ml) water
½ cup (3 ½ oz./100 g) sugar
2 unwaxed or organic clementines

Almond shortcrust pastry

1 stick (120 g) butter, room temperature,
plus a little extra for the molds
Scant ½ teaspoon (2 g) salt
⅔ cup (3 ¼ oz./90 g) confectioners' sugar
3 tablespoons (½ oz./15 g) ground
blanched* almonds
1 egg
Cake flour, divided as follows: ⅔ cup (2 ¼ oz./60 g)
plus 2 cups (6 ⅓ oz./180 g)

Milk chocolate-clementine *crémeux*

5 oz. (140 g) milk chocolate, 40 percent cocoa
2 egg yolks
2 tablespoons (1 oz./25 g) granulated sugar
½ cup (125 ml) milk
½ cup (125 ml) whipping cream
Zest* of 1 unwaxed or organic clementine

Orange blossom-scented Chantilly cream

1 cup (250 ml) whipping cream, well chilled
¼ vanilla bean
2 tablespoons (1 oz./25 g) granulated sugar
A few drops of orange blossom water

For garnish (optional): a few roughly chopped
roasted hazelnuts

Equipment

8 tartlet molds†
1 piping bag† fitted with a plain tip†
1 kitchen thermometer†
2 sheets of food-safe acetate† or parchment paper
1 rolling pin†
1 immersion blender†
1 flexible spatula†
1 whisk†
Plastic wrap

Techniques
Almond Shortcrust Pastry ›› p. 72
Chocolate *Crémeux* ›› p. 100

Chocolate, Clementine, and Orange Blossom Water Tartlets ★★

Serves 6–8
Preparation time: 1 hour
Cooking time: 55 minutes
Refrigeration time: 3 hours 40 minutes

Prepare the dried clementines.
Bring the water and sugar to the boil; leave to boil for 1 minute. Slice the clementines very thinly, leaving the skin on, and cook the slices for about 10 minutes in the syrup. Preheat the oven to 250°F (120°C). Remove them from the saucepan and arrange them in an ovenproof dish. Dry them out in the oven for about 35 minutes.

Prepare the almond shortcrust pastry (see p. 172).
Butter the tartlet molds. Roll the dough out to a thickness of ⅛ in. (3 mm) and line the tartlet molds. Chill for 30 minutes. Preheat the oven to 300°F-325°F (150°C-160°C) and bake until the pastry is a nice golden color, about 15 to 20 minutes.

Prepare the milk chocolate-clementine *crémeux*.
Chop the chocolate and melt it slowly in a bain-marie* or in the microwave oven (on "defrost" or at 500 W maximum, stirring from time to time). Whip* the egg yolks and sugar together. Add the milk, cream, and grated* clementine zest. Pour the mixture into a saucepan and cook over low heat, stirring constantly, until the mixture thickens slightly and coats the back of a spoon. The temperature will be 180°F-183°F (82°C-84°C) Remove from the heat and filter into a mixing bowl. Process for a few seconds with an immersion blender until the texture is smooth and creamy. Gradually pour one-third of the hot custard over the melted chocolate. Using a flexible spatula, mix it in energetically, drawing small circles to create an elastic, shiny "kernel."
Incorporate the second third of the custard, using the same procedure. Repeat with the last third. Pour it into a bowl, cover with plastic wrap flush with the surface, and chill.
When the tartlet shells are ready, pour in the chocolate-clementine *crémeux* and leave to set in the refrigerator for at least 2 hours.

Prepare the orange blossom-scented Chantilly cream.
Pour the well-chilled cream into a mixing bowl. Slit the ¼ vanilla bean lengthways and scrape the seeds out into the cream. Add the sugar and orange blossom water. Whip until the texture reaches that of a light Chantilly cream. Spoon the cream into a piping bag fitted with a plain tip and pipe out rounds of scented Chantilly cream. Garnish with a slice of dried clementine.

● **Chef's note**
For an interesting textural contrast, sprinkle the chocolate-clementine crémeux *with roughly chopped roasted hazelnuts.*

Tropézienne Redux
with White Chocolate ★★

Serves 6-8

Preparation time: 30 minutes, plus cooling time
Cooking time: 25 minutes
Resting time: 1 hour 30 minutes
Refrigeration time: 3 hours minimum

Three hours ahead, or–preferably–a day ahead, prepare the white
chocolate ganache.
Chop the chocolate and melt it slowly in a bain-marie* or in the microwave
oven (on "defrost" or at 500 W maximum, stirring from time to time).
Bring the ½ cup minus 1 tablespoon (110 ml) cream to the boil in a saucepan.
Gradually pour one-third of the boiling cream over the melted chocolate.
Using a flexible spatula, energetically mix the cream into the chocolate, drawing small, quick circles in the center to create a shiny, elastic "kernel." Incorporate the second third of the cream and mix in exactly the same way. Pour in
the remaining third, using the same stirring technique. Stir in the remaining
cold whipping cream as well as a little orange blossom water. Cover with plastic wrap flush with the surface of the ganache and chill for at least 3 hours in
the refrigerator.

Prepare the brioche.
Preheat the oven to 350°F (170°C). Cut out an 8 ½ in. (22 cm) disk of raw brioche dough. Leave it to rise* for 1 hour 30 minutes. Brush it with the egg wash,
sprinkle with pearl sugar and/or cocoa nibs, and bake for about 25 minutes.
Leave to cool and then cut it into two horizontally.

Prepare the syrup.
Bring the water and sugar to the boil and add the orange blossom water.
Remove immediately from the heat.

To assemble.
Moisten the cut surfaces of the brioche halves with a pastry brush. Whisk* the
ganache until its texture is creamy. Using a piping bag or a spatula, spread the
whisked ganache over the lower half of the brioche. Cover it with the top half,
dust with confectioners' sugar, and serve.

● Chef's note

*Pearl sugar can be found in the sugar aisle of the supermarket or in specialty
stores. If you can't find pearl sugar, substitute crystallized sugar.*

Techniques
Brioche Dough ›› p. 78
Whipped Ganache ›› p. 97

Ingredients
14 oz. (400 g) raw brioche dough, homemade
(see recipe p. 78)
1 egg for an egg wash
Pearl sugar and/or cocoa nibs*
Confectioners' sugar for dusting

Whipped ivory ganache*
with orange blossom water
5 ⅔ oz. (160 g) white chocolate, 35 percent cocoa
Whipping cream, divided as follows: ½ cup minus
1 tablespoon (110 ml) plus 1 cup
plus 1 tablespoon (270 ml)
A few drops of orange blossom water

Syrup
2 tablespoons (30 ml) water
2 ½ tablespoons (1 oz./30 g) granulated sugar

Equipment
1 flexible spatula†
Plastic wrap
1 pastry brush†
1 whisk†
1 spatula† or piping bag†

Ingredients

Milk chocolate ganache*

8 oz. (225 g) milk chocolate, 40 percent cocoa
Scant ⅔ cup (150 ml) whipping cream
1 heaped tablespoon (1 oz./25 g) honey

Almond shortcrust pastry

1 ½ sticks (6 ⅓ oz./180 g) unsalted butter,
plus a little extra for the mold
1 pinch table salt
1 cup (5 oz./140 g) confectioners' sugar
Generous ½ cup, (1 ¾ oz./50 g) ground
blanched* almonds
1 egg
Cake flour, divided as follows: 1 cup (3 ¼ oz./90 g)
plus 3 cups (9 ½ oz./270 g)

Vanilla pastry cream

½ vanilla bean
1 egg yolk
2 ½ tablespoons (1 oz./30 g) granulated sugar
1 ½ tablespoons (¼ oz./8 g) cake flour
1 ½ teaspoons (5 g) cornstarch
½ cup (125 ml) whole milk

Hazelnut cream

7 tablespoons (3 ½ oz./100 g) butter
¾ cup (3 ½ oz./100 g) confectioners' sugar
1 tablespoon (⅓ oz./10 g) cornstarch
1 cup plus 3 tablespoons (3 ½ oz./100 g) finely
ground hazelnuts
1 egg

Equipment

1 rolling pin†
1 flexible spatula†
1 baking sheet
1 piping bag† fitted with a V-shaped tip†,
known as a Saint-Honoré tip

Techniques

Ganaches ›› p. 32
Almond Shortcrust Pastry ›› p. 72
Vanilla Pastry Cream ›› p. 102

Hazelnut Waves ★ ★

Serves 6–8

Preparation time: 1 hour 30 minutes
Cooking time: 40 minutes
Setting time: 3 hours
Refrigeration time: 4 hours

Prepare the milk chocolate ganache.

Chop the chocolate and melt it slowly in a bain-marie* or in the microwave oven (on "defrost" or at 500 W maximum, stirring from time to time).
Bring the cream and honey to the boil in a saucepan. Gradually pour one-third of the boiling cream over the melted chocolate. Using a flexible spatula, energetically mix the cream into the chocolate, drawing small, quick circles in the center to create a shiny, elastic "kernel."
Incorporate the second third of the cream and mix in exactly the same way. Pour in the remaining third, using the same stirring technique. Leave to set for 3 hours in a cool place, but do not chill in the refrigerator.

Prepare the almond shortcrust pastry (see p. 72).

Use the proportions given opposite. Preheat the oven to 300°F–325°F (150°C–160°C). Roll the dough out to a thickness of ⅛ in. (3 mm) to make a square or rectangular shape and bake for about 20 minutes, until golden. Leave to cool.

Prepare the vanilla pastry cream (see p. 102).

Use the proportions given opposite. Cover with plastic wrap flush with the surface and chill for about 1 hour.

Prepare the hazelnut cream.

Soften the butter in a mixing bowl (see p. 134). Sift the confectioners' sugar and cornstarch together and add to the butter, stirring constantly. Stir as you add the ground hazelnuts. Then add the egg, and finally, stir in the cold pastry cream.

Preheat the oven to 375°F (190°C).

Spread the hazelnut cream over the entire surface of the cooled almond pastry and bake for about 20 minutes, until a nice golden color. Leave to cool completely.
Spoon the chocolate ganache into a piping bag fitted with a V-shaped or angled tip, and pipe out to form a wave pattern. Leave the pastry to set in the refrigerator for about 3 hours.
Remove from the refrigerator, and using a heated knife (dip it in hot water and then dry it carefully), cut out rectangles measuring 1 ¼ × 3 in. (3 × 8 cm).

● Chef's notes

As soon as you remove the pastry from the oven, place a sheet of parchment paper topped with a baking sheet over the top. This will ensure that the surface will remain perfectly smooth as it cools.

Instead of milk chocolate ganache, you might prefer a bittersweet chocolate ganache.

Mandarin Marvels ★

Makes 20-30 mini-tartlets

Preparation time: 2 hours
Cooking time: 15 minutes
Resting time: 40 minutes
Refrigeration time: 2 hours

Prepare the spiced dough.
Take the butter out of the refrigerator several hours before you begin baking and place it in a mixing bowl. Mix it energetically with a flexible spatula.
Soften it further with the spatula or a whisk (the final texture is known as *beurre pommade**).
Preheat the oven to 350°F (170°C). Sift the flour with the cinnamon and set aside.
Add the brown sugar and white granulated sugar to the butter and mix in well. Incorporate the egg and sifted flour and cinnamon. Lastly, stir in the milk and mix until the dough is smooth.
Cover the dough in plastic wrap and chill for about 1 hour.
Roll the dough out, preferably between 2 sheets of acetate, to a thickness of just under $\frac{1}{16}$ in. (2 mm) and cut it out to fit the molds. Bake for about 15 minutes and leave to cool.

Prepare the bittersweet chocolate ganache.
Chop the chocolate and melt it slowly in a bain-marie* or in the microwave oven (on "defrost" or at 500 W maximum, stirring from time to time). Bring the cream and honey to the boil in a saucepan. Gradually pour one-third of the boiling cream over the melted chocolate. Using a flexible spatula, energetically mix the cream into the chocolate, drawing small, quick circles in the center to create a shiny, elastic "kernel."
Incorporate the second third of the cream and mix in exactly the same way. Pour in the remaining third, using the same stirring technique. Process with an immersion blender until the mixture is smooth and perfectly emulsified*. Pour the ganache into the cooled tart shells.

Prepare the mandarin segments.
Using a well-sharpened paring knife, peel the mandarins, making sure you remove all the white pith. Extract the segments. Hold the mandarin in the hollow of your hand and slip the knife along the membrane that encloses the segment until you reach the center of the fruit. Repeat on the other side of the segment, all along the membrane to the center. The segment will come out on its own. Repeat with the remaining segments and reserve them on some sheets of paper towel.
Arrange 4 or 5 segments on each tartlet to reproduce the shape of a half-mandarin. Decorate with a few chocolate shavings: scrape them off from the bar of chocolate using the tip of a vegetable peeler. Reserve in the refrigerator until serving.

● **Chef's note**
For a final, elegant touch, top with a small piece of edible gold leaf.

Ingredients

Spiced dough
1 stick (4 ½ oz./125 g) butter
2 ¾ cups (9 oz./250 g) cake flour
½ teaspoon ground cinnamon
⅔ cup (4 ½ oz./125 g) light brown sugar
⅓ cup (2 ⅔ oz./75 g) granulated sugar
½ beaten egg
1 tablespoon plus 1 teaspoon (20 ml) whole milk

Bittersweet chocolate ganache*
3 ½ oz. (100 g) bittersweet chocolate, 60 percent cocoa
½ cup plus 1 ½ tablespoons (150 ml) whipping cream
1 heaped tablespoon (1 oz./25 g) honey

Decoration
10 seedless mandarins
1 bar bittersweet chocolate, 60 percent cocoa

Equipment
1 flexible spatula†
1 whisk† (optional)
Plastic wrap
2 sheets of food-safe acetate†
20-30 mini-tartlet molds†
1 immersion blender†
1 well-sharpened paring knife
1 vegetable peeler

Techniques
Melting Chocolate ›› p. 19
Spiced Dough ›› p. 76
Ganache for Tarts and Desserts ›› p. 96

Ingredients

Chocolate-almond streusel

Scant cup (2 ⅔ oz./75 g) cake flour
1 ½ tablespoons (10 g) unsweetened cocoa powder
1 cup minus 1 tablespoon (2 ⅔ oz./75 g)
ground blanched* almonds
Generous ⅓ cup (2 ⅔ oz./75 g) light brown sugar
Generous pinch (3 g) fleur de sel
5 tablespoons plus 1 teaspoon (2 ⅔ oz./75 g)
butter, chilled

Light ivory and passion fruit mousse

1 ½ sheets (3 g) gelatin
5 ½ oz. (150 g) white chocolate, 35 percent cocoa
Scant ½ cup (90 ml) milk
Generous ½ cup (160 g) whipping cream
Half a passion fruit

Garnish

Half a pineapple
1 mango
A few sprigs of fresh cilantro (coriander)

Equipment

Cookie cutters†, square or any other shape
of your choice
1 baking sheet lined with parchment paper
1 kitchen thermometer†
1 flexible spatula†
1 whisk† or hand-held electric beater†

Cilantro-Scented Pineapple and Mango Tart ★★

Serves 6–8

Preparation time: 2 hours
Cooking time: 10 to 15 minutes
Freezing time: 30 minutes
Refrigeration time: 2 hours 30 minutes

Prepare the chocolate-almond streusel.
Sift the flour and cocoa powder together. Combine them with the ground almonds, brown sugar, and fleur de sel. Cut the chilled butter into small cubes and using your hands, mix it into the preparation until it forms a crumbly texture. Chill for at least 30 minutes. Preheat the oven to 300°F-325°F (150°C-160°C).
Place the cookie cutters on the lined baking sheet and spread the streusel mixture at the base. If you wish to consolidate the crumbly mixture, lightly spray it with water before baking. Bake for about 10 to 15 minutes, until nicely browned. Leave to cool at room temperature.

Prepare the light ivory and passion fruit mousse.
Soften the gelatin in a bowl of cold water.
Chop the chocolate and melt it slowly in a bain-marie* or in the microwave oven (on "defrost" or at 500 W maximum, stirring from time to time).
Bring the milk to the boil in a saucepan. Wring the water out of the gelatin and incorporate it into the hot milk. Immediately remove from the heat.
Slowly pour one-third of the hot milk over the melted chocolate. Using a flexible spatula, briskly mix it in with a small circular movement to create an elastic, shiny "kernel." Then incorporate another third of the hot liquid, using the same circular movement, and finally, the last third, still mixing with a circular movement.
Using either a whisk or an electric beater, lightly whip* the well-chilled cream (see p. 108). When the milk, gelatin, and chocolate mixture has cooled to 86°F (30°C), carefully fold in* the lightly whipped cream, incorporating the passion fruit seeds as well. As soon as the mixture is thoroughly combined, pour it into the cookie cutters over the cooled cocoa streusel. Chill for 1 to 2 hours.
Peel the pineapple and mango and cut them into differently sized cubes. Pick the leaves from the cilantro stalks and chop them finely. Combine the differently sized cubes of fruit in a mixing bowl and toss them with the cilantro leaves. Remove the cookie cutters from the layered desserts and garnish with cilantro-flavored fruit cubes. Keep in the refrigerator until serving.

Techniques
Chocolate-Almond Streusel >> p. 88
Egg-Free Chocolate Mousse >> p. 111

Warm Chocolate Tart ★★

Serves 6
Preparation time: 1 hour
Cooking time: 25 minutes
Refrigeration time: 2 hours 30 minutes

Prepare the almond shortcrust pastry.

In a mixing bowl, soften the butter and mix with the salt, confectioners' sugar, ground almonds, egg, and ⅔ cup (2 oz./60 g) cake flour.

As soon as the ingredients are mixed through, add the remaining flour and mix until just combined. Cover in plastic wrap and chill for about 1 hour.

Roll the dough out to a thickness of ⅛ in. (3 mm) between two sheets of acetate and chill it for about 30 minutes, ensuring that it is flat. Preheat the oven to 300°F-325°F (150°C-160°C) and bake for about 20 minutes, until it is a nice golden color.

Prepare the bittersweet chocolate ganache.

Chop the chocolate and melt it slowly in a bain-marie* or in the microwave oven (on "defrost" or at 500 W maximum, stirring from time to time).

Bring the milk, cream, and sugar to the boil in a saucepan.

Gradually pour one-third of the boiling liquid over the melted chocolate.

Using a flexible spatula, energetically mix the liquid into the chocolate, drawing small, quick circles in the center to create a shiny, elastic "kernel."

Incorporate the second third of the liquid and mix in exactly the same way. Pour in the remaining third, using the same stirring technique. Incorporate the egg yolks and chill for at least 1 hour.

Preheat the oven to 350°F-375°F (180°C-190°C). Spoon the ganache into a piping bag and pipe it out into the tart shell. Bake for 5 to 7 minutes. Dust lightly with cocoa powder and serve immediately.

Techniques
Almond Shortcrust Pastry ≫ p. 72
Lining a tart dish ≫ p. 133

Ingredients

Almond shortcrust pastry
1 stick (4 oz./120 g) butter, room temperature, plus a little extra for the molds
Scant ½ teaspoon (2 g) table salt
⅔ cup (3 ¼ oz./90 g) confectioners' sugar
3 tablespoons (½ oz./15 g) ground blanched* almonds
1 egg
Cake flour, divided as follows: ⅔ cup (2 oz./60 g) plus 2 cups (6 ⅓ oz./180 g)

Baked bittersweet ganache*
4 ¼ oz. (120 g) bittersweet chocolate, 70 percent cocoa
½ cup plus 2 tablespoons (150 ml) milk
½ cup plus 2 tablespoons (150 ml) whipping cream
3 ½ tablespoons (1 ½ oz./40 g) sugar
2 egg yolks

A little unsweetened cocoa powder for dusting

Equipment
Plastic wrap
2 sheets of food-safe acetate†
1 flexible spatula†
1 tart mold† or pan, 7 in. (18 cm) diameter
1 piping bag†

Shared delights

Cyril Lignac
presents his recipe

I truly came to know chocolate when I
was working as a pastry apprentice. That
was when I discovered the grands crus:
Araguani, Nyangbo, Manjari, and others.
I understood that it was not accurate to
talk of "chocolate," but "chocolates." Each
one has its terroir, aromas, and story—a
lot like wine. For me, as a cook and pastry
chef, it is a product that gives manifold
opportunities to create. What's more,
we are living at a time when consumers
are increasingly well informed and are
becoming more and more demanding. It's
important to know the provenance of a
chocolate, just as it is important to know
where one's lamb and cherries come from.
My menus include all these details, and my
clients appreciate it.

Twisted Nyangbo Ganache with Roasted Sesame Tuiles and Poire Williams Sorbet

Nyangbo chocolate ganache (prepare a day ahead). Soak the gelatin in very cold water until softened. Chop the chocolate on a board. Bring the sorbitol, agar-agar, and water to the boil in a saucepan. Wring the water out of the gelatin and add it to the boiling mixture with the glucose. Bring to the boil again and add the whipping cream. Bring to the boil yet again and pour the hot mixture over the chopped chocolate.
Pour it into a baking pan or onto a tray. Cover with plastic wrap flush with the surface and chill. When the surface has hardened, freeze overnight.

Pear sorbet. Bring the water and sugar to the boil in a saucepan, and pour the hot liquid over the Williams pear pulp. Blend, then pour into the bowl of the ice-cream maker, following the manufacturer's instructions. Freeze—but be careful: home-made ice creams and sorbets should not stay too long in the freezer because they harden quickly.

Sesame tuiles. Preheat the oven to 350°F (180°C). Bring the water and sugar to boil in a saucepan. Add the honey and bring to the boil again. Pour on to the silicone mat, spreading the mixture out evenly with an offset spatula. Sprinkle generously with the sesame seeds. Bake for about 14 minutes. As soon as you remove it from the oven, cut into 2 × ½ in. (5 × 1 cm rectangles). Reserve any extra tuiles for another dessert. Stored in an airtight container, they will keep for three days.

Pear coulis. Bring the pear pulp to the boil with the potato starch, then chill.

Diced poached pears. Peel the pear. Cook the sugar until it forms a dark golden caramel*. Deglaze with the water, add the orange zest, and poach the pear in the liquid. Leave to cool and cut into ¼ in. (5 mm) cubes.

To assemble and finish. Remove the ganache from the freezer and leave at room temperature for 30 minutes so that you can work with it. Put on the gloves so that you don't leave any traces on the ganache and cut it into 10 equal rectangles.
Twist the rectangles and place them on a tray. Place in the refrigerator for 15 minutes to chill them. Spray them with the velvet spray.
Arrange the ganache twists in the center of each plate. Arrange three pear cubes at the top of the left of the twist and three other cubes on the right. Place a sesame tuile below the top cube and another just above the last one. Draw 3 dots of pear coulis on each side of the plate and garnish with a scoop of pear sorbet.

Serves 10

Ingredients

Nyangbo chocolate ganache*
⅜ sheet (0.75 g) gelatin
4 ⅔ oz. (130 g) Valrhona Nyangbo chocolate, 68 percent cocoa
1 oz. (30 g) sorbitol (sugar substitute available at specialty stores)
½ teaspoon (1 g) agar-agar (powder)
1 tablespoon plus ½ teaspoon (17 g) water
⅔ oz. (17 g) glucose
1 ¼ cups (300 ml) whipping cream

Pear sorbet
¼ cup (60 ml) water
⅓ cup (2 ¼ oz./60 g) granulated sugar
1 lb. 6 oz. (630 g) pear pulp, preferably Williams or Bartlett

Sesame tuiles
Scant ½ cup (100 ml) water
½ cup (3 ½ oz./100 g) sugar
2 tablespoons (40 g) honey
4 ¼ oz. (120 g) sesame seeds

Pear coulis
4 ½ oz. (125 g) pear pulp
¾ teaspoon (2.5 g) potato starch

Diced poached pears
1 pear, preferably Conference
2 ½ tablespoons (1 oz./30 g) granulated sugar
½ cup (125 g) water
Zest* of 2 unwaxed oranges

To finish
Chocolate velvet spray (from specialty stores)

Equipment
1 confectionary frame† or baking pan, 4 in. × 8 in. (10 cm × 20 cm)
1 ice-cream maker†
1 silicone baking mat†
1 offset spatula†
A pair of disposable gloves to work with the ganache

Ingredients

Breton shortbread
1 cup plus 1 scant ¼ cup (4 ¼ oz./120 g)
all-purpose flour
1 teaspoon (4 g) baking powder
1 pinch salt
2 egg yolks
Scant ½ cup (2 ¾ oz./80 g) sugar
5 ½ tablespoons (2 ¾ oz./80 g) butter, softened

Basic pouring custard (crème anglaise)
8 egg yolks
Scant ½ cup (2 ¾ oz./80 g) sugar
1 ½ cups (380 ml) whole milk
1 ½ cups (380 ml) whipping cream

Coffee cream
1 lb. (500 g) basic pouring custard,
made using ingredients above
3 tablespoons (⅓ oz./10 g) instant coffee

Chocolate crémeux
1 lb. (500 g) basic pouring custard,
made using ingredients above
7 oz. (200 g) bittersweet chocolate,
60 percent cocoa

Vanilla-scented milky foam
3 sheets (6 g) gelatin
¼ vanilla bean
2 ½ tablespoons (⅔ oz./20 g) confectioners' sugar
1 ¼ cups (300 ml) milk, well chilled

Equipment
2 sheets of food-safe acetate† or parchment paper
1 baking sheet
1 immersion blender†
1 flexible spatula†
8 shot glasses or small bowls
1 kitchen thermometer†
1 chinois†, 1 whisk†

● Chef's note
The milky foam can also be flavored with a few ground cardamom seeds and/or finely grated orange zest.*

Techniques
Breton Shortbread with Chocolate Chips >> p. 74
Basic Custard (crème anglaise) >> p. 98
Chocolate Crémeux >> p. 100

Coffee, Chocolate, and Vanilla Creams with Breton Shortbread ★★

Serves 6–8
Preparation time: 1 hour
Refrigeration time: 3 hours 30 minutes
Cooking time: 15 minutes

Prepare the Breton shortbread.
Preheat the oven to 350°F (170°C). Sift the flour with the baking powder and the salt.
Beat the egg yolks with the sugar until the mixture is thick and pale. Soften the butter and incorporate it, then the sifted dry ingredients.
Roll out the dough, between two sheets of acetate paper if possible, to a thickness of ¼ in. (5 mm). Chill for 30 minutes. Remove the dough from the refrigerator and cut out small ½ in. (1 cm) cubes. Place them on a baking sheet and bake for about 15 minutes, until a nice gold color. Leave to cool and then place a few cubes at the base of each of the glasses or bowls.

Prepare the pouring custard (see p. 98).
Use the proportions given opposite; this is used as the base for the coffee cream and the chocolate crémeux.

Prepare the coffee cream.
Weigh out 1 lb. (500 g) of hot pouring custard. Stir in the instant coffee until it is completely dissolved. Set aside in the refrigerator.

Prepare the chocolate crémeux.
Use another 1 lb. (500 g) of the pouring custard.
Chop the chocolate and melt it slowly in a bain-marie* or in the microwave oven (on "defrost" or at 500 W maximum, stirring from time to time). Heat the pouring custard to 183°F (84°C). Gradually pour one-third of the hot custard over the melted chocolate. Using a flexible spatula, mix it in energetically, drawing small circles to create an elastic, shiny "kernel."
Incorporate the second third of the custard, using the same procedure. Repeat with the last third and process briefly with an immersion blender.
Pour the crémeux into glasses or glass bowls over the cubes of shortbread and chill for 2 to 3 hours. When the crémeux has set, pour the coffee cream over it and return the glasses to the refrigerator.

Just before serving, prepare the vanilla-scented milky foam.
Soften the gelatin in a bowl of very cold water. When it has softened, wring out the water. Dissolve it in the microwave oven for 10 seconds at 500 W. Slit the quarter vanilla bean lengthways and scrape out the seeds into a mixing bowl. Combine the sugar, vanilla seeds, and well-chilled milk. Filter the liquid through a chinois and gradually pour it over the melted gelatin, whisking* briskly until it becomes frothy. Carefully place a dollop of vanilla-scented cream on top of the coffee cream and serve immediately.

Ingredients

Churros
¾ cup (185 ml) milk
Heaped ½ teaspoon (3 g) salt
1 teaspoon (4 g) sugar
5 tablespoons plus 1 teaspoon (2 ⅔ oz./75 g) butter
Generous ½ cup (1 ¾ oz./50 g) cake flour
3 eggs

Ginger-scented milk chocolate sauce
3 ¾ oz. (110 g) milk chocolate, 40 percent cocoa
1 cup minus 1 tablespoon (235 ml) whipping cream
2 teaspoons (½ oz./15 g) glucose syrup
1 small piece of ginger rhizome,
just over 1 in. (3 cm)
Scant ⅔ cup (4 ¼ oz./120 g) sugar
2 tablespoons plus 2 teaspoons (1 ½ oz./40 g) butter

Flavored sugar
1 unwaxed lime
1 cup (7 oz./200 g) sugar

2 cups (500 ml) oil for frying

Equipment

1 piping bag† fitted with a star-shaped tip†
1 blender or fine grater†
1 baking sheet lined with parchment paper
or silicone baking mat†
1 flexible spatula†
1 immersion blender†
1 deep fry pot
1 kitchen thermometer†

Techniques
Chocolate-Caramel Sauce ›› p. 129
Filling a piping bag ›› p. 132

Cactus-Shaped Churros and
Ginger-Scented Milk Chocolate Sauce ★★

Serves 6–8
Preparation time: 1 hour
Cooking time: 10 minutes
Freezing time: 3 hours

Prepare the churros.
Bring the milk, salt, sugar, and butter to boil in a saucepan. Pour the flour into the mixture and stir for 1 minute over high heat to dry out the dough. Remove from the heat and incorporate the eggs, one by one, stirring well each time, until the dough is smooth and forms a soft ball.
Spoon the dough into a piping bag and pipe out small cactus shapes using a star-shaped tip onto a lined baking sheet. Freeze for about 3 hours.

Prepare the ginger-scented milk chocolate sauce.
Chop the chocolate and melt it slowly in a bain-marie* or in the microwave oven (on "defrost" or at 500 W maximum, stirring from time to time).
Bring the cream to the boil with the glucose syrup. Peel the ginger and extract the juice using a blender, or reduce it to fine pulp with a grater.
In another saucepan, prepare a caramel* with the sugar using the dry method. Incorporate the butter, being careful not to burn yourself, and then the heated cream and glucose mixture. Gradually pour one-third of the mixture over the melted chocolate. Using a flexible spatula, mix it in energetically, drawing small circles to create an elastic, shiny "kernel."
Incorporate the second third of the liquid, using the same procedure. Repeat with the last third. Process for a few seconds using an immersion blender so that the mixture is smooth and perfectly emulsified*, and then stir in the ginger juice or pulp.
Prepare the lime zest* by grating it on a fine grater, or chop it very finely. Combine it thoroughly with the granulated sugar.
Heat the oil to 356°F (180°C) in a deep pot or deep fryer. Carefully drop in 2 to 3 frozen churros at a time and fry them until a nice golden color.
Drain them on paper towel and sprinkle them with the flavored sugar.
Serve the cactus-shaped churros with warm ginger-scented sauce.

● **Chef's note**
You may also make the churros into shapes that are easier to form.

Ingredients

Bittersweet chocolate mousse
10 ½ oz. (300 g) bittersweet chocolate,
70 percent cocoa
⅔ cup (150 g) whipping cream
3 egg yolks (2 ¼ oz./60 g)
6-7 egg whites (7 oz./200 g)
¼ cup (1 ¾ oz./50 g) granulated sugar

Garnish
1 oz. (25 g) walnuts
1 oz. (25 g) unpeeled* whole almonds
1 oz. (25 g) peeled* whole hazelnuts
½ oz. (15 g) pine nuts, preferably Mediterranean
1 Reinette apple, or Cox's Orange Pippin
1 pear, not too ripe
Scant ¼ cup (50 ml) whipping cream
Scant ½ cup (2 ¾ oz./80 g) sugar
2 tablespoons (30 ml) water

Whipped cream
¾ cup (200 ml) whipping cream

Equipment

1 kitchen thermometer†
1 piping bag†
1 flexible spatula†
1 whisk†

Techniques
Egg White-Based Chocolate Mousse >> p. 110
Filling a piping bag >> p. 132

Chocolate Crown with Winter Fruit and Nuts ★

Serves 8
Preparation time: 45 minutes
Refrigeration time: 12 hours

A day ahead, prepare the chocolate mousse.
Chop the chocolate and melt it slowly in a bain-marie* or in the microwave oven (on "defrost" or at 500 W maximum, stirring from time to time).
Bring the cream to the boil in a saucepan. As soon as it reaches the boil, remove from the heat. Slowly pour one-third of the hot cream over the melted chocolate. Using a flexible spatula, briskly mix it in with a small circular movement to create an elastic, shiny "kernel." Then incorporate another third of the hot cream, using the same circular movement, and finally, the last third, still mixing with a circular movement.
Stir in the egg yolks until the mixture is smooth.
In the meantime, start whisking* the egg whites with a little of the sugar. When they form soft peaks, incorporate the remaining sugar. When the chocolate mixture reaches 113°F-122°F (45°C-50°C), fold in* one quarter of the whisked egg whites, then carefully fold in the rest. Chill the mousse for 12 hours.

The next day, prepare the garnish.
Roughly chop the nuts. Peel and finely dice the apple and the pear. Heat the cream in a saucepan. Place the sugar and water in a heavy-bottomed saucepan and cook until it forms a caramel* (the temperature will be 343°F-347°F (173°C-175°C) and small bubbles will form). Remove the saucepan from the heat, and being careful not to splash yourself, pour in the hot cream. Leave to simmer for a few moments. Add the diced apple and bring back to a gentle simmer, then add the diced pear and roughly chopped nuts. Leave to chill in the refrigerator so that the nuts can soften and absorb all the aromas of the caramel.
In a mixing bowl, lightly whip* the well-chilled cream (see p. 134).

To assemble.
Spoon the mousse into a piping bag and pipe out rounds of chocolate mousse onto the plates. Serve with the caramelized fruit and nuts and a dollop of whipped cream.

● Chef's notes
You might want to spice up the caramel with a little cinnamon, star anise, or gingerbread spice mix if you're making this dessert at Christmas time.
Pair with a Roussillon wine, such as Maury, or good, hot black coffee.

Chocolate-Vanilla Marbled Waffles ★ ★

Serves 6–8

Preparation time: 45 to 50 minutes
Cooking time: 4 minutes per batch of waffles

Prepare the chocolate and maple syrup sauce.
Heat the maple syrup in a saucepan to 250°F (120°C). While it is cooking, slightly warm the cream. When the maple syrup has reached the right temperature, stir in the cream and bring back to the boil.
Chop the chocolate and melt it gently in a bain-marie* or in the microwave oven (on "defrost" or at 500 W maximum, stirring from time to time).
Gradually pour one-third of the boiling liquid over the melted chocolate. Using a flexible spatula, mix it in energetically, drawing small circles to create an elastic, shiny "kernel."
Incorporate the second third of the liquid, using the same procedure. Repeat with the last third.

Prepare the vanilla waffle batter.
Sift the flour into a mixing bowl. Bring the milk to the boil, then add the vanilla extract, sugar, butter, and salt. Pour the mixture into the sifted flour, stirring as you do so, until the batter is smooth. Whisk* the egg whites to soft peaks (see p. 134) and fold* them in carefully. Set aside at room temperature.

Prepare the chocolate waffle batter.
Sift the flour into a mixing bowl. Chop the chocolate and melt it slowly in a bain-marie or in the microwave oven (on "defrost" or at 500 W maximum, stirring from time to time). In a saucepan, bring the milk to the boil, then add the vanilla extract, sugar, butter, and salt. Incorporate the chocolate, third by third, into the hot liquid, stirring energetically each time. Then pour the mixture into the sifted flour and combine. Whisk the egg whites to soft peaks and fold them in carefully.

Heat the waffle maker. When it is hot, spoon the two batters over the grids fairly irregularly, to create an attractive marble pattern. Cook for about 4 minutes.
Place the waffles on plates and serve with a scoop of vanilla ice cream, drizzled with chocolate-maple syrup sauce.

● Chef's notes

You can prepare the waffles ahead of time. Sprinkle them with confectioners' sugar for added crunch, and reheat them in the oven on "broil."
Bringing the maple syrup to 250°F (120°C) brings out its aromas and makes it more syrupy. The cream must be warmed separately.

Ingredients

Vanilla waffle batter
1 generous cup (110 g) all-purpose flour
½ cup (125 ml) whole milk
1 tablespoon plus 1 teaspoon (20 g or 20 ml)
vanilla extract
2 tablespoons (1 oz./25 g) granulated sugar
1 stick (4 ½ oz./125 g) butter
Scant ½ teaspoon (2 g) table salt
3 egg whites

Chocolate waffle batter
1 generous cup (110 g) all-purpose flour
1 ¾ oz. (50 g) bittersweet chocolate,
70 percent cocoa
½ cup (125 ml) whole milk
1 tablespoon plus 1 teaspoon (20 g or 20 ml)
vanilla extract
¼ cup (1 ¾ oz./50 g) granulated sugar
1 stick plus 1 teaspoon (4 ⅔ oz./130 g) butter
Scant ½ teaspoon (2 g) table salt
3 egg whites

Milk chocolate and maple syrup sauce
1 cup (10 ½ oz./300 g) maple syrup]
Scant ⅔ cup (150 ml) whipping cream
3 ½ oz. (100 g) milk chocolate, 40 percent cocoa

Vanilla ice cream

Equipment

1 kitchen thermometer[†]
1 flexible spatula[†]
1 whisk[†]
1 waffle maker

Techniques

Melting Chocolate ›› p. 19
Chocolate-Caramel Sauce ›› p. 129

Mini Molten Chocolate Cakes
With *Verrines* of Softened Bananas and Chocolate Granita ★★

Serves 6-8
Preparation time: 1 hour 40 minutes
Refrigeration time: overnight
Cooking time: 15 minutes
Freezing time: overnight

A day ahead, prepare the molten chocolate cakes.
Chop the chocolate and melt it slowly in a bain-marie* or in the microwave oven (on "defrost" or at 500 W maximum, stirring from time to time). Add the butter to the melted chocolate and stir until thoroughly combined and smooth. Beat the eggs and sugar until thick and pale, and then stir in the flour. Stir the chocolate into the eggs and chill overnight.

Prepare the chocolate granita (see p. 123).
Blend for a few seconds using an immersion blender so that the mixture is smooth and perfectly emulsified*. Pour it into a dish to just over 1 in. (3 cm) thick. Place in the freezer for at least 3 hours, scratching regularly to form crystals that are just the right size.

The next day, prepare the softened bananas.
Preheat the oven to 400°F (200°C).
Melt the butter in the microwave oven. Cut open the passion fruit and extract the juice and, if you wish, the seeds. Peel the bananas and slice them into rounds that are not too thin. Combine the melted butter, brown sugar, and orange and passion fruit juice, and grind in the Sarawak pepper. Pour this marinade over the bananas and stir carefully to combine. Place the bananas with the marinade in an ovenproof dish and bake for 6 to 8 minutes. Set aside at room temperature.

Prepare the almond streusel (see p.88).
Use the proportions given opposite.

Preheat the oven to 375°F (190°C).
Remove the chocolate batter from the refrigerator and warm it up briefly in the microwave oven at 500 W. Butter the pastry circles with softened butter and place them on a baking sheet lined with parchment paper. Spoon the batter into a piping bag and pipe it out into the pastry circles. Bake for 6 to 7 minutes. While they are baking, arrange the softened bananas in the *verrines* (shot glasses) and spoon in the chocolate granita above it. Garnish with a few pieces of streusel. Place in the freezer while you finish preparing the dessert. Remove the molten chocolate cakes from the oven, wait for about 30 seconds, and turn them out into plates. Serve accompanied by the iced *verrines*.

Ingredients

Molten chocolate cakes
5 ⅔ oz. (160 g) bittersweet chocolate, 70 percent cocoa
1 ⅓ sticks (5 ⅔ oz./160 g) butter, plus a little extra for the pastry circles
5-6 eggs, total weight 10 oz. (280 g)
⅔ cup (4 ½ oz./125 g) sugar
Scant cup (2 ¾ oz./80 g) cake flour

Chocolate granita
6 oz. (170 g) bittersweet chocolate, 70 percent cocoa
2 ⅔ cups (650 ml) water
1 ½ tablespoons (⅓ oz./10 g) powdered milk
⅔ cup (4 ½ oz./125 g) sugar
1 heaped tablespoon (1 oz./25 g) honey

Softened bananas
1 tablespoon (15 g) butter
2 passion fruits
2 or 3 bananas, total weight approx. ¾ lb. (340 g)
1 ½ tablespoons (⅔ oz./20 g) brown sugar
¼ cup (60 ml) orange juice
2 grinds of the pepper mill with Sarawak pepper

Almond streusel
Scant cup (2 ¾ oz./80 g) cake flour
5 ½ tablespoons or ¾ stick (2 ¾ oz./80 g) butter
1 cup (2 ¾ oz./80 g) ground almonds
Scant ½ cup (2 ¾ oz./80 g) sugar
Generous pinch (3 g) fleur de sel

Equipment
1 immersion blender†
1 piping bag†
Individual pastry circles†,
2-2 ¼ in. (5-6 cm) diameter, 2 in. (5 cm) high
1 baking sheet lined with parchment paper
8 shot glasses or small bowls

● Did you know?
Sarawak pepper, which comes from Borneo, has a flavor that sets off desserts to great advantage. Its fresh, woody notes pair well with banana and chocolate.

Techniques
Chocolate-Almond Streusel >> p. 88
Chocolate Granita >> p. 123

Almond Mousse, Milk Chocolate Heart, and Honey-Softened Pears ★ ★ ★

Serves 6-8
Preparation time: 1 hour 30 minutes
Refrigeration time: 3 to 4 hours
Freezing time: overnight

A day ahead.
Prepare the egg-free chocolate mousse (see p. 111), using the proportions given opposite.
Pour it into the silicone ice-cube trays and leave to harden in the freezer for 2 to 3 hours.

A few hours later, prepare the almond mousse.
Soften the gelatin in a bowl filled with cold water. Bring the milk to the boil and remove immediately from the heat. Wring the water out of the gelatin and dissolve it in the milk.
Soften the almond paste: place it for about 40 seconds in the microwave oven. Process the almond paste with an immersion blender, gradually pouring in the milk combined with the gelatin. As soon as the mixture is completely smooth, set it aside to cool down.
Whisk* the whipping cream to soft-peak stage. When the milk and almond paste mixture has cooled to 104°F-113°F (40°C-45°C), carefully fold in* the lightly whipped cream.
Fill the individual molds three-quarters full with the almond mousse. In the center, insert an iced portion of milk chocolate mousse, taken from the ice tray. Leave to harden in the freezer for at least 3 to 4 hours.

The next day.
Peel the pears, cut them in halves, and then cut them into four or five pieces, depending on their size. Using a paring knife, remove the core and seeds, making sure the cut pieces are all the same size. Heat the honey in a pan and add the pear pieces, turning them over regularly until they are all slightly caramelized*. Drain the honey, and reserve it if you wish to use it as a sauce. Set aside the pears at room temperature.

Prepare the puff pastry arlettes (see p. 61).
Use the proportions given opposite.

Turn the frozen mousses out of their molds onto the serving dish and place in the refrigerator for 3 to 4 hours.
Serve them with a few pieces of honey-softened pears, arlettes, and chocolate shards. If you have kept the honey from the pears, you can now use it as a sauce.

Ingredients

Milk chocolate mousse
6 oz. (170 g) milk chocolate, 40 percent cocoa
½ sheet (1 g) gelatin
½ cup minus 1 tablespoons (100 ml) whole milk
1 cup minus 2 ½ tablespoons (200 ml) whipping cream

Almond mousse
2 sheets (4 g) gelatin
¾ cup (170 ml) whole milk
5 oz. (140 g) homemade almond paste (see p. 41)
¾ cup (170 ml) whipping cream

Honey-softened pears
2 pears, not too ripe
3 ½ tablespoons (2 ⅔ oz./75 g) chestnut honey

Arlettes
3 ½ oz. (100 g) puff pastry
¼ cup (1 ¾ oz./50 g) granulated sugar

Equipment
Silicone ice trays
1 immersion blender†
8 individual molds†, shape of your choice
1 whisk†
1 kitchen thermometer†

Techniques
Almond Paste ›› p.41
Arlettes ›› p. 61
Egg-Free Chocolate Mousse ›› p. 111

Ingredients

Chocolate cake

1 ¼ oz. (35 g) bittersweet chocolate,
60 percent cocoa
4 tablespoons (½ stick, 60 g) butter
3 eggs
1 heaped tablespoon (1 oz./25 g) honey
½ cup plus 1 tablespoon (3 ¾ oz./110 g)
granulated sugar
Generous ½ cup, (1 ¾ oz./50 g) ground
blanched* almonds
Scant cup (2 ¾ oz./80 g) cake flour
1 teaspoon plus 1 heaped ¼ teaspoon (5 g)
baking powder
2 ¼ tablespoons (½ oz./16 g) unsweetened
cocoa powder
⅓ cup (50 ml) whipping cream

Chocolate crémeux

4 ⅔ oz. (130 g) bittersweet chocolate,
70 percent cocoa
2 large egg yolks (1 ¾ oz./50 g)
2 tablespoons (1 oz./25 g) granulated sugar
½ cup (125 ml) whole milk
½ cup (125 ml) whipping cream

Whipped white chocolate-coffee ganache*

2 ¾ oz. (80 g) white chocolate, 35 percent cocoa
3 tablespoons plus 1 teaspoon (50 ml) espresso coffee
½ cup minus 1 tablespoon (115 ml) whipping cream

Coffee granita

¼ cup (1 ¾ oz./50 g) granulated sugar
1 ¼ cups (300 ml) black coffee

Chocolate opalines

½ lb. (225 g) pouring fondant*
(online or at specialty stores)
5 ½ oz. (150 g) glucose syrup
⅔ oz. (20 g) bittersweet chocolate,
70 percent cocoa, chopped

Chocolate sauce

¾ cup (200 ml) whole milk
6 oz. (170 g) bittersweet chocolate, 70 percent cocoa

Equipment

1 jelly (Swiss) roll pan lined with parchment paper
6–8 pastry circles†, 2 in. (5 cm) diameter
1 silicone baking mat†
1 immersion blender†
1 large freezer-proof dish
1 whisk†

White Chocolate-Coffee Dessert with a Whiff of Dark Chocolate ★ ★ ★

Serves 6–8

Preparation time: 2 hours 30 minutes
Cooking time: 10 minutes
Refrigeration time: overnight
Freezing time: overnight

A day ahead, prepare the chocolate cake batter (see p. 85).
Use the proportions given opposite. Pour out the batter onto a pan lined with parchment paper and bake for 10 minutes. When it has cooled, cut out disks and place them at the bottom of the pastry circles on a silicone baking mat.

Prepare the chocolate *crémeux* (see p. 100).
Use the proportions given opposite. Pour the mixture over the sponge layers and leave to set overnight in the refrigerator.

Prepare the whipped white chocolate-coffee ganache.
Chop the chocolate and melt it slowly in a bain-marie* or in the microwave oven (on "defrost" or at 500 W maximum, stirring from time to time). Prepare the espresso and pour it gradually over the melted chocolate. Process with an immersion blender to a smooth emulsion. Pour in the cold cream and process again. Chill to harden, preferably overnight.

Prepare the coffee granita.
Dissolve the sugar in the hot coffee and pour it into a large freezer-proof dish. Freeze overnight, scraping regularly with a fork.

The next day, prepare the chocolate opalines (see p. 50).
Store them in an airtight container.

Prepare the chocolate sauce (see p. 127).
Remove the ganache from the refrigerator and whisk* it until the texture is creamy.

To serve, remove the pastry circles from the sponge base* and chocolate cream. Drizzle the sauce attractively round the base of the plates. Place the sponge base with the cream in the center of each plate, top with a small scoop of white chocolate-coffee ganache and decorate with the chocolate opalines. Accompany with a small glass of coffee granita.

Techniques

Opalines ›› p. 50
Chocolate Cake Batter ›› p. 85
Whipped Ganache ›› p. 97
Chocolate *Crémeux* ›› p. 100
Chocolate Granita ›› p. 123
Chocolate Sauce ›› p. 127

Chocolate Cream with Jelled Coffee ★ ★

Serves 8
Preparation time: 20 minutes
Cooking time: 12 minutes
Refrigeration time: 2 hours 30 minutes

Prepare the chocolate creams.
Chop the chocolate and melt it slowly in a bain-marie* or in the microwave oven (on "defrost" or at 500 W maximum, stirring from time to time). Heat the milk in a saucepan, removing it from the heat just before it comes to the boil. Gradually pour one-third of the hot milk over the melted chocolate. Using a flexible spatula, mix it in energetically, drawing small circles to create an elastic, shiny "kernel." Incorporate the second third of the liquid, using the same procedure. Repeat with the last third until the mixture is quite smooth and creamy. Beat the egg and extra yolk together and stir into the chocolate mixture.
Pour the cream into the small glasses or bowls and cover them with plastic wrap. Place them in a steamer basket or colander. Put them over gently sim-mering water, cover the pot with the lid, and cook for 10 to 12 minutes. This is the time required for a glass with a diameter of 2 in. (5 cm) containing just over 1 in. (3 cm) of cream. The cream is done when the surface offers a little resistance to the touch; the interior should not be liquid.
Immediately chill the creams by placing them in a bowl of ice water and then leave to set in the refrigerator.

Prepare the jelled coffee.
Soften the gelatin in a bowl of cold water. Prepare a scant ½ cup (100 ml) of very strong coffee, preferably espresso. Wring the water out of the gelatin and incorporate it into the hot coffee until it is dissolved. Pour it into a small dish so that it is just under ½ in. (1 cm) deep. Chill for at least 2 hours, until quite set. Cut into small dice.

Serve the chocolate creams well chilled and accompany with the small cubes of jelled coffee.

Technique
Melting Chocolate >> p. 19

Ingredients
Chocolate cream
5 oz. (140 g) bittersweet chocolate
60 percent cocoa
Or 4 ¼ oz. (120 g) bittersweet chocolate
70 percent cocoa
Scant ½ cup (100 ml) milk
1 egg
1 egg yolk

Jelled coffee
1 sheet (2 g) gelatin
Scant ½ cup (100 ml) strong espresso coffee

Equipment
8 shot glasses or small bowls
1 steamer basket or couscous pot with colander
1 flexible spatula†

Ingredients

Lime-scented white chocolate *crémeux*

Zest* of 2 unwaxed limes

1 ½ sheets (3 g) gelatin

5 egg yolks

¼ cup (1 ¾ oz./50 g) granulated sugar

1 cup (250 ml) whole milk

1 cup (250 ml) whipping cream

8 oz. (225 g) white chocolate, 35 percent cocoa

Exotic fruit syrup

Zest of 1 unwaxed lime

Zest of ½ unwaxed orange

Scant ⅓ cup (70 ml) water

¼ cup (1 ¾ oz./50 g) granulated sugar

½ passion fruit

Phyllo roses

5 to 6 sheets phyllo pastry

3 tablespoons plus 1 teaspoon (50 g) butter

Confectioners' sugar for dusting

Exotic fruit salad

1 banana

½ grapefruit

½ pineapple

1 orange

1 mango

Equipment

1 kitchen thermometer†

1 baking sheet

1 immersion blender†

1 zester†

1 chinois†

1 flexible spatula†

1 pastry brush†

1 whisk†

Techniques

Melting Chocolate ›› p. 19

Chocolate *Crémeux* ›› p. 100

Exotic Fruit with Lime-Scented White Chocolate *Crémeux* ★ ★

Serves 6–8

Preparation time: 1 hour 30 minutes

Refrigeration time: overnight

Cooking time: 10 minutes

Resting time: 15 minutes

A day ahead, prepare the lime-scented white chocolate *crémeux*.

Finely chop the zest of the limes. Soften the gelatin in a bowl of cold water. While it is softening, whisk* the egg yolks, sugar, and zest in a mixing bowl. Pour the mixture into a saucepan and add the milk and cream. Simmer gently, stirring constantly, until the mixture coats the back of a spoon. It should reach a temperature of 180°F–183°F (82°C–84°C). Remove from the heat and pour the custard into a deep mixing bowl. Process for a few seconds with an immersion blender for a smooth, creamy texture. Incorporate the gelatin, stirring until completely dissolved. Strain the custard through a chinois. Chop the chocolate and melt it slowly in a bain-marie* or in the microwave oven (on "defrost" or at 500 W maximum, stirring from time to time). Gradually pour one-third of the hot custard over the melted chocolate. Using a flexible spatula, mix in energetically, drawing small circles to create an elastic, shiny "kernel." Incorporate the second third of the liquid, using the same procedure. Repeat with the last third. Process with an immersion blender for a smooth, creamy texture. Chill overnight.

The next day, prepare the exotic fruit syrup.

Finely grate the zest of the lime and orange. Bring the water and sugar to the boil and add the finely grated zest. Remove from the heat and leave to infuse for 5 to 10 minutes. Strain through a chinois and add the seeds scooped out of the half passion fruit. Set aside in the refrigerator.

Prepare the phyllo pastry roses.

Preheat the oven to 350°F (180°C). Unroll the sheets of phyllo pastry and cut each one into half. Crumple them up to give them some volume–they should look like a rose. Place them on a baking sheet and leave to dry out for about 15 minutes. While they are drying out, melt the butter and then lightly brush the crumpled sheets of phyllo. Dust them generously with confectioners' sugar and bake for a few minutes, until golden and lightly caramelized*.

Peel the fruit and cut them into fine dice. Arrange the diced fruit in soup plates, or other deep plates. Pour the exotic fruit syrup over the diced fruit.

To serve, arrange a scoop of lime-scented white chocolate *crémeux* in each plate and garnish with a crisp phyllo rose.

● **Chef's notes**

Place the phyllo roses in the plates at the last moment so that they don't go soggy in the syrup.

Tonka Bean-Scented Ivory Panna Cotta with Strawberry Coulis ★

Serves 8
Preparation: 40 minutes
Refrigeration time: overnight

A day ahead, prepare the white chocolate panna cotta.
Soften the gelatin in a bowl of cold water. Chop the chocolate and melt it gently in a bain-marie* or in the microwave oven (on "defrost" or at 500 W maximum, stirring from time to time).
Bring the milk to the boil. Wring the excess water out of the gelatin and dissolve it in the hot milk. Remove from the heat immediately.
Slowly pour one-third of the hot mixture over the melted chocolate. Using a flexible spatula, briskly mix it in with a small circular movement to create an elastic, shiny "kernel." Then incorporate another third of the hot liquid, using the same circular movement, and finally, the last third, still mixing with a circular movement. Pour in the cold whipping cream and grate the half tonka bean into the mixture. Process with an immersion blender until the mixture is perfectly smooth and emulsified*. Before you pour it into silicone molds or small glasses, wait until it just starts to thicken. This will ensure that the grated tonka bean does not rise directly to the surface. Chill overnight.

Prepare the strawberry coulis.
Set aside several whole strawberries for garnish and cut the others into small pieces. Leave them in a mixing bowl. Bring the water and sugar to the boil and pour the syrup over the cut strawberries. Chill overnight.

The next day.
Carefully pour the strawberries into a colander over a bowl to catch the juice. It should be perfectly transparent, so make sure you don't crush any strawberries into it. Drizzle the juice over the panna cotta and garnish with a few strawberry halves, and even raspberries if you wish.

● Chef's note
For a refreshing dessert, serve this panna cotta cold with light green tea.

Techniques
Melting Chocolate ›› p. 19
Chocolate Panna Cotta ›› p. 105

Ingredients
Ivory panna cotta
1 sheet (2 g) gelatin
6 oz. (175 g) white chocolate, 35 percent cocoa
¾ cup (200 ml) milk
1 ¼ cups (300 ml) whipping cream
½ tonka bean

Strawberry coulis
4 ⅔ oz. (130 g) strawberries
1 cup (250 ml) water
2 tablespoons (1 oz./25 g) granulated sugar

Equipment
1 immersion blender†
8 silicone molds† or small glasses
1 flexible spatula†
1 colander
1 grater†

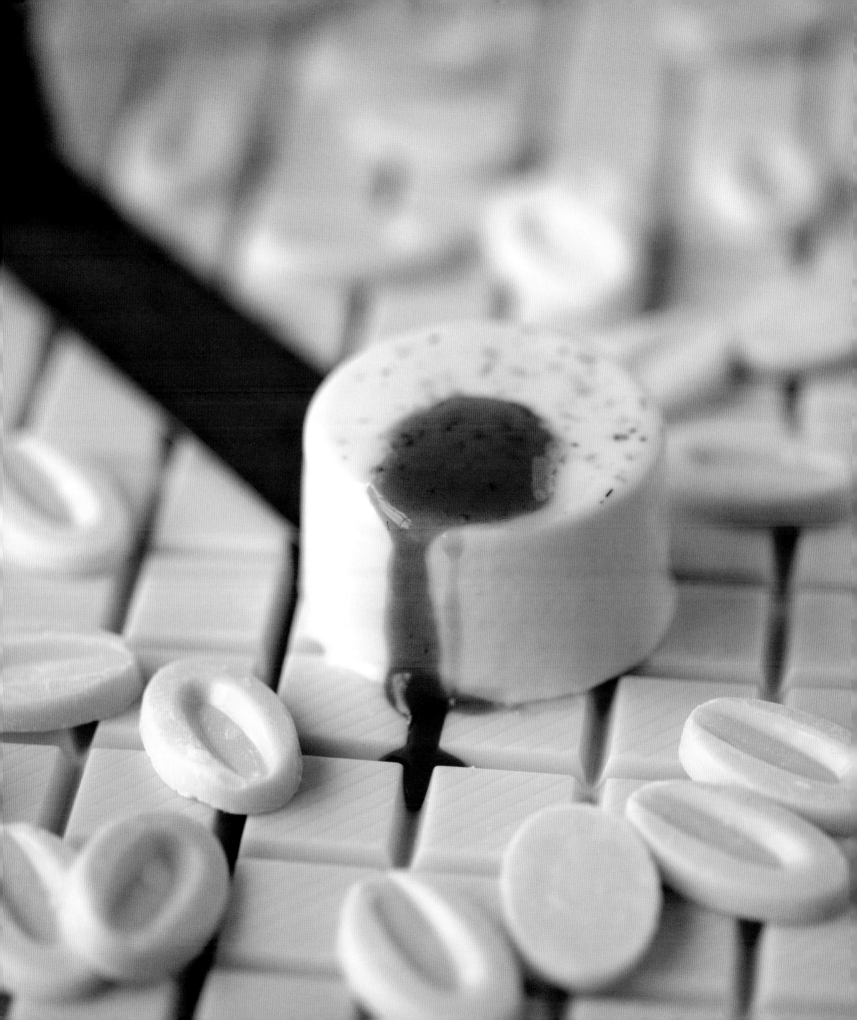

Ingredients

Bittersweet chocolate panna cotta

2 sheets (4 g) gelatin
4 ⅔ oz. (130 g) bittersweet chocolate,
60 percent cocoa
¾ cup (200 ml) milk
1 ¼ cup (300 ml) whipping cream

Pineapple sticks "sous vide"

⅔ cup (150 ml) pineapple juice
14 oz. (400 g) fresh pineapple
1 tablespoon plus 2 teaspoons (20 g)
light brown sugar (cassonade)
1 tablespoon (15 ml) brown rum

Thai-style lemongrass foam

2 cups (500 ml) whole milk
¼ cup (1 ¾ oz./50 g) granulated sugar
3 sticks lemongrass
½ vanilla bean
2 sheets (4 g) gelatin
½ cup (120 ml) unsweetened coconut milk

Equipment

1 immersion blender†
1 chinois†
1 siphon†
8 shot glasses, preferably square
1 kitchen thermometer†
1 flexible spatula†

Techniques
Melting Chocolate >> p. 19
Chocolate Panna Cotta >> p. 105

Bittersweet Chocolate Panna Cotta with Thai-style Lemongrass Foam ★★

Serves 6-8
Preparation time: 1 hour 45 minutes
Cooking time: 25 to 30 minutes
Refrigeration time: overnight

A day ahead, prepare the bittersweet chocolate panna cotta.
Soften the gelatin in a bowl of very cold water. Chop the chocolate and melt it slowly in a bain-marie* or in the microwave oven (on "defrost" or at 500 W maximum, stirring from time to time). Bring the milk and cream to the boil. When the gelatin has softened, wring out the water and dissolve it in the milk-cream mixture. Remove from the heat as soon as it has dissolved. Slowly pour one-third of the hot mixture over the melted chocolate. Using a flexible spatula, briskly mix it in with a small circular movement to create an elastic, shiny "kernel." Then incorporate another third of the hot liquid, using the same circular movement, and finally, the last third, still mixing with a circular movement.
Process with an immersion blender to ensure that the mixture is smooth and well emulsified*.
Pour into the shot glasses and chill overnight.

The next day, prepare the pineapple sticks.
Bring the pineapple juice to the boil and reduce by half. Peel the pineapple and cut it into little sticks. Combine the pineapple sticks with the light brown sugar and rum and then stir in the reduced juice. Place the combined ingredients in a plastic bag, expel the air, and seal with an elastic band. Put the bag into a pot of hot water heated to 167°F-176°F (75°C-80°C) and cook for 25 to 30 minutes.

Prepare the Thai-style lemongrass foam.
Bring the milk and sugar to the boil and reduce until 1 ½ cups (350 ml) remain. Thinly slice the lemongrass sticks, setting some aside for a garnish. Slit the half vanilla bean lengthways and scrape out the seeds. Incorporate these two flavorings into the reduced milk. Leave to infuse for 30 minutes and strain through a chinois. Soften the gelatin in a bowl of cold water. Wring out the excess water and dissolve it in the hot flavored milk. Stir in the coconut milk and pour the liquid into a siphon. Set aside in the refrigerator to chill for at least 3 to 4 hours.

To serve, arrange the pineapple sticks over the panna cotta in the glasses, then press out the foam from the siphon to fill the shot glasses. Garnish with thin slices of lemongrass.

● Chef's note
A good alternative to pineapple sticks is mango cubes. Cook them for about 20 minutes, depending on how ripe the mango is.

Verrines of Hot Chocolate Mousse, Cooked Cream, and Softened Berries ★★

Serves 6-8
Preparation time: 45 minutes
Cooking time: 20 minutes
Refrigeration time: 35 minutes

Prepare the cooked vanilla cream.
Preheat the oven to 200°F (90°C-100°C). Bring the milk and sugar to the boil in a saucepan. Slit the vanilla bean and scrape the seeds out into the hot milk. Leave to infuse for a few minutes and then filter through a sieve.
Combine the chilled cream with the egg yolks. Pour the vanilla-infused milk over this mixture and mix thoroughly. Pour it into the glasses and bake for about 17 to 20 minutes, until the surface offers some resistance to the touch but the interior is not liquid.

Prepare the softened raspberries and blueberries.
Combine the raspberries and sugar in a saucepan and heat to boiling point. Allow to simmer for 1 to 2 minutes then add the blueberries. Again, leave to simmer briefly. Set aside in the refrigerator.

Prepare the hot bittersweet chocolate mousse.
Chop the chocolate and melt it slowly in a bain-marie* or in the microwave oven (on "defrost" or at 500 W maximum, stirring from time to time).
Combine the sugar and agar-agar, then stir into the milk and bring to the boil. Gradually pour one-third of the boiling liquid over the melted chocolate. Using a flexible spatula, mix it in energetically, drawing small circles to create an elastic, shiny "kernel."
Incorporate the second third of the liquid, using the same procedure. Repeat with the last third. Pour the hot mixture into a siphon, keeping it in a bain-marie at 113°F-122°F (45°C-50°C) so that you can serve it hot.

When the cooked vanilla cream is done, cool it in the refrigerator for 30 minutes. Then place a spoonful of softened berries on the top and return it to the refrigerator. Just before serving, press out the hot chocolate mousse from the siphon.

● **Chef's notes**
It's essential to allow the agar-agar to boil, otherwise it will have no jelling strength.
Grate a few chocolate shavings over the mousse for a nice textural contrast— you'll have both melting softness and crunch.

Technique
Melting Chocolate >> p. 19

Ingredients

Cooked vanilla cream
¼ cup (65 ml) whole milk
¼ cup (1 ¾ oz./50 g) granulated sugar
1 vanilla bean
⅔ cup plus 2 teaspoons (190 ml) whipping cream, well chilled
4 egg yolks

Softened raspberries and blueberries
Scant ⅓ cup (2 ¼ oz./65 g) granulated sugar
2 ⅔ oz. (75 g) raspberries
1 ¾ oz. (50 g) blueberries

Hot bittersweet chocolate mousse
2 ¾ oz. (80 g) bittersweet chocolate, 70 percent cocoa
2 tablespoons (1 oz./25 g) granulated sugar
½ teaspoon (1 g) agar-agar powder
½ cup plus 2 teaspoons (135 ml) whole milk

Equipment
1 sieve†
8 shot glasses or small bowls
1 flexible spatula†
1 siphon†
1 kitchen thermometer†

Chocolate Mousse and
Creamy Caramel in a Spoon ★ ★

Serves 6-8
Preparation time: 1 hour 30 minutes
Refrigeration time: overnight

A day ahead, prepare the chocolate mousse.
Chop the chocolate and melt it slowly in a bain-marie* or in the microwave oven (on "defrost" or at 500 W maximum, stirring from time to time).
Soften the gelatin in a bowl of very cold water.
Bring the milk to the boil in a saucepan. Immediately remove from the heat. Wring the water out of the gelatin and incorporate it into the hot milk.
Slowly pour one third of the hot mixture over the melted chocolate. Using a flexible spatula, briskly mix it in with a small circular movement to create an elastic, shiny "kernel." Then incorporate another third of the hot liquid, using the same circular movement, and finally, the last third, still mixing with a circular movement.
Using either a whisk or an electric beater, whisk* the well-chilled cream until it forms soft peaks–it will be softly whipped (see p. 134).
When the chocolate mixture cools to 95°F-113°F (35°C-45°C) (otherwise the cream will melt), fold in* the softly whipped cream carefully with a flexible spatula. Chill overnight.

The next day, prepare the creamy caramel.
Bring the cream to the boil in a small saucepan. In a large saucepan, melt the honey, then gradually pour in the sugar, stirring constantly until you have a light caramel. Slowly pour in the hot cream, taking care that the caramel does not splutter, and bring the mixture to 217°F (103°C).
Leave to cool at room temperature.
Place small scoops of the mousse in Chinese-style soupspoons and drizzle with creamy caramel sauce. Sprinkle with nuts of your choice.

Technique
Egg-Free Chocolate Mousse >> p.111

Ingredients
Chocolate mousse
6 ⅓ oz. (180 g) bittersweet chocolate,
60 percent cocoa
1 ½ sheets (3 g) gelatin
⅔ cup (170 ml) whole milk
1 ½ cups (350 ml) whipping cream

Creamy caramel*
¾ cup (200 ml) whipping cream
1 tablespoon (20 g) honey
Scant ½ cup (3 ¼ oz./90 g) granulated sugar

Nuts of your choice

Equipment
1 flexible spatula[†]
1 hand-held electric beater[†] or whisk[†]
1 kitchen thermometer[†]
8 Chinese-style soupspoons for serving

Teatime treats

Christophe Felder

presents his recipe

There are many advantages to serving a chocolate dish: you're practically sure that it will be liked, for one thing, and for another, chocolate is a product that adapts to innumerable easy recipes. I notice when I teach nonspecialized pastry classes that the technique required to make a ganache* is generally easily learned. Only cutting and decorating it require professional skills.

I'm an advocate of simplicity, of mastering the taste of the final product. In pastry making, one should remain classic: a pastry or dough and a cream are the bases of the most popular recipes. Next, the quality of the ingredients affects the outcome and the way in which they are appreciated.

Here, I have chosen to interpret a recipe for the Gâteau basque, a specialty of the Basque region in south-west France. I have already made variations on this classic with strawberry, almond, cherries, and more.

Chocolate, when combined with a little almond paste, lemon, and orange takes on a whole new dimension.

I use Valrhona cocoa powder, and when it comes to the *grands crus*, I prefer Guanaja. Côte-Rôtie is one of the finest of Rhône wines; for me this is the chocolate equivalent.

Gâteau Basque with Chocolate

Pastry. Soften the butter, and place it with the granulated sugar and ground almonds in a mixing bowl. Combine with a flexible spatula, then add the finely grated lemon zest and mix again. Incorporate the egg and, when the mixture is thoroughly combined, add the flour, cocoa powder, and salt. Mix the ingredients in and cover the dough in plastic wrap. Chill for 1 hour.

Chocolate cream. Bring the milk and cream to the boil over medium heat in a saucepan. Whisk* the egg yolks, sugar, cocoa powder and cornstarch briefly together. Set aside.

When the milk-cream mixture reaches a simmer, add the whisked egg yolk, cornstarch and sugar mixture, whisking as you pour it in. Continue to stir the mixture until it thickens. When the cream has reached the right consistency, add the butter and chopped chocolate, stirring constantly.

Process with an immersion blender to emulsify*. Leave to cool. Soften the almond paste in the microwave oven on low power. Incorporate the rum into the almond paste. Then mix in the ground almonds and the orange zest. Add to the chocolate cream. Ensure the cream is smooth, cover it with plastic wrap; and reserve at room temperature.

To assemble. Preheat the oven to 350°F (180°C).
Roll out the dough to a thickness of ½ in. (1 cm). Cut out 2 squares, one 8 ½ × 8 ½ in. (22 × 22 cm) and the other 9 ½ × 9 ½ in. (24 × 24 cm). Butter the cake pan. Place the smaller square in the pan, reserving the larger one for the top.
Cut off 3 oz. (80 g) of the leftover dough and roll it evenly to form a log shape to surround the inside of the cake pan. Prick the dough base lightly with a fork. Using a piping bag with a plain tip, pipe the chocolate cream over the pastry base. Place the larger square over this, taking care that there are no air bubbles. Press down firmly at the edges to close securely so that none of the cream escapes during baking. Chill for 10 minutes.

Red glaze. To prepare the red glaze, beat the egg yolks with the red coloring. Brush the top layer of pastry with the glaze. To decorate, make shallow incisions in the pastry with a knife tip. Bake for about 30 minutes. Leave the cake to cool in the pan for a few minutes before removing it carefully.

Equipment
1 flexible spatula†
1 whisk†
1 pastry brush†
1 immersion blender†
1 rolling pin†
1 square baking pan, 10 × 10 in. (25 × 25 cm)
1 piping bag† fitted with a plain tip†

Serves 8

Ingredients
Pastry
1 ½ sticks (6 oz./175 g) unsalted butter, softened
⅔ cup (4 ½ oz./125 g) granulated sugar
1 cup (3 oz./85 g) ground blanched* almonds
Finely grated zest* of ½ unwaxed lemon
1 egg
2 ¼ cups (7 oz./200 g) cake flour
3 tablespoons (¾ oz./20 g) Valrhona cocoa powder
1 pinch salt

Chocolate cream
⅔ cup (150 g) milk
⅓ cup (80 g) whipping cream, 32 percent butterfat
2 egg yolks (1 ½ oz./40 g)
1 ½ oz. (40 g) sugar
2 tablespoons (20 g) cornstarch
1 ½ tablespoons (⅓ oz./10 g) Valrhona cocoa powder
1 tablespoon plus 1 teaspoon (¾ oz./20 g) butter
1 ¾ oz. (50 g) Guanaja chocolate, 80 percent cocoa
2 ¾ oz. (80 g) almond paste, 70 percent almonds
1 teaspoon (5 g) rum
Generous ½ cup, (1 ¾ oz./50 g) finely ground blanched almonds or almond meal
⅓ oz. (10 g) orange zest

Red glaze
½ teaspoon (0.4 g) carmine red food coloring
2 egg yolks (1 ½ oz./40 g)

Chocolate-Pecan Ladyfingers ★

Serves 8

Preparation time: 35 to 40 minutes
Cooking time: 25 minutes
Chilling time: 4 hours

Prepare the ganache 3 to 4 hours ahead of time.
This is so it can be chilled. Chop the chocolate and melt it slowly in a bain-marie* or in the microwave oven (on "defrost" or at 500 W maximum, stirring from time to time). Bring the whipping cream to the boil and add the butter and honey.
Gradually pour one third of the boiling mixture over the melted chocolate. Using a flexible spatula, mix it in energetically, drawing small circles to create an elastic, shiny "kernel." Incorporate the second third of the mixture, using the same procedure. Repeat with the last third. Add the butter. Process for a few seconds using an immersion blender so that the mixture is smooth and perfectly emulsified*.
Chill for 3 to 4 hours.

Prepare the biscuit layer.
Preheat the oven to 325°F (160°C).
In a large mixing bowl, combine the egg yolks, muscovado sugar, honey, and scant ¼ cup (1 ⅔ oz./45 g) sugar until the ingredients are just mixed. Set aside. Soften the butter. Chop the chocolate and melt it slowly in a bain-marie or in the microwave oven (on "defrost" or at 500 W maximum, stirring from time to time).
Add the softened butter to the melted chocolate.
Whip* the egg whites, gradually pouring in the ⅓ cup (2 ½ oz./70 g) sugar until the whites are shiny.
Fold* the chocolate-butter mixture into the egg yolk and sugar mixture. Stir in the flour and the chopped nuts. Then carefully fold in the whipped egg whites. Spread out the batter on the lined baking sheet to a thickness of about ⅔ in. (1.5 cm) and sprinkle with sesame seeds. Bake for about 25 minutes, until the tip of a knife inserted into the biscuit comes out dry. Remove from the oven and leave to rest for 5 minutes. Then turn it out onto a sheet of parchment paper. Place in the freezer for a few minutes and then cut out into finger shapes, 3 × ¾ in. (8 × 2 cm).

To finish:
Once the fingers have cooled, pipe a strip of ganache along each one.

● **Chef's note**
Hardening the sponge in the freezer makes it easy to cut it out into finger shapes.

● **Did you know?**
Muscovado sugar is brown sugar made from sugar cane in Mauritius. Its high molasses content gives it a very marked taste.

Ingredients

Biscuit layer
3 eggs, separated
4 lightly packed tablespoons plus 1 teaspoon (1 ⅔ oz./45 g) muscovado sugar
2 slightly heaped tablespoons (45 g) chestnut or pine honey
Granulated sugar, divided as follows: scant ¼ cup (1 ⅔ oz./45 g) plus ⅓ cup (2 ½ oz./70 g)
1 ⅓ stick (5 ½ oz./150 g) butter
3 ¼ oz. (90 g) bittersweet chocolate, 70 percent cocoa
7 tablespoons (1 ½ oz./40 g) cake flour
2 ½ oz. (70 g) chopped pecan nuts
2 ½ oz. (70 g) chopped cashew nuts
White sesame seeds for sprinkling

Bittersweet ganache*
4 ⅔ oz. (130 g) bittersweet chocolate, 70 percent cocoa
Generous ⅓ cup (90 ml) whipping cream
3 tablespoons plus 1 teaspoon (1 ¾ oz./50 g) butter
1 ½ tablespoons (1 oz./30 g) honey

Equipment
1 baking sheet lined with parchment paper, or 1 silicone baking mat†
1 piping bag†
1 flexible spatula†
1 immersion blender†
1 whisk†

Techniques
Melting Chocolate ›› p. 19
Ganache for Hand-Dipped Centers ›› p. 33

Ingredients

Almond and Anise Streusel
2 ½ teaspoons (10 g) light brown sugar (*cassonade*)
1 tablespoon plus 1 scant tablespoon (⅓ oz./10 g)
ground blanched* almonds
1 tablespoon plus 2 ½ teaspoons (⅓ oz./10 g)
cake flour
Small pinch salt
1 pinch ground green anise
2 teaspoons (⅓ oz./10 g) butter, well chilled

Pistachio loaf cake
1 tablespoon (½ oz./15 g) butter
⅓ cup (2 ⅔ oz./75 g) granulated sugar
1 egg
1 pinch table salt
2 tablespoons plus 1 teaspoon (35 ml)
whipping cream
⅔ cup (2 oz./60 g) cake flour
¼ teaspoon (1 g) baking powder
1 oz. (30 g) pistachio paste (see p. 42)

Light chocolate cake
1 tablespoon plus 1 teaspoon (⅔ oz./20 g) butter
⅓ cup (1 oz./30 g) cake flour
½ teaspoon (2 g) baking powder
1 tablespoon (¼ oz./8 g) unsweetened cocoa powder
1 egg
¼ cup (1 ¾ oz./50 g) granulated sugar
¼ cup (⅔ oz./20 g) ground blanched almonds
1 ¼ oz. (35 g) bittersweet chocolate,
60 or 70 percent cocoa
2 tablespoons (30 ml) whipping cream
1 egg white

A few candied cherries, such as Amarena cherries

Equipment
1 baking sheet or 1 silicone baking mat†
1 whisk†
1 loaf pan, 10 in. (25 cm)
Parchment paper

Techniques
Melting Chocolate ›› p. 19
Pistachio Paste ›› p. 42
Chocolate-Almond Streusel ›› p. 88

Chocolate-Pistachio Loaf
with Almond and Anise Streusel ★

Serves 6
Preparation time: 45 minutes
Cooking time: 1 hour 10 minutes

Prepare the almond and anise streusel.
Preheat the oven to 300°F-325°F (150°C-160°C). In a mixing bowl, combine the brown sugar, ground almonds, flour, salt, and ground anise. Finely dice the chilled butter and incorporate it into the mixture using your fingers until it forms a crumbly texture. Spread it out on a baking sheet or silicone baking mat. Bake for about 10 minutes, until it is a nice amber color.

Prepare the pistachio loaf cake.
Heat the butter in a saucepan until it is just melted. In a mixing bowl, combine the sugar with the egg, salt, and whipping cream until the texture is liquid. Sift the flour with the baking powder and stir it into the mixture until it forms a dough.
Lightly soften the pistachio paste in the microwave oven and mix a little of it into the batter. When this mixture is quite smooth (the pistachio paste will have softened, so it will be easier to incorporate), mix it in to the remaining batter with the melted butter.

Prepare the light chocolate cake.
Heat the butter in a saucepan until it is just melted. Sift the flour with the baking powder and cocoa powder and set aside. Whisk* the egg with the sugar until thick and pale. Add the ground almonds and the other, sifted dry ingredients. Stir them in until just mixed. Set aside at room temperature.
Chop the chocolate and melt it slowly in a bain-marie* or in the microwave oven (on "defrost" or at 500 W maximum, stirring from time to time).
Heat the whipping cream and combine it with the melted chocolate. Add the chocolate-cream mixture to the dough, then stir in the melted butter. Whisk the egg white and fold* it in carefully.

Preheat the oven to 300°F (150°C).
Line the loaf pan with parchment paper. Pour the pistachio batter into the bottom of the pan. Scatter a few cherries over the batter, taking care that they do not touch the sides of the pan. Pour in the chocolate batter, and then sprinkle the baked streusel over it. Bake for about 1 hour. Check for doneness with the tip of a knife. The cake is ready when it comes out dry.

● Chef's note
This cake will develop its aromas overnight. Wrap it in plastic wrap so that it keeps well. If you like a crisp crust, wrap the cake once it has cooled down. On the other hand, if you prefer it soft, wrap it while it is still warm.

Chocolate-Banana Loaf Cake
with Rum-Soaked Raisins ★ ★

Serves 6

Preparation time: 20 minutes
Cooking time: 40 to 50 minutes
Chilling time: overnight

A day ahead.
Rinse the sultanas under boiling water and plump them up by simmering over low heat in the white rum and water until the liquid has been completely absorbed.

Prepare the cake batter.
Place the butter in a saucepan over low heat until just melted. Chop the chocolate and melt it slowly in a bain-marie* or in the microwave oven (on "defrost" or at 500 W maximum, stirring from time to time). Pour the melted butter over the chocolate and then pour the mixture into the bowl of a food processor. Add the granulated and muscovado sugar. Process until smooth, then add the egg yolk and process again. Add the eggs, one by one, combining each time–the batter must remain smooth while you prepare it. Add the puréed bananas. Add the ground hazelnuts, cocoa nibs, flour, and baking powder and process again until just combined.
Chill for 15 minutes to allow the batter to harden.

Preheat the oven to 350°F (180°C).
While the batter is chilling, chop the milk chocolate. Take the batter out of the refrigerator and stir in the rum-flavored sultanas and chopped milk chocolate. Line a loaf pan with parchment paper; alternatively, butter it and dust it with flour, rapping it upside down to remove any excess. Bake for about 45 minutes, until it is well risen.
When you remove the cake from the oven, moisten it with the brown rum and grate a little nutmeg over the top. While it is still hot, cover it tightly in plastic wrap. All the rum flavors will penetrate the cake and none of the taste or the alcohol will evaporate. Leave to chill overnight in the refrigerator.

● Chef's notes

The batter is placed in the refrigerator to allow it to harden; this is so that the sultanas and chocolate pieces do not sink to the bottom of the pan.
This cake takes rather long to bake because of the puréed bananas. Baking time will vary depending on their ripeness.
Because there are so few dry ingredients in this recipe, the cake will always remain moist, however it is stored.

Ingredients
Generous ⅓ cup (2 ¼ oz./60 g) golden sultanas
3 tablespoons plus 1 teaspoon (50 ml) white rum
Scant tablespoon water

Cake batter
2 ¾ oz. (80 g) bittersweet chocolate,
60 percent cocoa
7 tablespoons (3 ½ oz./100 g) butter, plus a little
extra to grease the pan
3 ½ tablespoons (1 ½ oz./40 g) granulated sugar
2 lightly packed tablespoons (⅔ oz./20 g)
muscovado, light brown sugar (*cassonade*),
or other brown sugar
1 egg yolk
3 eggs
7 oz. (200 g) very ripe, almost black bananas
(about 2 bananas), puréed
Scant ½ cup (1 ½ oz./40 g) ground hazelnuts
1 ½ oz. (40 g) cocoa nibs*
Generous ½ cup (1 ¾ oz./50 g) cake flour
1 teaspoon (4 g) baking powder
5 ½ oz. (150 g) milk chocolate, 40 percent cocoa

A little brown rum
A little grated nutmeg

Equipment
1 loaf pan, 10 in. (25 cm)
1 food processor fitted with a blade attachment
Parchment paper
Plastic wrap

Technique
Melting Chocolate ≫ p. 19

Chocolate, Coconut, and Passion Fruit Cakes ★ ★ ★

Serves 6-8
Preparation time: 50 minutes
Cooking time: 10 minutes
Chilling time: 2 hours
Freezing time: overnight

A day ahead, prepare the almond nougatine.
Melt the butter with the glucose syrup in a saucepan. Combine the granulated sugar with the pectin and add this mixture to the saucepan. Then stir in the cocoa powder, and lastly, the finely chopped almonds. Remove immediately from the heat and pour the mixture onto a sheet of parchment paper. Cover it with a second sheet and roll it out thinly using a rolling pin. Place it flat (on a baking sheet if preferred) in the freezer for about 30 minutes.

Prepare the jelled passion fruit.
In a saucepan, heat the passion fruit pulp, glucose syrup, pectin, 1 ½ tablespoons (⅔ oz./20 g) granulated sugar, and honey. Then add the remaining ½ cup (3 ½ oz./100 g) sugar and bring the mixture to a temperature of 221°F (105°C). Immediately stir in the citric acid and pour the fruit mixture into a confectionery frame placed on a lined baking sheet (or lined brownie pan). It should be just under ½ in. (1 cm) thick. Freeze overnight.

The next day, prepare the soft coconut-chocolate sponge.
Sift the flour and baking powder together. Combine the sugar, honey, milk, egg, and finely ground coconut with the sifted dry ingredients.
Melt the butter. Chop the chocolate and melt it slowly in a bain-marie* or in the microwave oven (on "defrost" or at 500 W maximum, stirring from time to time). Combine the melted butter with the melted chocolate and stir this mixture into the batter. Leave to rest for about 2 hours in the refrigerator.

Preheat the oven to 350°F-360°F (170°C-180°C).

To assemble, cut out the nougatine into the same sized shapes as the molds. Spoon the batter into a piping bag. Place the pieces of nougatine at the base of each mold and pipe out the batter over the nougatine–you should have a layer just under ½ in. (1 cm) thick. Cut out a rectangle of jelled passion fruit and place it on the sponge batter. To finish, pipe out some more of the coconut-chocolate sponge. Bake for about 10 minutes, until a nice golden color.

● **Chef's note**
The apple pectin is essential for the nougatine to hold in this recipe, so be sure to use it.

● **Did you know?**
Apple pectin, yellow pectin, and citric acid can often be found in specialized baking stores and on Internet baking sites.

Ingredients

Almond nougatine
4 tablespoons (60 g) butter
1 heaped tablespoon (1 oz./25 g) glucose syrup
⅓ cup (2 ⅔ oz./75 g) granulated sugar
½ teaspoon (1 g) apple pectin
(from specialty stores or online)
1 tablespoon (¼ oz./8 g) unsweetened cocoa powder
3 ¼ oz. (90 g) finely chopped almonds

Jelled passion fruit (*pâte de fruits*)
6 oz. (175 g) passion fruit pulp
(available from specialty store or online)
3 tablespoons (1 ½ oz./45 g) glucose syrup
½ teaspoon (1 g) yellow pectin (slow-hardening pectin, from specialty stores or online)
Granulated sugar, divided as follows:
1 ½ tablespoons (⅔ oz./20 g)
plus ½ cup (3 ½ oz./100 g)
1 tablespoon (20 g) honey
¼ teaspoon (1 g) citric acid solution, 50 percent

Soft coconut-chocolate sponge
7 tablespoons (1 ½ oz./40 g) cake flour
½ teaspoon (2 g) baking powder
¼ cup (1 ¾ oz./50 g) granulated sugar
2 slightly heaped tablespoons (45 g) honey
¼ cup (60 ml) whole milk
1 extra large egg (2 ¼ oz./60 g)
2 ¼ oz. (60 g) finely ground coconut (powder form)
3 tablespoons (1 ⅔ oz./45 g) butter
1 ¾ oz. (50 g) bittersweet chocolate, 70 percent cocoa

Equipment
1 kitchen thermometer†
Rectangular silicone molds†,
2 ¾ in. × ⅔ in. (7 cm × 2 cm)
1 confectionery frame† or brownie pan
1 baking sheet
1 piping bag†
1 rolling pin†

Techniques
Melting Chocolate ›› p. 19
Pâte de Fruits (jelled fruits) ›› p. 45
Nougatine with Cocoa Nibs or Nuts ›› p. 59

Cookies ★

Makes about 30 cookies

Preparation time: 15 minutes
Cooking time: 12 minutes per baking sheet

Preheat the oven to 350°F (170°C). In a mixing bowl, soften the butter (see p. 134). Then cream it with the light brown sugar. Add the egg. Sift the flour and baking powder together into the mixture and incorporate. Stir in the chopped chocolate, nuts, and pieces of caramel and mix until thoroughly combined.
Shape small balls of dough, about 1 ½ in. (4 cm) in diameter, and flatten them very lightly on the baking sheet. Place them about 3 in. (8 cm) apart and bake for about 12 minutes.

● Chef's note
Don't flatten the cookies too much when you place them on the baking sheet: that way, they will remain soft inside and crisp outside.

Ingredients
1 ½ sticks (6 ⅓ oz./180 g) unsalted butter
Scant ⅔ cup (4 ¼ oz./120 g) light brown sugar (*cassonade*)
1 egg
2 cups (6 ⅓ oz./180 g) cake flour
1 teaspoon plus 1 heaped ¼ teaspoon (5 g) baking powder
5 ½ oz. (150 g) chopped chocolate
5 ½ oz. (150 g) mixed nuts (pecans, macadamia, cashew, walnuts, etc), roughly chopped
3 Carambar candies (a French caramel and cocoa toffee about 3 in./8 cm long), cut into pieces, or other similar chewy candy

Equipment
1 baking sheet lined with parchment paper.

Ingredients

Milk chocolate Genoa loaf

3 tablespoons plus 1 teaspoon (1 ¾ oz./50 g) butter

2 ⅔ oz. (75 g) milk chocolate, 40 percent cocoa

5 ⅔ oz. (160 g) almond paste (see p. 41)

⅓ cup (1 oz./30 g) cake flour

½ teaspoon (2 g) baking powder

3 eggs

2 teaspoons (10 ml) anise liqueur,
such as raki, pastis, arak, or ouzo (optional)

1 Granny Smith apple

Water with a little lemon juice squeezed in

2 ½ oz. (70 g) pearl sugar (coarse sugar grains)

Equipment

1 kitchen thermometer†

12 small silicone molds†

1 Japanese mandolin

1 whisk†

Mini Apple Chocolate Genoa Cakes ★★

Makes 12 small cakes

Preparation time: 20 minutes

Cooking time: 14 minutes

Prepare the milk chocolate Genoa loaf.

Melt the butter. Chop the chocolate and melt it slowly in a bain-marie* or in the microwave oven (on "defrost" or at 500 W maximum, stirring from time to time). Stir in the melted butter.

Soften the almond paste slightly in the microwave oven so that it is easier to incorporate into the batter. Sift the flour and baking powder together and set aside. Whisk* the eggs in a bowl placed over simmering hot water until the temperature reaches 122°F (50°C). Gradually pour the beaten eggs over the almond paste, stirring constantly. As soon as the mixture is quite smooth, carefully fold in* the sifted dry ingredients. Then stir in the liqueur, if using, and the mixture of melted chocolate and butter.

Fill the molds to three-quarters with the batter. Preheat the oven to 325°F–350°F (160°C-170°C)

Prepare the julienned apple.

Wash and peel the apple. Prepare a julienne (fine strips) with the mandolin. Dip the strips of apple in the water with the lemon juice to prevent them from oxidizing. Drain them and dry them on paper towel. Scatter the julienned apple over tops of the Genoa loaves and then sprinkle with the pearl sugar.

Bake for about 14 minutes. They should be soft to the touch (though not liquid) and lightly colored.

● Chef's notes

When the mini-cakes have cooled, they may be frozen and defrosted as you require.

Techniques

Melting Chocolate ≫ p. 19

Almond Paste ≫ p. 41

Chocolate Genoa Loaf ≫ p. 89

Crisp Shortbread and Nuts
with Chocolate ★ ★ ★

Serves 6–8
Preparation time: 45 minutes
Cooking time: 20 minutes
Freezing time: 1 to 2 hours
Setting time: 12 hours

A day ahead, prepare the almond nougatine.
Combine the sugar with the pectin in a mixing bowl. Melt the butter and glucose syrup in a saucepan and add the sugar-pectin mixture. Then stir in the cocoa powder, and lastly, the chopped almonds. Remove from the heat and immediately pour the nougatine over a sheet of parchment paper. Cover with another sheet and roll it out thinly using a rolling pin. Carefully place it, completely flat, in the freezer for 1 to 2 hours. Cut out small 1 ¼ in. (3 cm) diameter rounds with the cookie cutter.

Prepare the piped shortbread pastry.
Sift the confectioners' sugar. Soften the butter (see p. 134) and cream it with the confectioners' sugar. Incorporate the egg and the cream. Lastly, add the flour, cornstarch, salt, and vanilla. Be careful not to overmix.
Preheat the oven to 300°F-325°F (150°C-160°C).
Pipe out a circle of shortbread pastry into each silicone mold. Place a round of frozen almond nougatine above the circle of pastry and scatter with a few whole pistachios. Bake for 15 to 20 minutes, until a light gold color. Leave for 2 to 3 minutes before turning them out of the molds to cool.

Temper* the chocolate using the method of your choice (see p. 20). When the shortbread cookies have cooled, dip the smooth side in the tempered chocolate. Leave to harden for 12 hours.

● Chef's note
To make thicker chocolate disks, wait until you have turned out the shortbread from the molds. Pipe out the chocolate into the bottom of the mold just used for baking and place the cookies above. Leave to harden and turn out of the mold.

Techniques
Tempering ≫ p. 20
Nougatine with Cocoa Nibs or Nuts ≫ p. 59
Piped Shortbread Pastry ≫ p. 73

Ingredients
Piped shortbread pastry
¾ cup (3 ½ oz./100 g) confectioners' sugar
1 ⅓ stick (5 ½ oz./150 g) butter
1 egg
1 tablespoon (15 g) whipping cream
2 ¼ cups (7 oz./200 g) cake flour
2 tablespoons (⅔ oz./20 g) cornstarch
1 pinch salt
1 pinch vanilla seeds or ground vanilla

Almond nougatine
⅓ cup (2 ⅔ oz./75 g) granulated sugar
½ teaspoon (1 g) apple pectin
(from specialist stores or online)
4 tablespoons (2 ¼ oz./60 g) butter
1 heaped tablespoon (1 oz./25 g) glucose syrup
(from specialist stores or online)
1 tablespoon (¼ oz./8 g) unsweetened cocoa powder
3 ¼ oz. (90 g) chopped almonds

A few green pistachios
10 ½ oz. (300 g) bittersweet chocolate,
60 or 70 percent cocoa

Equipment
1 rolling pin†
2 sheets of parchment paper
8 silicone molds†, 2 ¾ in. (7 cm) diameter
1 piping bag† fitted with a star-shaped
½ in. (12 mm) tip†
1 cookie cutter†, 1 ¼ in. (3 cm) diameter

Chocolate *Financiers*, Citrus Streusel, and Candied Orange Peel ★ ★

Serves 6–8

Preparation time: 30 minutes
Cooking time: 30 minutes
Refrigeration time: 2 to 3 hours

Prepare the chocolate *financiers*.

Combine the ground almonds, confectioners' sugar, cornstarch, and cocoa powder in a mixing bowl. Lightly beat the egg whites with a fork to liquefy them. Incorporate the egg whites and whipping cream into the dry ingredients. Set aside the batter.

Chop the chocolate and melt it slowly in a bain-marie* or in the microwave oven (on "defrost" or at 500 W maximum, stirring from time to time).

Pour a little of the batter over the melted chocolate, stirring energetically with a flexible spatula to combine. Then fold* this mixture back into the remaining batter carefully. Chill for at least 2 to 3 hours. This is an important stage in the recipe, as it will allow the *financiers* to rise well when baked.

Prepare the citrus-flavored almond streusel.

Combine the brown sugar, ground almonds, flour, and finely grated* zests in a mixing bowl. Cut the butter into small dice and mix it into the preparation using your hands until it reaches a crumbly texture.

Chill for at least 30 minutes. Preheat the oven to 300°F–325 °F (150°C-160°C). Arrange the crumbly dough on a baking sheet or silicone baking mat. Bake for about 10 minutes, until nicely browned.

Prepare the *financiers* for baking.

Preheat the oven to 350°F (170°C).

Pour the chocolate batter into the molds and sprinkle with diced candied orange and baked streusel crumbs. Total baking time is 15 to 20 minutes. However, to ensure that the streusel and diced orange peel stay at the top of these little cakes, you may bake them in two stages. Bake the *financier* batter for 4 minutes, then sprinkle them with the two ingredients, and return to the oven for about 10 minutes.

● **Did you know?**

Silicone molds need no buttering. However, if the cakes do not come out of the molds, leave them to cool until they do, or place them briefly in the freezer.

Techniques

Melting Chocolate >> p. 19
Chocolate *Financier* Batter >> p. 83
Chocolate-Almond Streusel >> p. 88

Ingredients

Chocolate *financiers**

2 ¼ cups (6 ¾ oz./190 g) ground blanched* almonds
1 generous cup (5 ½ oz./150 g) confectioners' sugar
1 tablespoon (⅓ oz./10 g) cornstarch
1 ½ tablespoons (⅓ oz./10 g)
unsweetened cocoa powder
9 egg whites
⅓ cup (75 ml) whipping cream
1 ¾ oz. (50 g) bittersweet chocolate,
60 percent cocoa

Citrus-flavored almond streusel

4 tablespoons (1 ¾ oz./50 g) light brown sugar
Generous ½ cup (1 ¾ oz./50 g) ground
blanched almonds
Generous ½ cup (1 ¾ oz./50 g) cake flour
Zest* of ½ unwaxed orange
Zest of ½ unwaxed lemon
3 tablespoons plus 1 teaspoon (50 g) butter

8 ½ oz. (240 g) diced candied orange peel

Equipment

1 piping bag†
Baking sheet with *financier* molds†
1 baking sheet or 1 silicone baking mat†
1 flexible spatula†

Ingredients

3 ½ oz. (100 g) candied lemon peel
(alternatively, use orange peel)
¾ cup (5 ½ oz./150 g) granulated sugar
2 ½ tablespoons (1 ¾ oz./50 g) honey
½ cup plus 2 ½ tablespoons (160 ml)
whipping cream
1 ¾ oz. (50 g) pine nuts
3 ½ oz. (100 g) sliced almonds
14 ½ oz. (400 g) bittersweet chocolate,
70 percent cocoa, divided

Equipment

1 kitchen thermometer†
12 stainless steel pastry circles†, about
4 in. (10 cm) diameter or silicone molds†
1 silicone baking mat†
1 food processor fitted with a blade attachment
1 spatula†

Florentines ★ ★ ★

Serves 10-12
Preparation time: 10 minutes
Cooking time: 12 minutes

Preheat the oven to 300°F (150°C).
Cut the candied lemon peel into fine dice. Place the 12 pastry circles on a silicone baking mat.
In a thick-bottomed saucepan, combine the sugar, honey, and cream. Heat to a temperature of 244°F (118°C), then stir in the nuts and diced lemon peel.
Divide this mixture into the pastry circles, flattening it so that it is smooth and evenly distributed. Place in the oven and bake the Florentines for 10 to 15 minutes, until they turn a nice amber color. Remove from the oven and take off the pastry circles. Leave to cool.

Temper* the chocolate.
Finely chop 3 ½ oz. (100 g) of the chocolate, or process it in a food processor. Set aside. Chop the remaining chocolate using a knife with a serrated edge. Better still, use chocolate pistoles, buttons, or fèves. Melt it slowly in a bain-marie*, or in the microwave oven on "defrost" or at 500 W maximum.
Stir the chocolate at regular intervals so that it melts smoothly.
Check the temperature. When it reaches 131°F-136°F (55°C-58°C), remove the bowl from the bain-marie. Set aside one-third of the melted chocolate in a bowl in a warm place. Add the finely 3 ½ oz. (100 g) chopped or processed chocolate into the two-thirds of the melted chocolate, stirring constantly. The chocolate should reach a temperature of 82°F-84°F (28°C-29°C). Gradually add the remaining hot chocolate to increase the temperature to 88°F-90°F (31°C-32°C), stirring as you do so.

Use a spatula to cover the smooth surface (the under side) of each Florentine with the melted tempered chocolate.

● Chef's notes
Remove the florentines from their circles using a knife as soon as you take them out of the oven, when they are still pliable. If they start to harden, just pop them back into the oven very briefly.
These delicious classic cookies keep in an airtight container, in a dry place, for two to three days.

Technique
Tempering >> p. 20

Cupcakes ★★

Makes 18 cupcakes

Preparation time: 40 minutes
Cooking time: 15 minutes
Refrigeration time: 3 hours

Prepare the chocolate cupcakes.

Preheat the oven to 325°F (160°C). Melt the butter and set it aside. Chop the chocolate and melt it slowly in a bain-marie* or in the microwave oven (on "defrost" or at 500 W maximum, stirring from time to time). Stir in the melted butter. Sift the almonds, flour, cocoa, and baking powder ingredients together. Whisk* the eggs, honey, and sugar together until thick. Stir in the dry ingredients. Then stir in the whipping cream, and lastly, the melted chocolate and butter.
Spoon the batter into a piping bag and pipe it out into the cups to two-thirds of their height. Bake for about 15 minutes, until the tip of a knife or cake tester comes out dry.

Prepare the cupcake batter with your choice of flavoring.

Preheat the oven to 325°F (160°C). Melt the butter and set it aside. Combine the sugar, eggs, salt, and cream. Sift the flour with the baking powder and stir it into the egg mixture. Stir in the melted butter and your flavoring.
Spoon the batter into a piping bag and pipe it out into the cups to two-thirds of their height. Bake for about 15 minutes, until a nice golden color and the tip of a knife or cake tester comes out dry.

Make the whipped ganache (to flavor or color).

Chop the white chocolate and melt it slowly in a bain-marie or in the microwave oven (on "defrost" or at 500 W maximum, stirring from time to time). Bring the scant ½ cup (110 ml) cream to the boil. Gradually pour one-third of the boiling cream over the melted chocolate. Using a flexible spatula, mix it in energetically, drawing small circles to create an elastic, shiny "kernel." Incorporate the second third of the cream, using the same procedure. Repeat with the last third.
Stir the remaining cream (cold) into the ganache. Flavor or color it as you wish. Leave to set for at least 3 hours in the refrigerator, then whip* it until the texture softens.
To prepare the whipped bittersweet chocolate ganache, use the same procedure.

Ice and decorate.

Pipe out a decorative rosette of whipped ganache over the cupcakes using a piping bag fitted with a star-shaped tip. Follow your whims for the decoration.

● Chef's note

Whipped ganache must be eaten within 2 days.

Techniques
Basic Cake Batter ›› p. 84
Chocolate Cake Batter ›› p. 85
Whipped Ganache ›› p. 97

Ingredients

Chocolate cupcake batter
5 ½ tablespoons (2 ¾ oz./80 g) butter
1 ¾ oz. (50 g) bittersweet chocolate,
70 percent cocoa
1 cup minus 1 tablespoon (2 ⅔ oz./75 g) ground
blanched* almonds
1 ⅓ cups (4 ¼ oz./120 g) cake flour
3 ½ tablespoons (1 oz./25 g)
unsweetened cocoa powder
2 level teaspoons (8 g) baking powder
5 eggs
3 ½ tablespoons (2 ⅔ oz./75 g) honey
⅔ cup (4.4 oz./125 g) sugar
½ cup (120 ml) whipping cream

Or Plain cupcake batter (to flavor)
5 ½ tablespoons (2 ¾ oz./80 g) butter
1 ⅔ cups (11 oz./310 g) granulated sugar
5 eggs
1 pinch table salt
Generous ½ cup (135 ml) whipping cream
2 ⅔ cups (8 ½ oz./240 g) cake flour
1 level teaspoon (4 g) baking powder
Flavor of your choice, such as spices or citrus zest

Whipped ganache*, to flavor or color
5 ⅔ oz. (160 g) white chocolate, 35 percent cocoa
Whipping cream, divided as follows: ½ cup minus 1
tablespoon (110 ml) plus 1 cup plus 1 tablespoon (170 g)
Your choice of flavoring, such as citrus zest*,
spices, essential oils, etc.

Or
Whipped bittersweet chocolate ganache
Whipping cream, divided as follows: ½ cup minus
1 tablespoon (110 ml) plus 1 cup minus
3 tablespoons (200 ml)
3 ¼ oz. (90 g) bittersweet chocolate,
70 percent cocoa

Decorations
Crystallized* flowers, pearls,
chocolate sprinkles, fruit, etc.

Equipment
1 piping bag† fitted with a star-shaped tip†
1 flexible spatula†
1 whisk†
18 cupcake liners

Saint-Génix Brioche with Chocolate-Coated Almonds and Hazelnuts ★ ★ ★

Serves 8
Resting time: about 24 hours
Preparation time: 1 hour 30 minutes
Cooking time: 40 minutes

A day ahead, prepare the sourdough starter.
Early in the morning (at about 7 a.m.), combine the yeast, milk, and flour in a mixing bowl. Leave the starter to rise* at room temperature for about 5 to 6 hours.

Coat the almonds and hazelnuts.
Roast the almonds and hazelnuts (see p. 134). Leave them to cool.
Temper* the chocolate (see p. 20) and pour it into a mixing bowl. Using a dipping fork, dip small quantities of almonds and hazelnuts into the chocolate, allow the excess to drip off, and place on a sheet of parchment paper. Leave to harden. Repeat the operation until you have used all the nuts.

Prepare the dough for the Saint-Génix.
At about 2 p.m., knead* all the ingredients together with the yeast starter using the dough hook of your stand-alone mixer. Knead for 20 minutes at the lowest speed. Leave the dough to rest for 20 minutes, then knead again for 30 minutes at the next lowest speed. Cover with a clean, damp cloth and leave to rise until the dough has doubled in volume. Depending on the room temperature, this should take 3 to 5 hours.
When it has doubled in volume, punch down the dough to remove the air bubbles until it has returned to its initial volume. Incorporate the chocolate-coated nuts, using your hands. To do this, roll the dough into a square, add some nuts, fold, add more nut, and fold again. Shape the dough into a ball and place it on a baking sheet lined with parchment paper.
Cover with a clean, damp cloth and leave to rise overnight (about 12 hours).

The next morning, preheat the oven to 325°F-350°F (160°C-170°C).
Dip a pastry brush into a beaten egg and brush the surface of the dough. Then make incisions 4 to 6 incisions, just under ½ in. (1 cm) deep, and sprinkle with sugar pearls.
Bake for about 40 minutes.

● **Chef's note**
It's best to wait until the Saint-Génix is lukewarm before eating it, as the flavors only develop fully when it has cooled down considerably.

Techniques
Tempering » p. 20
Roasting Nuts » p. 134

Ingredients
Yeast starter
⅓ oz. (10 g) compressed yeast
¼ cup (60 ml) milk
½ cup (1 ¾ oz./50 g) all-purpose flour

Saint-Génix dough
2 eggs
Scant ½ cup (3 ¼ oz./90 g) granulated sugar
2 teaspoons (10 ml) orange blossom water
6 tablespoons (3 ¼ oz./90 g) butter
2 tablespoons (30 ml) rum
3 pinches salt
2 ½ cups (9 oz./250 g) all purpose-flour

Coated almonds and hazelnuts
5 oz. (150 g) whole almonds and hazelnuts, peeled*
5 oz. (150 g) bittersweet chocolate, 60 percent cocoa

1 egg (for the egg wash)
Pearl sugar for sprinkling

Equipment
1 stand-alone mixer† fitted with a dough hook
1 kitchen thermometer†
1 dipping fork†
1 rolling pin†
1 pastry brush†

Hot Chocolate Drinks ★

Traditional Hot Chocolate

Serves 6
Preparation time: 10 minutes
Cooking time: 10 minutes

Bring the milk to the boil with the cocoa powder.
Chop the chocolate and melt it slowly in a bain-marie* or in the microwave oven (on "defrost" or at 500 W maximum, stirring from time to time).
Pour one-third of the boiling cocoa-flavored milk over the melted chocolate, whisking* as you do so, until the texture is smooth, elastic, and shiny. Pour in the remaining liquid, whisking continuously.
Return the liquid to the heat, whisking energetically to form a light, creamy foam with small, compact air bubbles.

Almond-Flavored Hot Chocolate

Serves 6
Preparation time: 15 minutes
Cooking time: 10 minutes

Bring the milk to the boil. To soften the almond paste, place it in the microwave oven on low power (400 to 500 W) for about 40 seconds. Blend it with the milk.
Chop the chocolate and melt it slowly in a bain-marie* or in the microwave oven (on "defrost" or at 500 W maximum, stirring from time to time).
Pour one-third of the boiling liquid over the melted chocolate, whisking* as you do so, until the texture is smooth, elastic, and shiny. Pour in the remaining liquid, whisking continuously.
Return the liquid to the heat, whisking energetically to form a light, creamy foam with small, compact air bubbles.

Spiced Hot Chocolate

Serves 6
Preparation time: 20 minutes
Cooking time: 10 minutes

Bring the milk to the boil with the spices. Remove from the heat and leave to infuse for a few minutes before filtering through a fine-mesh sieve.
Chop the chocolate and melt it slowly in a bain-marie* or in the microwave oven (on "defrost" or at 500 W maximum, stirring from time to time).
Pour one-third of the boiling liquid over the melted chocolate, whisking* as you do so, until the texture is smooth, elastic, and shiny. Pour in the remaining liquid, whisking continuously.
Return the liquid to the heat, whisking energetically to form a light, creamy foam with small, compact air bubbles.

Ingredients

Traditional Hot Chocolate
3 cups plus scant ½ cup (850 ml)
whole or partially skimmed milk
1 tablespoon unsweetened cocoa powder
6 ½ oz. (185 g) bittersweet chocolate,
70 percent cocoa

Almond-Flavored Hot Chocolate
3 cups plus generous ⅓ cup (840 ml)
whole or partially skimmed milk
1 ¾ oz. (50 g) almond paste (see p. 41)
5 ⅔ oz. (160 g) bittersweet chocolate,
60–70 percent cocoa

Spiced Hot Chocolate
4 cups (1 liter) whole or partially skimmed milk
1 scant teaspoon (2 g) mixed spices,
either store-bought or homemade,
containing star anise, nutmeg (or mace),
cardamom, cloves, cinnamon, and ginger.
2 sticks cinnamon
3 ½ oz. (100 g) bittersweet chocolate,
60 percent cocoa
3 ½ oz. (100 g) milk chocolate, 40 percent cocoa

Ingredients

Earl Grey-Scented Hot Chocolate
3 cups plus 1 scant ¼ cup (800 ml)
whole or partially skimmed milk
¾ cup (200 ml) whipping cream
⅓ oz. (2 tablespoons, 10 g) Earl Grey tea leaves
6 ⅓ oz. (180 g) bittersweet chocolate,
65 percent cocoa

Hazelnut-Flavored Hot Chocolate
3 cups plus 1 scant ¼ cup (800 ml) whole
or partially skimmed milk
¾ cup (200 ml) whipping cream
⅔ oz. (20 g) homemade hazelnut paste
(see recipe p. 42)
9 oz. (250 g) milk chocolate, 40 percent cocoa

Equipment
1 whisk† or blender
1 fine-mesh sieve†

Earl Grey-Scented Hot Chocolate

Serves 6
Preparation time: 20 minutes
Cooking time: 10 minutes

Bring the milk and the cream to the boil. Infuse the Earl Grey tea leaves for a few minutes and filter through a fine-mesh sieve.
Chop the chocolate and melt it slowly in a bain-marie* or in the microwave oven (on "defrost" or at 500 W maximum, stirring from time to time).
Pour one-third of the boiling liquid over the melted chocolate, whisking* as you do so, until the texture is smooth, elastic, and shiny. Pour in the remaining liquid, whisking continuously.
Return the liquid to the heat, whisking energetically to form a light, creamy foam with small, compact air bubbles.

Hazelnut-Flavored Hot Chocolate

Serves 6
Preparation time: 10 minutes
Cooking time: 10 minutes

Chop the chocolate and melt it slowly in a bain-marie* or in the microwave oven (on "defrost" or at 500 W maximum, stirring from time to time).
Bring the milk, cream, and hazelnut paste to the boil and stir well to mix.
Gradually pour one-third of the boiling liquid over the melted chocolate, whisking* as you do so, until the texture is smooth, elastic, and shiny. Pour in the remaining liquid, whisking continuously.
Return the liquid to the heat, whisking energetically to form a light, creamy foam with small, compact air bubbles.

● Chef's note
To obtain a very creamy foam for all these recipes, use a blender.

Techniques
Melting Chocolate >> p. 19
Almond Paste >> p. 41
Hazelnut Paste >> p. 42

Ingredients
3 ½ oz. (100 g) bittersweet chocolate,
70 percent cocoa
1 ½ oz. (40 g) milk chocolate,
40 percent cocoa
2 cups (500 ml) whole milk
1 ¼ cups (300 ml) espresso coffee
Ice cubes

Equipment
1 flexible spatula†
1 chinois†
1 shaker†

Cafe con Choco ★

Serves 6-8
Preparation time: 15 minutes plus 1-2 hours chilling time
Cooking time: 10 minutes

Chop the bittersweet and milk chocolate and melt it slowly in a bain-marie* or in the microwave oven (on "defrost" or at 500 W maximum, stirring from time to time).
Bring the milk to the boil. Gradually pour one-third of the boiling liquid over the melted chocolate. Using a flexible spatula, mix in energetically, drawing small circles to create an elastic, shiny "kernel." Incorporate the second third of the liquid, using the same procedure. Repeat with the last third. Strain through a chinois and chill.
When the chocolate is cold, prepare the espresso coffee and pour it into a shaker. Add ice cubes, cool, and shake the coffee. Pour the cold chocolate into the shaker and shake again. To serve, add ice cubes to the glasses.

● **Chef's note**
You can drink this in summer just as you can in winter, at breakfast or at teatime. It's a delicious alternative to iced milk coffee.

Technique
Melting Chocolate >> p. 19

Teh Tarik with Chocolate ★

Serves 6
Preparation time: 20 minutes
Cooking time: 10 minutes

Chop the chocolate and melt it slowly in a bain-marie* or in the microwave oven (on "defrost" or at 500 W maximum, stirring from time to time).

Heat the water until it is simmering. Pour it over the tea leaves and leave to infuse for 5 minutes, then filter through a sieve.

Pour one-third of the hot tea over the melted chocolate, whisking* so that you have a smooth, elastic, and shiny texture. Then pour in the remaining liquid, whisking continuously.

Lastly, add the cold sweetened condensed milk, and process it with an immersion blender or in the blender to make a nice foam. Serve immediately.

● Chef's note
If you prefer this drink cold, don't add the sweetened condensed milk.

● Did you know?
The word tarek refers to the way in which the tea is mixed and poured in a thin stream so that it bubbles. It is drunk in Southeast Asia, particularly Malaysia.
Pu-Erh tea takes its name from the city of Pu'er in the Chinese province of Yunnan. It is very rare and highly sought after. Unlike other teas, it increases in quality as it ages.
When this drink is taken cold, the tea accentuates the bitterness of the chocolate.

Technique
Melting Chocolate >> p. 19

Ingredients
5 oz. (140 g) bittersweet chocolate,
70 percent cocoa
2 cups (500 ml) water
1 oz. (2 ½ tablespoons, 25 g)
Pu-Erh tea, or other fine black tea
¼ cup (60 ml) sweetened condensed milk

Equipment
1 immersion blender† or blender
1 sieve†
1 whisk†

Ingredients

½ vanilla bean
3 ¼ cups (800 ml) whole milk
¾ cup (200 ml) whipping cream
1 ½ cups (10 ½ oz./300 g) granulated sugar
5 ½ oz. (7 tablespoons, 150 g) glucose syrup
2 ½ tablespoons (1 ¾ oz./50 g) honey
3 ½ oz. (100 g) milk chocolate,
40 percent cocoa

Equipment

1 kitchen thermometer[†]
Small jelly jars

Milky Chocolate Jelly ★ ★

Serves 6-8

Preparation: 40 to 60 minutes
Cooking time: 30 minutes

Sterilize your jars before using them: leave them in a 200°F (90°C-95°C) oven for 20 minutes.

Slit the ½ vanilla bean lengthways and scrape out the seeds into the milk. Bring the milk, cream, sugar, glucose syrup, vanilla seeds and bean, and honey to the boil. Leave to simmer for about 30 minutes, until the mixture caramelizes* slightly and coats the back of a spoon. The temperature at this stage will be about 215°F-217°F (102°C-103°C). Remove the vanilla bean.

Chop the chocolate and melt it slowly in a bain-marie* or in the microwave oven (on "defrost" or at 500 W maximum, stirring from time to time). Stir the melted chocolate into the milk mixture.

Fill the pots immediately with the hot mixture and place in the refrigerator. Keeps for 1 week.

Technique
Melting Chocolate >> p. 19

Milk Chocolate *Palets* with Caramel ★★

Serves 6-8
Preparation time: 45 minutes
Cooking time: 9 minutes
Resting time: 4 hours 30 minutes

Prepare the caramel bonbon filling.
Chop the chocolate.
In a saucepan, heat the water, then stir in the 1 ¼ cups (240 g) sugar.
Dip a pastry brush in water and brush the sugar crystals away from the sides to dissolve all the sugar. Bring the syrup to a temperature of 350°F (180°C). While it is heating, combine the cream, glucose syrup, salt, and scant ½ cup (80 g) sugar in another saucepan and bring to the boil. When the water, glucose, and sugar mixture reaches the desired temperature of 350°F (180°C), carefully add the cubed butter. Stir briefly and then add the hot cream mixture and the chopped chocolate. The temperature of the mixture will be lowered. Stir continuously until the mixture reaches 250°F (120°C). Pour the caramel into the confectionery frame or prepared brownie pan. Leave to cool at room temperature for about 4 hours. Cut into 1 ¾ in. (2 cm) squares.

Prepare the sponge cake.
Chop the chocolate and melt it slowly in a bain-marie* or in the microwave oven (on "defrost" or at 500 W maximum, stirring from time to time). In a mixing bowl, soften the butter (see p. 134).
Pour the melted chocolate over the softened butter and mix until the ingredients have combined smoothly. Add the eggs one by one, stirring each time and ensuring that the mixture remains smooth. Slightly heat the milk. Take 4 oz. (115 g) of the cut-out caramels and melt them in the heated milk. Incorporate the milk-caramel mixture into the chocolate-egg mixture. Sift in the flour, and combine.

To assemble.
Preheat the oven to 350°F (180°C). Place one caramel bonbon in each mold. Spoon the caramel sponge cake coating into a piping bag and pipe it out over the bonbon. Bake for about 9 minutes, until the tip of a knife comes out dry. Remove from the oven and leave to cool for 30 minutes before turning out of the molds.

Techniques
Melting Chocolate ≫ p. 19
Caramel Filling for Hand-Dipped Centers ≫ p. 43

Ingredients
Sponge cake
1 ¾ oz. (50 g) milk chocolate, 40 percent cocoa
1 stick (4 ½ oz./125 g) butter
2 eggs
4 oz. (115 g) caramel filling (see below)
2 teaspoons (10 ml) whole milk
Scant ⅔ cup (2 ¼ oz./60 g) all-purpose flour

Caramel* bonbon filling
3 ½ oz. (100 g) milk chocolate, 40 percent cocoa
Scant ¼ cup (50 g) water
Granulated sugar divided as follows: 1 ¼ cup (8 ½ oz./240 g) plus scant ½ cup (80 g)
⅔ cup (180 g) whipping cream
2 ⅔ oz. (75 g) glucose syrup
2 pinches table salt
2 tablespoons (30 g) butter, cubed

Equipment
1 pastry brush†
1 kitchen thermometer†
6 to 8 silicone molds†
1 confectionery frame†, 8 in. (20 cm) square brownie pan, or 4 confectionery rulers†
1 baking sheet lined with parchment paper
1 piping bag†

Ingredients

3 eggs

Scant ⅔ cup (4 ¼ oz./120 g) granulated sugar

Scant ⅔ cup (4 ¼ oz./120 g) light brown sugar (*cassonade*)

3 ¼ oz. (90 g) bittersweet chocolate, 60 percent cocoa

1 ½ sticks (6 oz./170 g) butter

7 tablespoons (1 ½ oz./40 g) cake flour

1 ½ tablespoons (10 g) unsweetened cocoa powder

A handful of walnuts and/or pecan nuts, macadamia nuts, or Valrhona chocolate pearls, chopped chocolate or chocolate chips

Equipment

1 brownie pan, 8 in. (20 cm) square

or 1 tart pan, 8 in. (20 cm) diameter

lined with parchment paper

Brownies ★

Serves 8

Preparation time: 10 minutes

Cooking time: 20 minutes

Preheat the oven to 325°F (160°C).

In a mixing bowl, combine the eggs with the two types of sugar, being careful to ensure that the mixture does not bubble.

Chop the chocolate with the butter and melt slowly in a bain-marie* or in the microwave oven (on "defrost" or at 500 W maximum, stirring from time to time).

Stir the melted chocolate and butter into the egg and sugar mixture.

Sift in the flour and cocoa together and stir in until just mixed.

Pour the batter into the lined brownie pan or tart pan. Sprinkle with nuts of your choice, or chocolate pearls, or any of the alternatives. Bake for about 20 minutes. The brownies should be softly cooked, almost molten.

Leave to cool in the pan.

Serve when cooled.

● Chef's notes

To make it easier to cut up the brownies, place the pan in the freezer for a few minutes.

These brownies are even more delicious with a scoop of vanilla ice cream, salted butter caramel sauce, and a little Chantilly cream.*

Technique
Melting Chocolate ›› p. 19

Chocolate-Filled Croissant Cubes ★ ★ ★

Makes 8–10 croissant cubes

Preparation time: 5 hours
Resting time: 3 hours 30 minutes
Refrigeration time: 1 hour
Freezing time: 5 minutes
Cooking time: 14 minutes

Prepare the croissant dough (see p. 79).
When the dough is ready, chill it for 1 hour before rolling it out.

In the meantime, prepare the chocolate pastry cream (see p. 103).
Spread out three strips of pastry cream on a sheet of plastic wrap. They should each measure 11 × 2 ¾ in. and be ⅛ in. thick (28 cm × 7 cm, thickness 3 mm). Chill for 1 hour.

Prepare the croissant cubes.
Roll out the croissant dough to a thickness of ⅛ in. (3 mm). Cut out four strips, each 11 × 2 ¾ in., with a thickness of ⅛ in. (3 mm).
Spread a strip of pastry cream over the first layer of croissant dough. Cover it with another layer of dough. Continue, alternating pastry cream and croissant dough, and finishing with a layer of dough. Chill for 5 minutes to harden.
Cut out four slices, each measuring 1 ½ in. (4 cm), and then cut them in half.
Leave to rise* in the cube-shaped molds for 2 hours 30 minutes in a warm place, at 77°F (25°C).
Brush them with the egg yolk.
Preheat the oven to 350°F (175°C). Bake for 14 minutes.

● Chef's notes

Make sure you cut the slices just a little smaller than the cube-shaped molds so they do not completely lose their shape when they bake.
To make pains au chocolat, all you need to do is roll out the croissant dough into a strip 6–8 in. (15–20 cm) wide and cut out rectangles 3–4 in. (8–10 cm) wide. Place a stick of chocolate (if possible, the type specially made for pains au chocolat) near one end and start rolling the dough over. Then place another stick on the dough and roll until the end. The chocolate sticks should be well-enclosed within the rolled dough. Leave to rise for 2 hours, brush with egg yolk, and bake at 350°F (175°C) for about 15 minutes.

Techniques
Croissant Dough ›› p. 79
Chocolate Pastry Cream ›› p. 103

Ingredients

Croissant dough
6 cups (1 ⅓ lb./600 g) all-purpose flour
2 teaspoons (⅓ oz./10 g) salt
⅓ cup (2 ½ oz./70 g) granulated sugar
⅖ oz. (12 g) fresh (compressed) yeast
¾ cup (200 ml) very cold water
2 ⅘ sticks (11 ¼ oz./320 g) butter, well chilled

Chocolate pastry cream
3 oz. (85 g) bittersweet chocolate, 70 percent cocoa
Or 3 ⅓ oz. (95 g) bittersweet chocolate, 60 percent cocoa
1 tablespoon (⅓ oz./10 g) cornstarch
2 ½ tablespoons (1 oz./30 g) granulated sugar
2 egg yolks
1 cup minus 2 tablespoons (220 ml) whole milk
Scant ¼ cup (50 ml) whipping cream
1 egg yolk (to brush the top of the croissants)

Equipment
1 stand-alone mixer† fitted with a dough hook
1 rolling pin†
Plastic wrap
1 pastry brush†
8–10 cube-shaped molds†, 2 in. (5 cm)

Ingredients

Plain macaroon* shells
1 ¾ cups (5 ½ oz./150 g) blanched* ground almonds
1 generous cup (5 ½ oz./150 g) confectioners' sugar
¾ cup (5 ½ oz./150 g) granulated sugar
Scant ¼ cup (50 ml) water
3 ½ oz. (100 g) egg whites, weighed carefully
and divided into two equal parts
Powdered food coloring (optional)

Chocolate macaroon shells
1½ cups (4 ½ oz./125 g) ground almonds
3 ½ tablespoons (1 oz./25 g), cocoa powder, unsweetened
1 generous cup (5 ½ oz./150 g) confectioners' sugar
¾ cup (5 ½ oz./150 g) granulated sugar
3 ½ oz. (100 g) egg whites, weighed carefully
and divided into two equal parts
Scant ¼ cup (50 ml) water

Whipped* ivory ganache* (to flavor)
2 ¾ oz. (80 g) white chocolate, 35 percent cocoa
Whipping cream, divided as follows: 3 tablespoons
plus 1 teaspoon (50 ml) plus ½ cup
minus 1 tablespoon (110 ml)
Suggested flavorings: 1 tablespoon pistachio,
hazelnut, sesame, or other paste; or 1 tablespoon
(15 ml) orange blossom water, or grated zest* of
1 unwaxed lemon; or grated zest of 1 unwaxed orange;
or 1 vanilla bean; or a liqueur of your choice; or an
essential oil; or another flavoring of your choice

Bittersweet tonka bean ganache
3 ½ oz. (100 g) bittersweet chocolate,
70 percent cocoa
1 tonka bean
½ cup (120 ml) whipping cream, divided

Equipment
1 flexible spatula†
Plastic wrap, 1 spatula†, 1 piping bag†
1 kitchen thermometer†
1 baking sheet lined with parchment paper
or silicone baking mat†
1 stand-alone mixer† fitted with a whisk attachment

Techniques
Melting Chocolate >> p. 19
Macaroon Batter >> p. 82
Chocolate *Financier* Batter >> p. 83
Whipped Ganache >> p. 97
Piping out round macaroons >> p. 132

Assorted Macaroons ★ ★ ★ 🎬

Makes about 40 macaroons
Preparation time: 1 hour
Cooking time: 12 minutes per batch (one sheet per batch)
Total refrigeration time: 15 hours

A day ahead, prepare the bittersweet tonka bean ganache.
Chop the chocolate and melt it slowly in a bain-marie* or in the microwave oven
(on "defrost" or at 500 W maximum, stirring from time to time). Grate the tonka
bean into the cream. Bring the flavored cream to the boil in a saucepan. Gradually
pour one-third* of the boiling cream over the melted chocolate. Using a flexible
spatula, energetically mix the cream into the chocolate, drawing small, quick circles in the center to create a shiny, elastic "kernel." Incorporate the second third
and mix in the same way. Pour in the remaining third, using the same technique.
Leave to set at room temperature for 45 minutes.

Prepare the whipped ivory ganache.
Infuse the flavoring of your choice in the 3 tablespoons plus 1 teaspoon (50 ml)
whipping cream. Follow the directions for the ganache above, then stir in the
cold cream (½ cup minus 1 tablespoon (110 ml) whipping cream. Cover with
plastic wrap flush with the surface of the ganache, and chill for a minimum of
3 hours. Whisk* the ganache at medium speed until it reaches the consistency
of a thick cream that can be worked with a spatula or piping bag. If you whisk
it at high speed, it will lose its light, creamy texture and become fatty.

Prepare the plain macaroon shells.
Preheat the oven to 300°F (140°C). If your oven has smaller Fahrenheit increments, heat it to 285°F (preferable). Combine the ground almonds with the
confectioners' sugar, but mix only briefly so that the almonds do not exude
their oil. Cook the granulated sugar with the water to 230°F (110°C). While the
mixture is heating, start whisking half the egg whites to soft peaks. When
the syrup has reached the right temperature, pour it over the whisked egg
whites, whisking continuously. Continue beating until the mixture cools to
113°F (45°C), then stop the beater. Pour in the other half of the egg whites (1
¾ oz./50 g), add the coloring if using, and add the ground almonds combined
with the confectioners' sugar. Stir in energetically with a flexible spatula until
the batter is liquid and forms a ribbon.
Spoon the mixture into a piping bag and pipe it out (see p. 132) onto the baking
sheet or mat, an equal distance apart. Bake for about 12 minutes, depending
on the size of your macaroons. Leave to cool at room temperature.
To prepare the chocolate shells, combine the ground almonds with the cocoa
powder and confectioners' sugar, and proceed as for the plain macaroons.

To assemble the macaroons.
Turn the shells over. Spoon the ganache into a piping bag and pipe out a knob
onto the base of half the shells. Sandwich together using another shell of the
same size, pressing lightly so you do not crush them. Chill overnight and eat
the next day. Macaroons can also be frozen to eat later.

Gianduja-Topped Madeleines ★★

Makes about 20 average-sized madeleines
Preparation time: 15 minutes
Cooking time: 10 minutes
Chilling time: 4 minutes

Melt the butter and set aside to cool to 113°F (45°C). Beat the eggs, vanilla, sugar, and honey in a mixing bowl until all the ingredients are thoroughly mixed.
Sift in the flour and baking powder and fold in*. Stir in the melted, cooled butter. Chill the batter for 3 to 4 hours.
Prepare the madeleine baking pan. Grease the molds and dust them lightly with flour, tapping the pan upside down to remove any excess flour.
Preheat the oven to 400°F (200°C).
Pipe out the madeleine batter into the pan and bake for 8 to 10 minutes. They should peak in the center and be a nice golden color.
Melt the gianduja gently over the bain-marie* or in the microwave oven (on "defrost" or at 500 W maximum, stirring from time to time.) When it has thickened a little, spoon it into the piping bag with a very small tip.
Remove the madeleines from the oven and garnish with the gianduja. You'll have to wait until the madeleines have cooled down before you can eat them!

● **Chef's note**
We strongly recommend chilling the batter for a few hours so that the madeleines rise nicely in the oven.

Technique
Gianduja ≫ p. 40

Ingredients
2 ¼ sticks (9 oz./250 g) butter plus a little extra to grease the baking pan
5 eggs
½ teaspoon vanilla seeds or ground vanilla bean
1 ¼ cups (9 oz./250 g) sugar
2 teaspoons (15 g) honey
2 ¾ cups (9 oz./250 g) cake flour, plus a little extra for dusting the madeleine pan
2 level teaspoons (8 g) baking powder
7 oz. (200 g) gianduja (see p. 40)

Equipment
1 sieve†
1 baking sheet with madeleine molds
1 piping bag† fitted with a very small tip†

Iced desserts

Gilles Marchal

presents his recipe

I was born into the world of cooking and have remained in it ever since. My uncle and my godfather were both chefs; we would have big family dinners; fetching the milk from the farm was a ritual. My mother and grandmother were inveterate bakers. Such a world leaves a lasting imprint on a chef. And as for chocolate, well, I grew up with it: my father was regional director of the chocolate factory owned by Poulain, one of the oldest chocolate manufacturers in France. Today, my desserts are variations on the themes of my childhood memories. One example is my grandmother's chocolate mousse, a miracle of creaminess and flavor. I serve it individually or in a spoon topped with a fine leaf of chocolate as a nod to the little chocolate bits that were sprinkled on our desserts at home. Behind each of my desserts, there is story of a delicious memory.

For this dessert of bittersweet chocolate and red berries served in a glass, I have sought to create the best balance possible between the chocolate and the fruit. It's a subtle combination where the degree of acidity must be just right.

The time it takes to prepare pales in comparison with the time I take to bring an idea to fruition. When an idea takes root in my mind, I nourish it. When a new creation is born, that calls for a drink!

Bittersweet Chocolate Ice Cream with Red Berries

Caraïbes chocolate ice cream. Chop the chocolate finely. Bring the milk and whipping cream to the boil in a saucepan. Remove the liquid from the heat and add the berry-flavored tea to infuse for 15 minutes, then filter. Slit the vanilla bean and scrape out the seeds. Add the bean and seeds to the hot mixture and bring to the boil again. Whisk* together the egg yolk, honey, brown sugar, and cocoa powder until thick. Incorporate this mixture into the hot liquid and, stirring constantly, simmer until it reaches 181°F (83°C), the temperature at which it will coat the back of a spoon. Pour this simmering mixture over the chopped chocolate and the cocoa paste. Mix together and process briefly to emulsify*. Leave to rest for 6 hours in the refrigerator before placing in the ice-cream maker.

Strawberry and red berry sorbet with sansho pepper. Place the strawberry pulp in a pot. Add the red currants, raspberries, sugar, glucose syrup or honey, and pepper. Bring quickly to the boil and remove from the heat. Leave to cool and blend. Pour the mixture into the ice-cream maker bowl and follow the manufacturer's instructions.

Chocolate almond sponge. Preheat the oven to 400°F (200°C). Beat the almond paste together with the egg yolks using an electric beater until the mixture becomes foamy. Whisk the egg whites to firm peaks. Mix in the granulated sugar. Chop the chocolate finely and place it over a bain-marie* with the cocoa powder. Using a flexible spatula, carefully fold in* the egg whites, then the melted chocolate, into the almond paste and egg yolk mixture. Spread out the batter onto the lined baking sheet. It should be less than ½ in. (1 cm) thick. Bake for about 5 minutes, leave to cool, and cut to the desired shape.

Lorraine Mirabelle plum parfait. Whisk the egg yolks until thick and pale. Soften the gelatin sheet in a bowl of cold water. Cook the sugar and water in a saucepan to 257°F (125°C). Pour the syrup over the egg yolks, whisking as you do so. Wring the excess water out of the gelatin sheets and stir them into the hot mixture until just dissolved. Leave to cool and add the eau-de-vie. In another mixing bowl, whisk the whipping cream until it reaches a foamy, lightly whipped consistency. Using a flexible spatula, fold the whipped cream into the other mixture. Pour into the pastry circle and freeze.

To assemble. Arrange the preparations in layers in shot glasses (verrines). Begin with the chocolate ice cream, then a layer of almond-chocolate sponge. Spoon in some Mirabelle plum parfait, and top with another layer of chocolate ice cream. If you wish, drizzle over a little bittersweet chocolate sauce and scatter a few fresh berries on top. You may also add a disk of chocolate at the edge of the glass. Place a scoop of berry and pepper sorbet in the plate.

Serves 6–8

Ice cream with Caraïbes chocolate
7 oz. (200 g) bittersweet Caraïbes chocolate, 66 percent cocoa
2 cups (500 ml) whole milk
1 cup (250 ml) whipping cream, 35 percent butterfat
⅔ oz. (20 g) red berry-flavored tea
½ Bourbon vanilla bean
4 ¼ oz. (120 g) egg yolks
3 tablespoons plus 1 teaspoon (2 ½ oz./70 g) honey
⅓ cup (2 ¼ oz./70 g) brown sugar
2 tablespoons plus ½ teaspoon (½ oz./15 g) cocoa powder, unsweetened
⅔ oz. (20 g) cocoa paste, 70 percent cocoa

Strawberry and red berry sorbet with sansho pepper
1 ½ lbs (700 g) pulp of fresh strawberries
3 ½ oz. (100 g) fresh red currants
7 oz. (200 g) fresh raspberries
¾ cup (5 ½ oz./150 g) granulated sugar
2 ½ tablespoons (50 g) glucose syrup or honey
1 g (2 generous pinches) sansho pepper

Chocolate almond sponge
5 oz. (140 g) almond paste
4 ½ oz. (125 g) egg yolks
7 oz. (200 g) egg whites
¾ cup (5 ½ oz./150 g) granulated sugar
3 ¼ oz. (90 g) Guanaja chocolate, 70 percent cocoa
3 ½ tablespoons (1 oz./25 g) unsweetened cocoa powder

Lorraine Mirabelle plum parfait
3 ½ oz. (100 g) egg yolks
1 sheet (2 g) gelatin
Scant ⅔ cup (4 ¼ oz./120 g) sugar
3 tablespoons (40 g) water
¼ cup (60 ml) Lorraine Mirabelle plum eau-de-vie
2 cups (500 ml) whipping cream, 35 percent butterfat

Equipment
1 kitchen thermometer†, 1 ice-cream maker†
1 baking sheet lined with parchment paper
1 pastry circle †, 8 shot glasses (verrines)
1 flexible spatula†, 1 electric hand-held beater†

Chocolate-Coated Cocoa Nib Ice Cream with Roasted Almonds and Peanuts ★★

Serves 10
Preparation time: 40 minutes
Freezing time: 2 hours 30 minutes to 5 hours, depending on the ice-cream maker
Cooking time: 20 minutes
Refrigeration time: overnight

A day ahead, prepare the cocoa nib ice cream.
Preheat the oven to 300°F (150°C). Heat the cocoa nibs for about 10 minutes. Combine the milk, cream, powdered milk, sugar, egg yolks, and honey in a saucepan. When warm, add the cocoa nibs. Stir constantly until the mixture reaches a temperature of 185°F (85°C).
Cool rapidly by pouring it into a bowl placed over a larger bowl filled with ice cubes. Leave to rest overnight in the refrigerator so that the flavors develop.

The next day.
Filter the mixture and pour it into the ice-cream maker, following manufacturer's directions for setting time. When the ice cream is ready, spoon it into a piping bag and fill the molds. Insert the ice cream sticks and freeze for at least 2 hours.

Prepare the coating.
Roast the nuts (see p. 134).
Preheat the oven to 350°F (150°C) and roast the chopped almonds and/or peanuts for about 10 minutes, until they are a nice amber color right through.
Chop the chocolate and melt it slowly in a bain-marie* or in the microwave oven (on "defrost" or at 500 W maximum, stirring from time to time).
Stir in the grape-seed oil and then the roasted nuts. Remove the ice creams one by one from their molds and dip them immediately in the chocolate coating. Place them in a dish lined with parchment paper and return them quickly to the freezer until you serve them. They will keep for a maximum of two weeks.

● **Chef's note**
An attractive way of serving these ice creams is to place them in a bowl made of ice. A day ahead, pour some water into a mixing or salad bowl and then place a smaller bowl into it, so that the water comes up to the top of the sides of the larger bowl. This will create a cavity. Place in the freezer and unmold just before serving. Use your imagination to decorate it.

● **Did you know?**
We use grape-seed oil for chocolate coating to liquefy it; the oil helps form a thin chocolate shell that snaps pleasantly and melts quickly.

Ingredients
Cocoa nib* ice cream (or another ice cream of your choice)
5 ½ oz. (150 g) cocoa nibs*
3 cups (750 ml) whole milk
Scant cup (225 ml) whipping cream
Scant ½ cup (2 oz./55 g) powdered milk
Scant cup (6 oz./170 g) granulated sugar
2 egg yolks
2 teaspoons (15 g) honey

Coating
5 ½ oz. (150 g) chopped almonds and/or peanuts
1 lb. 2 oz. (500 g) bittersweet chocolate, 60 or 70 percent
3 tablespoons plus 1 teaspoon (50 ml) grape-seed oil

Equipment
1 kitchen thermometer†
1 ice-cream maker†
1 piping bag†
1 cold-water bath
10 silicone or other ice cream molds†
10 wooden ice cream sticks

Techniques
Melting Chocolate ›› p. 19
Cocoa Nib Ice Cream ›› p. 121
Roasting Nuts ›› p. 134

Iced Chocolate Parfait
and Cappuccino Sauce ★★

Serves 6-8
Preparation time: 30 minutes
Freezing time: 6 hours
Chilling time: 2 hours

Prepare the iced chocolate parfait.
Make a Swiss meringue–in a heatproof mixing bowl, combine the egg whites and the sugar. Place the bowl over a bain-marie* and continue whisking* until the temperature reaches 131°F-140°F (55°C-60°C). Remove from the heat and continue whisking until the mixture cools to room temperature.
Chop the chocolate and melt it slowly in a bain-marie or in the microwave oven (on "defrost" or at 500 W maximum, stirring from time to time).
Whisk the cream lightly until it thickens (see p. 108). Fold* one-quarter of this cream into the chocolate and stir until the texture is elastic and shiny.
Fold the Swiss meringue in* carefully. Lastly, fold in the remaining whisked cream. Spoon into the glasses and freeze for about 6 hours.

Prepare the cappuccino sauce.
Measure out the required quantity of espresso coffee. Pour the coffee into a saucepan and add the granulated sugar, jelly sugar, and glucose syrup. Bring to the boil, remove from the heat, and chill.
Take the parfaits out of the freezer half an hour before serving and drizzle them with the cold cappuccino sauce just before serving.

● Chef's note
You may want to add a dash of amaretto liqueur to the cappuccino sauce. Serve these parfaits with Breton shortbread (page 74) or cocoa cigarette (see p. 60) for an interesting texture contrast.

Technique
Chocolate Parfait >> p. 122

Ingredients
Iced chocolate parfait
3 egg whites
1 cup minus 3 tablespoons (5 ⅔ oz./160 g) granulated sugar
5 ¾ oz. (165 g) bittersweet chocolate, 70 percent cocoa
1 ¼ cups (310 ml) whipping cream

Cappuccino sauce
⅓ cup (85 ml) espresso coffee
2 ½ tablespoons (35 g) granulated sugar
⅓ oz. (10 g) jelly (jam) sugar
(sugar containing pectin)
⅔ oz. (20 g) glucose syrup

Equipment
1 kitchen thermometer†
1 whisk†
If possible, 1 stand-alone mixer†

Ingredients

Iced hazelnut-chocolate mousse

2 ⅔ oz. (75 g) bittersweet chocolate,
60 percent cocoa
3 egg yolks
Scant ⅓ cup (2 ¼ oz./65 g) granulated sugar
Scant ½ cup (100 ml) whole milk
3 oz. (85 g) glucose syrup
2 ⅔ oz. (75 g) hazelnut paste (see p. 42)
Generous ⅔ cup (170 ml) whipping cream,
well chilled

Light lemon-lime cream

1 lemon
½ vanilla bean
Scant ½ cup (50 ml) water
Generous ⅔ cup (4 ⅔ oz./130 g) granulated sugar
2 egg whites
½ cup (125 ml) whipping cream
1 ¾ oz. (50 g) lime pulp (available in professional
stores, or see chef's notes)
1 heaped tablespoon (1 oz./25 g) glucose syrup
1 oz. (25 g) diced candied lemon peel

Roasted hazelnuts for garnish

Limoncello glaze

1 lemon
4 ½ oz. (125 g) lemon marmalade
½ cup (3 ½ oz./100 g) sugar
2 teaspoons (10 g or 10 ml) Limoncello

Equipment

1 kitchen thermometer†
Attractive glasses for serving, such as shot glasses
or martini glasses
1 flexible spatula†
1 electric hand-held beater†
1 whisk† (optional)

● Chef's notes

*Take the glasses out of the freezer a few minutes
before serving so that the textures can soften
slightly.*
*If you cannot find ready-made frozen lime pulp,
you can make it yourself in the blender. Be careful
to remove all the seeds and to add a little sugar.*

Techniques

Pistachio/Hazelnut Paste >> p. 42
Custard-Based Chocolate Mousse >> p. 114

Iced Hazelnut-Chocolate Mousse and Lemon-Lime Cream ★★

Serves 6-8
Preparation time: 45 minutes, excluding hazelnut paste preparation
Freezing time: overnight

A day ahead, prepare the iced hazelnut-chocolate mousse.
Chop the chocolate and melt it slowly in a bain-marie* or in the microwave oven (on "defrost" or at 500 W maximum, stirring from time to time).
Prepare a pouring custard (*crème anglaise*).
In a mixing bowl, beat the egg yolks with the sugar.
Pour this mixture into a saucepan, add the milk and glucose syrup, and simmer over low heat. The liquid should thicken slightly and coat the back of a spoon. The temperature should be between 180°F-183°F (82°C-84°C).
Gradually pour one-third of the hot custard over the melted chocolate. Using a flexible spatula, mix in energetically, drawing small circles to create an elastic, shiny "kernel." Incorporate the second third of the liquid, using the same procedure. Repeat with the last third. Using a whisk or an electric beater, lightly whip* the well-chilled cream (see p. 108). Fold* the chocolate custard into the frothy cream.

Prepare the light lemon-lime cream.
Squeeze a scant ¼ cup (50 ml) of lemon juice. Slit the half vanilla bean lengthways and scrape out the seeds. Cook the lemon juice, vanilla seeds, water, and sugar in a saucepan until the mixture reaches the consistency of a syrup. The temperature should be 250°F (121°C). While it is cooking, whisk* the egg whites with an electric beater. Pour the syrup gradually over the whisked egg whites, continuing to beat until the mixture cools down to room temperature. Whip the cream (see p. 108) until it is frothy. Slightly warm the lime pulp in a saucepan and add the glucose syrup to dissolve it. Stir in the diced candied lemon peel. Carefully fold this pulp mixture into the Italian meringue, and then fold this into the lightly whipped cream.

To assemble.
Spoon the hazelnut-chocolate mousse into the bottom of the glasses. Place in the freezer to harden. Scatter a few roasted hazelnuts over the mousse, and then pour in the lemon-lime cream. Return to the freezer while you prepare the glaze.

Prepare the Limoncello glaze.
Squeeze the lemon (you should have a scant ¼ cup, 50 ml). In a mixing bowl, combine the lemon juice, marmalade, granulated sugar, and Limoncello. Leave to cool for a few minutes and then pour it over the lemon-lime cream. Chop a few hazelnuts and scatter them on the top.
Freeze at least overnight, a minimum of 12 hours.

Iced Raspberry-Filled Meringues and Hot Chocolate Sauce ★★

Serves 6-8
Preparation time: 1 hour
Freezing time: 4 hours minimum
Cooking time: 2 hours

Prepare the raspberry sorbet.
Bring the water and sugar to the boil in a saucepan, remove from the heat, and leave to cool. Blend the raspberries with the prepared, cooled syrup and the juice of half a lemon. Filter the pulp to remove the seeds and pour into ice cube trays. Freeze for at least 4 hours.

Prepare the meringue.
Preheat the oven to 230°F (110°C).
Sift the confectioners' sugar and set aside. Whisk* the egg whites to soft peaks, gradually adding the sugar. When you have the desired consistency–the egg whites will be glossy and firm–carefully fold in* the confectioners' sugar using a flexible spatula.
Either use a piping bag or a spoon dipped in cold water to place small rounds of meringue batter on a lined baking sheet. Bake for about 2 hours. The meringues are done when they are crisp on the outside but still chewy inside.

Prepare the chocolate sauce.
Chop the chocolate and melt it slowly in a bain-marie* or in the microwave oven (on "defrost" or at 500 W maximum, stirring from time to time).
Bring the milk to the boil. Gradually pour one-third of the boiling liquid over the melted chocolate. Using a flexible spatula, mix in energetically, drawing small circles to create an elastic, shiny "kernel."
Incorporate the second third of the liquid, using the same procedure. Repeat with the last third. Blend for a few seconds using an immersion blender.

When the sorbet has frozen, cut it into pieces and process it in a blender until the texture is creamy.
Scoop out balls of sorbet and place them in individual serving dishes with a few meringues, or sandwich meringues halves together with disks of sorbet. Garnish with raspberries and drizzle with chocolate sauce, hot or cold, as you prefer, when you serve the dessert.

● **Chef's notes**
The advantage of this "not-quite sorbet" is that no ice-cream maker is required. The texture is very creamy but it must be eaten immediately and can't be returned to the freezer.
This raspberry sorbet recipe can also be transformed into a granita: just scratch it with a fork at regular intervals while it is in the freezer.

Ingredients
Raspberry sorbet
1 ½ cups (10 ½ oz./300 g) granulated sugar
1 ¼ cup (300 ml) water
1 lb. (500 g) fresh raspberries
Juice of ½ lemon

Meringue
¾ cup (3 ½ oz./100 g) confectioners' sugar
3 egg whites
½ cup (3 ½ oz./100 g) granulated sugar

Chocolate sauce
6 ⅓ oz. (180 g) bittersweet chocolate, 60 percent cocoa
¾ cup (200 ml) whole milk

For garnish
9 oz. (250 g) fresh raspberries

Equipment
Ice cube trays
1 baking sheet lined with parchment paper
1 piping bag† (optional)
1 flexible spatula†
1 immersion blender†
1 whisk†

Technique
Chocolate Sauce >> p. 127

Ingredients

Chocolate ice cream
6 ⅓ oz. (180 g) bittersweet chocolate,
70 percent cocoa
2 ⅔ cups (660 ml) whipping cream
¼ cup (1 oz./30 g) powdered milk
⅓ cup (2 ½ oz./70 g) granulated sugar
3 tablespoons (2 ¼ oz./60 g) honey

Crisp almond cookies
7 oz. (200 g) whole almonds
2 egg whites
1 ½ cups (7 oz./200 g) confectioners' sugar
2 tablespoons (½ oz./15 g) unsweetened
cocoa powder

Caramel* and passion fruit sauce
3 ¾ oz. (110 g) milk chocolate, 40 percent cocoa
1 cup minus 1 tablespoon (235 ml) whipping cream
1 ½ teaspoons (10 g) glucose syrup
Scant ⅔ cup (4 ¼ oz./120 g) sugar
2 tablespoons plus 2 teaspoons (1 ½ oz./40 g) butter
Scant ¼ cup (50 ml) passion fruit juice

Equipment
1 ice-cream maker†
1 kitchen thermometer†
1 baking sheet lined with parchment paper
1 flexible spatula†

Crisp Almond Cookies with Chocolate Ice Cream and Caramel and Passion Fruit Sauce ★★★

Serves 6–8
Preparation time: 2 hours
Cooking time: 1 hour
Freezing time: 30 minutes to 3 hours 30 minutes, depending on the
ice-cream maker
Refrigeration time: overnight

A day ahead, prepare the bittersweet chocolate ice cream (see p. 120).
Leave to rest overnight in the refrigerator so that the flavors develop (professionals call this "maturing"). Pour the mixture into the ice-cream maker, following the manufacturer's instructions for your machine, and store at 0°F (-18°C).

Prepare the crisp almond cookies.
Preheat the oven to 325°F (160°C).
Chop the almonds–not too roughly, but not too small either, so that the cookie has a good crunch–and roast them for a few minutes. Lightly beat the egg whites to liquefy them and combine them with the confectioners' sugar and cocoa powder in a stainless steel bowl. Stir in the chopped almonds and place the bowl over a pot of simmering water. Heat the mixture, stirring from time to time, until it reaches a temperature of 176°F (80°C). Spoon the batter onto a baking sheet lined with parchment paper and flatten out to a diameter of about 2 ¾ in. (7 cm), leaving at least 2 in. (5-6 cm) between them. Bake for about 1 hour, until dry to the touch, and cool on a rack.

Prepare the caramel and passion fruit sauce.
Chop the chocolate and melt it slowly in a bain-marie* or in the microwave oven (on "defrost" or at 500 W maximum, stirring from time to time).
Heat the cream with the glucose syrup. While the mixture is heating, prepare a caramel using the dry method in another saucepan, bringing the sugar up to 356°F-365°F (180°C-185°C). Add the butter very carefully so that you do not burn yourself, then gradually pour in the hot cream and glucose mixture. Bring this to the boil. Gradually pour one-third of the boiling liquid over the melted chocolate. Using a flexible spatula, mix it in energetically, drawing small circles to create an elastic, shiny "kernel." Incorporate the second third of the liquid, using the same procedure. Repeat with the last third. Stir in the passion fruit juice.

To assemble and serve.
Place a cookie in the plate and then place a scoop of chocolate ice cream over it. Top it with a second cookie. Drizzle the sauce over the cookies.

Techniques
Chocolate Ice Cream >> p. 120
Chocolate-Caramel Sauce >> p. 129

Special occasions

Christophe Michalak
presents his recipe

I simply adore working with forms and colors, and take great pleasure in making shapes with my ingredients. When I was a child, I dreamed of going to fine arts school , but in the end, my passion for food took the upper hand and I chose the world of desserts.

I like to revisit the great classics of the pastry making tradition and create surprises by changing the flavors within. This is how the *religieuses* with salted butter caramel, the Pêche Melba macaroons*, and the marshmallow teddy bears were born—all a tribute to the sweets I ate as a child.

Choco-Crunch Tart

Linzer Shortcrust Pastry. Preheat the oven to 300°F–325°F (150°C–160°C). Crush the egg yolk cooked in the microwave oven and sift it through a sieve. Combine it with the flour and potato or cornstarch. Soften the butter and combine it with the confectioners' sugar, fleur de sel, lemon zest, and then with the mixture of egg yolk, flour, and starch. Roll the dough out to a thickness of ⅟₁₆ in. (2 mm).
Cut out a rectangle measuring 4 × 16 in. (10 × 40 cm). Bake until golden brown, about 15 minutes.

Chocolate sponge. Line a 16 × 24 in. (40 × 60 cm) jelly roll pan with parchment paper. Preheat the oven to 400°F (200°C). Sift the flour, starch, and cocoa powder together. Melt the butter. Whisk* the egg whites in a bowl placed over simmering water until they form soft peaks. When whisked, incorporate the sugar using a spatula. Combine the egg yolks with the whisked egg whites, then carefully fold in* the sifted dry ingredients and the melted butter. Pour the batter on to the lined baking sheet and bake for 8 minutes. Allow to cool and cut out a strip measuring 3 × 14 ½ in. (8 × 37 cm). Cut the remaining sponge into small cubes.

Cooked chocolate cream. Preheat the oven to 250°F (120°C). Chop the chocolate. Combine the milk, sugar, egg yolks, and eggs. Bring the cream to the boil and pour it over the chopped chocolate. Incorporate the milk mixture with the cream and chocolate and combine until the texture is smooth. Pour the mixture into a rectangular dish, 4 × 14 in. (10 × 35 cm), switch off the oven, and place the cream in the oven to cook for 30 minutes. Cool rapidly by placing it in the freezer.

Shiny gianduja glaze. Melt the Araguani chocolate and gianduja. Bring the whipping cream, syrup, and glucose syrup to the boil. Gradually pour the boiling liquid over the melted chocolate. Process the mixture until smooth, adding the oil and coloring.

Jivara milk chocolate Chantilly cream. Melt the Jivara chocolate. Bring the whipping cream to the boil. Gradually pour the cream over the chocolate. Chill for at least 4 hours.

Bittersweet chocolate truffles. Melt the two types of chocolate. Bring the whipping cream to the boil. Gradually pour the cream over the chocolate. Incorporate the butter and invert sugar and leave to set for a few hours. Shape the mixture into truffles and roll them in the cocoa powder.

To assemble and finish. Place the strip of chocolate sponge over the piece of Linzer shortcrust. Take the cooked cream from the freezer, cover it with Gianduja glaze, and place it atop the sponge. Roll the cubes of sponge in the sparkling ruby red food coloring and place them attractively around the base. Whip the Jivara Chantilly cream. Make six scoops and arrange them on the glazed chocolate cream. Garnish with truffles and shards of tempered* chocolate. Serve when still well chilled.

Serves 8

Ingredients

Linzer Shortcrust Pastry
⅓ oz. (10 g) cooked egg yolk (prepare in microwave oven)
2 ¾ cups (9 oz./250 g) cake flour
⅓ cup (1 ¾ oz./50 g) potato starch or cornstarch
2 ¼ sticks (9 ¾ oz./275 g) butter
Scant ⅔ cup (3 ¼ oz./90 g) confectioners' sugar
1 slightly heaped teaspoon (6 g) salt
A good pinch (3 g) fleur de sel
Zest* of 2 unwaxed lemons, finely grated*

Chocolate sponge
½ cup (1 ¾ oz./50 g) all-purpose flour
⅓ cup (1 ¾ oz./50 g) potato starch or cornstarch
Scant ½ cup (2 oz./55 g) unsweetened cocoa powder
2 teaspoons (10 g) butter
9 oz. (250 g) egg whites
1 ¼ cups (8 ½ oz./240 g) sugar
8 ½ oz. (240 g) egg yolks
Sparkling ruby red food coloring

Cooked chocolate cream
⅔ cup (175 g) whole milk
Scant ½ cup (3 oz./85 g) granulated sugar
1 oz. (30 g) egg yolk
2 oz. (60 g) eggs
1 ½ cups plus 2 tablespoons (375 g) whipping cream, 35 percent fat content
9 ¾ oz. (275 g) bittersweet Guanaja chocolate (70 percent cocoa)

Shiny gianduja glaze
10 ½ oz. (300 g) Araguani bittersweet chocolate (72 percent cocoa)
1 ½ lb. (750 g) gianduja (see p. 40)
2 cups plus 1 scant cup (700 ml) whipping cream
5 ¼ oz. (160 g) 30° Baume syrup
Scant ⅓ cup (4 ½ tablespoons or 100 g) glucose syrup
7 ½ tablespoons (3 ½ oz./100 g) grape-seed oil
1 teaspoon (5 g) red food coloring

Jivara milk chocolate Chantilly cream
1 lb. (500 g) Jivara milk chocolate
4 cups (1 liter) whipping cream

Bittersweet chocolate truffles
10 oz. (280 g) Caraïbes bittersweet chocolate (66 percent cocoa)
10 oz. (280 g) Manjari bittersweet chocolate (64 percent cocoa)
2 cups (500 ml) whipping cream
7 tablespoons (3 ½ oz./100 g) butter
3 oz. (87 g) invert sugar
Unsweetened cocoa powder for dusting

Ingredients

Whipped ivory ganache* with Tahiti vanilla
1 Tahiti vanilla bean
1 ⅔ oz. (45 g) white chocolate, 35 percent cocoa
Whipping cream, divided as follows: ⅓ cup plus
2 teaspoons (90 ml) plus ½ cup plus 1 teaspoon (130 ml)

Almond shortcrust pastry
1 stick (4 ½ oz./120 g) butter, room temperature,
plus a little extra for the molds
Scant ½ teaspoon (2 g) table salt
⅔ cup (3 oz./90 g) confectioners' sugar
3 tablespoons (½ oz./15 g) ground blanched* almonds
1 egg
Cake flour, divided as follows: ⅔ cup (2 oz./60 g)
plus 2 cups (6 ⅓ oz./180 g)

Vanilla-scented almond cream
2 tablespoons plus 1 teaspoon (1 ¼ oz./35 g) butter
Scant ¼ cup (1 oz./30 g) confectioners' sugar
½ beaten egg (35 g)
½ cup (1 ⅔ oz./45 g) ground blanched* almonds
½ vanilla bean
1 scant teaspoon (3 g) cornstarch

Jelled pears
7 oz. (200 g) pears
A little lemon juice
2 ¾ oz. (80 g) pear pulp, store bought or prepared
at home with 10 percent sugar
1 oz. (30 g) preserving sugar

Chestnut spaghetti
2 ⅔ oz. (75 g) chestnut paste (*pâte de marron*)
2 ¼ oz. (60 g) creamed chestnuts (*crème de marron*)
2 tablespoons plus 2 teaspoons (1 ½ oz./40 g) butter
1 tablespoon plus 2 teaspoons whipping cream

Decoration
Glacéed chestnuts
1 pear

Equipment
1 pastry circle†, 7 in. (18 cm) and 1 baking sheet
lined with parchment paper, 1 pastry circle†, 8 in.
(20 cm) (or silicone cake mold†), 1 food processor
fitted with a blade attachment, 1 piping bag† fitted
with a small plain tip† or potato ricer, 1 kitchen
thermometer†, 1 flexible spatula†, 1 rolling pin†

Techniques
Almond Shortcrust Pastry >> p. 72
Whipped Ganache >> p. 97

Mont Blanc, Revisited ★ ★ ★

Serves 6-8
Preparation time: 1 hour 30 minutes
Refrigeration time: minimum 3 hours
Cooking time: 20 minutes
Freezing time: overnight

A day ahead, prepare the whipped ivory ganache.
Slit the Tahiti vanilla bean and scrape the seeds into the cream. Melt the chocolate (see p.19). Bring the ⅓ cup plus 2 teaspoons (90 ml) whipping cream to
the boil with the vanilla seeds. Gradually pour one-third of the cream over
the chocolate. Using a flexible spatula, mix it in energetically, drawing small
circles to create an elastic, shiny "kernel." Continue according to the "three
thirds rule*" (see p. 95). Stir in the remaining cream and leave to set for at
least 3 hours in the refrigerator. Whisk* the ganache to soften the texture.

Prepare the almond shortcrust pastry (see p. 72).
Preheat the oven to 300°F (150°C). Roll the dough out to a thickness of about
⅛ in. (4 mm) and cut out a 7 in. (18 cm) base. Place it on a lined baking sheet or
in the cake pan and bake for about 10 minutes, until it turns a nice golden color.

Prepare the vanilla-scented almond cream.
Increase the oven temperature to 350°F (170°C). Soften the butter. Combine
the egg with the confectioners' sugar. Add the ground almonds, vanilla seeds,
and softened butter. Whisk lightly, then incorporate the cornstarch. Spread it
out on the almond shortcrust base and bake for about 7 to 8 minutes, until a
nice golden color.

Prepare the jelled pears.
Cut the pears into small dice and squeeze lemon juice over them immediately.
Bring the pear pulp and preserving sugar to the boil. Boil for 2 minutes and
pour into a bowl. Leave to cool, and when the temperature has reached 122°F
(50°C), stir in the diced pears. Pour over the almond cream layer and freeze
for 1 hour.

Place the larger pastry circle on a lined baking sheet. Pour in the whipped
ganache and position the pear-almond cream component over it with the
pastry on the top. Freeze overnight. The next day, turn it out of the mold so
that the pastry base is at the bottom.

At the last minute, make the chestnut spaghetti.
Process the chestnut paste, chestnut cream, and butter together in the bowl
of a food processor until the texture is smooth and creamy and the color is
slightly paler. Incorporate the whipping cream. Fill a piping bag fitted with a
small plain tip or use a potato ricer. Press out the chestnut spaghetti, covering
the cake entirely, and decorate with glacéed chestnuts and a cut-up pear.

● Chef's note
*You can replace the pear with apple for a different but equally harmonious
dessert.*

Hazelnut Praline Christmas Log ★ ★

Serves 6–8
Preparation time: 1 hour
Cooking time: 7 minutes
Refrigeration time: 3 hours.

Prepare the jelly roll.
Sift the flour and set aside. Beat the 2 whole eggs and 2 egg yolks with the scant ½ cup (2 ¾ oz./80 g) sugar until the mixture is pale and thick. Whisk* the 2 egg whites with the 2 ½ tablespoons (1 oz./30 g) sugar to soft peaks. Carefully fold* the whisked egg whites into the first mixture and pour in the sifted flour. Stir until just combined.
Spread the batter out onto the pan and bake for about 5–7 minutes. It should be only very lightly colored. When cooled, leave at room temperature.

Prepare the whipped chocolate-hazelnut ganache.
Chop the chocolate and melt it slowly in a bain-marie* or in the microwave oven (on "defrost" or at 500 W maximum, stirring from time to time). Add the praline. Bring the ⅔ cup (160 ml) whipping cream to the boil. Gradually pour one-third of the boiling cream over the melted chocolate and praline. Using a flexible spatula, mix it in energetically, drawing small circles to create an elastic, shiny "kernel." Incorporate the second third of the cream, using the same procedure. Repeat with the last third.
Stir in the remaining 1 ⅔ cups (400 ml) cold cream. Process until the mixture is smooth and thoroughly emulsified*. Chill for at least 3 hours, and then whip* the ganache at medium speed until it is creamy. If you whip it any faster, it will lose its light, creamy texture and will become fatty

To assemble.
Turn the jelly roll sponge out of the pan. Spread one-third of the ganache over it and sprinkle with a few roughly chopped hazelnuts. Roll up the sponge and cover completely with the remaining whipped ganache. Decorate with roasted chopped hazelnuts and dust with confectioners' sugar.

Techniques
Melting Chocolate ›› p. 19
Homemade Praline ›› p. 38
Plain Jelly Roll (Swiss Roll) ›› p. 90
Whipped Ganache ›› p. 97

Ingredients
Plain jelly roll sponge
Generous ½ cup (1 ¾ oz./50 g) cake flour
2 eggs, whole
2 eggs, separated
Granulated sugar, divided as follows: scant ½ cup
(2 ¾ oz./80 g) plus 2 ½ tablespoons (1 oz./30 g)

Whipped chocolate hazelnut ganache*
5 ½ oz. (150 g) milk chocolate, 40 percent cocoa
4 ¼ oz. (120 g) hazelnut praline*, homemade
(see p. 38) or store bought
Whipping cream, divided as follows: ⅔ cup (160 ml)
plus 1 ⅔ cups (400 ml)

7 oz. (200 g) chopped hazelnuts
Confectioners' sugar for dusting

Equipment
1 jelly (Swiss) roll pan
1 flexible spatula†
1 electric hand-held beater† or whisk†

Klemanga ★★

Serves 6-8
Preparation time: 1 hour 20 minutes
Cooking time: 10 minutes
Total freezing time: 4 hours
Defrosting time: 6 hours

Prepare the soft coconut sponge (see p. 90).
Preheat the oven to 350°F (180°C). Lightly beat the two egg whites. Combine the ground coconut, flour, and confectioners' sugar with the two egg whites and the whipping cream.
Whip* the four remaining egg whites to soft peaks, gradually pouring in the sugar as you whip. Carefully fold* the beaten egg whites into the first mixture. Spread out the batter on a lined baking sheet or silicone mat and bake for about 10 minutes.
Using the pastry circle as a cutter, cut out two disks of sponge.

Prepare the mango-passion fruit coulis.
Soften the gelatin in a bowl of cold water. Finely dice the mango. Heat the mango and passion fruit pulps in a saucepan to 122°F (50°C), adding a little sugar if necessary. Wring the water out of the gelatin and dissolve it in the fruit pulp. Stir in the small mango cubes and set aside in the refrigerator.

Place the pastry circle on a silicone mat or lined baking sheet. Place one disk at the base of the ring. Pour out the mango-passion fruit coulis, ensuring that you leave a little for the finishing. Top that with the second disk of sponge. Flatten lightly so that it is smooth. Freeze for 1 hour.

Prepare the chocolate Chantilly mousse (see p. 113).
Use the proportions given opposite.
Remove the dessert from the freezer. Spoon the Chantilly mousse into a piping bag and pipe out large balls of chocolate Chantilly on the top layer of sponge. Return to the freezer for a further 3 hours.

Remove the pastry circle and place the dessert on a serving dish. Dust it with unsweetened cocoa powder. Slightly melt the mango-passion fruit coulis in the microwave oven, ensuring that you do not heat it, and decorate the dessert with it. This should not be eaten icy, so allow plenty of time–about 6 hours–for it to defrost in the refrigerator.

● **Chef's note**
As soon as you have prepared the Chantilly mousse, pipe it out. That way, you'll be sure of making attractive shapes.

Techniques
Melting Chocolate >> p. 19
Soft Almond or Coconut Sponge >> p. 90
Chocolate Chantilly Mousse >> p. 113

Ingredients

Soft coconut sponge
6 egg whites, divided (2 plus 4)
⅔ cup (2 oz./55 g) finely ground coconut
Generous ¼ cup (1 oz./25 g) cake flour
Scant ½ cup (2 oz./55 g) confectioners' sugar
1 tablespoon (15 ml) whipping cream
⅓ cup (2 ½ oz./70 g) granulated sugar

Mango-passion fruit coulis
¾ sheet (1.5 g) gelatin
5 ¾ oz. (165 g) fresh mango, peeled and stone removed (net weight)
2 ⅔ oz. (85 g) mango pulp, store bought, or homemade, with 10 percent sugar
1 ¾ oz. (50 g) passion fruit pulp (if using fresh passion fruit, it's best to strain it)
A little granulated sugar (optional)

Chocolate Chantilly mousse
4 ⅔ oz. (130 g) bittersweet chocolate, 70 percent cocoa
Whipping cream, divided as follows: ½ cup plus 1 tablespoon (140 ml) plus ⅓ cup (80 ml)
A little unsweetened cocoa powder for dusting

Equipment
1 pastry circle†, 7-8 in. (18-20 cm) diameter
1 silicone baking mat† or a baking sheet lined with parchment paper
1 jelly (Swiss) roll pan
1 kitchen thermometer†
1 piping bag†
1 whisk†

Crisp Triple Chocolate Cake ★ ★ ★

Serves 6-8

Preparation time: 1 hour 45 minutes
Refrigeration time: overnight
Cooking time: 15 minutes

A day ahead, prepare the whipped white chocolate and vanilla ganache.
Chop the white chocolate and melt it slowly in a bain-marie* or in the microwave oven (on "defrost" or at 500 W maximum, stirring from time to time).
Slit the vanilla bean lengthways, scrape the seeds out into the ¼ cup (60 ml)
whipping cream, and bring it to the boil. Strain through a chinois. Gradually
pour one-third of the boiling cream over the melted chocolate. Using a flexible spatula, mix it in energetically, drawing small circles to create an elastic,
shiny "kernel." Incorporate the second third of the cream, using the same procedure. Repeat with the last third. Add the remaining cream and process with
an immersion blender until smooth and entirely emulsified*. Set aside in the
refrigerator and leave to harden, preferably overnight.

Prepare the basic custard (see p. 98).
Use the proportions given opposite.

Prepare the bittersweet and milk chocolate *crémeux* (see p. 100).
Use the proportions given opposite. Set aside in the refrigerator.

The next day, prepare the brownie-style base.
Chop and roast the almonds in a 325°F (160°C) oven. When they are done,
increase the temperature to 350°F (175°C). In a mixing bowl, briefly mix the
brown sugar with the egg, just enough to dissolve the sugar crystals. Set
aside. Soften the butter (see p. 134). Chop the chocolate and melt it slowly in a
bain-marie or in the microwave oven. Incorporate the softened butter into the
melted chocolate and mix until smooth. Gradually mix in the egg and brown
sugar mixture until smooth. Sift in the flour and mix until combined. Stir
in the roasted chopped almonds. Pour the batter into the unbuttered frame
placed on a lined baking sheet or a silicone baking mat. Bake for 14 minutes.
Trim the edges so they are neat and allow to cool completely.

To finish
Remove the whipped ganache from the refrigerator. Whisk it until it reaches
a creamy texture. Place a thin sheet of tempered chocolate over the cooled
brownie base. Spoon the bittersweet chocolate *crémeux* into a piping bag and
pipe it out over the sheet of chocolate. Place another sheet of chocolate atop the
crémeux and using the second piping bag, pipe out the whipped white chocolate ganache. Dot milk chocolate *crémeux* here and there over the top and garnish with chocolate shards. Keep in the refrigerator until ready to serve.

Ingredients

Whipped white chocolate and vanilla ganache*
1 ¼ oz. (35 g) white chocolate, 35 percent cocoa
1 vanilla bean
Whipped cream, divided as follows: ¼ cup (60 ml)
plus ½ cup minus 2 tablespoons (100 ml)

Basic pouring custard
3 egg yolks
¼ cup (1 ¾ oz./50 g) granulated sugar
1 cup (250 ml) whole milk
1 cup (250 ml) whipping cream

Bittersweet chocolate *crémeux*
1 cup minus 1 ½ tablespoons (225 ml)
pouring custard (see above)
3 oz. (85 g) bittersweet chocolate, 70 percent cocoa

Milk chocolate *crémeux*
½ cup minus 2 tablespoons (100 ml)
pouring custard (see above)
1 ¾ oz. (50 g) milk chocolate, 40 percent cocoa

Brownie-style base* with roasted almonds
1 ⅔ oz. (45 g) whole almonds
Scant ⅓ cup (2 ¼ oz./60 g) light brown sugar
1 small egg (1 ⅔ oz./45 g)
3 tablespoons plus 1 teaspoon (1 ¾ oz./50 g) butter,
room temperature
1 oz. (25 g) bittersweet chocolate, 70 percent cocoa
Generous ¼ cup (1 oz./25 g) cake flour

Decoration
2 thin squares of tempered* chocolate,
6 ⅔ in. (16 cm) square (see p. 20)
A few shards of tempered chocolate

Equipment

1 chinois†, 1 baking pan
1 baking sheet lined with parchment paper or
1 silicone baking mat†
1 kitchen thermometer†
2 piping bags †, 1 flexible spatula†
1 immersion blender†

Techniques

Melting Chocolate ›› p. 19
Tempering ›› p. 20
Whipped Ganache ›› p. 97
Basic Custard (*crème anglaise*) ›› p. 98
Chocolate *Crémeux* ›› p. 100

Ingredients

Raisins soaked in whisky
Scant ½ cup (100 ml) whisky
4 ¼ oz. (120 g) sultanas

Almond *dacquoise**
⅓ cup (1 oz./30 g) cake flour
1 cup (3 oz./85 g) blanched* ground almonds
¾ cup (3 ½ oz./100 g) confectioners' sugar
3 egg whites
¼ cup (1 ¾ oz./50 g) granulated sugar

Custard-based bittersweet chocolate mousse
5 ¾ oz. (165 g) bittersweet chocolate,
70 percent cocoa
⅓ cup minus 1 teaspoon (75 ml) whole milk
Whipping cream, divided as follows: ⅓ cup
minus 1 teaspoon (75 ml) plus 1 cup minus
1 ½ tablespoons (225 ml)
1 egg yolk
1 heaped tablespoon (15 g) sugar

Whisky whipped cream
¾ cup (200 ml) whipping cream
2 ½ tablespoons (⅔ oz./20 g) confectioners' sugar
1 tablespoon plus 2 teaspoons (25 ml) whisky

Equipment

16 small oval silicone molds†,
length approx. 3 in. (7 cm)
1 kitchen thermometer†
1 baking sheet lined with parchment paper
or 1 silicone baking mat†
1 offset spatula†
1 whisk†
1 tuile mold† (optional)

Glasgow Cakes ★★

Make 16 small oval cakes
Preparation time: 45 minutes
Cooking time: 45 minutes
Soaking time: 1 hour 30 minutes
Freezing time: overnight

A day ahead, prepare the whisky-soaked sultanas.
Bring the whisky to the boil and pour it immediately over the sultanas. Cover and leave them to plump for about 1 hour 30 minutes.

Prepare the almond *dacquoise* (see p. 86).
Preheat the oven to 350°F-375°F (180°C-190°C). Using an offset spatula, spread the batter out over a lined baking sheet or silicone mat, setting aside 2 tablespoons of batter for decoration. Bake for 10 minutes, until golden. Lower the oven temperature to 250°F (120°C). Spread out sixteen teardrop shapes of the remaining *dacquoise* batter on a lined baking sheet. Bake for about 35 minutes. Leave to cool and store in an airtight container.

Prepare the custard-based chocolate mousse (see p. 114).
Use the proportions given opposite. Pour the mousse into the molds and divide the whisky-plumped raisins evenly over the mousse, keeping some for garnish.
Cut out sixteen *dacquoise* bases* just slightly smaller than the size of the molds and place them atop the mousse. Freeze overnight.

The next day, prepare the whisky whipped cream.
Whip* the cream with the confectioners' sugar until it barely forms a Chantilly consistency. Add the whisky and whip further if the cream is too liquid.

Turn the cakes out of their molds and decorate with whisky Chantilly cream, sultanas, and a teardrop of dried *dacquoise*.

● Chef's note
If you would like curved dried dacquoise *shapes, use a tuile mold. However, if you don't have one, you can make do with an empty can. Open it at both ends and place strips of parchment paper at the ends. Drop the batter in teardrop shapes over the can and bake at 250°F (120°C). for about 35 minutes.*

Techniques
Almond *Dacquoise* ≫ p. 86
Custard-Based Chocolate Mousse ≫ p. 114

Bittersweet Chocolate Fondue ★

Serves 6-8
Preparation time: 40 minutes
Freezing time: 3 hours

Prepare the bittersweet chocolate fondue.
Bring the milk to the boil with the cream, glucose syrup, and honey. Slit the vanilla bean lengthways and scrape out the seeds. Leave the bean and seeds to infuse in the hot mixture.
Chop the chocolate and melt it slowly in a bain-marie* or in the microwave oven (on "defrost" or at 500 W maximum, stirring from time to time). Gradually pour the hot liquid over the melted chocolate, one-third* at a time, using the procedure described on p. 95. Pour the fondue into bowls and chill, or use immediately at a temperature between 108°F-113°F (42°C-45°C).

Prepare the raspberry marshmallow.
Grease a sheet of plastic wrap and set out the wooden skewers on it. Soften the gelatin in a large bowl filled with cold water. Bring the 10 oz. (280 g) raspberry purée to the boil with the sugar, 2 slightly heaped tablespoons (45 g) honey, and glucose syrup. Place the remaining honey in the bowl of a stand-alone mixer fitted with the whisk attachment. Pour the boiling syrup over. Wring the water out of the gelatin and place it in the mixer bowl. Whisk* until the mixture cools to 86°F (30°C), then add the remaining raspberry purée and the liqueur. Spoon the marshmallow into a piping bag and pipe out the marshmallow unevenly over wooden skewers.

Prepare the milk chocolate ganache.
Soften the gelatin in a large bowl of cold water. Bring the milk to the boil. Chop the chocolate and melt it (see p. 19). Wring the excess water out of the gelatin sheets and incorporate them into the milk. Pour the hot milk over the melted chocolate by thirds, using the procedure on p. 95.
Pour the ganache into a frame positioned over a lined baking sheet to a thickness of about ½-¾ in. (1.5 cm). When the ganache has set, cut out rectangles ¾ × 2 in. (2 × 5 cm) and freeze for 3 hours. Just before serving, heat an oil bath to 300°F-350°F (150°C-170°C), beat the egg, and fill a dish with breadcrumbs. Dip the frozen ganache into the beaten egg, then into the breadcrumbs, repeating for each rectangle, and fry for about 1 minute. Serve immediately. Accompany the fondue with strawberries, cubes of marshmallows, sticks of ganache, pâtes de fruits, macaroons, etc.

● Chef's note
You may want to flavor the fondue. Use spices, tea, or fruit pulp. For a spice fondue, add 1 slightly heaped teaspoon (4 g) of mixed spices for ginger bread to the hot milk and cream mixture. For a tea-flavored fondue, infuse ⅔ oz. (20 g) Blue Flower Earl Grey in the cream and milk overnight in the refrigerator. Just before straining the mixture through a chinois† the next morning to eliminate the tea leaves, add 2 teaspoons (10 ml) orange blossom water to the chocolate. The glucose syrup is not absolutely essential to this recipe; however, it provides the viscosity that optimizes this type of texture.

Ingredients

Bittersweet chocolate fondue
Generous ¾ cup (210 ml) milk
½ cup plus 2 tablespoons (150 ml) whipping cream
1 tablespoon (⅔ oz./20 g) glucose syrup
1 tablespoon (⅔ oz./20 g) honey
½ vanilla bean
13 ¼ oz. (375 g) bittersweet chocolate, 70 percent cocoa

Raspberry marshmallow
5 sheets (10 g) gelatin
Unsweetened raspberry purée, divided:
10 oz. (280 g) plus ⅔ oz. (20 g)
⅓ cup (2 ½ oz./70 g) granulated sugar
Honey, divided as follows: 2 slightly heaped tablespoons (1 ½ oz./45 g) plus 1 ⅔ tablespoons (1 ¼ oz./35 g)
5 teaspoons (1 ¼ oz./35 g) glucose syrup
2 teaspoons (10 ml) raspberry liqueur, 30° alcohol

Milk chocolate ganache*
4 sheets (8 g) gelatin
⅔ cup (160 ml) milk
9 oz. (250 g) milk chocolate, 40 percent cocoa
¾ stick (2 ¾ oz./80 g) butter
1 egg
Breadcrumbs
Oil for frying

Raspberry *pâte de fruits* (jelled fruit) (see p. 45)
Strawberries
Assorted Macaroons* (see p. 283)

Equipment
1 kitchen thermometer†
1 stand-alone mixer† fitted with a whisk attachment
1 confectionery frame†
1 baking sheet lined with parchment paper
1 piping bag†
Wooden skewers
Lollipop sticks

Techniques
Melting Chocolate ≫ p. 19
Pâte de Fruits (jelled fruit) ≫ p. 45

Ingredients
2 packets of rectangular dry butter cookies

Whipped milk chocolate-coffee ganache*
3 ¾ oz. (110 g) milk chocolate, 40 percent cocoa
⅓ cup (80 ml) espresso coffee
⅔ cup plus 2 teaspoons (190 ml) whipping cream

Coffee syrup
1 ¼ cups (300 ml) espresso coffee
¼ cup (1 ¾ oz./50 g) granulated sugar

A few chopped, roasted almonds for decoration

Equipment
1 silicone baking mat† or sheets of food-safe acetate†
1 flexible spatula†
1 whisk† or electric hand-held beater†

Manhattan Cappuccino ★ ★

Serves 6–8
Preparation time: 1 hour
Refrigeration time: 3 hours minimum

Prepare the whipped milk chocolate-coffee ganache.
Chop the chocolate and melt it slowly in a bain-marie* or in the microwave oven (on "defrost" or at 500 W maximum, stirring from time to time). Prepare the espresso coffee and gradually pour one-third of the hot liquid over the melted chocolate. Using a flexible spatula, mix it in energetically, drawing small circles to create an elastic, shiny "kernel."
Incorporate the second third of the coffee, using the same procedure. Repeat with the last third. Mix in the cold whipping cream and leave to set in the refrigerator for at least 3 hours, but preferably overnight.

Prepare the coffee syrup.
Make some very strong espresso coffee and stir in the sugar. Leave to cool to room temperature before dipping the cookies.

Dip five cookies into the cooled coffee syrup and immediately place them side by side on a sheet of acetate or a silicone baking mat.

Remove the ganache from the refrigerator and whip* it at medium speed until it reaches a creamy consistency.
Spread out a thin layer of ganache over the cookies. Soak another five cookies in the coffee and repeat the operation twice more. Set aside a little whipped ganache to cover the edges.
Then construct the elements that will represent the buildings and high-rises with single and sandwiched pairs of cookies. Insert chopped toasted almonds into the gaps. Chill.
To serve, place the various components horizontally or vertically to evoke the Manhattan skyline.

● Chef's note
This architecturally structured dessert is delicious served with chocolate sauce (see p. 127) or chocolate-caramel sauce (see p. 129).

Techniques
Melting Chocolate >> p. 19
Whipped Ganache >> p. 97

Orange Blossom Ivory Mousse
with a Praline Heart ★ ★

Serves 12
Preparation time: 40 minutes
Cooking time: 12 minutes
Refrigeration time: 2 hours
Total freezing time: 6 hours

Prepare the almond-praline sponge.
Sift the flour and baking powder together. Combine the eggs, honey, and sugar. Mix in the praline, and then the ground almonds. Stir in the sifted dry ingredients. Heat the cream to 113°F-122°F (45°C-50°C) and incorporate the butter. Then pour the cream-butter mixture into the batter. Leave in the refrigerator for 2 hours.
Preheat the oven to 350°F (180°C). Pour the batter over a lined baking sheet or silicone baking mat and bake for about 12 minutes, until a cake tester of knife tip comes out dry. Leave to cool and cut out disks using the cookie cutter.

Prepare the praline heart.
Soften the gelatin in a bowl of cold water. Bring the whipping cream to the boil in a saucepan, remove from the heat, wring the water from the gelatin, and incorporate it into the hot cream. Pour the cream over the praline by thirds*, using the procedure explained on p. 95. Spoon it into a piping bag and pipe it out into twelve silicone ice-cube cavities. Freeze for a minimum of 3 hours.

Prepare the orange blossom ivory mousse.
Chop the chocolate and melt it slowly in a bain-marie* or in the microwave oven (on "defrost" or at 500 W maximum, stirring from time to time). Soften the gelatin in a bowl of cold water. Bring the milk to the boil, remove from the heat, wring the water out of the gelatin, and incorporate it into the milk. Gradually pour the boiling milk over the melted chocolate, one-third at a time, using the procedure described on p. 95. In a mixing bowl, whisk* the cold cream until it is lightly whipped (see technique p. 134). When the chocolate mixture has cooled to 95°F-104°F (35°C-40°C), fold in* the lightly whipped cream using a flexible spatula. Stir in the orange blossom water.

Place the small pastry circles on a baking sheet lined with parchment paper. Place the sponge bases* at the base of the circles. Turn the iced praline creams out of the ice trays onto the sponge base. Then pour the orange blossom ivory mousse over the iced praline cream and freeze for 3 hours. Remove the circles and decorate as you wish, for example with a few caramelized* hazelnuts and chocolate pearls.

● **Chef's note**
Serve these small mousses with a clementine sauce, or accompanied by slices of clementines.

Ingredients

Almond-praline* sponge
Generous ¼ cup (1 oz./25 g) cake flour
¾ teaspoon (3 g) baking powder
2 eggs
1 heaped tablespoon (1 oz./25 g) multi-floral honey
2 ½ tablespoons (1 oz./30 g) granulated sugar
1 ⅔ oz. (45 g) praline, homemade (see p. 38)
or store-bought
Generous ⅓ cup (1 oz./30 g) ground
blanched* almonds
Scant ¼ cup (50 ml) whipping cream
2 tablespoons (30 g) butter

Praline heart
½ sheet (1 g) gelatin
½ cup minus 1 ½ tablespoons (100 ml)
whipping cream
4 ¼ oz. (150 g) praline, homemade (see p. 38)
or store-bought

Orange blossom ivory mousse
4 ⅔ oz. (130 g) white chocolate, 35 percent cocoa
2 sheets (4 g) gelatin
Scant ⅓ cup (70 ml) whole milk
Scant ⅔ cup (150 ml) whipping cream, well chilled
1 teaspoon (5 ml) orange blossom water

Whole hazelnuts
Chocolate pearls

Equipment
1 kitchen thermometer[†]
1 baking sheet lined with parchment paper
or 1 silicone baking mat[†]
1 ¼ in. (3 cm) diameter cookie cutter[†]
1 piping bag[†]
Silicone ice-cube tray (tray of 12)
12 individual pastry circles[†]
1 flexible spatula[†]
1 whisk[†]

Techniques
Homemade Praline ›› p. 38
Egg-Free Chocolate Mousse ›› p. 111

Ingredients

Almond Shortcrust Pastry

1 stick (4 oz./120 g) butter, room temperature
Scant ½ teaspoon (2 g) salt
⅔ cup (3 oz./90 g) confectioners' sugar
3 tablespoons (½ oz./15 g) ground blanched* almonds
1 egg
Cake flour, divided as follows: ⅔ cup (2 oz./60 g) plus 2 cups (6 ⅓ oz./180 g)

Chocolate-caramel*-vanilla mousse

3 ½ oz. (100 g) milk chocolate, 40 percent cocoa
½ vanilla bean
1 sheet (2 g) gelatin
2 ½ tablespoons (1 oz./30 g) granulated sugar
2 egg yolks
1 cup (250 ml) whipping cream, divided as follows:
3 ½ tablespoons (50 ml) plus 1 cup
minus 3 tablespoons (200 ml)

Lemon-scented crushed pear

1 pear
Juice of ½ lemon
A little granulated sugar

Caramel and white chocolate glaze

9 ⅓ oz. (265 g) white chocolate, 35 percent cocoa
2 sheets (4 g) gelatin
¾ cup (175 ml) whipping cream
3 tablespoons (40 ml) water
1 ½ tablespoons (1 oz./30 g) glucose syrup
¼ cup (1 ¾ oz./50 g) granulated sugar
1 tablespoon plus 2 teaspoons (25 ml)
grape-seed oil

Equipment

1 kitchen thermometer†
Small square silicone molds†
1 baking sheet lined with parchment paper
1 flexible spatula†
1 immersion blender†
1 whisk†

Techniques

Melting Chocolate ›› p. 19
Almond Shortcrust Pastry ›› p. 72
Chocolate Chantilly Mousse ›› p. 113

Pear and Milk Chocolate Petits Fours ★★

Serves 6–8

Preparation time: 1 hour 30 minutes
Cooking time: 10 minutes
Total freezing time: 3 hours 30 minutes

Preheat the oven to 300°F–325°F (150°C–160°C).
Prepare the almond shortcrust pastry (see p. 72). Cut the dough into squares that are just slightly smaller than the size of the silicone molds. Place them on a lined baking sheet and bake for about 10 minutes.

Prepare the chocolate-caramel-vanilla mousse.
Chop the chocolate and melt it (see p. 19). Slit the vanilla bean and scrape out the seeds. Soften the gelatin in a bowl filled with cold water. Cook the sugar in a saucepan until it forms a light caramel (small bubbles will begin to form and the temperature should be 343°F–347°F (173°C–175°C). While it is cooking, beat the egg yolks. Carefully stir 3 ½ tablespoons (50 ml) whipping cream into the caramelized sugar. Pour the liquid over the beaten egg yolks, add the vanilla seeds, and return to the heat. Stir until it thickens and coats the back of a spoon. Wring the excess water from the gelatin and incorporate it into the custard. Process for a few seconds with an immersion blender until smooth and creamy. Incorporate the hot custard into the melted chocolate by thirds*, using the procedure on p. 95. Process briefly again until completely emulsified*. In a mixing bowl, lightly whip* the remaining 1 cup minus 3 ½ tablespoons (200 ml) whipping cream (see p. 134). When the chocolate-custard mixture has cooled to 113°F–122°F (45°C–50°C), fold in* one-third of the lightly whipped cream. Then carefully fold in the remaining cream using a flexible spatula. Pour the mousse into the small molds and top with a small square of baked shortcrust pastry. Freeze for about 3 hours.

Prepare the lemon-scented crushed pear.
Peel and core the pear. Cut it into pieces and place them in a bowl. Pour in the lemon juice and process. Adjust the taste, adding a touch of sugar if necessary. When the mousses are completely frozen, remove them from their molds and turn them upside down. Top them with a little crushed pear. Return to the freezer for 30 minutes.

Prepare the caramel and white chocolate glaze.
Chop the chocolate and melt it (see p. 19). Soften the gelatin in a bowl filled with cold water. In a saucepan, heat the whipping cream, water, and glucose syrup. Remove from the heat, wring the water from the gelatin, and incorporate it into the hot liquid. Place the sugar in a heavy-bottomed saucepan. Cook until it forms a light caramel, then pour it into the cream and glucose syrup mixture. Pour this hot cream gradually over the melted chocolate by thirds, according to the procedure on p. 95. Stir in the grape-seed oil. Process, ensuring you do not incorporate any air bubbles. Ice the petits fours with the caramel and white chocolate glaze and keep in the refrigerator until ready to serve.

Ingredients

Chocolate cake layer

1 stick (4 oz./120 g) butter, plus a little extra
for the mold
2 ½ oz. (70 g) bittersweet chocolate,
70 percent cocoa
6 eggs
Scant ⅓ cup (3 ½ oz./100 g) acacia honey
1 scant cup (6 oz./170 g) granulated sugar
1 cup plus 3 tablespoons (3 ½ oz./100 g)
blanched* ground almonds
1 ¾ cups (5 ⅔ oz./160 g) cake flour,
plus a little extra for the mold
2 ½ teaspoons (10 g) baking powder
¼ cup (1 oz./30 g) unsweetened cocoa powder
⅔ cup (160 ml) whipping cream

Bittersweet chocolate ganache*

7 oz. (200 g) bittersweet chocolate,
70 percent cocoa
1 ¼ cups (300 ml) whipping cream
2 ½ tablespoons (50 g) honey

Ultra-shiny glaze

6 sheets (12 g) gelatin
Scant ½ cup (100 g) water
1 scant cup (6 oz./170 g) granulated sugar
⅔ cup (2 ⅔ oz./75 g) unsweetened cocoa powder
⅓ cup plus 2 teaspoons (3 oz./90 g)
whipping cream

Decoration

1 sheet edible gold leaf

Equipment

1 cake mold†, 8 in. (20 cm) diameter
1 long serrated knife
1 pastry circle†, 8 ½ in. (22 cm) diameter
1 immersion blender†
1 baking sheet lined with parchment paper
1 cake rack

Techniques

Ultra-Shiny Glaze ›› p. 66
Chocolate Cake Batter ›› p. 85
Ganache for Tarts and Desserts ›› p. 96

Gold-Topped *Palet* Dessert ★ ★

Serves 6

Preparation time: 1 hour
Cooking time: 40 minutes
Refrigeration time: overnight plus 6 hours
Freezing time: overnight

A day ahead, prepare the ultra-shiny glaze (see p. 66).
Chill overnight.

Prepare the chocolate cake batter (see p. 85).
Use the ingredients given opposite. Preheat the oven to 325°F (160°C). Butter the cake mold, dust it lightly with flour, and pour in the batter. Bake for about 40 minutes, testing for doneness with the tip of a knife. The cake is done when it comes out dry. Turn out of the mold, leave to cool completely (otherwise it will be harder to cut), and cut it into three layers, using a long serrated knife, such as a bread knife.

Prepare the bittersweet chocolate ganache (see p. 96).
Use the proportions given opposite.

To assemble and decorate.
Place the pastry circle on a flat, lined baking sheet. Position the first layer of chocolate cake; its diameter will be smaller than that of the pastry circle. Spread out one-third of the ganache, then place another layer of chocolate cake over it, pressing down so that the ganache oozes out over the sides of the first cake layer. Spread out the second third of the ganache, and repeat the procedure, finishing with a layer of ganache.
Rap lightly to smooth out the surface and freeze, ideally overnight.

The next day.
Reheat the ultra-shiny glaze over a bain-marie* or gently in the microwave oven (on "defrost" or 500 W, stirring from time to time). Process with an immersion blender. Take the frozen dessert out of the freezer and place it on a cake rack over a sheet that will catch the glaze that runs off. Cover the dessert completely with glaze and very lightly shake the cake rack to eliminate any excess glaze. Transfer the dessert to a serving dish and place the gold leaf in the center. Keep in the refrigerator for about 6 hours to defrost, and take it out an hour before serving so it comes to room temperature, when its flavors will be at their best.

● Chef's note
Processing the glaze before using it eliminates air bubbles.

Flore ★★★

Serves 6-8

Preparation time: 1 hour 30 minutes
Freezing time: 1 hour plus 3 hours
Refrigeration time: 6 hours

A day ahead, prepare the chocolate cake batter (see p. 85).
Use the proportions given opposite. Preheat the oven to 350°F (180°C). Pour out the batter onto a jelly (Swiss) roll pan to a thickness of just under 1 in. (2 cm) and bake for about 10 minutes. When the sponge has cooled, cut out a circle slightly smaller than the 8 ½ in. (22 cm) cake mold.

Prepare the jasmine *crémeux*.
Leave the jasmine tea leaves to infuse in the cold cream for about 3 to 4 hours, or in hot cream for about 5 minutes. Filter the cream into a saucepan. Soften the gelatin in a bowl of cold water. Mix the egg yolks and sugar in a bowl to dissolve the sugar. Pour the mixture into the tea-flavored cream and leave to simmer, stirring constantly, until it coats the back of a spoon and has thickened slightly. The temperature should be 180°F-183°F (82°C-84) C). Remove from the heat. Wring the water out of the gelatin and stir it in until completely dissolved. Pour the *crémeux* into a deep mixing bowl. Process with an immersion blender until smooth and thoroughly emulsified*. Pour into the 7 in. (18 cm) mold. Freeze for about 3 hours, until completely hardened.

Prepare the egg-free chocolate mousse (see p. 111).
Use the proportions given opposite. Set aside in the refrigerator.

To assemble.
Position the layer of chocolate sponge in the center of the larger mold. Unmold the jasmine *crémeux* and place it in the center of the chocolate sponge. Arrange the raspberries around the rim of the chocolate sponge and pour the chocolate mousse into the mold. Place in the freezer, ideally overnight.

The next day.
Remove the frozen dessert from the mold and leave it in the refrigerator while you prepare the white chocolate glaze, using the instructions on p. 69. Glaze* the cake and decorate with crystallized jasmine flowers and pearl sugar. Return the dessert to the refrigerator for a minimum of 6 hours, until serving.

● **Chef's notes**
Cut the remaining sponge cake into small cubes and freeze for use in a verrine dessert.
It's best to leave the tea leaves to infuse overnight in cold cream to avoid the astringency of the tea and retain only the pleasant aromas.

Ingredients

Chocolate sponge
3 eggs
2 ½ tablespoons (50 g) honey
Scant ½ cup (3 oz./85 g) granulated sugar
Generous ½ cup (1 ¾ oz./50 g) ground blanched* almonds
⅓ cup (80 ml) whipping cream
Scant cup (2 ¾ oz./80 g) cake flour
1 ¼ teaspoons (5 g) baking powder
2 tablespoons (½ oz./15 g) unsweetened cocoa powder
¼ cup (60 ml) melted butter
2 tablespoons plus 1 teaspoon rum
1 ¼ oz. (35 g) bittersweet chocolate, 70 percent cocoa

Jasmine *crémeux*
⅓ oz. (10 g) jasmine tea leaves
1 cup (250 ml) whipping cream
1 sheet (2 g) gelatin
3 egg yolks
¼ cup (1 ¾ oz./50 g) granulated sugar

Bittersweet chocolate mousse
6 oz. (170 g) bittersweet chocolate, 60 percent cocoa
½ cup (125 ml) whole milk
1 cup (250 ml) whipping cream

4 ½ oz. (125 g) raspberries
White chocolate glaze (see p. 69)

Decoration
Crystallized* jasmine flowers
Pearl sugar

Equipment

1 kitchen thermometer†
1 immersion blender†
1 mold†, 7 in. (18 cm) diameter
1 mold†, 8 ½ in. (22 cm) diameter
1 jelly (Swiss) roll pan
1 sieve†

Techniques

White Chocolate or Colored Glaze ›› p. 69
Chocolate Cake Batter ›› p. 85
Basic *Crémeux* ›› p. 99
Egg-Free Chocolate Mousse ›› p. 111

Ingredients

Chocolate cake
1 ¼ oz. (35 g) bittersweet chocolate,
60 percent cocoa
4 tablespoons (2 ¼ oz./60 g) butter
3 eggs
2 ½ tablespoons (50 g) honey
Scant ½ cup (2 ¾ oz./80 g) granulated sugar
Generous ½ cup (1 ¾ oz./50 g) ground
blanched* almonds
Scant cup (2 ¾ oz./80 g) cake flour
1 ¼ teaspoons (5 g) baking powder
2 tablespoons (½ oz./15 g) unsweetened
cocoa powder
⅓ cup (80 ml) whipping cream

Bittersweet chocolate Chantilly mousse
6 ⅓ oz. (180 g) bittersweet chocolate,
60 percent cocoa
Whipping cream, divided as follows: 1 cup
minus 3 tablespoons (200 ml) plus ½ cup
minus 1 ½ tablespoons (100 ml)

Crunchy almond coating
2 ½ oz. (70 g) chopped almonds
10 ½ oz. (300 g) bittersweet chocolate,
60 percent cocoa
2 tablespoons (30 ml) grape-seed oil

Decoration
White and bittersweet chocolate , melted
Various fruit coulis, store bought or homemade, in
bowls, with brushes or, even better, with pipettes.

Equipment

1 kitchen thermometer†
1 confectionery frame† or rectangular cake mold†,
9 ½ × 13 ½ in. (24 × 34 cm)
1 baking sheet lined with parchment paper
or 1 baking mat†
8 pastry circles†, 3 in. (7 ½ cm) diameter
2 paper decorating cones†

Mister Clown ★

Serves 8
Preparation time: 1 hour 30 minutes
Cooking time: 10 minutes
Freezing time: 4 hours

Prepare the chocolate cake batter (see p. 85).
Use the ingredients given opposite. Place the rectangular frame on a lined baking sheet, or use a cake pan. Pour the batter into the pan or frame and bake for about 8 to 10 minutes, until a knife tip or cake tester comes out dry. Leave to cool and cut out eight disks the same size as the pastry circles.

Prepare the chocolate Chantilly mousse (see p. 113).
Use the ingredients given opposite.

To assemble.
Place the individual pastry circles on a baking sheet lined with parchment paper. In each one, place a disk of chocolate sponge and cover it with a layer about 1 in. (1-3 cm) thick of chocolate Chantilly mousse. Freeze for about 4 hours. Remove the rings from around these little *palets* and return them to the freezer.

Prepare the crunchy almond coating.
Heat the oven to 325°F (160°C) and roast the chopped almonds for a few minutes. Leave to cool. Melt the chocolate over a bain-marie* or in the microwave oven (on "defrost" or at 500 W, stirring from time to time). Stir in the oil and then the roasted almonds.

Insert the tip of a kitchen knife into the chocolate sponge to lift it up and dip it, still frozen, into the crunchy coating. Remove immediately, allowing the excess coating to drip off, and then place each cake on a serving plate.
Prepare two paper decorating cones (see p. 53) and fill one with melted bittersweet chocolate and the other with white chocolate. Draw the eyes and mouth on the top of the chocolate cake using the white chocolate, and, with the bittersweet chocolate, draw the bodies of the clowns on the plates. The children can then decorate their clowns with the various coulis.

● **Chef's note**
To coat the cakes well, they must be frozen when they are dipped.

Techniques
Paper Decorating Cones ›› p. 53
Chocolate Cake Batter ›› p. 85
Chocolate Chantilly Mousse ›› p. 113

Candies and confections

Jean-Paul Hévin
presents his recipe

Chocolate? It's all I think about! And I suppose you could call me a chocoholic, for I couldn't imagine a day without tasting it. It's a professional obligation, a pleasure, and a means to keep my taste buds awake. Chocolate is one of the finest products there is.

It can be adapted to any artistic creation, its range of tastes and pairings is limitless, it is good for our health. During my lifetime, I have experienced several revelations, including the moment when I "went into pastry" at professional high school, and when I discovered Japan, where I realized that desserts could be aesthetically simple without being simplistic. Working on that premise, one can dare to imagine that any kind of creation—the Louvre pyramid, stiletto heels, haute couture dresses—can be transfigured by the magic of chocolate.

Luscious Lollipops

Chocolate *palets*. Chop the bittersweet or milk chocolate into small pieces. Melt two-thirds of the chocolate in a bowl over a bain-marie* at low heat (122°F or 50°C). While it is melting, chop the remaining third very finely. It is preferable to let your chocolate melt off the heat to avoid spoiling it. Remove the bowl from the bain-marie and wait for a few minutes. Cool the chocolate down to 84°F (29°C) by adding the remaining third of finely chopped chocolate and mix with a spatula for a good few minutes. Return the bowl of chocolate to the bain-marie to gently heat the chocolate to 90°F–91°F (32°C–33°C).

Cover your baking sheet with waxed paper or a transfer sheet. Using a piping bag, pipe out several rows of chocolate *palets*, each about 2 in. (5 cm) in diameter. Rap the baking sheet a few times so that the chocolate spreads out evenly, at which stage the diameter should spread to 2 ¾ in. (7 cm). Leave the chocolate to set at room temperature; it will keep its sheen. To speed up the hardening process, you may even leave it on a shelf of the refrigerator briefly—in 10 minutes, the crystallization* should be visible.

Chocolate ganache. Bring the whipping cream and the invert sugar to the boil. Leave to cool. Chop the chocolate. When the cream reaches 167°F (75°C), pour it over the chopped chocolate and stir carefully until the mixture is perfectly smooth. Incorporate the butter. At this stage, you may incorporate a few drops of essential oils if you are using any. Pour the ganache onto a baking sheet to cool.

Place in the refrigerator for a minimum of 1 hour, or leave in a cool place, in which case more time will be required. Leave the ganache to harden.

To assemble the lollipop. Use the ganache like glue between 2 palets. Place a ball of ganache on each chocolate *palet*, then place a stick between 2 chocolate *palets* and press gently so that it all holds together.

Store your creations in a cool place until you are ready to savor them. They will keep for 2 to 3 days in a cool place, or 4 to 6 days in an airtight container on the highest shelf of your refrigerator.

● **Chef's note**
Ensure that the temperature of the water of the bain-marie does not exceed 131°F (55°C).

Candies and confections

Ingredients
For the chocolate *palets*
1 ½ lb. (700 g) bittersweet or milk chocolate
Transfer sheets with red lipstick pattern (optional)

For the chocolate ganache*
Scant ½ cup (115 ml) whipping cream, 30 percent butterfat
⅔ oz. (20 g) invert sugar
7 ½ oz. (215 g) chocolate, 63 percent cocoa
3 tablespoons plus 2 teaspoons (2 oz./55 g) unsalted butter, softened
A few drops of essential oils, such as bergamot orange, orange, orange blossom, fresh mint, petit-grain bigarade, rose, or a combination of oils such as mint with bergamot orange (optional)

Equipment
1 kitchen thermometer†
1 spatula†
1 piping bag†
1 baking sheet
20 lollipop sticks

Bittersweet Chocolate Bars, Salted Butter Caramel, and Crystallized Almonds ★ ★ ★

Makes 15 bars
Preparation time: 3 hours 30 minutes
Cooking time: 35 minutes
Refrigeration time: 30 minutes
Freezing time: 30 minutes

Prepare the salted butter caramel.
Place a square frame on a lined baking sheet. Bring the cream to the boil and set aside. Bring the glucose syrup gently to the boil in a large saucepan, then gradually add the sugar. Continue simmering until it forms a light caramel. Carefully add the salted butter, making sure it does not splash and burn you. Then stir in the hot cream and continue cooking until the caramel reaches 244°F (118°C). Pour it into the frame and leave to set.

Prepare the crystallized almonds with long pepper.
Preheat the oven to 300°F (150°C).
Roast the almonds (see p. 134) and leave them to cool. Place the sugar and water in a saucepan and bring to the boil. Leave to boil for 1 minute. Turn the oven temperature down to 195°F (90°C). Carefully stir the cooled almonds into the syrup and add a little long pepper.
Spread the almonds out over a lined baking sheet and dry in them in the oven for about 20 minutes, until they are crisp. Set aside in an airtight container.

Prepare the almond shortcrust pastry (see p. 72).
Use the ingredients given opposite. Roll it out between two sheets of food-safe acetate to a thickness of ⅛ in. (3 mm) and place it in the freezer for 30 minutes. When the dough has hardened, carefully remove the sheets of acetate and cut it into 4 × 1 in. (10 × 2 cm) strips. Chill for 30 minutes. Preheat the oven to 300°F-325°F (150°C-160°C) and bake for about 15 minutes, until a nice golden color.

To finish.
Cut the caramel into 4 × 1 in. (10 × 2 cm) strips and place them on the strips of baked pastry. Using a piping bag, pipe out the ganache over the caramel. Place the caramel bars on a rack positioned over a baking sheet and set aside.
Temper* the chocolate (see p. 20). Pour it into a jug and add the hazelnut oil. Mix thoroughly. Pour it over the bars, covering them completely. Sprinkle generously with crystallized almonds before the chocolate sets, and carefully place the bars on parchment paper or a silicone baking mat.

Ingredients

Almond shortcrust pastry
1 ¼ sticks (5 ¼ oz./145 g) butter
1 pinch salt
¾ cup (3 ½ oz./100 g) confectioners' sugar
¼ cup (⅔ oz./20 g) ground blanched* almonds
2 eggs
Cake flour, divided as follows: ¾ cup (2 ½ oz./70 g) plus 2 ½ cups (8 ¼ oz./230 g)

Bittersweet chocolate ganache*
12 ⅔ oz. (360 g) bittersweet chocolate, 60 percent cocoa
1 ¼ cups (300 ml) whipping cream
3 tablespoons (2 ¼ oz./60 g) honey
1 tablespoon plus 1 teaspoon (20 g) butter

Salted butter caramel*
Generous ⅔ cup (185 ml) whipping cream
3 tablespoons (2 ¼ oz./60 g) glucose syrup
Scant cup (6 ½ oz./185 g) granulated sugar
3 ½ tablespoons (1 ¾ oz./50 g) salted butter

Crystallized* almonds with long pepper
Scant ½ cup (3 ¼ oz./90 g) granulated sugar
Generous ⅓ cup (90 ml) water
9 oz. (250 g) whole almonds
A little long pepper

To finish
1 lb. 2 oz. (500 g) milk chocolate, 40 percent cocoa
Scant ⅓ cup (70 ml) hazelnut oil

Equipment
1 square frame or pan , 8 in. (20 cm)
1 baking sheet lined with parchment paper
1 kitchen thermometer†
1 piping bag†
2 sheets of food-safe acetate †
Parchment paper or 1 silicone baking mat†
1 cake rack

Techniques
Tempering » p. 20
Ganache for Hand-Dipped Centers » p. 33
Almond Shortcrust Pastry » p. 72
Roasting Nuts » p. 134

Crisp, Melting Bonbons ★ ★ ★

Make 15 tartlets or 60 small bonbons
Preparation time: 1 hour
Refrigeration time: 7 hours

Prepare the crisp praline.
Chop the chocolate and melt it slowly in a bain-marie* or in the microwave oven (on "defrost" or at 500 W maximum, stirring from time to time). Stir in the praline and bring the temperature to 79°F (26°C), stirring constantly. At this stage, the mixture will begin to thicken slightly. Stir in the crushed *crêpes dentelles* and immediately pour into the tartlet molds. Give the molds a rap or two to ensure that the surface is flat and smooth. Place in the refrigerator for 1 hour.

Prepare the bittersweet chocolate ganache.
Chop the chocolate and melt it slowly in a bain-marie* or in the microwave oven (on "defrost" or at 500 W maximum, stirring from time to time). Bring the whipping cream to the boil with the honey. Pour one-third gradually over the melted chocolate. Using a flexible spatula, mix it in energetically, drawing small circles to create an elastic, shiny "kernel."
Incorporate the second third of the liquid, using the same procedure. Repeat with the last third. Process for a few seconds and leave to cool down. As soon as the temperature reaches 95°F-104°F (35°C-40°C), incorporate the diced butter. Spoon the ganache into a piping bag and pipe it out over the crisp praline. Leave to harden for 6 hours in the refrigerator.

Prepare the coating.
Temper* the chocolate (see p. 20). When it reaches 88°F (31°C), pour it into a large mixing bowl and stir in the grape-seed oil until combined.
Turn the tartlets out of their molds. Cut the tartlets into quarters, if you are making the small size, and dip them in the coating mixture which should still be at 88°F (31°C). Transfer them to a baking sheet lined with parchment paper and scatter with crushed *crêpes dentelles*.

Techniques
Melting Chocolate ›› p. 19
Tempering ›› p. 20
Coating ›› p. 25
Ganache for Hand-Dipped Centers ›› p. 33
Homemade Praline ›› p. 38

Ingredients
Crisp praline*
1 oz. (26 g) milk chocolate, 40 percent cocoa
3 ¼ oz. (90 g) praline, homemade (see p. 38)
or store bought
1 ¼ oz. (35 g) crushed *crêpes dentelles*, an extremely friable, fine wafer-like biscuit, a Breton specialty, plus a little extra for the decoration

Bittersweet chocolate ganache*
5 oz. (140 g) bittersweet chocolate, 70 percent cocoa
½ cup plus 1 teaspoon (130 ml) whipping cream
1 heaped tablespoon (1 oz./25 g) honey
1 tablespoon (15 g) butter, diced

Coating
8 ¼ oz. (230 g) bittersweet chocolate,
70 percent cocoa
2 tablespoons (30 ml) grape-seed oil

Equipment
Silicone tartlet molds†
1 kitchen thermometer†
1 piping bag†
1 baking sheet lined with parchment paper
1 flexible spatula†

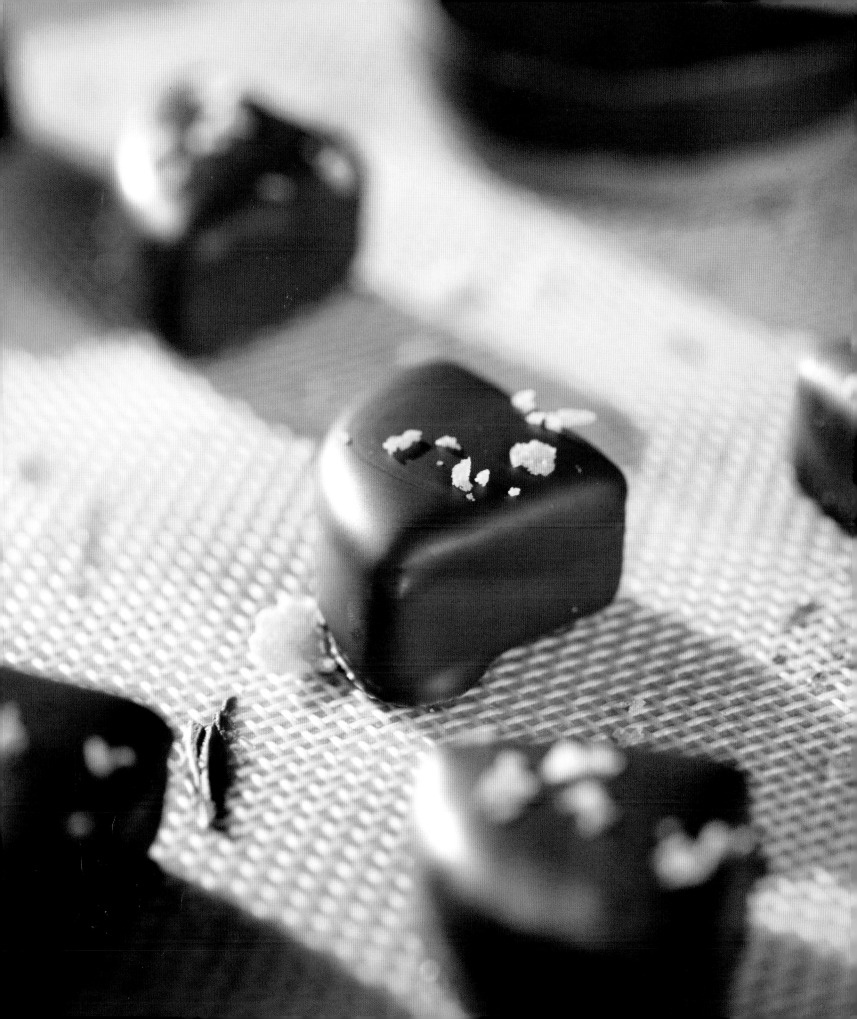

Ingredients

5 ½ oz. (150 g) bittersweet chocolate,
70 percent cocoa

1 cup (250 ml) whipping cream

1 pinch salt

1 ¼ cups (9 oz./250 g) granulated sugar

2 teaspoons (15 g) honey

1 tablespoon butter, diced

Equipment

1 confectionery frame† and 1 baking sheet

Or silicone molds†

1 kitchen thermometer†

Chocolate-Flavored Caramel Bonbons ★★★

Makes 30-40 caramels

Preparation time: 30 minutes

Setting time: overnight

A day ahead.

Chop the chocolate and melt it slowly in a bain-marie* or in the microwave oven (on "defrost" or at 500 W maximum, stirring from time to time).

Add the salt to the cream and heat in the microwave oven so that it is warm enough to be added to the caramel*.

In a large saucepan, caramelize the sugar with the honey to make a nice, light caramel.

Being very careful, slowly pour the hot cream over the caramel so that it does not splash.

Heat the mixture to 239°F (115°C) and pour it over the melted chocolate. Add the diced butter and mix it in quickly.

Pour into a confectionery frame or silicone molds and leave to harden overnight. Cut into small squares the next day.

● **Chef's note**

If you wish, you can substitute the 5 ½ oz. (150 g) bittersweet chocolate with 7 oz. (200 g) milk chocolate, and then roll the caramels in finely chopped peanuts.

 Technique
Melting Chocolate ≫ p. 19

Chocolate-Honey Marshmallow ★★

Makes 10 strips of marshmallow
Preparation time: 20 minutes
Resting time: overnight

A day ahead, prepare the chocolate-honey marshmallow.
Soften the gelatin in a bowl filled with cold water. Prepare the baking sheet: line it with lightly greased parchment paper (use a neutral oil or spray), and grease the sides, or line an oiled baking pan with plastic wrap, making sure you remove all wrinkles and air bubbles.
In a saucepan, bring the sugar, the smaller quantity of honey, and the water to 230°F (110°C). Place the larger quantity of honey in a mixing bowl and pour in the hot syrup. Squeeze the excess water from the gelatin and melt it in the microwave (for 10 seconds at 500 W, without adding any liquid), then combine it with the syrup-honey mixture and whisk* until it reaches a foamy texture.

Chop the chocolate and melt it slowly in a bain-marie* or in the microwave oven (on "defrost" or at 500 W maximum, stirring from time to time).
When the marshmallow mixture is lukewarm, use a flexible spatula to incorporate the melted chocolate. Pour it immediately into the frame or pan and cover with another sheet of lightly greased paper, greased side downward.
Leave to set overnight, then cut out strips using an oiled knife.
Roll them in the cocoa powder or colored sugar and store in an airtight container.

Techniques
Melting Chocolate ›› p. 19
Chocolate Marshmallow ›› p. 44

Ingredients
8 ½ sheets (17 g) gelatin
1 cup plus 3 tablespoons (8 oz./225 g) granulated sugar
Honey, divided as follows: 3 tablespoons plus 1 scant teaspoon (2 ½ oz./70 g) plus scant ⅓ cup (4 ½ tablespoons, 3 ½ oz./ 100 g)
⅓ cup (75 ml) water
3 ½ oz. (100 g) chocolate, 70 percent cocoa
Cocoa powder for dusting
Colored sugar for decoration

Equipment
2 baking sheets lined with lightly greased parchment paper
1 extra sheet of lightly greased parchment paper
1 square frame or pan, 8 in. (20 cm)
1 whisk†
1 flexible spatula†

Ingredients

10 ½ oz. (300 g) bittersweet chocolate,
70 percent cocoa
Or 10 ½ oz. (300 g) white chocolate,
35 percent cocoa
Or 10 ½ oz. (300 g) milk chocolate,
40 percent cocoa
Your choice of dried fruit and nuts
(dried apricots, almonds, walnuts, pistachios, etc)

Equipment

1 kitchen thermometer†
Baking sheets lined with parchment paper
1 piping bag†

Mendiants ★★★

Makes about 30 mendiants
Preparation time: 45 minutes

Line a baking sheet with parchment paper. Place your dried fruits and nuts in small bowls or ramekins, a separate bowl for each type.

Temper* the chocolate.
Chop the chocolate and melt it slowly in a bain-marie* (see p. 19).
Prepare a cold-water bath with a few ice cubes in it. When the chocolate reaches 131°F-136°F (55°C-58°C), remove it from the hot bain-marie and place it over the cold-water bath.
Stir constantly to prevent the chocolate from crystallizing* too fast at the edges, and the cocoa butter* from overcrystallizing. Keep checking the temperature.
When the chocolate cools to about 95°F (35°C), remove it from the cold bain-marie, still stirring until the bittersweet chocolate cools to 88°F-90°F (31°C-32°C); milk chocolate cools to 81°F-82°F (27°C-28°C); white or colored chocolate cools to 82°F-84°F (28°C-29°C)
Fill a piping bag with the chocolate and pipe out identically sized chocolate drops, just under 1 in. (2 cm) in diameter. Rap the baking sheet lightly so that the drops spread out to form small disks (*palets*). Very quickly, top them with the dried fruit and nuts, and leave to set.

● Chef's note
Do not pipe out too many drops of chocolate at the same time so that you have time to place the dried fruit and nuts before the chocolate sets.

Techniques
Melting Chocolate ›› p. 19
Tempering ›› p. 20

Orangettes ★ ★ ★

Serves 6-8
Preparation time: 1 hour 30 minutes
Cooking time: 45 minutes
Resting time: overnight

A day ahead, prepare the orangettes.
Clean and brush the oranges under cold running water. Cut the peel into four quarters without making an incision into the flesh of the fruit. Carefully pull away the quarters of peel and place them in a large pot. Cover with cold water and bring to the boil. Leave to boil for 5 minutes. Drain, leave to cool, and repeat the procedure. Drain again and leave to cool in a colander. In a heavy bottomed pot, combine the sugar and water and bring to the boil. When the syrup begins to boil, drop the orange skins in. When the water comes to the boil again, leave it to simmer for 5 minutes. Remove from the heat and leave the syrup with the orange peel to cool down again completely. Bring to the boil again twice, leaving the syrup to simmer 5 minutes each time and allowing it to cool down completely each time. The candied peel should be transparent after these three steps.
When the syrup and peel have finally cooled down, cut the peel into thin strips about ¼ in. (5 mm) wide. Place them on a rack, ensuring that they do not overlap and leave them to dry out, uncovered, for at least 12 hours.

Temper* the chocolate using the technique of your choice (see p. 20).
Use a dipping fork to coat the orange peel (see p. 25). Dip the strips of candied peel one by one in the tempered bittersweet chocolate. Leave to harden before serving.

● Chef's note
If you prefer, you can find strips of candied orange peel ready to be coated at fine grocery stores.

Techniques
Melting Chocolate ›› p. 19
Tempering ›› p. 20

Ingredients
3 large oranges, unwaxed
1 ¼ cups (9 oz./250 g) sugar
2 cups (500 ml) water
1 lb. (450 g) bittersweet chocolate,
70 percent cocoa

Equipment
1 kitchen thermometer†
1 dipping fork†
1 colander
1 heavy bottomed pot
1 wire rack

Candies and confections

Rose and Raspberry Lollipops ★★★

Serves 6–8
Preparation time: 1 hour 30 minutes
Refrigeration time: overnight
Freezing time: 2 hours

A day ahead, prepare the white chocolate and raspberry ganache.
Chop the chocolate and melt it slowly in a bain-marie* or in the microwave oven (on "defrost" or at 500 W maximum, stirring from time to time). Bring the cream to the boil in a saucepan. Gradually pour one-third of the boiling cream over the melted chocolate. Using a flexible spatula, mix it in energetically, drawing small circles to create an elastic, shiny "kernel." Incorporate the second third of the cream, using the same procedure. Repeat with the last third. Add the rose water and raspberry pulp and mix well. Process briefly with an immersion blender so that the mixture is smooth and well emulsified*. Leave to harden overnight in the refrigerator.
The next day, spoon the ganache into a piping bag fitted with a plain tip onto a lined baking sheet and pipe it out into truffle shapes. Insert a lollipop stick into the center of each truffle and freeze for 2 hours.

Prepare the white chocolate coating.
Chop the chocolate and melt it slowly in a bain-marie or in the microwave oven (on "defrost" or at 500 W maximum, stirring from time to time). Pour it into a large mixing bowl and incorporate the oil. To chop the sugar-coated almonds, crush them with the bottom of a sturdy saucepan.
Take a sheet of food-safe acetate, or even better, a transfer sheet and spread it out on a perfectly smooth, flat baking sheet.
Dip the frozen lollipops into the coating mixture. Allow the excess to drip off quickly and then transfer them immediately to the transfer sheet, holding the stick vertically. Scatter them with chopped sugar-coated almonds.
Leave to harden before you remove them from the sheet. Transfer the lollipops to the refrigerator until you serve them.

● **Did you know?**
The chocolate transfer sheets can be found in cake decorating shops or online. The transfers are made of colored cocoa butter.*

Techniques
Melting Chocolate ›› p. 19
Coating ›› p. 25
Raspberry Pulp Ganache for Hand-Dipped Centers ›› p. 34

Ingredients
White chocolate and raspberry ganache*
14 oz. (400 g) white chocolate, 35 percent cocoa
Generous ⅔ cup (180 ml) whipping cream
1 ⅛ teaspoon (6 ml) rose water
5 ⅔ oz. (160 g) raspberry pulp

White chocolate coating
10 ½ oz. (300 g) white chocolate, 35 percent cocoa
2 teaspoons (10 ml) grape-seed oil

Decoration
A few white sugar-coated almonds

Equipment
1 immersion blender†
1 kitchen thermometer †
Sheet of food-safe acetate† or
a chocolate transfer sheet of your choice
1 piping bag† fitted with a plain tip†
1 baking sheet lined with parchment paper
Lollipop sticks
1 flexible spatula†

Fresh Fruit Chocolate Bars ★ ★ ★

Makes 2-3 bars
Preparation time: 30 minutes
Refrigeration time: 1 hour

Temper* the milk and bittersweet chocolates separately.
Using a chopping board, chop half the chocolate with a serrated knife. You may also use couverture chocolate* in other forms, such as buttons, fèves, or pistoles. Finely chop the other half, or process it with the blade attachment of your food processor, and set it aside. Place the more coarsely chopped chocolate in a heatproof bowl, glass or metal.
If you have a double boiler, half fill the bottom part with hot water.
Otherwise, half fill a pot or saucepan with hot water. Place the bowl in this, ensuring that it does not touch the bottom of the saucepan. Place the saucepan (or double-boiler) over low heat and check that the water does not boil. Stir constantly. (You may also use the microwave oven, but only set at "defrost" or at 500 W maximum.) As soon as the chocolate begins to melt, stir it regularly using a flexible spatula so that it melts evenly.
Check the temperature with your thermometer. When it reaches 131°F-136°F (55°C-58°C) for the bittersweet chocolate and 113°F-122°F (45°C-50°C) for the milk chocolate, remove the chocolate from the bain-marie and add the 3 ½ oz. (100 g) finely chopped chocolate, stirring until the bittersweet chocolate cools to 82°F-84°F (28°C-29°C) and the milk chocolate, to 81°F-82°F (27°C-28°C).
Briefly return the bowl to the bain-marie to raise the temperature again. Remove after a few moments, and continue to stir until bittersweet chocolate reaches 88°F-90°F (31°C-32°C) and milk chocolate, 84°F-86°F (29°C-30°C).
In a mixing bowl, quickly combine the fruit (at room temperature) with the tempered chocolate. Immediately spoon into the molds and give them a little shake to ensure that the surface is flat.
Leave to rest for 1 hour in the refrigerator, turn out of the molds, and enjoy!

● **Chef's note**
Chocolate bars made with fresh fruit will keep no longer than 24 hours. You'll notice that they will marble because of the moisture contained in the fruit. The message is clear: you should eat this delicious treat without delay.

🥄 **Technique**
Tempering >> p. 20

Ingredients
Bittersweet chocolate bars
7 oz. (200 g) bittersweet chocolate,
60 or 70 percent cocoa
2 ½ oz. (70 g) fresh raspberries or 2 ¼ oz. (60 g)
fresh blueberries at room temperature

Milk chocolate bars
7 oz. (200 g) milk chocolate,
40 percent cocoa
2 ¼ oz. (60 g) fresh apricots,
each cut into 6 pieces, at room temperature

Equipment
1 serrated knife
1 food processor fitted with a blade attachment
(optional)
Chocolate bar molds†
1 kitchen thermometer†
1 flexible spatula†

Ingredients

14 oz. (400 g) white chocolate,
35 percent cocoa

White chocolate and coconut ganache*
1 teaspoon plus heaped ½ teaspoon (¼ oz./8 g)
grated unsweetened coconut
Scant ⅓ cup (70 ml) coconut milk
1 cup minus 2 tablespoons (220 ml)
coconut liqueur, such as Malibu
1 heaped tablespoon (16 g) granulated sugar
5 ¼ oz. (145 g) white chocolate, 35 percent cocoa

Equipment

Chocolate bar molds†
1 kitchen thermometer†
1 piping bag†
1 flexible spatula†

Coconut Bars ★ ★ ★

Makes 4 bars

Preparation time: 30 minutes
Setting time: 48 hours

Two days ahead, temper* (7 oz. (200 g) white chocolate using the method of your choice (see p. 20).
Pour a thin layer of chocolate into the 4 bar molds. Leave to harden at room temperature.

Prepare the white chocolate and coconut ganache.
Lightly toast the grated coconut (see p. 134). Gently heat the coconut milk and liqueur. In a heavy bottomed saucepan, cook the sugar until it forms a light caramel*. When the caramel is ready, carefully pour in the heated coconut milk and liqueur, making sure it does not splash and burn you.
Chop the white chocolate and melt it slowly in a bain-marie* or in the microwave oven (on "defrost" or at 500 W maximum, stirring from time to time). Gradually pour one-third of the coconut caramel over the melted chocolate. Using a flexible spatula, mix it in energetically, drawing small circles to create an elastic, shiny "kernel." Incorporate the second third of the liquid, using the same procedure. Repeat with the last third. Stir in the lightly toasted grated coconut.

When the ganache has cooled to 82°F (28°C), spoon it into a piping bag and partially fill the chocolate-lined molds. Make sure you leave a space of just under 1/16 in. (2 mm) below the rim so that you will be able to fit in the closing layer of the bar. Leave to harden for 24 hours in a cool room.

The next day, finish the bars. Temper the remaining 7 oz. (200 g) white chocolate and pour out the layer to enclose the filling. Leave to harden for 24 hours in a cool room.

● Chef's note

Make sure that the ganache is no hotter than 82°F (28°C) when you fill the bars, otherwise the white chocolate will become "de-tempered."

Techniques
Tempering ≫ p. 20
Roasting Nuts ≫ p. 134

Truffle Hearts ★ ★ ★

Serves 8
Preparation time: 1 hour
Refrigeration time: 3 hours

Prepare the bittersweet chocolate ganache.
Chop the chocolate and melt it slowly in a bain-marie* or in the microwave oven (on "defrost" or at 500 W maximum, stirring from time to time). Slit the half vanilla bean and scrape the seeds out into the cream. Bring the cream and honey to the boil with the half vanilla bean. Sieve.
Gradually pour one-third of the boiling cream over the melted chocolate. Using a flexible spatula, mix it in energetically, drawing small circles to create an elastic, shiny "kernel."
Incorporate the second third of the cream, using the same procedure. Repeat with the last third.
As soon as the ganache has cooled to 95°F-104°F (35°C-40°C), but no cooler, stir in the diced butter. Process with an immersion blender so that the mixture is smooth and thoroughly emulsified*. Leave to set for 3 hours in the refrigerator.
Spoon it into a pastry bag and pipe out balls. As soon as the texture is sufficiently hard, roll them with your hands to shape them. It's best to use thin disposable gloves for this.

Prepare the coating.
Temper* the bittersweet chocolate using the method of your choice (see p. 20). Pour the tempered chocolate into a large mixing bowl. Pour out a sufficient quantity of cocoa powder to cover a plate. Use a dipping fork to coat the truffles. Press down lightly with the tip of the fork to submerge the truffle completely in the tempered chocolate. Retrieve the truffle with the fork and dip it 3 or 4 times more. This will create suction so that the chocolate coating will not be too thick. Then scrape the excess chocolate off from the bottom of the truffle so that the coating is not too thick.
Carefully place the truffle in the cocoa powder and roll it immediately to cover it. Leave the truffles to harden in the cocoa powder. When the truffles have set, place them in a sieve or sifter to remove any excess cocoa powder.

● Chef's note
It's important not to let the ganache cool too much as its texture will become grainy.

Techniques
Melting Chocolate ›› p. 19
Tempering ›› p. 20
Coating ›› p. 25
Ganache for Hand-Dipped Centers ›› p. 33

Ingredients
Bittersweet chocolate ganache*
8 oz. (225 g) bittersweet chocolate, 70 percent cocoa
½ vanilla bean
1 cup minus 3 tablespoons (200 ml) whipping cream
2 tablespoons (1 ½ oz./40 g) acacia honey
3 ½ tablespoons (1 ¾ oz./50 g) butter, diced

Coating
10 ½ oz. (300 g) bittersweet chocolate, 70 percent cocoa
Unsweetened cocoa powder for dusting

Equipment
1 sieve†
1 kitchen thermometer†
1 immersion blender†
1 piping bag† fitted with a plain tip†, ¾ in. (2 cm) diameter
1 baking sheet
1 dipping fork†
1 pair of fine disposable gloves
1 flexible spatula†

Ingredients

Lemon sugar
3 unwaxed lemons
1 ½ cups (7 oz./200 g) confectioners' sugar

Colored sugar
Lemon-yellow powdered food color
A little 60° alcohol
1 cup (7 oz./200 g) sugar

Chocolate and jasmine tea ganache*
⅔ oz. (20 g) jasmine tea leaves
1 cup plus scant ½ cup (350 ml) whipping cream
3 tablespoons (2 ¼ oz./65 g) glucose syrup
11 ¾ oz. (335 g) bittersweet chocolate,
70 percent cocoa
5 tablespoons (2 ½ oz./70 g) butter, diced

Coating
10 ½ oz. (300 g) bittersweet chocolate,
70 percent cocoa

Equipment

1 kitchen thermometer†
1 piping bag† fitted with a plain ½ in. (12 mm) tip†
1 baking sheet lined with parchment paper
1 dipping fork†
1 chinois†
1 flexible spatula†

Techniques
Tempering ›› p. 20
Coating ›› p. 25
Ganache for Hand-Dipped Centers ›› p. 33

Jasmine Truffle Logs ★ ★ ★

Serves 6–8
Preparation time: 1 hour
Setting time: overnight
Resting time: overnight

Two days ahead, prepare the lemon sugar.
Remove the zest* of the three lemons. Cut it into fine dice or grate*, and mix thoroughly with the sugar. Spread the mixture out on a baking sheet to dry out.

Prepare the colored sugar.
Dilute the yellow powdered food color with a little 60° alcohol and use it to color the granulated sugar. Mix well and leave out to dry at room temperature.

Leave the jasmine tea leaves to infuse in the cold cream for 24 hours.

One day ahead, prepare the chocolate and jasmine tea ganache.
Heat the cream with the leaves to about 122°F (50°C) and strain through a chinois. Then stir in the glucose syrup and bring to the boil. Chop the chocolate and melt it slowly in a bowl over a bain-marie* or in the microwave oven (on "defrost" or at 500 W, stirring from time to time). Gradually pour one-third of the hot cream mixture over the melted chocolate. Using a flexible spatula, mix it in energetically, drawing small circles to create an elastic, shiny "kernel." Incorporate the second third of the liquid, using the same procedure. Repeat with the last third. As soon as the ganache cools to about 95°F–104°F (35°C–40°C), mix in the diced butter. Process briefly until the mixture is smooth and perfectly emulsified*. Leave to set for 3 hours.
Using a piping bag, pipe out small log shapes of ganache onto the lined baking sheet. Leave to harden overnight in a cool room.

The next day, temper* the chocolate using the method of your choice (see p. 20).
Spread out the lemon sugar and a little colored sugar onto a sheet of parchment paper. Using a dipping fork, coat the log-shaped truffles in the tempered chocolate (see p. 25). Then place them on the mixed sugars and roll them gently in them. Leave to harden completely for about 10 minutes before touching them.

● Chef's note
You can use orange zest instead of lemon zest.

Sesame-Topped Choco-Cinnamon Ganaches

★ ★ ★

Makes 40-50 bonbons
Preparation time: 2 hours
Refrigeration time: at least 3 hours

Prepare the cinnamon ganache.
Warm the cream a little in a saucepan and add the cinnamon sticks. Remove from the heat and leave to infuse for 15 to 20 minutes. Filter. Return the flavored cream to the saucepan. Pour in the milk and bring to the boil.
Chop the chocolate and melt it slowly in a bain-marie* or in the microwave oven (on "defrost" or at 500 W maximum, stirring from time to time). Incorporate the cream and milk mixture to the chocolate by thirds* (see p. 95). Process with an immersion blender so that it is smooth and perfectly emulsified*. When the ganache has cooled to 95°F-104°F (35°C-40°C), stir in the diced butter and process again. Place a confectionery frame over the silicone baking mat and pour out the ganache to a thickness of just under 1 in. (2 cm). Chill in the refrigerator for at least 3 hours. Cut out squares of just over 1 in. (3 cm).

Prepare the sesame nougatine.
Preheat the oven to 325°F (160°C). Roast the sesame seeds for about 8 to 10 minutes. Heat the honey in a saucepan and gradually add the sugar. Keep an eye on the temperature. When it reaches 325°F (160°C), add the still-warm sesame seeds. Remove from the heat and pour out the nougatine. Roll it between two sheets of acetate as thinly as possible. Remove the top sheet and with a paring knife, cut out squares measuring just under 1 in. (2 cm). Set aside.

Coat the bonbons.
Line a baking sheet with parchment paper, or, even better, a sheet of food-safe acetate. Temper* the chocolate using the method of your choice (see p. 20). Pour the tempered chocolate into a large mixing bowl, and use it to undercoat the bonbons (see p. 24). Place the bonbon with the coated side on the tines of a dipping fork and place it in the tempered chocolate. Press down lightly with the tip of the fork so that the bonbon is completely immersed in the chocolate. Retrieve it with the fork and dip the heel three or four times again to create a suction phenomenon, which will prevent a too-thick layer of chocolate from forming. Then scrape the bonbon against the rim of the mixing bowl so that only a fine layer of chocolate is left. Carefully place the bonbon on the prepared baking sheet. Place a square of sesame nougatine atop each bonbon and leave to set.

● **Chef's notes**
If the nougatine hardens too quickly, return it to the oven for a few minutes so that it becomes soft again.
If you prefer, you may just place a few nougatine shards on each bonbon.

Ingredients

Cinnamon ganache*
Scant ⅔ cup (150 ml) whipping cream
2 cinnamon sticks
½ cup minus 2 tablespoons (100 ml) milk
1 lb. (500 g) milk chocolate, 40 percent cocoa
3 ½ tablespoons (1 ¾ oz./50 g) butter, diced

Sesame nougatine
5 ⅔ oz. (160 g) white sesame seeds
¼ cup (3 ¼ oz./90 g) honey
¾ cup (5 ½ oz./150 g) granulated sugar

To coat and finish
1 lb. (500 g) milk chocolate,
40 percent cocoa

Equipment

1 kitchen thermometer†
1 immersion blender†
1 silicone baking mat†
1 baking sheet
1 confectionery frame†
1 dipping fork†
3 sheets of food-safe acetate†
or parchment paper

Techniques

Tempering ›› p. 20
Undercoating ›› p. 24
Coating ›› p. 25
Ganache for Hand-Dipped Centers ›› p. 33

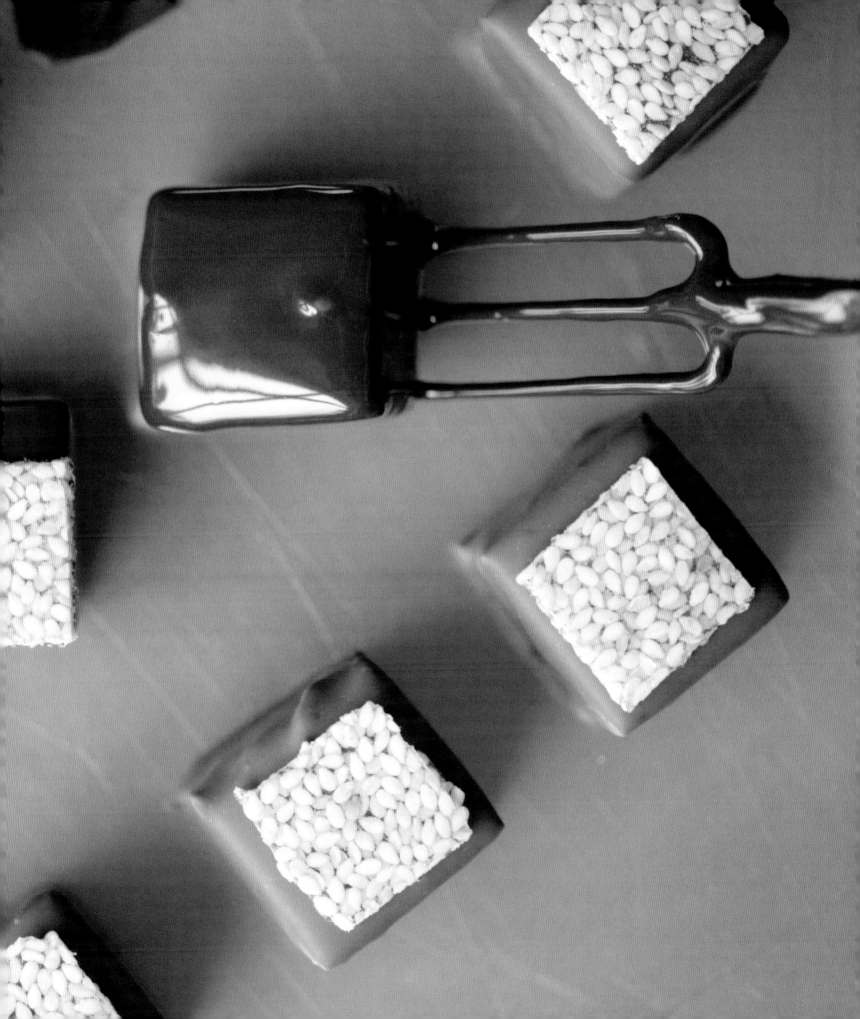

Ingredients
1 sheet of Valrhona ivory hollow balls (50)

Ivory chocolate plastic
3 ¼ oz. (90 g) white chocolate,
35 percent cocoa
2 ¼ oz. (60 g) glucose syrup

Lime jelly
6 oz. (170 g) store-bought neutral glaze
or apple jelly
⅓ cup (80 ml) lime juice
Zest* of ½ unwaxed lime

Lemon marshmallow
4 ½ sheets (9 g) gelatin
½ cup (3 ½ oz./100 g) sugar
Honey, divided as follows: 3 tablespoons
(2 ¼ oz./65 g) plus 2 ½ tablespoons (50 g)
⅓ cup (80 ml) lemon juice,
divided into two equal parts
2 ½ tablespoons (50 g) glucose syrup

7 oz. (200 g) white chocolate,
35 percent cocoa

Decoration
Yellow or green velvet spray

Equipment
1 food processor fitted with a blade attachment
1 kitchen thermometer†
1 piping bag†
1 whisk†
1 rolling pin†
Lollipop sticks
1 small flower-shaped cookie cutter†

Lollipops ★ ★ ★

Makes 50 lollipops
Preparation time: 1 hour 30 minutes
Resting and setting time: 24 hours

A day ahead, prepare the ivory chocolate plastic.
Chop the chocolate and melt it gently over a bain-marie* or in the microwave oven (on "defrost" or at 500 W, stirring from time to time). Warm the glucose syrup to about 104°F (40°C) in a saucepan and carefully stir in the melted chocolate. As soon as the two are smoothly mixed, remove from the heat and set aside at room temperature until the next day.

The next day, prepare the lime jelly.
Place the glaze (or jelly), lime juice, and lime zest in the bowl of a food processor. Blend until combined and then pour into a piping bag to pipe out into the hollow balls, filling just one-third.

Prepare the lemon marshmallow.
Soak the gelatin in a bowl of cold water. Cook the sugar, 3 tablespoons (2 ¼ oz./65 g) honey, and half the lemon juice until the mixture reaches the consistency of a syrup. Whip* the glucose syrup and 2 ½ tablespoons (50 g) honey until the texture is liquid and stir in the boiling syrup. Wring the excess water from the gelatin and dissolve it in the mixture.
Stop whisking* when the temperature has cooled to 86°F (30°C) and stir in the remaining half of the lemon juice. Fill the balls with this mixture and leave to dry in the open air in a dry place for 12 hours.

Temper* the white chocolate (see p. 20) and pipe it out with a piping bag to close the hole. Before the lollipops have completely set (this should take no longer than 4 to 5 minutes), insert a lollipop stick vertically in the center of the ball.
When they have set, insert the sticks into a piece of polystyrene and, using stencils, spray them with the velvet spray.
Knead* the chocolate plastic until it is softened. Roll it out on a board and cut out small flower shapes with the cookie cutter. Stick them onto the lollipops.

Techniques
Chocolate Plastic ›› p. 51
Melting Chocolate ›› p. 19
Tempering ›› p. 20

Chocolate-Coated Cherries
and Pineapple Cubes ★ ★ ★

Makes about 80 coated sweet snacks
Make ahead (see chef's note)
Preparation time: 2 hours
Resting and setting time: 24 hours

A day ahead, prepare the pineapples.
At least 1 day ahead, remove the skin from the pineapples. Cut them into 1 in.
(3 cm) cubes, avoiding the core, which is too hard. Slit the vanilla bean lengthways and scrape out the seeds. Place the sugar in a frying pan and prepare a
dry caramel*. Stir in the diced pineapple and vanilla seeds and leave for 2 to
3 minutes, until golden. Pour in the rum and flambé the cubes. Remove from
the heat, place in an airtight container, and refrigerate at least overnight, but
ideally for 2 to 3 days.

The next day.
Place the diced pineapple on a rack positioned over a larger dish to drain, allowing the juice to drip into the dish. Leave for 1 to 2 hours. Insert a wooden skewer
or toothpick into each cube so that you can dip them easily into the fondant.
Combine the fondant and 2 tablespoons of the pineapple juice in a heatproof
bowl. Heat over a bain-marie* to 140°F-149°F (60°C-65°C), stirring constantly.
Dip the pineapple cubes into the fondant and place them on a baking sheet.
When the fondant has set, temper* the chocolate (see p. 20). Coat the pineapple
cubes, one by one, in the chocolate (see p. 25). Leave to set for at least 12 hours,
and then serve as soon as possible.

Prepare the cherries.
Position a rack over a dish large enough to catch the *eau-de-vie* from the cherries. Drain the cherries on the rack for 1 to 2 hours, and finish drying them off
on some sheets of paper towel. Slit the vanilla bean in half lengthways and
scrape out the seeds. In a heatproof bowl, combine the fondant, vanilla seeds,
and 2 tablespoons of *eau-de-vie*. Heat over a bain-marie to 140°F-149°F (60°C-
65°C), stirring constantly. Hold the cherries by their stalks and dip them in
the fondant mixture, taking care to leave a little ring without any fondant.
Place them on a baking sheet.
When the fondant has set, temper the chocolate (see p. 20). Dip the cherries,
including as much of the stalk as possible, one by one, in the chocolate (see p.
25). Then place them in the colored sugar and leave to set for at least 12 hours.

● Chef's note
*For optimal taste, prepare the cherries about 2 weeks before you intend serving
them. The fondant will have melted, imbuing the cherries with heightened
flavor. The pineapples too are best prepared 2–3 days ahead of serving.*

Techniques
Melting Chocolate ›› p. 19
Tempering ›› p. 20
Coating ›› p. 25

Ingredients
For the pineapple cubes
2 Victoria pineapples
1 vanilla bean
Scant ½ cup (3.1 oz./90 g) granulated sugar
½ cup (3 ½ oz./100 g) sugar
Scant ⅔ cup (150 ml) brown rum
10 ½ oz. (300 g) pastry fondant*
10 ½ oz. (300 g) bittersweet chocolate,
60 or 70 percent cocoa

For the cherries
50 cherries in eau-de-vie with their stalks
½ vanilla bean
10 ½ oz. (300 g) pastry fondant *
10 ½ oz. (300 g) bittersweet chocolate,
60 or 70 percent cocoa

For decoration
Colored sugar

Equipment
1 cake rack or other rack
1 dish, larger than the cake rack
1 kitchen thermometer†
Wooden skewers or toothpicks
1 baking sheet

Betty the Baby Bear ★★★

Makes 1 bear

Preparation time: 2 hours
Refrigeration time: 35 minutes

Clean the molds with cotton wool soaked with 90° alcohol. Place two confectionery rulers on a lined baking sheet.

Temper* the chocolate using the method of your choice (see p. 20).

Prepare the chocolate balls.
When the tempered chocolate has reached the right temperature, completely fill a half-sphere mold from a ladle so that the entire surface is covered. Turn it upside down over a mixing bowl so that the excess chocolate can drain out of the mold.
Shake the mold gently to remove the excess and place it over the two rulers.
When the chocolate begins to set, turn the mold the other way round and scrape off the excess chocolate from the edges of the mold using a paring knife. This will ensure that the edges are clean. Repeat this procedure with each of the half-sphere molds.
Place the molds in the refrigerator for about 20 minutes.
Take them out of the refrigerator, but wait for a few minutes before turning the chocolate pieces out of their molds.

To assemble
To stick the half spheres of chocolate together, gently heat the bottom of a saucepan and turn it upside down. You will need it to lightly place the edges of the half-spheres of chocolate on the hot surface to melt their rims slightly. Stick the edges of the two largest half-spheres together to form one large sphere and lightly melt the base so that it can hold on a surface. To form the head, stick the two 1 ¾-in. (4.5-cm) diameter half-spheres together, using the same procedure. Very lightly melt the base of the head so that you can stick it to the top of the body. Then stick the 1 ¼-in. (3-cm) diameter half molds to the body to make the ears and the arms. Prepare the legs in the same way as the body and head, and place them on either side of the body.
Chill the assembled bear for about 15 minutes. Decorate first with the chocolate velvet spray, and then with the red velvet spray.

Ingredients
1 lb. 2 oz. (500 g) bittersweet chocolate, 60 or 70 percent cocoa
1 chocolate velvet spray
1 red velvet spray

Equipment
1 kitchen thermometer†
2 half-sphere molds†, 2 ¾ in. (7 cm) diameter
2 half-sphere molds†, 1 ¾ in. (4.5 cm) diameter
8 half-sphere molds†, 1 ⅕ in. (3 cm) diameter
2 confectionery rulers†
1 baking sheet lined with parchment paper
1 paring knife
1 ladle
Cotton wool and 90° alcohol to clean the molds

Techniques
Melting Chocolate ›› p. 19
Tempering ›› p. 20
Classic Molding ›› p. 26

Candies and confections

Sam the Snowman ★ ★ ★

Makes 10 snowmen
Preparation time: 1 hour
Refrigeration time: 45 minutes

Clean the molds with cotton wool soaked with 90° alcohol. Place two confectionery rulers on a lined baking sheet.

Temper* the chocolate using the method of your choice (see p. 20).

Make the molds and assemble.
When the chocolate is ready, fill the half-spheres using a ladle–the entire surface must be covered. Turn the molds upside down over the mixing bowl to remove the excess chocolate. To drain completely, shake the molds gently and place over the two rulers (or other objects) to drip.
When the chocolate begins to set, turn the mold the right way up and use a paring knife to scrape off the excess chocolate from the edges of the mold. This will ensure that the edges are clean. Repeat this procedure with each of the half-sphere molds.

Place the molds in the refrigerator for about 30 minutes. Take them out of the refrigerator but wait for a few minutes before turning the chocolate pieces out of their molds.

Gently heat a baking pan and slightly melt one edge of the balls so that they will stay in place. Then stick two half-spheres together and place them on parchment paper.
Place either in the freezer or the refrigerator for 15 minutes, and then spray with white velvet.

Color the almond paste and prepare the decorative elements: scarves, caps, buttons, and so on. Stick them on with melted white chocolate.

Ingredients
White chocolate, 35 percent cocoa, divided as follows:
14 oz. (400 g) plus 3 oz. (100 g)
1 white velvet spray
Almond paste (see p. 41)
Food colorings

Equipment
1 kitchen thermometer†
2 confectionery rulers†
Half-sphere molds†, 1 ½ in. (4 cm) diameter
1 ladle
1 paring knife
Cotton wool and 90° alcohol to clean the molds
1 baking sheet lined with parchment paper
1 baking pan

Techniques
Melting Chocolate ≫ p. 19
Tempering ≫ p. 20
Classic Molding ≫ p. 26
Almond Paste ≫ p. 41

Daisy Easter Egg ★ ★ ★

Serves 6-8
Preparation time: 30 minutes
Refrigeration time: 1 hour
Freezing time: 15 minutes

Clean the molds with cotton wool soaked with 90° alcohol. Place the two confectionery rulers on a lined baking sheet.

Temper* the 14 oz. (400 g) chocolate (see p. 20).
Pour it into a large mixing bowl.

To make the molds and assemble
When the chocolate is at the right temperature, fill the egg molds with a ladle. Turn them upside down over the mixing bowl to remove the excess chocolate. To drain completely, shake the molds gently and place over the two rulers.
When the chocolate begins to set, turn the molds the right way up and use a paring knife to scrape off the excess chocolate from the edges. This will ensure that the edges are clean.
Chill the molds in the refrigerator for about 1 hour. Remove them, but wait for a few minutes before turning the chocolate pieces out of their molds.
To assemble the shells, lightly melt the edges on a warmed baking sheet and stick the edges together carefully.

Decorate the eggs.
For a velvet finish, place the eggs in the freezer for 15 minutes and spray them as soon as you remove them with the green and yellow sprays to make an attractive coating that will remind you of spring.
Roll out the colored almond paste or the chocolate plastic and cut out small flowers using the cookie cutter. Melt the 3 oz. (100 g) of white chocolate and use it to glue the flowers on.

● Chef's notes
*Make sure you clean the molds with cotton wool and alcohol each time you reuse them. This will ensure that there will be no stains or whitening.
The molds should not be too cold when you use them.*

Techniques
Melting Chocolate >> p. 19
Tempering >> p. 20
Classic Molding >> p. 26
Chocolate Plastic >> p. 51

Ingredients
White chocolate, 35 percent cocoa, divided as follows:
14 oz. (400 g) plus 3 oz. (100 g)
1 green chocolate velvet spray
1 yellow chocolate velvet spray
Colored almond paste or ivory chocolate plastic (see p. 51)

Equipment
1 kitchen thermometer[†]
2 confectionery rulers[†]
1 baking sheet
1 paring knife
Egg-shaped molds[†]
1 rolling pin[†]
1 flower-shaped cookie cutter[†]
1 ladle
Cotton wool and 90° alcohol to clean the molds

Rochers ("rock" cookies) ★ ★ ★

Makes about 1 lb. (500 g) of *rochers**

Preparation time: 50 minutes
Setting time: 3 hours

Chop the chocolate and melt it slowly in a bain-marie* or in the microwave oven (on "defrost" or at 500 W maximum, stirring from time to time). Combine the melted chocolate with the praline. Place the mixing bowl in a larger bowl of ice water and cool the mixture down to 75°F (24°C), stirring constantly. Remove immediately from the water.
Stir in the crumbled *crêpes dentelles*, and pour the mixture on to a lined baking sheet. Leave to harden for a few hours.
When it has hardened, break it into small pieces.

Place a few of the hardened pieces in a mixing bowl and begin whisking* with an electric beater. Gradually incorporate the remaining pieces until you have a smooth mixture.
Spoon it into a piping bag and pipe out small walnut-sized balls on to a lined baking sheet. Leave to harden before you coat them.

Roast the almonds (see p. 134) and allow them to cool. Then pour them into a plate.

Temper* the chocolate using the method of your choice (see p. 20).
Dip the *rochers* in the tempered chocolate and then roll them in the plate of chopped almonds. Leave to harden for a few minutes. Coat them once again in the tempered chocolate. If the chocolate has cooled, it is advisable to reheat it to 91°F (33°C) so that it doesn't crack.

Techniques
Melting Chocolate ›› p. 19
Tempering ›› p. 20
Coating ›› p. 25
Homemade Praline ›› p. 38
Roasting Nuts ›› p. 134

Ingredients
3 ½ oz. (100 g) milk chocolate,
40 percent cocoa
9 oz. (250 g) praline*, homemade (see p. 38)
or store bought
⅓ oz. (10 g) crumbled *crêpes dentelles*,
an extremely friable, fine wafer-like biscuit,
a Breton specialty

Coating
3 ½ oz. (100 g) chopped almonds
1 lb. (500 g) bittersweet chocolate,
60 percent cocoa, or milk chocolate,
40 percent cocoa

Equipment
1 kitchen thermometer†
1 baking sheet lined with parchment paper
1 hand-held electric beater†
1 piping bag†
1 dipping fork†
1 large bowl with ice water

Ingredients

10 ½ oz. (300 g) bittersweet chocolate,
60 or 70 percent cocoa content

Concentrated cinnamon water
Scant ½ cup (100 ml) water
5 cinnamon sticks, crushed

Cinnamon marshmallow
Scant ¼ cup (50 ml) water
Scant ¼ cup cinnamon water (see above),
divided into two equal parts
1 cup plus 3 tablespoons (8 oz./225 g)
granulated sugar
Honey, divided as follows: 1 ½ teaspoons (10 g)
plus ⅓ cup (4 ½ oz./125 g)
10 sheets (⅔ oz./20 g) gelatin
8 oz. (225 g) white chocolate,
35 percent cocoa content

To finish
Equal quantities of:
Ground cinnamon
Cornstarch
Confectioners' sugar

Equipment

1 stand-alone mixer†
1 kitchen thermometer†
6 to 8 plastic or metal cylinders, 6-8 in. (15-20 cm)
length and ¾ in. (2 cm) diameter
Parchment paper
Plastic wrap
1 piping bag†
1 chinois†
1 confectionery framer† (optional)

Techniques
Tempering » p. 20
Chocolate Marshmallow » p. 44

Crisp Tubes of Cinnamon Marshmallow
 ★ ★ ★

Serves 6-8
Begin a day ahead
Preparation time: 2 hours
Refrigeration time: 1 hour
Resting time: overnight

A day ahead, prepare the chocolate tubes.
Line the insides of the cylinders with parchment paper and close one end with
plastic wrap.

Temper* the chocolate (see p. 20)
Using the piping bag, fill each tube with tempered chocolate and immediately
empty out the excess chocolate. Roll the tube back and forth so that the chocolate lines the interior evenly. Leave to set in the refrigerator.

Prepare the concentrated cinnamon water.
Bring the water and the cinnamon to the boil, then leave to simmer gently
until it has reduced to one-half. Strain through a chinois.

Prepare the cinnamon marshmallow.
Place the water, half the cinnamon water (1 tablespoon plus 2 teaspoons or
25 ml), sugar, 1 ½ teaspoons (10 g) honey and heat to 230°F (110°C). Soften
the gelatin in a bowl of cold water. Wring out the excess water and melt it
in the microwave oven. Pour the remaining honey and the cooked syrup into
the bowl of a stand-alone mixer and begin whisking* on high speed. Gradually reduce the speed to half, and when it has cooled down a little, add the
remaining half of cinnamon water and continue to whisk until the mixture
cools to room temperature.
While the stand-alone mixer is whisking, chop the white chocolate and gently
melt it over a bain-marie* or in the microwave oven (on "defrost" or at 500
W, stirring from time to time). As soon as the marshmallow mixture is at
room temperature, remove it from the bowl and incorporate it rapidly into the
melted chocolate. Pour it into a piping bag and fill the chocolate tubes with the
mixture. Leave to set overnight in a cool room.

The next day
Remove the chocolate tubes from the plastic cylinders and peel off the parchment paper. Slightly heat a kitchen knife (if you dip it in hot water, be sure
to dry it thoroughly) and cut the tubes into cork sizes. Combine the ground
cinnamon, cornstarch, and confectioners' sugar in a plate. Dip the end of each
"cork" into the mixture and serve.

● Chef's note
*To simplify this recipe, just pour the marshmallow mixture into a confectionery
frame. When it has set, cut it up and coat it in tempered chocolate.*

Golden *Palets* ★ ★ ★ 🎬

Makes about 50 *palets*
Preparation time: 40 minutes
Setting time: overnight plus 5 hours

A day ahead, prepare the bittersweet chocolate ganache.
Chop the chocolate and melt it slowly in a bain-marie* or in the microwave oven (on "defrost" or at 500 W maximum, stirring from time to time).
Slit the half vanilla bean and scrape out the seeds. Place the whipping cream, honey, and vanilla seeds and bean in a saucepan and bring to the boil. Leave to infuse for a few minutes and strain.
Gradually pour a third of the boiling liquid over the melted chocolate. Using a flexible spatula, mix in energetically, drawing small circles to create an elastic, shiny "kernel."
Incorporate the second third of the liquid, using the same procedure. Repeat with the last third. As soon as the ganache reaches a temperature of 95°F-104°F (35°C-40°C), incorporate the diced butter. Process briefly with an immersion blender until the mixture is completely emulsified*. Leave to set for at least 3 hours.

Pipe out the ganache *palets*.
As soon as the ganache is thick enough to be piped out, fill a piping bag and pipe out small, truffle-sized balls onto a silicone mat or lined baking sheet.
Place a sheet of parchment paper over the baking sheet of truffle balls and then place a baking sheet on top of this, pressing lightly to flatten the balls of ganache. This will create the *palet* shape.
Remove the baking sheet and leave to set overnight.

Coat the ganache.
Line a baking sheet with a sheet of acetate if you have some, otherwise use parchment paper. Temper* the chocolate using the method of your choice (see p. 20).
Pour the tempered chocolate into a large mixing bowl. Very carefully peel off the sheet of paper protecting the ganache *palets*.

Make the undercoating–a fine layer of tempered chocolate–for the palets (see p. 24).
Place a *palet*, coated side downward, on a dipping fork and dip into the tempered chocolate. Press the ganache down with the tines of the fork. Retrieve the *palet* with the fork and dip it three or four times to create the suction that will prevent the chocolate from forming a coating that is too thick. Then scrape on the edge of the mixing bowl so that the layer of chocolate left on the *palet* is thin. Carefully place the coated *palet* on the prepared baking sheet.
Place a small amount of gold leaf on each *palet* and leave to set. Cover each one, if possible, with a strip of food-safe acetate.

● **Chef's note**
We use honey in this ganache to improve the texture and to lengthen its storage time.

Ingredients
Bittersweet chocolate ganache*
8 oz. (225 g) bittersweet chocolate,
70 percent cocoa
½ vanilla bean
¾ cup (200 ml) whipping cream
2 tablespoons (40 g) honey
3 tablespoons plus 1 teaspoon (50 g) butter, diced

Coating and decoration
1 lb. (500 g) bittersweet chocolate,
70 percent cocoa
Edible gold leaf

Equipment
1 sieve[†]
1 flexible spatula[†]
1 kitchen thermometer[†]
1 immersion blender[†]
1 piping bag[†]
1 silicone baking mat[†] or 1 baking sheet lined with
parchment paper
An additional baking sheet
1 sheet of parchment paper, large
enough to cover the baking sheet
If possible, strips of food-safe acetate [†]
1 dipping fork[†]

Techniques
Tempering ›› p. 20
Undercoating ›› p. 24
Coating ›› p. 25

New trends

Christophe Adam
presents his recipe

Chocolate is difficult for the young pastry chef and the novice. It's a product that has to be tamed, as it were, and one can start creating freely with it only once one has mastered the basics. This serious, "professional" approach is, in my opinion, essential, and cannot be dissociated from a thorough knowledge of the product. Having worked for over twenty years now with Valrhona, I pay careful attention to the character of the chocolate, defined by its percentage of cocoa, its provenance, and its cru. I have learned to taste it, to seek out its bitter, fruity, spicy, smoked flavors, all nuances that come into play when a dessert is in the process of being created.

So-Choc

Bitter chocolate sponge. Preheat the oven to 425°F (210°C).
Whisk* the egg whites to soft peaks. Add half the granulated sugar. Whisk the egg yolks energetically with the other half of the sugar. Sift the cocoa powder and stir it into the thickened egg yolk and sugar mixture. Fold* the egg yolk and cocoa mixture into the sweetened whisked egg whites. Place a steel pastry circle over a sheet of parchment paper and butter it. Pour in the sponge batter. Bake for 10 minutes and allow to cool.

Cocoa gianduja pastry. Incorporate the finely grated orange zest with the granulated sugar. Soften the butter and add the sugar mixed with the zest, the ground hazelnuts, cocoa powder, flour, and *fleur de sel*. Leave to rest for 1 hour in the refrigerator. Preheat the oven to 325°F (160°C).
Roll out thinly with a rolling pin, or use a laminator, and bake for 12 minutes. Using the blade attachment of your food mixer, crush the paste into powder form and then gradually add the milk gianduja. Pour it into the pastry circle and chill for 30 minutes.

Gold-dusted chocolate shards. Melt the 70 percent bittersweet chocolate and spread it out thinly over a sheet of food-safe acetate. Leave to harden in the refrigerator and gently dust with the gold dust. Cut out the shards to the desired sizes.

Bittersweet chocolate *crémeux*. Soak the gelatin in cold water for 20 minutes. Chop the chocolate. Energetically whisk together the egg yolk and sugar. Bring the milk and cream to the boil and prepare a basic custard (*crème anglaise*) with the egg yolks (see p. 98). When it is ready, strain through a chinois† into a mixing bowl. Drain and rinse the gelatin and incorporate it into the custard. Gradually pour the custard over the cocoa paste and the chopped chocolate. Set aside in the refrigerator.

Cocoa syrup. Mix the gelatin powder into the ½ tablespoon of water and leave it to swell. Heat the 3 tablespoons (45 g) water with the syrup and then add the cocoa powder. Incorporate the gelatin into the hot mixture.

Chocolate mousse. Soak the gelatin sheet in cold water for 20 minutes. Chop the chocolate. Bring the milk to the boil and incorporate the gelatin. Pour it in several stages over the chopped chocolate. Whisk the cream to a Chantilly texture and incorporate it into the chocolate mixture.

To assemble the cake. Remove the pastry circles from the bitter chocolate sponge and cocoa gianduja pastry. Clean one of the circles and place it on a baking sheet lined with parchment paper. Slip the strip of acetate around the inside. Pipe out a line of mousse around the sides. Place the cocoa gianduja pastry at the base. Add the mousse and then pipe out the bittersweet chocolate *crémeux* using a piping bag.

Serves 8

Ingredients
For the bitter chocolate sponge
2 ⅓ oz. (65 g) egg white
⅓ cup (2 ½ oz./70 g) granulated sugar, divided
1 ⅔ oz. (45 g) egg yolks
3 tablespoons (⅔ oz./20 g) unsweetened cocoa powder

For the cocoa gianduja pastry
Grated zest* of 1 unwaxed orange
Scant ¼ cup (1 ⅔ oz./45 g) sugar
2 tablespoons (30 g) butter
Generous ½ cup (1 ⅔ oz./45 g) ground hazelnuts
2 tablespoons plus ½ teaspoon (½ oz./15 g) unsweetened cocoa powder
⅓ cup (1 oz./30 g) all-purpose flour
1 pinch (1.5 g) *fleur de sel*
2 oz. (60 g) milk gianduja

For the gold-dusted chocolate shards
7 oz. (200 g) bittersweet chocolate, 70 percent cocoa
⅓ oz. (10 g) edible gold dust

For the bittersweet chocolate *crémeux*
¾ sheet (1.5 g) sheet gelatin
¾ oz. (20 g) egg yolk (about 1 egg yolk)
½ tablespoon (6 g) granulated sugar
½ cup (115 ml) milk
⅓ cup (75 g) whipping cream, 30 percent butterfat
¼ oz. (5 g) cocoa paste
1 ¾ oz. (52 g) bittersweet chocolate, 70 percent cocoa

Add another layer of mousse. Moisten the bitter sponge with the cocoa syrup. Finish with a final layer of mousse and smooth the top. Freeze for 4 hours.

Chocolate glaze. Soak the gelatin for 20 minutes in cold water. Prepare a syrup with the water and sugar. Combine the syrup with the cocoa powder. Bring the cream to the boil and then incorporate the gelatin. Combine the cream and syrup until smooth. Leave it to cool to 68°F–77°F (20°C–25°C).

To finish. Remove the circle from the dessert and glaze* it with the chocolate glaze. Wait for the cake to come to room temperature to add the shards of gold-dusted chocolate.

For the cocoa syrup
Water, divided as follows: ½ tablespoon (8 g) plus 3 tablespoons (45 g)
Scant ¼ teaspoon (1 g) powdered gelatin
6 tablespoons (90 g) 30° Baume syrup
2 tablespoons plus ½ teaspoon (½ oz./15 g) unsweetened cocoa powder

For the chocolate mousse
1 sheet (2 g) gelatin
½ cup plus 1 tablespoon (140 ml) milk
1 cup plus 1 teaspoon (255 g) whipping cream, 30 percent fat
7 oz. (200 g) bittersweet chocolate, 70 percent cocoa

For the chocolate glaze
3 tablespoons (40 g) water
Scant ⅔ cup (4 ¼ oz./120 g) sugar
6 tablespoons (1 ½ oz./40 g) unsweetened cocoa powder
⅓ cup (80 g) whipping cream
2 sheets (4 g) gelatin

Equipment
1 whisk†
1 rolling pin†
1 food mixer with blade attachment
1 chinois†
1 piping bag†
2 steel pastry circles†, 1 ½ in. (4 cm) high and 6 ⅔ in. (16 cm) diameter
1 strip food-safe acetate†, 1 ½ in. (4 cm) wide
1 kitchen thermometer†

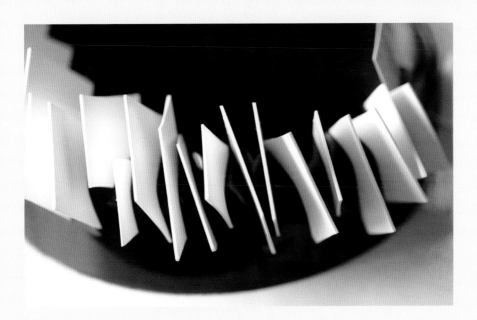

Jelled Milk Chocolate, Chestnuts, and Soy Foam ★★

Serves 6–8
Preparation time: 45 minutes
Baking time: 10 minutes
Refrigeration time: overnight

A day ahead, prepare the soy milk foam.
Soften the gelatin in a bowl filled with cold water. Combine the milk, sugar, soy milk, and cream in a saucepan and bring to the boil. Remove from the heat, wring the water out of the gelatin, and incorporate it into the hot liquid. Leave to cool and pour the mixture into the siphon. Chill overnight. When it is time to garnish the glasses with the foam, add two gas cartridges for Chantilly cream.

The next day, prepare the jelled milk chocolate.
Soften the gelatin in a bowl filled with cold water.
Chop the chocolate and melt it slowly in a bain-marie* or in the microwave oven (on "defrost" or at 500 W maximum, stirring from time to time).
Bring the milk and sugar to the boil in a saucepan. Remove from the heat, wring the water out of the gelatin, and incorporate it into the hot mixture. Gradually pour one-third of the hot milk over the melted chocolate. Using a flexible spatula, mix in energetically, drawing small circles to create an elastic, shiny "kernel." Incorporate the second third of the liquid, using the same procedure. Repeat with the last third. Process for a few seconds using an immersion blender so that the mixture is smooth and perfectly emulsified*. Pour the chocolate mixture into the glasses and set aside in the refrigerator.

Prepare the almond streusel.
Preheat the oven to 300°F–325 °F (150°C–160°C). In a mixing bowl, combine the molasses (or alternative) sugar, ground almonds, and flour. Cut the chilled butter into small dice and add it to the mixture. Rub the butter in with your fingers until you have a crumble texture. Spread out on a baking pan and bake for about 10 minutes, until the crumbs are a nice golden color.

Just before serving, prepare the chestnut vermicelli mixture.
Combine the chestnut cream with the softened butter and add a little rum, if using. Spoon it into the piping bag.

To serve
Place 1 chocolate disk wedged in at a slight angle in the jelled milk chocolate. Sprinkle with streusel and cover with the chestnut mixture, piped out from the bag. Top with soy foam.

● **Did you know?**
Kurozato is a dark brown sugar that comes from Okinawa. You can find it at Japanese groceries.

Ingredients
Soy milk foam
2 sheets (4 g) gelatin
⅓ cup (75 ml) milk
3 ½ tablespoons (1 ½ oz./40 g) sugar
⅔ cup (180 ml) soy milk
2 tablespoons (30 ml) whipping cream

Jelled milk chocolate
1 sheet (2 g) gelatin
2 ⅔ oz. (75 g) milk chocolate, 40 percent cocoa
⅔ cup (175 ml) milk
2 ½ teaspoons (10 g) sugar

Almond streusel
2 ¼ tablespoons (1 ¾ oz./50 g) molasses sugar, soft dark brown sugar, or kurozato sugar (dark sugar from Japan)
Generous ½ cup, (1 ¾ oz./50 g) ground blanched* almonds
Generous ½ cup (1 ¾ oz./50 g) cake flour
3 ½ tablespoons (1 ¾ oz./50 g) butter, well chilled

Chestnut vermicelli
4 ¼ oz. (120 g) creamed chestnut (*crème de marron*, at specialty stores or online)
5 ½ tablespoons (2 ¾ oz./80 g) butter, softened
Rum, according to taste (optional)

8 disks of milk chocolate, 40 percent cocoa (see p. 48)

Equipment
1 siphon† for Chantilly cream
6–8 shot glasses (*verrines*)
1 flexible spatula†
1 immersion blender†
1 piping bag† fitted with a plain ⅛ in. (3 mm) tip†

Techniques
Melting chocolate ≫ p. 19
Disks ≫ p. 48
Almond Streusel ≫ p. 88

Ingredients

Almond streusel

1 tablespoon plus 2 teaspoons (1 oz./25 g) butter
2 tablespoons (1 oz./25 g) light brown sugar
Generous ¼ cup (1 oz./25 g) cake flour
Generous ¼ cup (1 oz./25 g) ground
blanched* almonds

Almond *dacquoise**

3 egg whites
¼ cup (1 ¾ oz./50 g) granulated sugar
1 cup (3 oz./85 g) blanched* ground almonds
⅓ cup (1 oz./30 g) cake flour
¾ cup (3 ½ oz./100 g) confectioners' sugar

Semi-confit mandarins

4 mandarin oranges
1 heaped tablespoon (1 oz./25 g) multi-floral honey

Crème brûlée

½ cup plus 2 tablespoons (150 ml)
partially skimmed milk
½ cup minus 2 tablespoons (100 ml) whipping cream
¾ vanilla bean
2 tablespoons (1 oz./25 g) granulated sugar
½ teaspoon (1 g) agar-agar
2 egg yolks

Bittersweet chocolate *suprême*

2 ⅔ oz. (75 g) bittersweet chocolate,
70 percent cocoa
1 cup (250 ml) whole milk
Whipping cream, 30-35 percent fat,
divided as follows:
1 tablespoon plus 2 teaspoons (25 ml)
½ cup minus 2 tablespoons (100 ml)
1 ½ tablespoons (⅔ oz./20 g) granulated sugar
½ teaspoon (1 g) agar-agar

Equipment

1 square 5 in. (12 cm) frame
1 square 6 in. (15 cm) frame
1 baking sheet lined with parchment paper
1 kitchen thermometer†
1 immersion blender†
1 whisk†

Techniques

Melting Chocolate ›› p. 19
Almond *Dacquoise* ›› p. 86
Chocolate-Almond Streusel ›› p. 88

Almond *Dacquoise* with Semi-Confit Mandarins and Bittersweet Chocolate *Suprême* ★★★

Serves 6-8
Preparation time: 1 hour 30 minutes
Cooking time: 25 minutes
Refrigeration time: 3 hours; freezing time: 1 hour

Prepare the almond streusel (see p. 88).
Use the proportions given opposite. Set aside.

Prepare the almond *dacquoise* (see p. 86).
Use the proportions given opposite. Preheat the oven to 375°F (190°C). Pour the mixture into the square 5 in. (12 cm) frame placed over the lined baking sheet and bake for about 15 minutes, until golden. Set aside.

Prepare the semi-confit mandarin oranges.
Place the whole mandarins, unpeeled, in a pot, and cover them with water. Bring to the boil, drain, and return to the pot to cover with water a second time. Bring to the boil again. Remove the fruit from the water, slice thinly, and remove the seeds if any. Place the sliced mandarins with the honey in a pot and reduce over very low heat so that as much water as possible evaporates. When they are ready, arrange them over the *dacquoise* and freeze for 1 hour.

Prepare the crème brûlée.
Combine the milk and cream in a saucepan. Slit the vanilla bean lengthways and scrape the seeds into the liquid. Leave to infuse for 10 minutes. Remove the bean, combine the sugar with the agar-agar and dissolve them in the hot liquid. Return to the heat and bring to the boil. Place the 2 egg yolks in a mixing bowl and pour the hot liquid over, stirring as you do so. Return this liquid to the pot. When the liquid reaches 183°F (84°C), remove from the heat and pour it over the mandarins. Place in the refrigerator for 2 hours.

Prepare the mold.
Place the square 6 in. (15 cm) frame on a baking sheet lined with parchment paper. Unmold the *dacquoise*-tangerine-crème brûlée component and position it squarely in the center. Set aside in the refrigerator.

Make the bittersweet chocolate *suprême*.
Melt the chocolate (see p. 19). In a saucepan, heat the milk and 1 tablespoon plus 2 teaspoons (25 ml) whipping cream. Add the combined sugar and agar-agar and bring to the boil. Leave to simmer for a few minutes. Gradually pour one-third of the hot mixture over the chocolate (see p. 95). Process with an immersion blender until emulsified*. Leave to cool to 95°F (35°C). Whip* the ½ cup minus 1 tablespoon (100 ml) cream until it starts to thicken (see p. 108). Fold* this cream into the chocolate preparation and pour it into the prepared mold over the three-layered component. Scatter the streusel over the top. Chill until serving, when you should remove the larger cake frame.

Sweet and Tangy Strawberry Cloud with White Chocolate Mousse ★★

Serves 8
Preparation time: 50 minutes
Refrigeration time: 6 hours
Freezing time: 1 hour

Prepare the homemade strawberry coulis.
Hull the strawberries, wash them, dry them carefully, and blend them with the sugar and lemon juice. Taste to see if extra sugar is required. Strain through a chinois and weigh out 10 ½ oz. (300 g) for the strawberry cloud.

Prepare the strawberry cloud.
Soften the gelatin in a bowl of cold water. Heat the strawberry coulis. Wring the excess water out of the gelatin and add it to the hot coulis. Stir until dissolved and chill for 2 hours.

Prepare the lemon and white chocolate mousse.
Soften the gelatin in a bowl of cold water. Chop the chocolate and melt it slowly in a bain-marie* or in the microwave oven (on "defrost" or at 500 W maximum, stirring from time to time). Bring the soy milk to the boil in a saucepan and leave the lemon zest to infuse for 5 minutes. Strain, wring the water from the gelatin and dissolve it in the hot soy milk.
Gradually pour one-third of the hot liquid over the melted chocolate. Using a flexible spatula, mix it in energetically, drawing small circles to create an elastic, shiny "kernel."
Incorporate the second third of the liquid, using the same procedure. Repeat with the last third. Leave to cool.
In a mixing bowl, whisk* the soy cream until it thickens and is lightly whipped (see p. 108). When the chocolate mixture has cooled to 95°F-104°F (35°C-40°C), carefully fold in* the whipped soy cream.

Prepare the strawberry brunoise.
Hull the strawberries, setting aside several bases with their stems, if you wish, for decoration. Finely dice the strawberries to make a brunoise and add a little sugar if necessary.

To assemble.
Carefully pour the strawberry coulis into the glasses. Place in the refrigerator for 1 hour. Pour the lemon and white chocolate mousse over the set coulis. Chill for 4 hours. Spoon the strawberry cloud mixture into the siphon, add two gas cartridges, and shake well. Arrange the finely diced strawberries over the mousse. Just before serving, press out some strawberry foam into each glass. Decorate, if you wish, with some remaining diced strawberry.

Techniques
Melting Chocolate >> p. 19
Egg-Free Chocolate Mousse >> p. 111

Ingredients
Homemade strawberry coulis
1 lb. 5 oz. (600 g) strawberries
⅓ cup (2 ¼ oz./60 g) granulated sugar
Juice of ½ lemon

Strawberry cloud
1 ½ sheets (3 g) gelatin
10 ½ oz. (300 g) homemade strawberry coulis
(see above)

Lemon and white chocolate mousse
1 sheet (2 g) gelatin
5 ¼ oz. (150 g) white chocolate, 35 percent cocoa
⅓ cup (80 ml) soy milk
Zest* of 1 unwaxed lemon
⅔ cup (160 ml) soy cream

Strawberry brunoise
5 oz. (140 g) strawberries

Equipment
1 kitchen thermometer†
1 siphon†
8 shot glasses (verrines)
1 chinois†
1 whisk†
1 flexible spatula†

Truffled Ivory Macaroons ★ ★ ★ 🎬

Makes about 40 filled macaroons

Preparation time: 1 hour
Refrigeration time: 3 hours plus overnight
Cooking time: 12 minutes per batch (one tray at a time)

A day ahead, or at least 3 hours ahead.
Prepare the whipped ivory-truffle ganache.
Chop the chocolate and melt it slowly in a bain-marie* or in the microwave oven (on "defrost" or at 500 W maximum, stirring from time to time). Bring the ⅓ cup (80 ml) whipping cream to the boil.
Gradually pour one-third of the boiling cream over the melted chocolate. Using a flexible spatula, mix it in energetically, drawing small circles to create an elastic, shiny "kernel."
Incorporate the second third of the cream, using the same procedure. Repeat with the last third. Stir in the hazelnut oil and chopped truffle and process for a few seconds. Then stir in the remaining cold cream. Leave to set for at least 3 hours in the refrigerator.

Prepare the macaroon batter (see p. 82).
Preheat the oven to 285°F (140°C). Spoon the mixture into a piping bag and pipe it out in 1-in. (3-cm) diameter rounds onto the baking sheet or mat. Bake for about 12 minutes. Store at room temperature.

When the shells have cooled, whisk* the ganache until the texture is creamy. Spoon it into a piping bag, turn the shells over, and pipe out a knob of ganache onto each one. Place a shard of tempered chocolate over the ganache on half of the macaroons. Sandwich them together and place them on their sides. Garnish with a truffle shaving slightly inserted into the ganache.
Chill overnight.

● Chef's notes
Precision is all-important to make this recipe successfully. Most importantly, the egg whites should be weighed.
Use the finest black truffles available.
Macaroons are best when left to chill overnight so that their flavors develop. This will give them a nice crust, a melting interior, and bring out the flavor of the truffle to the full.

Ingredients

Macaroon* shells
1 ½ cups (4 ½ oz./125 g) ground almonds
3 ½ tablespoons (1 oz./25 g),
unsweetened cocoa powder
1 generous cup (5 ¼ oz./150 g) confectioners' sugar
3 ½ oz. (100 g) egg whites,
divided into two equal parts
¾ cup (5 ¼ oz./150 g) granulated sugar
Scant ¼ cup (50 ml) water

Whipped ivory-truffle ganache*
3 ¾ oz. (110 g) white chocolate, 35 percent cocoa
Whipping cream, divided as follows: ⅓ cup (80 ml)
plus generous ¾ cup (190 ml)
2 tablespoons (30 ml) hazelnut oil
⅔ oz. (20 g) chopped black truffle

Decoration
Shards of tempered* chocolate
About 40 black truffle shavings

Equipment
1 piping bag† fitted with a plain ⅓ in. (1 cm) tip†
1 baking sheet lined with parchment paper
or 1 silicone baking mat†
1 kitchen thermometer†
1 stand-alone mixer† (for the Italian meringue)
1 flexible spatula†
1 whisk†

Techniques
Melting Chocolate ›› p. 19
Tempering ›› p. 20
Macaroon Batter ›› p. 82
Whipped Ganache ›› p. 97
Filling a piping bag ›› p. 132
Piping out round macaroons ›› p. 132

Soy Milk Nama Choco ★★

Serves 6-8
Preparation time: 15 minutes
Chilling time: 3 hours

Prepare the bittersweet chocolate ganache.
Chop the chocolate and melt it slowly in a bain-marie* or in the microwave oven (on "defrost" or at 500 W maximum, stirring from time to time).
Bring the soy milk to the boil with the honey and glucose syrup. Gradually pour a third of the boiling mixture over the melted chocolate. Using a flexible spatula, mix in energetically, drawing small circles to create an elastic, shiny "kernel."
Incorporate the second third of the liquid, using the same procedure. Repeat with the last third.
Process for a few seconds using an immersion blender so that the mixture is smooth and perfectly emulsified*.
Pour the mixture into the frame positioned on the lined baking sheet, or into the prepared brownie pan. Chill for a minimum of 3 hours.
Remove the frame, sprinkle the ganache with light brown or colored sugar, and cut out 1 in. (2 cm) cubes.

● Chef's note
This is a version of a ganache that is popular in Japan. Prepared in this way, it can be used as a bonbon.

Ingredients
Bittersweet chocolate ganache*
¾ lb. (350 g) bittersweet chocolate, 70 percent cocoa
1 cup (250 ml) soy milk
1 ½ teaspoons (10 g) honey
1 ½ teaspoons (10 g) glucose syrup

Decoration
1 cup minus 1 ½ tablespoons (6 ⅓ oz./180 g) light brown or colored sugar

Equipment
1 immersion blender†
1 flexible spatula†
1 confectionery frame† or brownie pan, lined with plastic wrap
1 baking sheet lined with parchment paper

Technique
Melting Chocolate ›› p. 19

Ingredients
6 cod fillets, skin left on

Fish fumet
1 ¼ lb. (600 g) fish bones
2 oz. (50 g) shallots
2 oz. (50 g) onions
2 oz. (50 g) leek, white part only
2 oz. (50 g) carrots
1 bouquet garni, comprising thyme,
bay leaf, and parsley
4 cups (1 liter) water
Scant ⅔ cup (150 ml) white wine
Peppercorns

White chocolate-matcha tea oil
4 ¼ oz. (120 g) white chocolate,
35 percent cocoa
8 tablespoons (120 ml) olive oil
4 tablespoons (60 ml) grape-seed oil
⅓ oz. (10 g) matcha tea

Milk chocolate ganache* with fish fumet
3 ½ oz. (100 g) milk chocolate,
40 percent cocoa
Scant ½ cup (100 ml) fish fumet (see above)
2 teaspoons (3 g) Lapsang souchong tea

Matcha and white chocolate béarnaise sauce
1 small shallot, finely chopped
1 garlic clove, chopped
2 teaspoons (10 g) butter
1 small glass (150 ml) dry white wine
Scant ⅔ cup (150 ml) fish fumet (see above)
1 egg yolk
White chocolate-matcha tea oil
(see above)

Whipped cream
Scant ½ cup (100 ml) whipping cream
2 tablespoons (30 ml) fish fumet (see above)

Equipment
1 chinois†
1 immersion blender†
1 whisk†
1 spatula†
1 flat, cold plate

Technique
Melting Chocolate ›› p. 19

Cod Fillet, Green Tea Béarnaise, Smoked Milk Chocolate Sauce ★ ★

Serves 6-8
Preparation time: 1 hour
Cooking time: 35 minutes
Chilling time: 2 hours

Prepare the fish fumet.
Crush the fish bones, rinse and drain them. Peel, wash, and dice the vegetables. Place the fish bones, shallots, onions, leek whites, carrots, and bouquet garni in a large pot. Pour in the water and white wine and add a few peppercorns. Bring to the boil, and then lower the heat, skimming regularly. Leave to simmer for 25-30 minutes, without stirring, as this would cloud the fumet. Strain through a chinois and chill rapidly over ice before placing in the refrigerator.
Use within three days.

Prepare the white chocolate-matcha tea oil.
Chop the chocolate and melt it in a bain-marie* or in the microwave oven (on "defrost" or at 500 W maximum, stirring occasionally). Slightly warm the two types of oil and mix them, with the matcha tea, into the melted chocolate. Process with an immersion blender and set aside at room temperature.

Prepare the milk chocolate ganache with fish fumet.
Chop the chocolate and melt it slowly. Heat the fish fumet in a saucepan, remove from the heat, and add the Lapsang souchong. Leave to infuse for 2 minutes and strain through a chinois. Gradually incorporate the fish fumet into the melted chocolate, one-third at a time, using the procedure on p. 95. Process for a few seconds. Leave to set in the refrigerator for about 2 hours.

Prepare the matcha and white chocolate béarnaise sauce just before serving. Gently sweat the shallot and garlic with the butter. When the aromatics are translucent, deglaze with the white wine and leave to reduce until almost dry. Pour in the fish fumet. Reduce once again by half and strain through a chinois into a mixing bowl.
Add the egg yolk to the mixture and whip* the sauce using a small whisk. Gradually pour in the flavored oil, whisking* constantly until it has the consistency of a béarnaise sauce (mayonnaise-like). Set aside at room temperature.

Prepare the whipped cream with fish fumet.
Whip the well-chilled cream and incorporate the fumet. Whip until it reaches a Chantilly texture.

Over high heat, begin cooking the fish fillets, skin side down. Press down firmly with a spatula so they remain flat. When they are well seared and the skin begins to crisp, reduce the heat and finish cooking. Use a flat, cold plate to serve (if it is warm, the ganache will melt). Place a small spoonful of chocolate ganache with fish fumet, and then draw out a circle of matcha béarnaise. Carefully place the fillet skin side upward, and accompany with a few rounds of sautéed new potatoes and a spoonful of whipped cream with fish fumet.

Filet Mignon, East Meets West ★ ★

Serves 6-8
Marinating time: 24 hours
Cooking time: 1 hour 45 minutes

A day ahead, prepare the filets mignons.
Remove the fat from the meat and prepare the marinade. Thinly slice the sticks of lemongrass and peel and grate the ginger. In a bowl, combine the white wine, soy sauce, and lemon juice. Heat in a saucepan without allowing it to boil. Chop the chocolate and melt it slowly in a bain-marie* or in the microwave oven (on "defrost" or at 500 W maximum, stirring from time to time). Gradually incorporate the hot liquid over the melted chocolate, one-third at a time, according to the method given on p. 95. Add the sliced lemongrass and cilantro leaves and pour into a dish. Leave to cool. Place the filets mignons in the marinade and leave to marinate for 24 hours in the refrigerator.

The next day.
Preheat the oven to 375°F (190°C).
Drain the filets mignons, reserving the liquid to use later in the sauce, and dry them well using paper towel. Otherwise, any excess marinade will burn when you sear the meat in the skillet.
Melt the butter in the skillet and when it is sizzling, sear the filets, coloring them on each side. Finish cooking them in the oven for about 15 minutes. They should reach a core temperature of 145°F (63°C). Remove them from the oven and leave them to rest in a dish, covered with plastic wrap, for about 15 minutes.

Prepare the sauce.
Deglaze the skillet in which you have cooked the meat with the sherry vinegar and white wine. Reduce briefly and then pour in the reserved marinade. Bring to the boil and simmer for a few minutes, then filter through a sieve or chinois. Incorporate the chopped chocolate. Adjust the seasoning with the salt and pepper, and if necessary, add a few drops of lemon juice. Keep the sauce warm.

Prepare the arugula salad with cilantro.
Prepare a light vinaigrette using vinegar or soy sauce, oil, salt, and pepper. Combine the arugula and cilantro leaves. Do not season with the vinaigrette until the last minute.

Prepare the lemongrass-scented rice.
While the filets mignons are resting, slit the stick of lemongrass and place it in the water with the salt. Bring to the boil. Gently sauté the rice in the oil in a large pot until the grains are translucent. Pour in the scented water, cover, and leave to cook over medium heat until the water is completely absorbed, about 10 to 12 minutes. This should be served immediately.

Slice the filets mignons finely and arrange them in a serving dish or on individual plates. Accompany with lemongrass-scented rice and drizzle with the sauce. Add a serving of arugula salad.

Ingredients
Filets mignons
1 ½ lb. (750 g) pork filet mignon
1 tablespoon plus 2 teaspoons (25 g) butter

Marinade
2 sticks lemongrass
1 ⅔ oz. (45 g) fresh ginger
1 cup plus 1 scant ½ cup (350 ml)
dry white wine, such as Noilly Prat
7 tablespoons (105 ml) soy sauce
Juice of ½ unsprayed lemon
2 ¾ oz. (80 g) bittersweet chocolate,
60 percent cocoa
A few sprigs, leaves picked of fresh cilantro
(coriander), approx. ¼ oz. (8 g)

Lemongrass-scented rice
3 cups (750 ml) water
2 pinches salt
1 stick lemongrass
½ lb. (500 g) basmati rice
4 tablespoons (60 ml) oil (neutral,
such as canola or grape seed)

Sauce
4 tablespoons (60 ml) sherry vinegar
Scant ½ cup (100 ml) dry white wine,
such as Noilly Prat
1 oz. (25 g) bittersweet chocolate,
60 percent cocoa, chopped
1 pinch salt
1 pinch black pepper
A few drops of lemon juice

Arugula salad with cilantro
10 oz. (300 g) arugula (rocket)
1 bunch fresh cilantro (coriander)
Vinegar or soy sauce to taste
Oil as needed
Salt and black pepper to taste

Equipment
1 sieve† or chinois†
1 skillet
Plastic wrap

Technique
Melting Chocolate ›› p. 19

Ingredients

Lobster cooking liquid
3 live lobsters, each weighing about 14 oz. (400 g)
6 ⅓ pints (3 liters) water
5 star anise
1 level teaspoon black peppercorns
1 level teaspoon piment d'Espelette

Lobster reduction
1 fennel bulb
1 leek, white part only
3 carrots
1 head of garlic
1 onion
1 celery stick
1 sprig thyme
7 tablespoons (3 ½ oz./100 g) unsalted butter,
well chilled and diced
3 ½ oz. (100 g) tomato paste (concentrate)
2 tomatoes
Salt to taste

Lightly whipped cream with bittersweet chocolate
3 ½ oz. (100 g) bittersweet chocolate,
70 percent cocoa
1 ¼ cups (300 ml) whipping cream

Garnish
Ground piment d'Espelette

Equipment
1 immersion blender†
1 whisk†

Lobster Jus under a Light Cloud of Bittersweet Chocolate ★★

Serves 6-8
Preparation time: 40 minutes
Cooking time: 10 minutes
Freezing time: 20 minutes

Prepare the lobsters.
Place the lobsters in the freezer for about 20 minutes.
During this time, bring the water to the boil with the spices. Drop the sleeping lobsters into the boiling water and cook for 10 minutes. Remove them and leave to cool for about 15 minutes, then extract the flesh. Keep the carcasses for the reduction.

Lobster reduction
Wash, peel, and cut all the vegetables for your aromatic garnish. In a sauté pan, gently fry the lobster carcasses with the aromatic base in butter. Make sure they are well cooked, but they must not burn as this would give the reduction an unpleasantly bitter taste. Stir in the tomato paste and simmer for a few minutes. Cut the tomatoes into quarters, add them to the pan, and cover with water. Season with salt. Reduce by half, filter, pressing down hard on the carcasses. Take the reduction and reduce it by a further one-third. Adjust the seasoning and incorporate the chilled, diced butter with an immersion blender.

Prepare the lightly whipped cream with bittersweet chocolate.
Chop the chocolate and melt it slowly in a bain-marie* or in the microwave oven (on "defrost" or at 500 W maximum, stirring from time to time).
Lightly whip* the cream (see p. 108). Carefully fold* the whipped cream into the melted chocolate and reserve in the refrigerator.
Slice the lobster flesh and place the slices in small bowls. Half fill them with the hot lobster reduction. Add a tablespoon of cold whipped cream with chocolate. Sprinkle with a pinch of ground piment d'Espelette and serve hot.

● **Chef's notes**
Check that the cooking liquid is well seasoned so that the lobsters acquire a good flavor during the cooking. The contrast between the hot lobster jus and the cold whipped cream is a tantalizing surprise.
Make sure that you allow the jus to reduce sufficiently to create a strong contrast with the chocolate-flavored whipped cream.

 Technique
Melting Chocolate ›› p. 19

Roasted Veal Sweetbread Medallions and Rosemary-Scented Chocolate Sauce ★★

Serves 6–8
Preparation time: 30 minutes
Cooking time: 15 minutes

Place the veal sweetbreads in a pot and cover them completely with cold water. Add a dash of white vinegar. Add salt and pepper and bring to the boil. Allow to boil for 1 minute. Immediately transfer the sweetbreads to a bowl filled with ice water and then remove the fine membrane surrounding them. Wash, peel, and cut the carrots into 24 large sticks. Bring the chicken stock to the boil and blanch the carrot sticks in it, then drain them and set aside.

Prepare the rosemary-scented veal jus.
Bring the veal stock to the boil in a saucepan with the tips of the rosemary sprigs. (Keep the thicker parts of the sprigs to cook the sweetbreads.) Leave to infuse for a few minutes.

Cook the veal sweetbreads.
Insert two sprigs of rosemary into the sweetbreads, one on each side, and cook them in a sauté pan with unsalted butter, spooning the rosemary-scented veal jus over regularly. Repeat this procedure until the sweetbreads are a nice light color and slightly caramelized*. Halfway through the cooking process, add the blanched carrot sticks to color them slightly.

Prepare the veal jus with chocolate.
Chop the chocolate and melt it slowly in a bain-marie* or in the microwave oven (on "defrost" or at 500 W maximum, stirring from time to time).
Bring the ¾ cup (200 ml) of rosemary-scented veal jus to the boil. Pour one-third of it over the chocolate, and using a flexible spatula, mix in energetically, drawing small circles to create an elastic, shiny "kernel." Incorporate the second third of the liquid, using the same procedure. Repeat with the last third. Process with an immersion blender for a few seconds and adjust the seasoning.
Heat the plates. Place the sweetbreads on paper towel and arrange 4 carrot sticks on each plate. Remove the sprigs of rosemary from the sweetbreads and place the sweetbreads atop the carrots. Pour one spoonful of chocolate veal jus over the dish and garnish with a sprig of fresh rosemary.

Technique
Melting chocolate ›› p. 19

Ingredients
Roasted veal sweetbreads
6 veal sweetbreads,
each weighing about 4 oz. (120 g)
White vinegar
Salt and pepper to taste
Butter as needed

Side dish
6 large carrots
Chicken stock (homemade or a diluted cube),
sufficient to blanch* the carrots

Rosemary-scented veal jus
1 ¼ cups (300 ml) homemade
or reconstituted veal stock
12 sprigs fresh rosemary

Veal jus with chocolate
3 ½ oz. (100 g) bittersweet chocolate,
70 percent cocoa
¾ cup (200 ml) rosemary-scented veal jus
(see above)

Garnish
Fresh rosemary

Equipment
1 sauté pan
1 flexible spatula†
1 immersion blender†

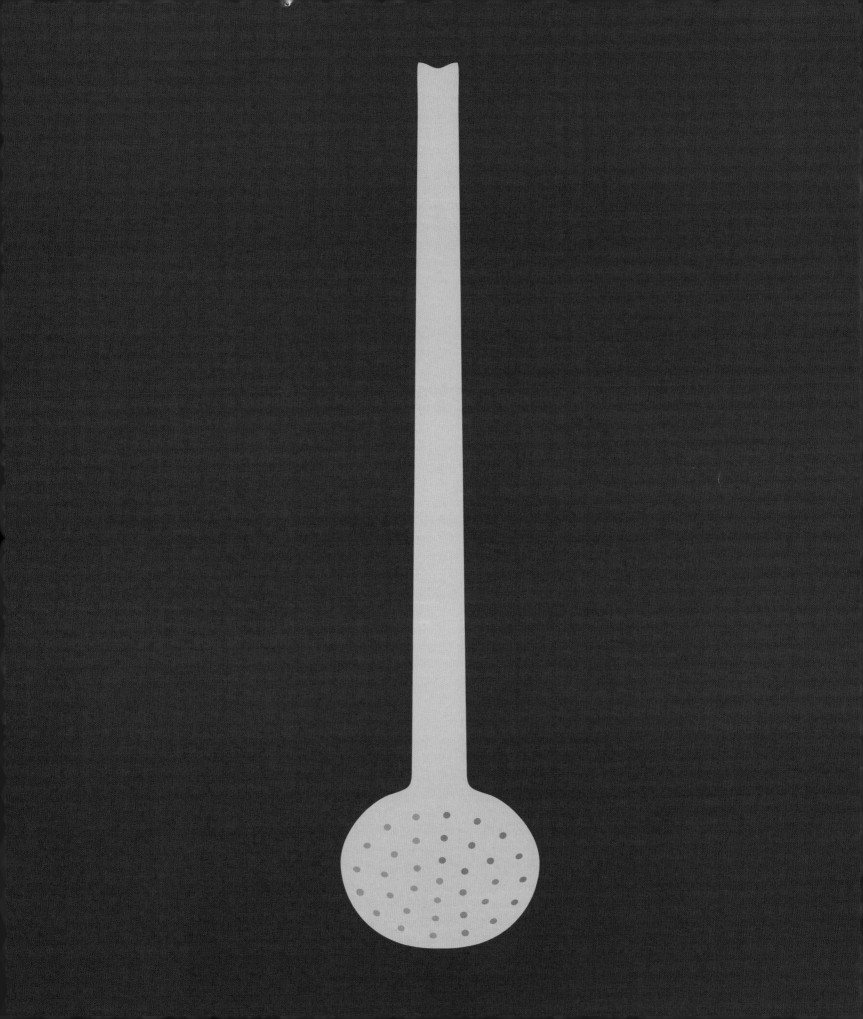

Appendixes

Equipment

Stand-alone mixer (1)
An investment, certainly, but one that is certainly worthwhile as it eases preparation in numerous pastry-making recipes, allowing you to whip*, knead*, and combine ingredients.

Hand-held electric beater (2)
To whip* egg whites and cream.

Electronic scale (3)
This is indispensable for accurate measurements of your ingredients.

Kitchen thermometer or instant-read thermometer (4)
A thermometer with a probe can measure the temperature at the very core of your preparation. It is one of the pastry-maker's best friends.

Immersion blender (5)
Immersion blenders are useful to finish emulsions such as ganaches* and blend other preparations.

Molds and pastry circles/rings (6)
Professionals make frequent use of molds and pastry rings. They give shape to desserts, and are used to bake or cook pastries, sponges, and creams. To make your pastry-making life easier, invest in silicone molds.

Silicone baking mat/Silpat (7)
An easily cleaned, anti-adhesive woven mat that is as useful in the oven as it is in the freezer.

Clear, food-safe acetate sheets (8)
These sheets are so practical to use that you will soon not be able to do without them. They allow you to make shiny chocolate decorations and roll out pastry dough without having to sprinkle your surface with flour.

Whisk or whip (9)
We use whisks† to whip cream and egg white, and to blend preparations that must remain light.

Triangular spatula/scraper (10)
This triangular shaped instrument is used to scrape flat surfaces and spread out tempered* chocolate.

Flexible spatula (11)
To gently combine all sorts of mixtures and batters, and to scrape out bowls.

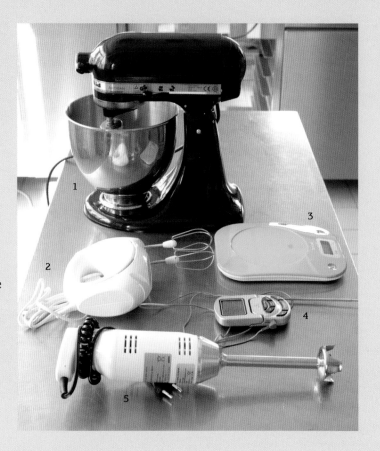

Pastry brush (12)
Use the pastry brush to butter molds* and pans, baste pastries, and moisten sponges.

Dipping forks (13)
Dipping forks are the appropriate instrument for coating chocolate bonbons in tempered* chocolate.

Rolling pin (14)
A rolling pin is useful for more than rolling out pastry; it can be used to create curved shapes in both dough and chocolate.

Pastry tips (15)
Pastry tips come in different diameters and shapes; they can be plain, star-shaped, or V-shaped (angled).

Piping/pastry bag
A bag in disposable plastic or plasticized (and therefore reusable) fabric that will allow you to pipe out macaroons*, meringues, éclairs, and more, using different tips†.

Sieve/chinois (16)
A sieve or sifter is used to sift flour, confectioners' sugar, and cocoa powder to remove lumps. A chinois is a conical sieve used to filter mixtures.

Cookie cutters (17)
From the simplest shapes to the most complex (here, flowers), cookie cutters will enable you to decorate to your heart's content.

Spatulas/offset spatulas (18)
Spatulas are useful to spread out chocolate, toppings, and glazes, and allow you to handle and transfer desserts without damaging them.

Zester/grater (19)
A zester is the ideal tool for finely grating citrus fruits, and gives you a superior result to that of a vegetable peeler.

Tuile mold
Tuile is French for "tile." A tuile mold is a curved mold over which cookies hot from the oven are placed to obtain curved cookies which resemble roof tiles. A rolling pin[†] or tin can can be substituted for a tuile mold.

Ice-cream maker (20)
This apparatus will allow you to make delicious homemade ice creams and sorbets. It lowers the temperature of your mixture and prevents crystals from forming.

Siphon (21)
With its gas cartridges, a siphon will transform hot and cold liquids into foam. The number of cartridges you'll need depends on the size of your siphon and the amount of liquid to foam. There are special cartridges for Chantilly cream.

Confectionery ruler/frame
Confectionery, or caramel, rulers are square rods of varying thickness. Confectionery rulers and frames are used when spreading fondant*, ganache*, caramel* etc. in order to obtain slabs of uniform thickness.

Paper decorating cone
A parchment paper cone for decoration. To make: cut the paper into a right-angled triangle, the shorter sides measuring 12 in. (30 cm) and 15 in. (38 cm). With the right angle toward you, hold the right corner with your right hand, the left hand holding down the center of the triangle. Roll your right hand inwards so that the top corner meets the center of the triangle. Hold this with your right hand and wind the loose end around with your left hand, with the point ending above the rim. The tip must be completely closed. Fold the edges securely over the rim, fill the cone, and snip a tiny hole at the tip.

Glossary

Bain-marie
When cooking with a bain-marie, or double-boiler, the bowl containing food is placed over a pot of simmering water. This cooking method surrounds the food with very gentle heat. It is used for melting chocolate and making custard (*crème anglaise*) in particular.

Blanch
To plunge a vegetable (or other ingredient) briefly into boiling water, to remove acidity or to prepare the food for freezing.

Caramel/caramelize
To cook sugar until it turns a lovely amber color (temperature about 350°F or 180°C). To caramelize sugar using the dry method (i.e. when only sugar is called for), use the following procedure: Place one-third of the sugar in a heavy-bottomed saucepan. Cook until it forms a light caramel. Add the next third of the sugar and stir. When this quantity has reached the same color, a light caramel, add the last third of the sugar. This ensures that the sugar is thoroughly cooked. It provides a rich flavor; though it is not used for decorative caramel as its color is not always suitable.

Cocoa butter
This is the fat that is naturally present in the cocoa bean. Cocoa butter can be added when couverture chocolate* is made. It is a solid fat that acts a hardener in certain preparations (see p. 144).

Cocoa nibs
Roasted cocoa beans that have been separated from the husks and broken into small pieces. Nibs may be added to sweet and savory dishes instead of nuts or chocolate chips.

Couverture chocolate
Professional quality chocolate with a marked gloss. Its percentage of cocoa butter means it can be used to make fine coatings.

Crystallization/crystallize
The transition from a liquid state to a solid state. We also say chocolate "hardens" or "sets."

Dacquoise
A light sponge made with egg whites and more nuts (usually hazelnuts or almonds) than flour, used as a base* for layered gâteaux.

Détrempe
A French term that designates the flour and water paste that is a base for pastry dough before the butter is added to make puff pastry, croissant dough, and so on.

Emulsify
To combine two liquids that normally do not mix, such as water and oil (see p. 95).

Financier
A cake made from almonds and whisked* egg white, usually formed into small ovals or rectangles.

Fold in, To (egg whites and cream)
The technique of adding beaten egg whites or cream (see pp. 108-134) to other ingredients in order to retain a light, airy texture. Use a flexible spatula†, starting in the middle and rotating the bowl as you work; take care not to apply pressure to the sides of the bowl. Stop folding in as soon as the mixture is smooth.

Fondant (*fondant pâtissier*)
A paste made from a sugar syrup mixture kneaded* as it cools to make a smooth paste. It can be used to make candies or heated to make a pouring *fondant* that can be used as an icing.

Ganache
A chocolate filling made from chocolate and whipping cream to which other ingredients may be added (see p. 32).

Glaze
To cover the top of a cake with an icing or glaze.

Kneading
A technique used for working dough, either by hand or using a mixer fitted with a dough hooks. Manual kneading requires pressing, folding, and turning using the heels of both hands, and then pushing away from the body. When dough is well kneaded, its texture will be smooth and elastic.

Macaroons (*macarons*)
Made with ground almonds, sugar, and egg white, these small round cakes are often colored and flavored and sandwiched in pairs. They are not to be confused with the coconut macaroon found in the USA and elsewhere.

Pâte à bombe

A whisked* preparation of eggs and sugar that is used as the base for buttercream and mousse recipes.

Peeling nuts

To peel hazelnuts, toast them until golden (see p. 134), leave to cool, and rub them between your hands or in a clean towel or cloth. The friction will flake the skins away. To peel almonds, place them in boiling water for a minute or two, then transfer them to cold water to cool down. Strain and then pop them out of the skin.

Pommade (beurre)

Beurre en pommade, softened butter, is worked with a spatula†
and/or a whip until it reaches the soft texture required for the recipe (see p. 134).

Praline

Here, praline refers to a nut paste that usually contains at least half almonds or hazelnuts, or a mixture of both, with sugar. It may also refer to a confection, candy, or filled chocolate.

Rise (prove)

The term used for a yeast dough that swells with the activity of the yeast.

Rochers

The grainy texture and jagged profile of these cookies give rise to their name, which means "rock."

Seeding

A method of tempering* chocolate (see p. 21).

Sponge bases

Sponge bases use flour, eggs, and sugar as their basic ingredients. French cakes and desserts often comprise numerous layers whose sponges are always very thin. When ready for baking, they are spread out thinly on baking sheets and cut to the desired shape when cooled, rather than being baked as a cake that rises* high and is then cut horizontally.

Tempering

The process of heating and cooling chocolate to make it ready for use in dipping, undercoating, and coating (see pp. 20-23).

Thermal inertia

This is the phenomenon whereby food retains heat and so continues to cook even after it is removed from the source of heat.

"Three-Thirds" Rule

The "Three-Thirds" rule refers to a method of mixing chocolate and cream or milk to make a ganache (see p. 95).

Whip/Whisk

To beat ingredients, such as cream or egg whites, to incorporate air bubbles into them until they are light.

Zest

The outer skin of a citrus fruit. Do not include the white pith just underneath the skin as it is bitter.

INDEX

Page numbers in italic refer to illustrations

About the authors

Valrhona

In the world of chocolate, Valrhona is a symbol of excellence. Founded by a pastry chef in the Rhône Valley in 1922, the company has become the official supplier of countless renowned pastry makers and chocolatiers, Michelin-starred restaurants, and fine grocery stores. The approach that starts with origins, *crus*, domain names, and the aromatic palette of flavors found in the chocolate collection makes it an outstanding brand. Its success in a highly profitable niche market is due to an equation that means that although just 1 percent of the world production comes out of its factory, 98 percent of its clientele are well-known names. Valrhona is present in sixty-six countries and sells more than half its production outside France.
Website: www.valrhona.com

The École du Grand Chocolat Valrhona

Chocolate is one of the most difficult basic ingredients for a pastry chef to work with. Until 1989, there was no school that taught the unique art of chocolate making. The École du Grand Chocolat was born of the ambition to become a benchmark in the field of training in chocolate. Today, it is a recognized training center, respected by professionals the world over. The wide range of training courses and the creativity of the recipes stem from highly sophisticated teaching techniques and the caliber of both the in-house teachers and those who come from elsewhere. The school comprises five training laboratories in three different locations: Tain l'Hermitage, Tokyo, and Versailles. For fifteen years, the school was open only to professionals, but since 2003 we have also been teaching the general public, and the members are proving to be increasingly expert

themselves. The contents of the courses are not restricted to the basics; rather, they are taught by theme and recipes that reflect–and even influence–trends in chocolate and pastry creation. The École du Grand Chocolat has a team of twenty pastry chefs who develop recipes, train and provide support for Valrhona clients, and offer consulting services and demonstrations for professionals working in the food trade in France and around the world.

Frédéric Bau and his team

Frédéric Bau is acknowledged by his peers as one of the finest pastry chefs and chocolate makers in the world. He was awarded the title of best apprentice in his region of the south of France and won the top prize for *Meilleur Apprenti de France*, a rigorous nationwide competition for France's best apprentice. In 1986 he began working at Fauchon, the Parisian gastronomic institution, soon after Pierre Hermé also started there, and was in charge of decoration. When Valrhona hired him in 1988, he founded the École du Grand Chocolat, becoming creative director and executive chef. He has created Valrhona's *Essentiels*, basic recipes for sponges, ganaches, mousses, and more; all a source of inspiration and a veritable bible for other pastry chefs. His passion for chocolate has led him to use chocolate in all its varying forms, including in savory recipes. In May 2009, he and his wife opened a restaurant in Tain l'Hermitage, Umia.

From left to right:

David Capy, Thierry Bridron, Philippe Givre, Vincent Bourdin, Julie Haubourdin, Frédéric Bau, Jérémie Runel, Fabrice David.

DVD contents

The sequences on the DVD show professionals at work and therefore the quantities, cooking times, and other specifics may vary slightly from the recipes in the book, which have been adapted for use in the home. When putting techniques into practice or making recipes, follow the precise indications given in the book.

To follow along in the book, the page numbers indicated below refer to the corresponding technique.

Acknowledgments

Frédéric Bau would like to thank all the artisan chocolatiers, pastry chefs, bakers, and cooks who, for decades, have been regaling us with their creativity and passion for their work. This book is first and foremost an homage to them all; I take my hat off to them.

And I have to thank all the great chefs who were kind enough to answer Flammarion's invitation to enrich this book with the recipes that reflect their talent:

Christophe Adam (Fauchon), Frédéric Cassel, Jean-Paul Hévin, Christophe Felder, Éric Léautey, Cyril Lignac, Gilles Marchal (Maison du chocolat), and Christophe Michalak (Plaza Athénée).

Sincere thanks to my colleagues, the magicians who have been running the École du Grand Chocolat for twenty years: Fabrice David, Philippe Givre, Jérémie Runel, David Capy, Thierry Bridron, Vincent Bourdin. And very special thanks to you, Julie Haubourdin, a brilliantly cut diamond in the rough world of cocoa who skillfully took the helm of the ship, transcribing the secrets and tricks of the trade that we want to share with our readers. Good food is also devoured with the eyes, and so thank you, Clay, for imparting so much gourmet magic to your photos, and to you, Eve-Marie, for finding just the right words to transmit our work to our readers. And lastly, and on behalf of us all, thank you to Pierre Hermé, for confirming in your foreword that the professionals who have compiled this book are continuing your vision.

The authors would like to thank you, the readers of *Cooking with Chocolate*, who have devoured the recipes with your eyes and will now go on, we hope, to regale your guests with your creations.

Thank you to all the team at Flammarion, in particular Liza Person for your patience and Valérie de Sahb for your confidence in us.

Much appreciation, of course, to Eve-Marie for the tender loving care you have shown our words in your texts and to Clay for showcasing our creations with such artistry.

To complete *Cooking with Chocolate* in such a short time we were privileged to have the precious help of all the staff of the École du Grand Chocolat in Tokyo and in Tain. Thank you to you all.

Lastly, we would like to pay tribute to the countless men and women who work behind the scenes, without whom that seemingly tasteless seed could not produce the aromatic, melting product–chocolate–with its multiple savors and innumerable uses: farm workers, planters, those who source the products, chocolate factory workers, researchers, and tasters.

Flammarion would like to thank the entire Valrhona team for their unfailing commitment, as well as Eve-Marie Zizza-Lalu for her editing, Clay McLachlan, photographer, for his artistic taste, and Alice Leroy, for her creativity in laying out the recipes and showing the techniques.